PIE ACADEMY

PIE ACADEMY

Master the Perfect Crust and 255 Amazing Fillings

with Fruits, Nuts, Creams, Custards, Ice Cream, and More

Expert Techniques *for* Making Fabulous Pies *from* Scratch

KEN HAEDRICH

The mission of Storey Publishing is to serve our customers by
publishing practical information that encourages
personal independence in harmony with the environment.

EDITED BY Deborah Balmuth and Lisa H. Hiley
ART DIRECTION AND BOOK DESIGN BY Carolyn Eckert
TEXT PRODUCTION BY Jennifer Jepson Smith
INDEXED BY Andrea Chesman

PHOTOGRAPHY BY © Emulsion Studio, except © ML Harris/Alamy Stock Photo, spine and endpapers
FOOD STYLING BY Torie Cox

Storey books are available at special discounts when purchased in bulk for premiums and sales promotions as well as for fund-raising or educational use. Special editions or book excerpts can also be created to specification. For details, please call 800-827-8673, or send an email to sales@storey.com.

STOREY PUBLISHING
210 MASS MoCA Way
North Adams, MA 01247
storey.com

Printed in China
10 9 8 7 6 5 4 3 2 1

LIBRARY OF CONGRESS CATALOGING-IN-PUBLICATION DATA
Names: Haedrich, Ken, 1954– author.
Title: Pie academy : master the perfect crust and 255 amazing fillings, with fruits, nuts, creams, custards, ice cream, and more : expert techniques for making fabulous pies from scratch / Ken Haedrich.
Description: North Adams, MA : Storey Publishing, 2020. | Includes index. | Summary: "Discover recipes for all types of crusts and pastry, including gluten-free, whole wheat, and extra-flaky. Learn about the best tools and gadgets to make dough and fillings. Step-by-step instructions with photos make it easy for bakers of all levels"-- Provided by publisher.
Identifiers: LCCN 2020008926 (print) | LCCN 2020008927 (ebook) | ISBN 9781635861112 (hardcover) | ISBN 9781635861129 (ebook)
Subjects: LCSH: Pies. | Pastry. | Baking. | LCGFT: Cookbooks.
Classification: LCC TX773 .H2197 2020 (print) | LCC TX773 (ebook) | DDC 641.86/52--dc23
LC record available at https://lccn.loc.gov/2020008926
LC ebook record available at https://lccn.loc.gov/2020008927

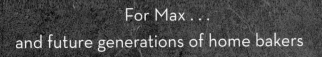

For Max . . .
and future generations of home bakers

Contents

PART TWO: THE WONDERFUL WORLD OF PIE

4   **A Panoply of Pie Doughs:** All the Dough You'll Ever Need 55

5   **Berry Pies:** Summer's Jewels in a Crust 87

6   **More Summer Delights:** A Profusion of Fruit Pies 117

7   **Make Mine Apple:** Variations on a Classic 163

8   **The Other Fall Classics:** Pear, Pumpkin, Cranberry, and More 203

9   **The Notable Nut:** Pecan Pie and Beyond 247

10 **Rich, Sweet, and Simple:** Chess, Buttermilk, and Other Custard Pies 275

11 **Small Packages:** Mini Pies, Turnovers, and Other Hand Pies 323

12 **Icebox Pies:** Chiffons, a Chocolate Silk, and Other Cool Pleasures 349

13 **Cream Pies:** The Diner Classics Come Home 375

14 **From the Freezer:** Inviting Ice Cream Pies and Other Icy Treats 393

15 **A Pie Potpourri:** Brownie Pies, Rice Pies, and Other Delicious Oddballs 413

16 **The Pie Maker's Pantry:** Sweet Sauces, Toppings, and Meringues 443

Troubleshooting Guide 454

Acknowledgments 457

List of Pies by Chapter 458

Index 460

Metric Conversion Chart 470

The Pie Preface

So you love baking pies and are ready to explore a wider world beyond apple, pumpkin, and pecan. Or you want to learn how to bake a pie from scratch and you don't know where to begin. Or you know where to begin and do so with the best of intentions, but your pies keep throwing you curve balls. Your dough cracks and falls apart. It sticks to your counter like superglue. Your pies are too ugly to bring out in public. This and more. I feel your pain. And you've come to the right place, because I can help.

By way of introduction, I've been writing cookbooks for nearly 40 years — 15 of them, in fact, including two collections of sweet pies and one of savory pies. This book is an updated, revised, and — if I may say so — totally awesome-ized edition of my outsize book, *Pie*, originally published in 2004.

I caught the pie-making bug early on from my dad, a regular weekend pie maker, and my mom, his loving pie partner. Even as a young child, it was clear to me that there was special magic happening in those shared moments. Whether the pie making enhanced their relationship or their relationship brought special joy to their pie making, I could not be sure. But I was lucky to be an observer of that Sunday tradition.

When I started making my own way in the world, I naturally gravitated toward the kitchen. Somewhere along the line I started cooking for a living, writing magazine articles and cookbooks, and teaching baking classes. After a number of years of this, I woke up one day and realized I had become the de facto Dear Abby for pie makers. Home cooks from around the globe were leaving their pie baggage in my email inbox, a heavy burden of pie woe. I'd unpack it and write back, trying to help sort out their issues.

So I started a website — ThePieAcademy.com — to expand my reach, help even more home bakers, and become a cheerleader for home pie baking. I created pie-making videos and online pie courses to help and encourage folks to find contentment and achieve mastery in our chosen craft.

Offline, The Pie Academy holds pie getaways in different parts of the country where our members come to hone their skills and enjoy the community of fellow pie makers. I hope you'll join us someday.

As the "dean" of The Pie Academy I've become acutely aware of the questions and quandaries that you have or will have as a pie maker. You may be frustrated, and understandably so. We've all been told that pie making is easy — as easy as pie, right? — but I can tell you for a fact that most home cooks encounter plenty of speed bumps and fender benders on the road to pie mastery. And I have about 10,000 emails to prove it.

I field questions from pie makers who want to know whether they should use butter, lard, or vegetable shortening for their crust; how to know when they've added enough water; if they have to refrigerate the dough; why the dough always sticks or falls apart on the way to the pan; why the berry pie is runny, the apples aren't tender, or the pastry cream didn't set up; why the pie shell shrunk — and I'm just getting warmed up. You will find the answers to all those questions, and many more, in the pages that follow.

One thing you won't find here are detailed instructions on creating labor-intensive pastry still lifes, the sort of pies that become Instagram starlets. I admire anyone who has the patience and talent to turn their top crusts into geometric masterpieces and stunning artwork. I'll even confess to a smidgen of jealousy; I'm more of a stick-figure artist myself. But this is pie we're talking about, the province of home cooks, and I'm afraid these fancy pies sometimes scare more people away from pie making than they attract.

That said, you will find instructions on making decorative lattice tops, attractive crimped edges, peekaboo crusts, and a good many other pastry flourishes, plus virtually everything else you need to know to make fabulous sweet pies in every category imaginable.

There are no shortcuts to learning how to make good pie. Pie making is part science, part "feel" or baker's intuition. Recipes alone can only take you so far. Beyond that, pie making requires practice and cultivated instincts for all the little nuances. You've got to roll up your sleeves and get into the flour. The fact that you're here tells me you're ready to go down this path. You've probably had a taste of the real deal — the flaky texture of a homemade crust, the creamy goodness of a velvety custard pie, or the sweet satisfaction of a fresh peach crumb pie in August — and you're unwilling to settle for anything less.

I'm excited to join you on your pie journey; thanks for choosing me as your guide. I hope you'll be patient with yourself and enjoy the trip. Nobody learns to make great pies in a couple of weekends; I sure didn't. Don't rush toward mastery. Take your time, observe, make notes in the margins, try stuff that makes you a little nervous, and don't be afraid to make mistakes or ugly pies. Enjoy the process, have a laugh, and share everything you make. One day you'll wake up and realize you've nailed this pie thing.

If I can make one more suggestion: unless you're an experienced pie maker, don't skip part one, where I walk you through the nuances of making pie dough from scratch. This mini baking class will teach you many of the fine points of making pie dough and assembling a pie, and steer you clear of the usual obstacles. I think you'll get a lot out of it.

From there, I hope you'll dive right into the recipes and get baking. Keep me in the loop, send me an email at The Pie Academy, and let me know how you're doing. I look forward to hearing from you.

— KEN HAEDRICH, *dean of The Pie Academy*

PART ONE

Behind the Scenes

1
The Pie Maker's Tools:
PINS, PANS, PASTRY BLENDERS, AND MORE

Making a good pie doesn't require a lot of stuff you probably don't already have. During my first years as a pie maker, I pretty much relied on a few dinged-up old pie pans, a rolling pin I picked up on the cheap, and a pastry blender whose wires bent at the mere sight of cold butter.

But I was having so much fun I hardly noticed how challenged my tools were.

I'm not recommending that you outfit yourself with substandard gear; decent tools make the job more enjoyable and easier to accomplish. But you don't have to spend a fortune on them, either. Here are the items to put on your wish list if you don't already have them. Let's start with the big stuff.

Rolling Pins

You may have heard the urban legend about the clever cook who used a bottle of wine to roll a perfect crust one snowy night in the Tetons — or in the Adirondacks or in Brooklyn — when the cupboard was bare, save for the exact ingredients needed to make an apple pie. No doubt it happened somewhere at least once. But you can be sure that for every baker who pulled off that trick, there are a thousand others who tried, threw in the towel, and polished off the wine instead.

So you need a rolling pin, not a wine bottle, and the first thing you should know is that not all of them are created equal. There are silly ones, like the kind you fill with ice cubes that sweat all over your dough. Or flimsy ones with handles that stick into the pin like an afterthought and break off the first time you exert pressure.

I have quite a collection of pins, but if I had to narrow it down to the two I use 99 percent of the time, it would be pretty easy: an American-style pin with a 12-inch barrel and handles and a tapered, single-piece French-style pin.

The former is hefty, which allows the pin to do some of the work for you; it's not necessary to push so hard. And the barrel glides smoothly over the dough, thanks to the ball bearing design. If you're serious about making pies, this is the one to get.

The solid French-style pin is 20 inches long and especially useful when you're just starting to roll the dough and it's firm from sitting in the fridge. This pin allows you to exert direct pressure on the dough during the first phase of your rolling and work it into a pliable consistency. And the pin's taper gives you the ability to sort of "steer" the dough if it starts to get out of round.

The other advantage of the narrower pin is that it allows you to better see what you're doing when you're rolling smaller circles of dough for mini pies or hand pies.

Plan on getting both styles.

Pie Pans

I could write an entire book about pie pans — I own about 50 of them, no kidding — but I'll take mercy on you since you're here to make pie, not listen to me ramble about the nuances of the perfect pie pan. Here's the straight skinny in as few paragraphs as possible.

Pie pans come in a variety of sizes, but the most common one is 9 to 9½ inches in diameter, measured from inside rim to outside rim. The "standard" ones referred to in this book are about 1 inch deep, while deep-dish pie pans are closer to 1¼ to 1½ inches deep. (Bear in mind that those

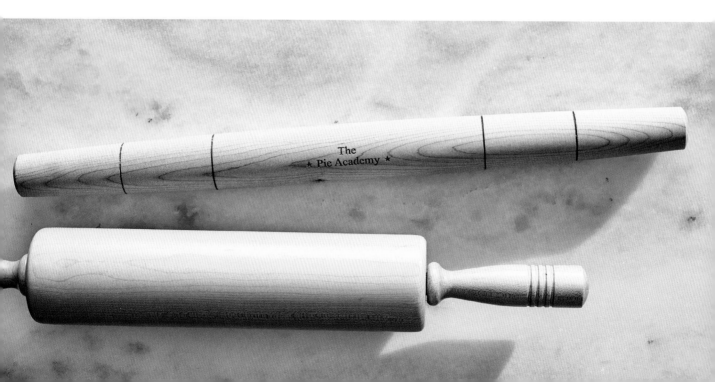

MEASURE DIAMETER FROM INSIDE RIM TO THE OPPOSITE OUTSIDE RIM

THE PIE PLATE

are actual sizes. The functional size, and thus the pan's capacity, is often considerably greater, taking into account that the upstanding edge of the piecrust can add an additional ½ inch of height.)

Pie pans can be made of glass, various metals, ceramic, and clay.

GLASS. It's hard to beat a basic tempered-glass pie pan, like the ones made by Pyrex or Anchor Hocking. They typically cost less than 10 dollars, and I have found some real beauties in thrift stores and at yard sales for a buck or two. I'm partial to the colorful vintage Pyrex pans you find on sites like eBay.

The best Pyrex pans have a wide rim or built-out handles so you can grab the pie securely when you remove it from the oven. Unless you drop them on a hard surface, these pans are pretty indestructible.

METAL. Metal pie pans are all over the map, material-wise. I like the old-fashioned stamped-tin ones you find at flea markets and antiques shops — Table Talk is one brand. They're rugged, and I love the well-used patina. Just avoid the rusty ones.

If I had to choose my favorite metal pan, however, I'd vote for one of the 9½-inch aluminized steel pie pans made by USA Pan. Their pans are tough and built to withstand years of heavy use. They have a release finish and a wafflelike bottom that help prevent pies from sticking.

CERAMIC. There are all sorts of ceramic pie pans out there, and most do a great job. Many are attractive enough to bring to the table — something to consider for special-occasion pies. Two of the best brands are Le Creuset and Emile Henry. My one beef with heavy ceramic or stoneware pans is that they're often so thick that the crust doesn't brown quickly enough, resulting in a less-than-crisp bottom crust. If you're using that type of pan, you might want to start with a slightly hotter oven than usual. Preheat the oven to 425°F (220°C) when you bake a fruit pie, then reduce the heat to 400°F (200°C) when you put the pie in the oven. That will give the bottom crust a helpful blast of heat to brown it.

CLAY. If you're looking for a special, top-notch clay pan, check out the ones handmade by Tom Hess of Hess Pottery. His pans are pieces of art. All things considered, it's my favorite higher-end pie pan.

AND EVEN DISPOSABLE. Finally, in the humble pie department, I used to be pretty vocal about my distaste for disposable aluminum pie pans. I called them things like "cheap" and "flimsy," but I've come around in recent years. Because I like to give pies away, I needed a way to do so without constantly worrying about getting my pans back. So I learned how to get the best out of these pans by putting the pie near the bottom of the oven, on a dark baking sheet, and leaving it there for about two-thirds of the bake. I've been amazed at how well this works.

How to Mail a Pie

Everyone loves receiving homemade cookies or brownies in the mail, so imagine the joy that a whole pie would bring. Believe it or not, it's possible to send a pie to a loved one, but you have to pick the right recipe. Firm, cookie-type pies are obvious candidates, and many nut pies also ship well. Because they're small and can be tightly wrapped, hand pies and tarts travel well, too. I've shipped small individual crumb-topped fruit pies with success, but large fruit pies with a pastry top crust don't hold up too well.

Follow these tips for successful pie packaging.

- Use a disposable aluminum pie pan, for obvious reasons. These pans can be a little tricky to remove from the oven, so lift the forward edge of the pie with a metal spatula. As you do, quickly slide a rimless cookie sheet under the pie. Swap the spatula for a potholder and steady the pie while you slide the sheet all the way under the pie.

- Freeze the pie overnight.

- Wrap it well in plastic wrap, then in aluminum foil, and pack it in a sturdy, well-padded box. Write FRAGILE and PERISHABLE about 100 times all over the box.

- Use one of the faster forms of delivery so the package arrives in 2 or 3 days and be extra nice to the postal clerk when you mail it.

Pies That Handle Shipping Well

- Canadian Butter Tarts (page 280)

- Chocolate Brownie–Pecan Pie (page 255)

- Chocolate Chip Cookie Pie (page 427)

- Fancy Chocolate Chess Pie (page 284)

- Oatmeal–Butterscotch Chip Cookie Pie (page 420)

- Oatmeal-Butterscotch Pie (page 421)

- Oatmeal-Raisin Pie (page 422)

- Race Day Chocolate-Pecan Pie (page 252)

- Roasted Virginia Peanut Pie (page 269)

- Sawdust Pie (page 258)

Pastry Blender and Fork

A PASTRY BLENDER is used to literally cut the fat into the dry ingredients. It's basically just a grip handle with blunted, curved blades or wires. You simply grasp the handle and push the wires or blades repeatedly into the dry mixture.

Over the years, I've seen a variety of pastry blenders come along with a new bell or whistle or the promise of making the process go faster and smoother. There's one with a little doohickey that you slide back and forth to push the pastry mixture through the blades as it builds up, and others with extrabeefy grips, fat blades, or a little platform for your thumb, for better leverage.

I've tried them all, and the one I still like best is simple and lightweight, with a grippy handle and curved wires that get the job done. I know some old-school pie makers who like to use two knives — you wield them like scissors, crisscross fashion, to cut in the fat — but I never could get the hang of that method.

A PASTRY OR BLENDING FORK is the perfect tool for mixing pie dough by hand. It rakes through the mixture and redistributes the moisture, whereas a big spoon just shovels everything around. I must reach for this thing half a dozen times a day, using it for everything from making an omelet to carving meat to mixing up veggie burgers.

Something about the blending fork, made by Endurance, works beautifully for pastry. Perhaps it's the larger grip, the width of and spacing between the tines, or the graceful arc of the business end. I haven't found anything else that's half as good for the job, but you can certainly use any large fork.

Food Processor

Not everyone is as big a fan of the food processor for mixing up pie dough as I am. Detractors will tell you that it doesn't make as flaky of a crust as hand mixing, which is a bunch of hooey, or that you can overmix the dough, which is true, but overall it has been a boon for home pie bakers.

Using the machine speeds up the mixing of dough quite a bit, no small consideration for someone who makes a lot of pies. For those who have arthritis or limited hand and arm mobility, it does much of the hard mixing work for you.

The caveat, as mentioned, is that it's easy to mix the dough too much and overwork it, resulting in a less tender crust. But if you pay close attention as you mix, you'll do just fine.

WHAT SIZE?

I occasionally take flack for saying this, but even though you'll find recipes here for double-crust processor doughs, I would rather use the processor to make two single-crust recipes than mix a double batch. Why? Because you still get better results with a smaller, single-crust batch of dough than you would even using a large food processor — say, one with a 12- to 14-cup capacity. Larger batches of dough tend to compact in the machine and get cramped, so the dough is not as evenly mixed. Smaller batches don't have that problem.

That said, I know some cooks prefer mixing a double-crust batch all at once to save a little time, so most of the doughs in the crust section have double-crust versions. In any event, the minimum-size food processor I recommend for pie dough is 10 cups, but I prefer one in the 12- to 14-cup range.

Nearly all food processors come with a plastic "dough blade." Though it sounds like you could, don't use this blade to make pie dough. You probably won't even use it for mixing bread dough, its actual purpose, because the metal blade does a better job.

It's worth mentioning that if you don't already own one, you should do some serious research before you plunk down good money for a new food processor. They aren't cheap, and it's easy to under- or overbuy for your particular needs. If you plan to use it for bread dough as well as pie dough, you definitely want all the capacity and power you can get. If you're still not sure which one is best for you, buy one that offers a little more oomph and

versatility than you think you need. It's better to have a machine you can grow into than to be stuck with one that turns out to be inadequate.

Electric Mixers

Even though I'm partial to the food processor, a stand mixer is a perfectly good tool for mixing pie dough (see page 71). A good stand mixer (KitchenAid is nearly synonymous with the term) is an almost indispensable tool for anyone who likes to bake. It frees up your hands so you can take care of other tasks, and it's all but required for making the Swiss Meringue (page 448) that people love on cream pies. I've had my own KitchenAid mixer for more than 30 years. It's gotten a bit noisy in its old age, but it shows no signs of slowing down. When I finally do replace it, I'll get one with a tilting head instead of the type with a bowl that is raised and lowered with a hand crank.

There are many small pie-related jobs (blending fillings or beating a few egg whites) that can be done quickly and don't require the power of a stand mixer, and for those occasions I use a basic electric handheld mixer.

Other Necessities and Niceties

MEASURING CUPS. You'll need both a set of graduated dry measuring cups, the kind you fill to the top and then level off, as well as a set of glass liquid measuring cups. You'll use the 1- and 2-cup measures most often, but I regularly use my 8-cup measure when I'm cutting up or measuring out fruit.

PASTRY BRUSH. A small bristle pastry brush gets a lot of use in the pie maker's kitchen. You'll use it to brush excess flour off dough. You'll use it to moisten the rim of the shell when attaching a top pastry. And it's indispensable for brushing an egg wash or milk glaze on a top crust. The ideal size is about 1 inch wide. Get two of them, one for wet work and one for dry.

Food Processor Tips

Safety first: all food processor blades are extremely sharp. I once warned a large crowd watching me at a pie-making demonstration to never reach carelessly into the bowl of the food processor to check the dough, then proceeded to do exactly that and sliced my hand open. It was like a scene from a horror flick. Bottom line: be careful.

- As with dough made by hand, chill the dry mixture, water, and fat for 10 to 15 minutes before mixing the dough.

- Unless otherwise instructed, use short pulses to mix the dough. A short pulse is about 1 second long. Pulsing tosses the mixture around inside the bowl; the result is a more even distribution of fat without the dough compacting under the blade.

- That said, it's inevitable that the dough mixture will compact a bit when you start adding the water, especially if you're mixing up a double-crust batch. When that happens, stop the machine, remove the lid, and loosen the ingredients with a large fork. I sometimes do this after I cut in the fat and before I add the water.

- If you do reach into the processor bowl to check the consistency of the dough, carefully remove a bit of dough from the top of the mixture. Or use a spoon to scoop a sample out. Don't reach down where the cutting blade is.

- If you're mixing consecutive batches of dough (as I often do, so I can put extra pie shells in the freezer), there's no need to wash the processor bowl between batches. A little pastry debris from a previous batch is not a problem.

A RULER. I have a couple of standard 12-inch rulers and one 16 inches long made from a sawed-off yardstick. Whenever I make a pie, I keep at least one within reach to measure pans, circles of dough for hand pies, oblongs for crostatas, and a hundred other little things.

PASTRY WHEEL OR CUTTER. There's little difference between a pastry wheel and a ravioli cutter. In many kitchens, they're one and the same — a short, straight handle with a fluted wheel at the end, almost like a tall unicycle. Use it to even up the edges of rolled dough and cut strips for a lattice top. You can do both of these things with an everyday paring knife, but that could cut a silicone mat, if you use one, and may well scratch your work surface. A knife also pulls on the dough, rather than shearing it evenly.

FLOUR SHAKER OR DUSTER. Often called a powdered sugar shaker, this looks like a mug, often handled, with some sort of screen or perforated screw-on lid. It's typically made of plastic or stainless steel and costs just a few bucks. I use it to sprinkle flour on my rolling surface, dough, and pin to keep things from sticking as I roll. A great little tool.

PARCHMENT PAPER. If there's any one thing that's made life easier for pie bakers, it's parchment paper. In my preparchment days, I spent countless hours soaking and scrubbing baking sheets to remove baked-on fruit goo. Now I just ball up the parchment and throw away the mess. I also use parchment to roll out dough and underneath virtually all of my prep work. I also use it on top of my rolling mat (see page 30 for more on that.)

Forget about those rolls of parchment paper you find in the supermarket. It's more expensive buying it that way, but even more irritating, the blessed stuff won't lie flat when you unroll it. Parchment paper that comes in sheets sized to fit full- and half-sheet pans is available from baking and restaurant supply stores.

OVEN LINER. Especially if you don't bake pies on a baking sheet, consider using an oven liner, a handy item that keeps the oven floor clean when pie filling — or anything else — misbehaves and spills over. Liners have a nonstick, wipe-clean surface: once the oven cools, you simply slide out the liner and rinse it off. You can find these liners in kitchenware shops for about 20 bucks. There are less expensive ones, but in my experience it's worth paying a little extra for the durability. Read the packaging and consult the owner's manual for your oven before using a liner; many liners aren't compatible with gas ovens.

TIP: If you make a point of baking fruit pies on a parchment-lined baking sheet, the way I recommend, your oven won't get dirty, at least not from your pies.

COOLING RACKS. One of the best gifts my wife ever bought me was a pair of cooling racks. They're large enough to hold a sheet pan, but my favorite feature is the folding legs: when unfolded, they hoist the racks about 4 inches above the surface they stand on. This gives your hot pies plenty of ventilation space when they're cooling and prevents moisture build-up underneath the rack, which could damage the table or other surface. If you can find racks like these, grab 'em.

1 CUP = 4½ OUNCES

Weights and Measures

Nowadays, many cookbooks provide weight measurements for ingredients in addition to traditional measures like cups and tablespoons, but back when I started my food writing career, weight measurements were uncommon. None of my early mentors and cookbook heroes — James Beard, Marion Cunningham, even Julia Child — did it, and their recipes taught generations of home cooks how to excel in the kitchen.

I think weight measurements got a foot in the door of home kitchens when professional chefs and bakers starting writing cookbooks for home cooks. Because professional bakers work in such large batches, weights are essential for them; you can't bake 100 loaves of bread using a measuring cup.

Having taught baking skills to home cooks for years, I realize how important it is not to throw up obstacles for bakers, and I'm afraid that weight measures often do that. They send the unwritten message that successful home cooking and baking requires them; it doesn't. And they can make cooking seem less accessible for those who don't own a kitchen scale.

That said, I do own a small digital kitchen scale that I use to weigh vegetable shortening from a bulk container and butter from 1-pound blocks. However, I only purchased it a few years ago, and I'd written a dozen cookbooks by then. If I didn't have a scale today, I could get along fine using measuring spoons and cups to measure bulk fats.

If you prefer to weigh flour rather than use a dry measuring cup, that's fine. But keep in mind that there is a wide discrepancy, even among reputable sources, about how much a cup of all-purpose flour weighs. Some say as it's as little as 4¼ ounces, others as much as 5 ounces. That's a considerable spread, and it only compounds the confusion home bakers often experience when baking by weight.

For what it's worth, 1 cup of flour, measured the way I do it, pretty consistently weighs 4½ ounces, so that's my point of reference.

2

In the Pantry:
FLOURS, FATS, AND FILLINGS

One of the things I've always liked about making piecrust
is that it doesn't involve anything exotic or hard to find.
All you need is fat, flour, salt, and sometimes sugar. With
the exception of butter, which seems to keep going up in
cost, nothing is too expensive, either.

Consequently, a good homemade piecrust is never more
than a few minutes away. Indeed, mixing up a batch of
pie dough is a lot quicker than making a trip to your local
supermarket to buy packaged pie dough. So homemade
pie dough is not only more convenient than a convenience
one, it's more economical.

Let's consider our basic piecrust ingredients, the
ingredients you'll want on hand so you can make a pie at
a moment's notice.

Flour

Everyday all-purpose flour makes a wonderful pie-crust. Of the major brands out there, I'm partial to Gold Medal, but others work great, too. I use bleached all-purpose flour, as much out of habit than anything else. Many bakers today prefer unbleached flour, and that's fine. Use whichever one you're partial to.

Do not substitute any kind of bread flour, coarse whole-grain flours, or self-rising flour for all-purpose flour. Those products aren't designed for making piecrust, and you simply won't get the results you're hoping for.

Please note that I do use whole-wheat pastry flour in my Whole-Wheat Pie Dough (page 66), but it is a specific brand — the Whole Foods Market house brand — that is finely textured and makes a fabulous crust. I recommend it highly and hope you try the recipe.

STORAGE. My preferred way of storing all-purpose flour is to transfer it from the bag into a plastic or Lucite storage container with a tight-fitting lid. Mine is rectangular and measures about 14 by 8 by 5 inches, the perfect size for holding a 5-pound bag of flour. I store it in a lower cabinet, in a relatively cool location.

A large container like this allows me to mea-sure flour easily and correctly: I hold the cup over the bin with one hand and "fluff" the flour with my other hand. Then I pick up flour by the handful, drop it in until the cup overflows, and level off the top with a knife or a finger. That's how you measure flour. I often see new pie mak-ers push the cup into the flour and cram it full, but that method results in too much flour. (See Weights and Measures, page 11, for a discussion of weighing flour.)

Fats

The most common fats for pie dough are butter, solid vegetable shortening, and lard. Lard used to be the fat of choice for pie makers, and it's making a comeback in some circles; it's hard to beat lard's

flakiness in a crust. Let's have a look at all of these options.

BUTTER. The butter of choice for pie makers is unsalted butter. Not only does unsalted butter have a cleaner, more natural flavor than salted butter, but it allows us to accurately regulate the salt content in our crust. Use whatever brand you prefer. As the price of butter has climbed, I've discovered that house brands can offer very good quality at about half the price.

In recent years, expensive European brands have gained in popularity. They're slightly higher in fat than traditional butter and make a delicious crust; it's fun to experiment with them. But I make a lot of pies and have a hard time justifying the expense.

VEGETABLE SHORTENING. Fats lubri-cate the flour — that's what "cutting in the fat" is all about — and make piecrust tender and flaky. But there are major differences between butter and vegetable shortening (Crisco being the iconic brand). Butter is an all-natural prod-uct that adds a delicate buttery flavor to crusts; vegetable shortening is flavorless. It's produced

by treating cooking oil with a process that solidifies the oil and makes it stable across a wide temperature range.

In other words, unlike butter — which hardens in the fridge and softens at room temperature — vegetable shortening maintains much the same solid consistency regardless of the ambient temperature.

One reason for Crisco's popularity is the fact that it's been around for a long time and is part of the American pie-making tradition. In spite of the fact that vegetable shortening has none of butter's flavor, a Crisco crust has a pleasant, almost nutty taste. For a great many of us, that flavor is synonymous with the pies our moms or grandmas used to make. A butter crust wants us to notice its lovely flavor; a Crisco crust is happy to be a supporting cast member in service of the filling.

In my day-to-day pie making, I almost always add a couple of tablespoons Crisco to my otherwise all-butter crust. Not only does the shortening soften the dough and make it easier to roll, it has a conditioning effect on the crust and renders it more tender than an all-butter crust. In that respect, a butter-shortening crust offers the best of both worlds.

LARD. Americans have a conflicted relationship with lard. It was a beloved staple in our ancestors' farm kitchens, but it earned a reputation as being bad for our health. More recently, animal fats have begun to enjoy a renaissance of sorts. I'm a cook, not a health cop, so if you have concerns about lard — or any other fat, for that matter — I encourage you to do your homework. Let me suggest *The Fat Kitchen: How to Render, Cure & Cook with Lard, Tallow & Poultry Fat* by Andrea Chesman.

But from a purely pie-making perspective, lard enjoys an enviable reputation for creating the flakiest of piecrusts. Lard's flavor is generally neutral, but many experienced pie makers will tell you that using butter and lard in more or less equal proportions creates the best piecrust you'll ever taste.

Like any other ingredient, it helps to know your source. Lard is available in supermarkets, but many home bakers prefer to seek out local farmers or other sources for top-quality lard. A dedicated few are rendering their own lard, a process of slow-melting pig fat on a pot on the stovetop.

Salt, Sugar, and Cornstarch

Plain old table salt comprises just a fraction of the total ingredients in a pie dough, but it plays an important role. Without it, piecrust will taste flat. So unless you're on a strict salt-limited diet, don't leave it out.

Sugar is usually considered an optional ingredient in a piecrust. If you're making a sweet pie, you really don't need it; the filling should provide all the sweetness that's required. And if you're making a savory pie, like a quiche, it's simply not necessary.

Sugar does help to brown the crust, but this is often a disadvantage for pies that take a while to bake, which most pies usually do, and results in an overbrowned edge. So pie bakers typically leave the sugar out of the crust. However, if you want to add a teaspoon or two of sugar to any of the basic pie dough recipes here, feel free to do so.

As for cornstarch, I use a spoonful or two in many of my pie dough recipes to make the crust a little more tender. A lot of pie makers don't bother with it, but I think it makes a small but worthwhile contribution.

Water and Other Liquids

You need just enough fresh water in piecrust to make the dough come together. Any water that's fit to drink is fine. Pie makers sometimes disagree on how to add the water — a little at a time, all at once, or somewhere in between. I have my own thoughts, which you'll read about in chapter 3, about how it should be done for both the hand method and food processor doughs.

You will find pie dough recipes here that include other types of liquid, like milk, one with puréed cottage cheese, and in other cases an egg or egg yolk for tenderness.

There is also a buttermilk pie dough in the piecrust chapter. Buttermilk is an acidic liquid that helps tenderize dough, much the way vinegar does, which is why I often add vinegar to my pie doughs.

Ingredients for Fillings

As I've mentioned, something that's always appealed to me about pie making is the fact that pie recipes rarely require exotic or hard-to-find ingredients. You can find virtually everything you need at your local supermarket or farm stand. Let's consider some pie filling staples.

FRUIT

Americans have grown accustomed to finding any sort of fresh produce virtually year-round on our supermarket shelves — strawberries in the dead of winter, peaches in April, and so on. There's a measure of comfort in knowing that the goods are always there, even if they come from halfway across the globe. But experienced pie makers know to set their calendars and baking schedule by what's happening closer to home.

When you think about making a fruit pie, the first thing to ask yourself is, "What's in season locally?" You can doctor the fruit all you want, but there's no substitute for the flavor and juiciness of ripe local berries, peaches and other stone fruits, and apples. Using good fruit will get you halfway to a great pie. (The other 50 percent is what this book is all about.)

When you crave a fruit pie in the middle of winter, however, consider frozen fruit. The bags of frozen fruit at your supermarket are known as IQF (individually quick frozen) fruit, and the name should give you a clue as to why the quality of the fruit is generally very good: the ripe fruit is quickly processed and frozen, capturing most of the juice and flavor. I watch for sales at my local supermarket and stock up when the price is right.

Be advised that whenever I specify frozen fruit in a recipe, I'm talking about frozen fruit in a bag, not frozen fruit packed in syrup.

Learn how to make a
fancy (but simple) lattice
topping on page 46.

EGGS AND DAIRY PRODUCTS

Where eggs are called for in this book, I use large ones. I keep a couple of dozen on hand at all times because I bake a lot of pies and quiches. I don't always buy cage-free eggs, but I try to because I think happy chickens make better-tasting eggs. Unless I'm separating eggs, which is easier to do when the eggs are cold, I prefer adding them to pies when they're at room temperature. The closer to room temperature the filling is when a pie goes in the oven, the faster it will bake.

Generally speaking, I prefer full-fat versions of cream cheese, sour cream, milk, and so on, but feel free to use low-fat products if that's your preference. For most people, pie is an occasional treat, not an everyday event, so to my mind a little extra richness is nothing to fret about. Because these dairy products are combined with other ingredients and don't have to stand on their own, I try to save money by buying house brands, where the savings can be significant. (See Butter, page 14.)

SUGARS AND SPICE

The predominant sweeteners throughout this collection are plain granulated sugar and light brown sugar. I buy these at warehouse clubs because I use a lot of both for recipe testing, but not everyone needs the quantities I do. Here are a few notes.

BROWN SUGAR. When you measure brown sugar, be sure to pack it firmly into the measuring cup; you'd be surprised how much that packing can make a difference in the amount of sugar you add to the recipe. I don't use dark brown sugar often — it's darker because it has more molasses in it — but on a few occasions I specify it. If you don't want to keep both kinds on hand, just substitute light brown sugar when a recipe calls for dark.

MAPLE SYRUP. I use pure maple syrup in many pie recipes. At some point, you'll get weary of me singing its praises. This is a holdover from my years of living in New England, where I became enamored of the stuff and never outgrew it. Real maple adds a subtle but distinct flavor to pie fillings; it's especially good in pear pies, custard pies, and any pie made with pecans. Once you've tried it, you'll never consider substituting pancake syrup for the real thing.

SPICES. Baking spices enhance pies with layers of flavor. Consider how a sprinkle of nutmeg elevates a custard pie and the way apple pie just isn't the same without cinnamon. Keep your baking cabinet stocked with an array of baking spices so they're always on hand when you need them. If it's been a while since you've inventoried your spices, go through your containers, give them a sniff, and check the date. Replace any that don't smell vibrant or are out of date. Your pies will thank you. Store spices away from the heat of the stove and they'll last much longer.

THICKENERS

First off, I want everyone to relax about thickeners. This is not a subject to get worked up about the way people sometimes do. Thickeners are your friend. They're there simply to help you end up with a full-bodied fruit filling instead of fruit soup between two crusts. They hold pastry cream together for cream pies and step in when a custard pie needs a boost.

Even if you didn't know the first thing about thickeners, you'd quickly develop an intuition about how much to use, and when, in your pie making. But let's jump-start your understanding by taking a closer look at our options.

CORNSTARCH. This fine powder is made from the kernel of the corn plant. It's inexpensive and readily available. I use cornstarch at least half the time in my pie making, especially in juicy fruit pies. In mildly juicy pies, like apple, you may need only 1½ to 2 tablespoons of cornstarch. A recipe for a deep-dish berry or peach pie may call for as much as 3 to 4 tablespoons. It's difficult to come up with a hard-and-fast quantity for a given fruit pie because, among other reasons, fruits vary in juiciness from season to season.

Pies made with frozen fruit, which contain ice crystals and tend to release a lot of liquid, require a little extra thickening.

When I add cornstarch to a fruit filling, I almost always mix it in a small bowl with a little sugar before adding it to the fruit. This disperses the cornstarch and breaks up any clumps, so it will spread evenly throughout the filling without clumping. Some might find this step a little fussy

Keep Those Pie Spices Fresh

Gone are the days of inexpensive spices; you've probably noticed. So it pays to buy smart and do what you can to keep them fresh. Here are some tips for doing just that.

- Rule of thumb: Only buy enough of a given spice that you'll use in 6 to 9 months.

- Buy smaller quantities from a bulk dealer, whose supplies typically are fresher.

- Give the spices the sniff test. If they don't tantalize your senses, throw them out and get fresh ones.

- Keep them away from the heat. The biggest mistake cooks make is storing spices too near the stove. Heat destroys the volatile oils that give spices their flavor.

- Don't store them in the sunlight. Direct sunlight will wreak havoc on their flavor. Find a dark, low-humidity cabinet to store them.

- If you really want your pies to sparkle, get a spice grinder and use whole spices.

or unnecessary, but it's an old habit that feels virtuous and I see no reason to change now.

I've heard pie makers say that they don't like to use cornstarch in their fruit fillings because it can cloud the filling and make it look less glossy, but I — quite literally — don't see their point. Or if I do, it's so minimal as to be moot.

FLOUR. Good old all-purpose flour works great for thickening apple and pear pies, but it is not as potent as cornstarch so you typically have to use more of it. The rule of thumb for flour is to use twice as much as the recommended amount of cornstarch in a fruit pie if you're making a substitution. That's a good estimate, but a little too extravagant, in my experience. Not to split hairs, but if I were going to substitute flour for 1 tablespoon cornstarch in an apple pie, I'd probably use 1½ tablespoons or 2 scant tablespoons flour.

While I don't have clouding issues with cornstarch, clouding can indeed be a concern with flour. I prefer not to use flour with dark berry or cherry pie fillings; it stands out more in dark fillings. With pear and apple fillings, the cloudiness isn't really noticeable.

TAPIOCA. There are two types of tapioca used in pie making: tapioca starch (a.k.a. tapioca flour) and quick-cooking tapioca, which I use in some fruit pies. Like cornstarch, tapioca starch is a fine powder that's added directly to the fruit filling; as with cornstarch, I'll mix it with a little sugar first. Most pie makers recommend substituting 1½ to 2 tablespoons tapioca starch per tablespoon cornstarch, and that formula has worked out for me. The juicier the fruit, the more you should favor doubling the amount.

There was a time when I used quick-cooking tapioca (or "minute tapioca," as it's sometimes called) almost exclusively for my fruit pies. But unlike the other powdery thickeners we're discussing, quick-cooking tapioca is granular, and a common complaint is that the granules do not fully dissolve into the filling when the pie bakes. You can usually minimize the problem by letting the filling sit for 10 to 15 minutes before assembling the pie so that the granules have a chance to soften.

Pie through the Ages

No one knows for certain who baked the first pie. Some historians believe that it was the Romans. The first written recipe for a pie, they tell us, came from Cato the Censor (234–139 BCE), who printed a recipe for a goat cheese and honey pie in a rye crust. Here are a few more things historians know about the evolution of pie.

- *The Oxford English Dictionary notes that the word* pie *was "evidently a well-known popular word in 1362," although it most likely referred to meat and fowl pies, not dessert pies.*

- *In 1475, the Italian writer Platina offered a recipe for a squash pie sprinkled with sugar and rose water. Could this have been an early ancestor of our pumpkin pie?*

- *Fruit pies likely did not exist much before the 1500s. In Tudor and Stuart times, English pies were made with pears, apples, and quinces.*

- *Pie came to America with the English settlers, who baked their pies in pans known as "coffyns." Pastry crust was not their forte. It was typically meant only to contain the filling, not to be eaten.*

- *Apple pie for breakfast is an old New England tradition. The 1877 diary of a Vermont housewife counts her annual output of pies at 427 — and this without refrigerated pie pastry!*

- *Pie is still America's favorite dessert, with apple leading the pack.*

How to Make a Pie:
A STEP-BY-STEP TUTORIAL
PLUS A WHOLE LOT MORE

If my years in the kitchen have taught me anything, it's that cooking is much more enjoyable and far less chaotic if you take the time to gather the necessary ingredients and tools before you begin. (Multiply that statement by two, or maybe ten, if kids are involved.)

You'll save yourself a gallon of grief if you have everything in its place before you start making a piecrust. The French call this concept *mise en place*, and virtually every restaurant and savvy cook practices it. I suggest doing it before you start making piecrust and then before rolling it out.

I know you're anxious to dive into the recipes, but if you're a new pie maker, I recommend that you read this entire section from start to finish before you actually head to the kitchen and begin making your dough and baking your pie. At the very least, read up to the point where we chill the dough. Think of it as a get-acquainted trip, where you have the luxury to be a passenger and look at the map and scenery without the distraction of having to pack or drive.

Making a Perfect Piecrust

This step-by-step illustrated recipe is written around a single-crust batch of the Perfect Pie Dough by Hand recipe on page 56.

HAVE READY

- 1½ cups all-purpose flour
- 1½ teaspoons cornstarch
- ½ teaspoon salt

- 10 tablespoons (1¼ sticks) cold unsalted butter, cut into ½-inch cubes, or 8 tablespoons (1 stick) cold, cubed unsalted butter plus 2 tablespoons vegetable shortening or lard
- 2 teaspoons white vinegar
- ¼–⅓ cup cold water

MEASURE THE DRY INGREDIENTS

Use a large mixing bowl that can accommodate both of your hands comfortably. Measure the flour and add it to the bowl. Add the cornstarch and salt. Whisk the dry mixture to combine, or just mix it by hand. Put the bowl in the refrigerator.

MEASURE THE FAT

Cut the butter into ½-inch cubes. If you're using stick butter, cut the stick into tablespoon-size pieces, then cut each piece into four equal cubes. Scatter the cubes around on a flour-dusted plate; the flour prevents the butter from sticking to the plate. Put the shortening on the same plate if you're using it, in several small lumps, then put the plate in the refrigerator. You don't need to cover it.

MEASURE THE LIQUID

When you measure the liquid — especially the liquid for piecrust — leave the cup on the counter and bend over so you're at eye level with the marks on the side of the cup. If you're standing above the cup, you won't get an accurate reading.

Using a 1-cup glass measuring cup, add the 2 teaspoons white vinegar and enough cold water to equal ⅓ cup total liquid. Put the cup in the refrigerator with the other ingredients and chill for 10 to 15 minutes.

Dough or Pastry?

Just in case you're wondering, the terms "dough" and "pastry" can be used interchangeably in the context of making a piecrust.

CUT IN THE FAT (A)

After everything has chilled for 10 to 15 minutes, take the dry ingredients and the fat out of the refrigerator. Dust your hands with the flour in the bowl, then add the fat to the bowl all at once. Toss the fat with the flour, coating it thoroughly.

Using firm finger pressure, pinch the butter cubes to flatten them out. Do this down in the bowl so you smear the fat with plenty of flour; the flour will help prevent the fat from rubbing onto your fingers. (Note: If the butter is too cold to pinch and flatten without difficulty, let the mixture sit for 5 minutes and then proceed.)

If you need a little more leverage, instead of pinching the butter and flour between your fingers, use your thumbs and simply press against the bottom of the bowl, which requires less finger strength.

"Cutting in the Fat"

Cutting in the fat is a term for combining the fat and the flour. The cutting motion coats the fat with the flour, smears them together, and helps prevent the dough from developing gluten — stretchy, weblike strands of wheat protein that would otherwise form when the water is added, resulting in a less tender crust.

The cutting also creates countless little particles of fat that get flattened out when you roll the dough. When the moisture in the fat turns to steam in the oven, it makes little pockets in the crust and creates that prized flakiness pie makers aspire to.

How Long Do I Keep Cutting?

The standard advice in recipes — and I've said it myself many times — is to cut until the mixture resembles small peas, green peas, or split peas. That description offers some guidance and is useful as recipe shorthand, but you should know that "small peas" is an average. In my experience, it's better to work in the fat a little too much than too little, or some of the flour will not be lubricated, which in turn will require you to add more liquid than you probably should.

Even after I stop cutting with my pastry blender, I like to rub the mixture between my fingers to ensure that everything is touched by the fat. Generally speaking, it will take you 3 to 4 minutes to do a thorough job of cutting in the fat.

CUT IN THE FAT (B)

Once most of the fat is smushed, start pushing it down into the mixture with the pastry cutter, cutting the fat into smaller and smaller pieces. As you work, occasionally scrape the ingredients from the edge of the bowl so everything gets "touched by the fat" — a phrase coined by my friend and mentor, the late food writer Marion Cunningham.

As you cut, notice how the mixture starts to build up on the wires or blades of the pastry blender. Take a moment, every few pushes, to push out the buildup with your fingers. Retoss everything together in the bowl so you end up with a nice even distribution of ingredients each time you do this.

ADD THE LIQUID (A)

Use your hands to mound the ingredients toward the center of the bowl, making a little mountain of it. Now drizzle half of the liquid down the sides of the bowl, but not in just one location; rotate the bowl as you pour it so the liquid doesn't end up all in one spot.

Using a large fork, begin tossing the mixture from the perimeter toward the center of the bowl. Work your way all around, tossing as you go. Don't start compressing the mixture at this early stage of the game; you're simply trying to distribute the moisture by moving the mixture around in the bowl.

Now sprinkle about half of the remaining liquid over the mixture, raining it down randomly here and there. Use the fork and toss the mixture again.

Please note that some bakers prefer to do the exact opposite of what I do. Instead of gathering the dry ingredients toward the middle of the bowl and pouring the water down the sides, they make a well in the middle of the dry ingredients and pour the water into the well. Both ways work, if you want to try another approach.

ADD THE LIQUID (B)

Sprinkle on the remaining liquid and stir the mixture more vigorously, until the dough starts to cohere. Before you stir the dough too much, however, try to determine if it needs more liquid. This is a judgment call that you'll get better at with practice, and frankly there's almost no way to "book learn" when you've added enough liquid. It's something you master by trial and error, and it's also something of a moving target because humidity, the ingredients, and other variables can alter the outcome. If more liquid is needed, add cold water a teaspoon or two at a time. By the time you add the final teaspoon, the dough should be gathering into good-size clumps.

One test for judging whether you've added enough water to the dough is to grab a small handful and squeeze it in the palm of your hand. If it holds together, and you can nudge it around with a finger without it crumbling apart, it's ready. If it still seems dry and crumbly, mix in a little more water.

GATHER THE DOUGH

Now it's time to gather up the dough and shape it, first into a ball, then into a disk. The easiest way is to simply gather and press it together, then pack it together gently like you're making a snowball. The trick is to shape it without overhandling it.

At this point, I like to give the dough a couple of gentle kneads on a lightly floured countertop — nothing vigorous, just a few pushes to smooth it out.

SHAPE THE DOUGH

Put the dough ball in the center of a sheet of plastic wrap, then flatten it with your palm to make a disk between ¾ and 1 inch thick. If the edge cracks a little, don't worry; just pinch it back together where needed. Wrap the dough in the plastic wrap and put it in the refrigerator.

Double Talk

When you make a double-crust batch of dough, you'll notice that the recipes tell you to divide the dough in two, making one part slightly larger than the other. The larger part is for the bottom crust, the shell, because it requires more dough. The other part, obviously, is for the top crust. Another possibility, of course, is to use the dough for two shells if you don't need a top crust. In that case, divide the dough into equal halves. In any event, both halves should be shaped and wrapped separately.

Rolling Out the Dough

Over the years, I've worked on all sorts of kitchen countertop surfaces, from Formica to butcher block and granite, and I've had good luck rolling dough on pretty much all of them. It's been a while since I rolled directly on the countertop itself, but I know many pie makers do, and it suits them just fine. I think it's a pain in the neck to clean, so here are some other options. If you don't have a favorite rolling method, try one or more of them and see which one works best for you.

WAXED PAPER. In my early pie-making years, waxed paper was my go-to choice for rolling. It has just enough built-in grip to grab the rolled-out dough and hold on to it while you invert the dough over the pie pan (and then peel off the paper). It's also 12 inches wide, and since most dough is rolled into a 12- to 13-inch circle, you pretty much know when the circle of dough is large enough.

When I roll on waxed paper, I dust the paper with flour before I begin. I don't use a second sheet of paper on top; I just flour the top of the dough as I work if the dough becomes sticky. As the dough circle starts to get bigger, it may stick a little to the paper, but I don't worry about that. You'll be able to peel the paper off the dough once you invert the dough over the pie pan.

Why Do I Chill the Dough?

For starters, fats soften as you mix them into the flour and chilling refirms the fats in the dough. If you didn't chill it, the dough would be a little sticky and more difficult to roll.

Also, remember that gluten I mentioned (see Cutting in the Fat, page 26), and how developing it can make a dough less tender? Well, in spite of our best efforts, some gluten always forms when we make pie dough. Chilling the dough and letting it rest relaxes the gluten so the dough is easier to roll and, ultimately, more tender.

HOW LONG SHOULD THE DOUGH REFRIGERATE? Generally speaking, about 1 hour, give or take. With experience you'll become adept at judging the "feel" of the dough when it's ready to roll — firmish and still slightly pliable without breaking, but not too hard. It should yield to medium finger pressure.

It's fine if the dough chills for several hours or overnight. Just take it out of the fridge about 10 minutes before you plan to roll it so it becomes softer and more pliable. You'll know if the dough is still too cold if it firmly resists when you start to roll. You shouldn't have to fight it.

WHAT ABOUT FREEZING IT? Pie dough freezes beautifully for up to 2 months. Simply overwrap the disc in plastic wrap, then slip it into a plastic freezer bag before freezing. Identify and date the bag: *Whole-Wheat Pie Dough (Single Crust) 9/14*. Transfer the dough to the refrigerator about 8 hours before rolling, or take it right from the freezer and let it sit at room temperature until it's ready. (I prefer the former because the dough will thaw more evenly in the fridge.)

Note: It's not unusual for pie dough to oxidize and change in color as it chills. It's especially noticeable when there's vegetable shortening in the dough. The coloring is minimal after one night, but after a couple of days it starts to take on a grayish shadow. It looks a bit unappetizing, but there's no impact on the flavor. So I suggest freezing the dough instead of refrigerating it if you won't be using it within 24 hours. Incidentally, this coloring is less noticeable after you bake the pie, so don't freak out if this happens to you. It's not the end of the world.

The one problem with waxed paper is that it has a tendency to scoot around the counter when you roll, so you may need to put a nonskid silicone baking mat under it.

PLASTIC WRAP. I've never been a huge fan of rolling between sheets of plastic wrap, but I understand why others are: the dough simply won't stick to it, which can be a big plus, especially for new pie makers, and doubly so when you're rolling a pie dough made with a large proportion of vegetable shortening. (I explain in more detail on page 61.)

My main complaint about this arrangement is the plastic has a maddening way of crimping and grabbing the dough; you have to stop frequently to stretch out the wrap and smooth it over. A bit of a hassle for sure, but don't write off this method altogether if other approaches don't work for you. Indeed, if you end up making the Gluten-Free Pie Dough (page 76), rolling between sheets of plastic may be your best option.

PARCHMENT PAPER AND BAKING MAT. This has been my default rolling arrangement for years. I keep a silicone mat on my counter at all times. (Silpat is one common brand name.) I lay a sheet of parchment paper on top of the mat, and the mat keeps the parchment from scooting around the countertop. Both the mat and the sheets of parchment measure 16½ by 24½ inches. The parchment is large enough to contain whatever mess I make; I just wad up the paper and toss it when I'm done. This leaves very little to clean up on the countertop itself.

FLATTEN THE DOUGH

Dust the work surface with flour, but don't overdo it. Put the chilled pie dough on the counter and dust the top of the dough with flour, too. Take the rolling pin, dust it with flour, and rock it over the dough a few times to wake it up. Don't push hard; pie dough likes to wake up slowly, like my wife, only my dough doesn't also require a fresh cup of coffee and the morning paper.

How Hard Do I Press on the Pin?

It won't take too much practice before you learn how much pressure to apply as you roll. Use too little and your progress will be slow; you'll start warming up the dough, and it will get tacky. Use too much pressure and the dough will stick or come out uneven. So use medium pressure, enough to see some progress with each pass of the pin.

And don't worry, even experienced pie makers roll a lopsided circle sometimes, so don't panic if the dough circle isn't perfect. Just trim off the errant dough with a pastry cutter and make the best circle you can. Keep the scraps handy to patch with, if necessary, or to make a mini pie shell.

From here on out, so I don't have to keep mentioning it, assume that you should dust the work surface, the top of the dough, and the rolling pin as needed, to prevent the dough from sticking. That goes for every recipe in the book.

BEGIN ROLLING

Once you've rocked the dough and flattened it out a little, begin rolling it from the center out. Only roll away from you, toward the 10:00, 12:00, and 2:00 positions. As you complete each sequence, give the dough about a quarter turn, then repeat the rolling sequence. Rotate another quarter turn and repeat. (If you're using waxed paper, at some point you'll likely be rotating the paper with the dough semistuck to it, instead of just turning the dough.)

The key thing is to keep the dough from sticking to the counter. That's the main reason for those quarter turns. At the first sign that it is sticking, run your fingers under the dough to loosen it, slide the dough off to the side, and reflour the rolling surface before you continue.

Before long you should have a circle of dough that's the perfect size for lining the pie pan. If you're using a standard 9- or 9½-inch pie pan, a 12-inch circle will be large enough. If you're using a deep-dish pie pan, make it 12½ to 13 inches in diameter.

At this point, take a pastry brush and brush the excess flour off the dough. Don't dawdle, because the longer the dough stays at room temperature, the more difficult it will be to handle.

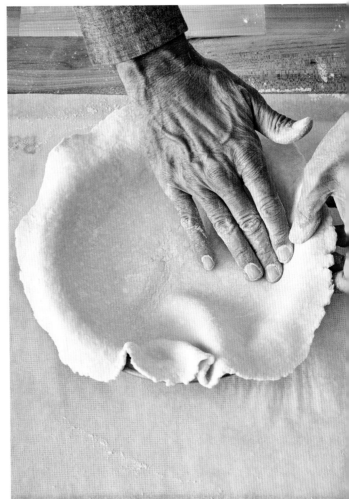

TURN THE DOUGH INTO THE PIE PAN

The easiest method is to simply run your hands under the dough — just scoot your fingers and palms under the dough on opposite sides — then lift it into the pan. This works fine if the dough is holding together nicely and not breaking apart on you. If you're feeling less than confident, borrow an extra set of hands to help lift it. Or consult the box below.

SETTLE THE DOUGH

The object of this next step is to fit the dough into the pan without stretching or tearing it. Begin by making sure that the dough is draped evenly over the pan. You don't want an overhang of 1½ inches on one side and half that much on the opposite side or the edge of the crust will be lopsided.

Once you've adjusted the circle of dough, start to gently nudge it down the sides of the pan and into the crease at the bottom. Do this gradually, working your way around as you go. To avoid stretching the dough, lift up on the overhanging pastry with one hand and use the other hand to nudge the dough into the pan. If you do this correctly, you should be able to see the crease of the pan imprinted clearly in the dough, some of which will still hang over the sides of the pan. With any luck, the overhang will be a fairly even ¾ to 1 inch all around.

What you do next with the pie shell depends on the type of pie you're going to make.

IF YOU'RE MAKING A SINGLE-CRUST PIE, you're likely making a crumb-topped fruit pie, custard pie, chess pie, or another kind of pie without a top crust. In that case, you'll probably want to make an attractive fluted edge. We'll talk about that next.

FOR A DOUBLE-CRUST FRUIT PIE, the overhanging dough is needed to attach the top crust; just refrigerate the shell. Then skip to page 39 for the double-crust technique. (Cover with plastic wrap if you won't be assembling the pie within 1 hour.)

Other Pie-Dough Transfer Methods

The distance from rolling mat to pie pan is measured in inches, but the journey can be a treacherous one. My inbox is full of piecrust transfer stories, and they aren't pretty. Not to worry: You have several options in addition to the one pictured here.

If you've rolled the dough onto waxed paper, simply invert the paper and dough over the pan, center it, then slowly peel off the paper.

Another option is to use a rimless cookie sheet. Flour the sheet, lift one edge of the dough, then carefully slide the sheet under the dough until you're supporting the entire thing. Position the sheet over the pan, then slide the dough into the pan.

I've never been crazy about it, but some bakers like to rest their rolling pin at one end of the dough and roll the dough onto the pin. Position the pin over one edge of the pan, then unroll the dough into the pan. This option has always felt clumsy to me, and it's especially tricky if you use a big, heavy pin. And if you like to make pie doughs with whole grains, like I do, they often lack the suppleness to withstand this rolling move. Overall, it works best with butter doughs. But if you like this method and it works for you, by all means stick with it.

One final option, if the dough is flexible enough, is to gently fold the rolled dough in half, then half again, forming equal quarters. Then put the dough in the pan, with the point of the folds in the middle, and unfold it. You should be able to do this with most all-butter doughs.

Do I Have to Do the Crimping Thing?

If you don't want to bother with a fluted edge, simply trim the overhanging edge by running a paring knife around the edge to trim off the excess flush with the outer edge of the pan. Leave the edge as is, or give it a simple decorative finish by pressing down along the edge with the tines of a fork. This is called a fork-crimped edge.

The drawback of not sculpting an upstanding ridge is that the shell won't hold as much filling. That extra capacity can come in real handy. The other drawback is that you'll have a larger pile of dough trimmings (be sure to save and use them to make mini pie shells).

Of course, you can always roll out the trimmings, cut them into shapes, and arrange them on a baking sheet. Brush with milk or cream, sprinkle with cinnamon and sugar, and bake at 375°F (190°C) until golden brown. Kids love making these piecrust cookies.

Fluting the Edge

The technique described here is referred to, variously, as a crimped, ruffled, fluted, or scalloped edge. There are probably other terms I'm not familiar with. No matter what you call it, here's how we do it.

Take the overhanging dough and fold it under (toward the outside of the pan) so any seam is hidden. As you fold, pinch the dough together while you sculpt it into an upstanding ridge. Work your way around the edge, making the ridge as consistently thick and even as possible. This ridge should be ½ to ¾ inch high. Place the shell in the freezer for 5 to 6 minutes to firm up the ridge. This makes it easier to flute and helps the flutes hold their shape.

To create the flute, form a V with the thumb and forefinger of one hand against the outside of the rim. With your other forefinger, press against the shell from the other side, pushing the dough into the V. (For slightly larger flutes, press with your thumb instead of your forefinger.) Apply equal pressure from both sides so the edge remains straight. Don't be afraid to push firmly; exaggerated flutes hold their shape better in the oven. Continue around the entire perimeter. Cover with plastic wrap and refrigerate the shell for at least 15 minutes.

VENTING FOR BLIND BAKING

If you need to prebake the shell (see Blind Baking, page 36), poke the bottom seven or eight times with a fork. When you poke, twist the fork slightly from side to side to enlarge the holes; small holes tend to close up when the shell prebakes. These holes act as little vents and allow trapped steam to escape from under the shell when you remove the pie weights (more about these weights in Blind Baking).

Freeze the Shell

In addition to freezing a disc of dough, you can also take the extra step of rolling it out then freezing the shell in the pan. Overwrap the shell with two layers of plastic and freeze until needed. Be very careful not to disturb that overhanging dough. It might tear off if you knock it against something in the freezer. (I often make and freeze several pie shells in advance during the holiday season.) When you're ready to use the shell, transfer it to the fridge or leave it at room temperature until the overhang is flexible enough to shape without breaking.

Blind Baking

The first step in blind baking is to weigh down the crust so it doesn't balloon in the oven. If the crust puffs up and loses contact with the pan, it won't brown properly. It becomes misshapen, too, and may not accommodate all of the filling.

Before turning on the oven, adjust the racks so one of them is in the bottom position and the other is in the middle of the oven. If you have only one rack, split the difference so it's in the position between those two. Preheat the oven to 375°F (190°C). (Incidentally, it's a good idea to double-check the oven's temperature with an oven thermometer, especially if your pies are getting overbrowned.)

TIP: If you put the pie pan in the freezer, especially a glass or ceramic one, make sure it sits at room temperature for 5 to 7 minutes before you place it in the oven. You don't want to shock the pie pan and cause it to shatter. Never put a cold glass or ceramic pan onto a hot baking sheet, either.

BEFORE YOU BEGIN

A pie shell will inevitably leak a little butter as it bakes, which is why you need to put it on a baking sheet. I typically use a dark rimmed baking sheet; dark transmits heat better. I highly recommend lining the sheet with parchment paper to soak up any leaking butter. The butter is less likely to smoke in the oven if it absorbs into the parchment rather than ends up directly on the baking sheet.

What Exactly Is Blind Baking?

Blind baking refers to the process of prebaking the pie shell — either partially or fully — to "set" the crust and keep it, well, as crusty as possible. It happens to be one of the most confusing and conflicting issues pie makers face. I get a ton of emails on the subject, and they're not typically about how well things are working out. Frustration reigns.

A prebaked pie shell will yield a noticeable definition between the crust and filling. Done properly, you get the crustiness you want, along with the contrasting softness of the filling. People will wonder what it is that makes your pies so darn good; this is one of your secrets.

When should you blind bake a piecrust? We'll get to that, but let's first talk about when you don't need to blind bake the crust, and that's pretty much whenever you're making a traditional fruit pie with either a top crust or a crumb topping.

If you're making a double-crust fruit pie, there's simply no way to attach the top pastry if the shell has already been baked; it would be too crusty to attach the raw dough.

But what about a crumb-topped fruit pie? Might there be some value in prebaking the

bottom crust before the fruit goes in, so it's less likely to become saturated by the juice?

The answer is "sort of, but not really." It's true that partially baking the crust will make it more moisture resistant. But there's a trade-off: by the time you prebake the crust, then add the filling and bake the pie for another 50 or 60 minutes — until the filling is fully cooked — the piecrust, and especially the top edge, will be overbaked and dry.

Pies that benefit the most from partially prebaking the shell include pumpkin and sweet potato, chess pie, custard pie, pecan pie, and buttermilk pie, to name a few — pies with loose, wet fillings will make the bottom crust soggy if it's not partially baked before the filling goes in.

On the savory side of pie, a quiche almost always calls for a partially prebaked pie or tart shell. All of these are baked at a lower temperature than fruit pies and for less time, so the risk of overbaking the shell is minimal.

Finally, certain pie shells are fully prebaked when the recipe call for no further baking, most notably cream pies, where the filling is cooked separately then added to the shell.

Tear off a sheet of aluminum foil about 16 inches long. Use standard foil, not heavy-duty foil; the former is more malleable and shapes more easily, so the foil fits the shell like a glove.

You'll need about 1½ pounds dried black beans, pinto beans, lima beans, or another large bean. Some folks swear by ceramic pie weights, but I've always been a bean guy. Use the beans over and over again for the same purpose. Cool thoroughly after each use, then store them in a sealed jar. (They may smell a bit toasty after a number of uses, but that won't hurt anything.)

WEIGH DOWN THE CRUST

To line the shell, center the foil over the shell, then gradually begin nudging it evenly into the pan. Scoot it down into the crease, pressing it snugly against the sides of the shell. The foil should fit like a second skin. You'll be left with several inches of foil overhang on opposite sides — don't cut it off. Simply fold it down so it looks like the pan has foil wings. Put the winged pie shell on the baking sheet. Add enough dried beans to fill the pan by about two-thirds, banking them up the sides until they are even with the top edge of the pan.

TIP: I used the foil method for years. More recently, I've been experimenting with really large coffee filters, like the ones used for the big urn-style coffee makers. The filters that measure 16 to 18 inches across fit perfectly in a pie pan. They're also more breathable — if that's the word for it — than foil, so I think they allow for better baking.

BAKE THE PIE SHELL (A)

Put the baking sheet and pie pan on the lower rack of the preheated oven and set the timer for 25 minutes. Don't open the oven until the time is up.

After 25 minutes, slide out the rack and carefully — so you don't accidentally touch the hot pan or sheet — grab the overhanging foil on opposite sides and lift out the beans. The foil will cool off almost immediately once you slide out the rack, but touch the foil gingerly, at first, just to be sure. If you're using a coffee filter, lift it out with two hands. Wear oven mitts for protection if needed. Lift slowly, so the foil or paper doesn't grab the shell, and pull the foil or paper up and out of the shell. If you'd rather do this step on top of the stove or in your work area instead of leaning over the oven, transfer the baking sheet to the stovetop and work from there.

BAKE THE PIE SHELL (B)

Once you've remove the beans, poke open the fork holes in the bottom of the shell if they look like they've filled in. The holes keep the bottom of the pastry from inflating like a balloon during the next stage. Transfer the baking sheet to the middle shelf, lower the heat to 350°F (180°C), and set the timer for 10 minutes. Again, no peeking except through the oven window.

Check the pie shell after 10 minutes. By now the bottom of the shell should have a dryish surface and the top edge should just be starting to turn golden. If not, slide it back in and bake for 3 or 4 minutes longer. You now have a partially prebaked pie shell.

If you need a fully prebaked pie shell — for a cream pie, for instance — bake for an additional 15 to 18 minutes after the initial bake, instead of 10, until golden brown and crusty all over.

TIP: If you find out later that the bottom of the shell is getting too dark when you prebake it, move the oven rack up one position for subsequent pies.

COOL BEFORE FILLING

Transfer the pie shell to a cooling rack and cool thoroughly before filling.

It's a good idea to plug those holes in the shell before adding a liquid filling. Even though they're small, I like to smear the smallest amount of cream cheese over them, applying it like putty to a tiny nail hole, to prevent the filling from leaking through and sticking to the pan.

Or you can use the old egg white wash trick: when the shell comes out of the oven, immediately brush the entire surface with lightly with an egg white beaten with 1 teaspoon water until frothy. The wash will harden right away and help seal the crust from moisture.

Assembling a Double-Crust Fruit Pie

Now that you know how to mix up and roll out a single crust and blind bake it, if that step is called for, you can proceed to take that pie shell and fill it with a lovely custard or cream filling. But what if you want to bake a double-crust fruit pie instead of a single-crust anything else?

Well, for starters, you need to make two batches of a single-crust recipe or follow the directions for a double-crust recipe. If you do the latter, divide the dough into two parts, making the portion for the bottom crust slightly larger than the other. Because it's rolled into a smaller circle and requires less dough, you will use the smaller part for the top crust. Put both portions in the refrigerator to chill, then proceed to roll out the bottom crust and line the pie pan as described previously.

The Delightful Dilemma of Pastry Trimmings

Inevitably, you will end up with little trimmings and pieces of dough when you bake a pie. Please don't toss them; you're throwing money away, and there are so many uses for them. So let's talk about strategies that minimize the waste and put these leftovers to good use.

First, treat the scraps delicately. It's dough, not Silly Putty. They've already been shaped and rolled, and now you're going to pat and roll them again, which is a recipe for a tough crust. So just gather the scraps into a heap, press down to flatten them, place in a quart freezer bag, and freeze.

Don't keep adding scraps to one larger pile of frozen trimmings forever. I recently had a fellow tell me he had a solid, frozen mound of dough scraps in the freezer about the size of a football. According to him, the mass was impenetrable, and — the real kicker — the pile had been growing for about 4 years. He was clearly attached, but I suggested it was time he let go of this iceberg and start from scratch.

I've found that the best use for these scraps is mini pies. I keep 4- and 5-inch disposable aluminum pie pans on hand, and if I have enough scraps from a pie session, I immediately roll them out, turn them into mini pie shells, and freeze them. They're ready and waiting when I have leftover filling from another pie or when I want to make some small pot pies.

FILL THE SHELL

Before you roll the smaller part for the top crust, take a moment to prep your tools so the assembly proceeds without delay. Set up your rolling station with whatever you need — pastry brush; pastry wheel and scissors for trimming the crust; a small bowl of water for moistening the rim of the shell; whatever glaze you might be using; a parchment-lined baking sheet for under the pie pan; and a lightweight pot lid or other round template for cutting the top pastry, if you're not freehanding it.

First and foremost, have the filling ready. For the purposes of this demo, we're making an imaginary apple pie. For most fruit pies, we'll start the pie on a lower rack and move it up to the middle rack later, so adjust the shelves accordingly. Then preheat the oven to 400°F (200°C).

ROLL THE TOP CRUST

Roll the top crust into a nice round 11- to 11½-inch circle. We'll make ours 11½ inches because our imaginary apple pie uses a big mound of apples. If you don't mound the filling, an 11-inch circle should be large enough. If you're using a template, place it over the dough and use a pastry wheel or paring knife to trim around it. If you don't have a suitable template, do some quick measurements with a ruler and just freehand it. Transfer the filling to the pie shell and even it out with a spoon or your hands.

COVER THE FILLING

Lightly moisten the edge of the pie shell with
water, using a pastry brush or your fingertip. Lift
the dough and drape it evenly over the filling.
Press gently along the edge to seal the dough.
At this point, you can either trim the dough flush
with the outside edge of the pan and crimp it,
or trim and flute the edge like you did for the
pie shell.

To simply crimp the crust, hold a sharp paring
knife perpendicular to the counter and slice off
the overhang, using the outside edge of the pan
as a guide. Then take a large fork and press the
tines into the pastry, working your way around
the entire rim. This improves the seal and leaves
a simple fork-crimped edge. See page 43 for
instructions on fluting.

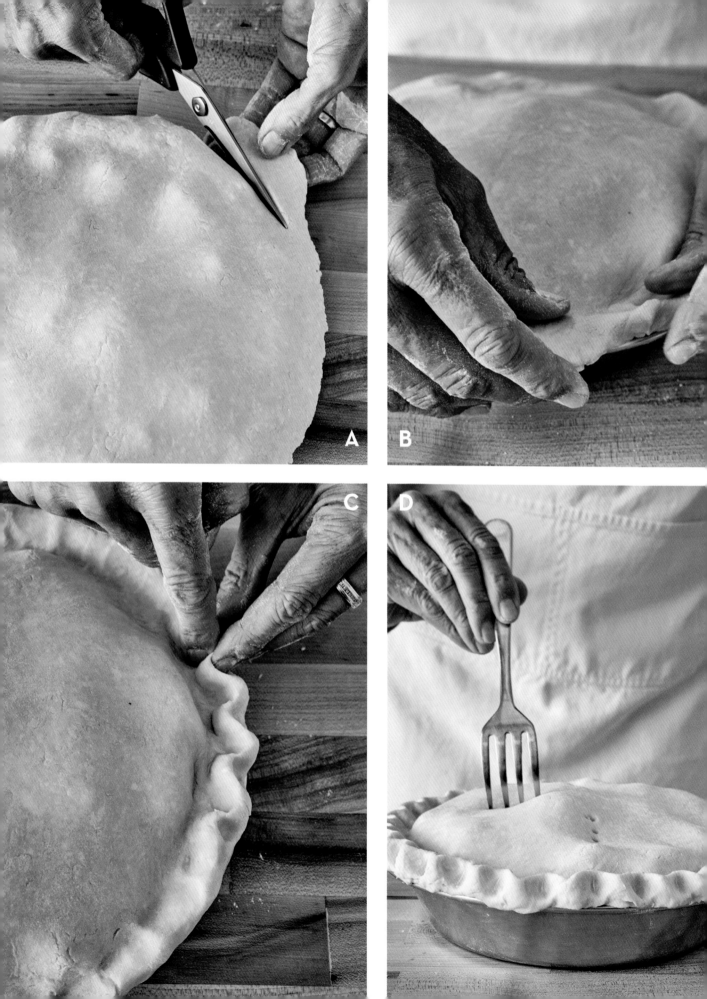

TO FLUTE THE EDGE

Follow the same technique as for the pie shell (page 34), but with some minor adjustments. First, use scissors to trim the shell and top crust so you have an even overhang of about ½ to ¾ inch all around. (A)

Starting anywhere along the edge, fold the overhang back toward the outside of the pan, to hide the seam, then pinch and sculpt the overhang into an upstanding ridge just as you would for a shell. The only difference here is that the ridge will be beefier because you're sculpting two layers of dough instead of one. (B)

Continue all the way around, sculpting the dough into an even ridge. Place the pie in the freezer for 5 to 7 minutes to firm up the ridge and make it easier to flute.

Remove the pie from the freezer and make flutes just as you would for a shell. (C)

VENT AND GLAZE

Using a large fork or the tip of a paring knife, make several holes — steam vents — in the top pastry, twisting the knife from side to side so the hole is about ¼ inch across. (D) I always put a couple of vents down near the edge so I can examine the fruit juices that gather there as the pie bakes. I'll explain why in the next section.

Using a pastry brush, lightly apply whatever glaze you're using, if any. Brush it on evenly; don't let it puddle. (E) Sprinkle the top with several big pinches of sugar, if using, then place the pie on a rimmed baking sheet, preferably one lined with parchment paper.

If you're making a fruit pie, put the baking sheet and pie in the oven on the lower rack and set the timer for half of the total baking time. Halfway through the baking, move the pie up to the middle rack and rotate the pie 180 degrees to help it bake evenly. Set the timer, and bake until done.

Tips for a Perfectly Baked Double-Crust Fruit Pie

It's exciting to make a pie, especially when you're a beginner. You're curious, naturally, to watch the crust start to brown and see the juices begin to bubble. But there's only so much you can see through that blasted oven window. I get it.

It's tempting to just pull open the oven door for a few seconds to check for signs of progress. Yet every time you do that, the oven cools off. You know what they say about a watched pot, don't you? It doesn't boil. And a watched fruit pie doesn't bake, either, at least not as fast as it should.

Bottom line: don't open the oven until you're at least halfway into the baking, and then only if the recipe tells you to or you need to change the pie's position. Every time you open that oven door, hot air spills out, the oven cools, and the pie loses momentum. This only increases the baking time and ultimately makes it more difficult to judge the pie's doneness.

IT'S ALL ABOUT THE JUICE

Here's a little secret that will immediately raise your pie IQ: the color of the top crust — or bottom crust, for that matter — can be an unreliable indicator of the doneness of a fruit pie. Yes, a gorgeously bronzed crust is worthy of a magazine cover or viral Instagram moment. But it's what's happening inside the filling that really matters.

Think about that fruit filling for a moment. First of all, it's well protected from the heat of the oven by the dough, which starts to bake and glaze over before the fruit even breaks a sweat. By the time the crust has developed a tan, the fruit is barely tepid. Juice is starting to ooze from the fruit, but not nearly enough to write home about.

After what seems like an eternity, the crust becomes beautifully golden. The fruit is beginning to cook, and there's an abundance of juice. But it's thin and runny juice, not the sweet, full-bodied juice of a properly baked fruit pie.

It's not until you behold thick fruit juice bubbling up through the top crust — remember those vent holes you made for just this purpose? — that you know your pie is done. (Note: On a crumb-topped fruit pie, the juices will usually bubble up thickly around the edge and, quite often, through cracks in the topping.)

As for the crust, no matter what shade of golden brown, it's time to get the pie out of the oven and onto a cooling rack when you see those thick, volcanic juices. (You can, however, cover the top of the pie with foil if it's getting too dark before the fruit filling is done. Try not to wait until the last second to make this determination, because the crust will still darken a little even with the pie covered.)

Cooling, Serving, and Storing Fruit Pies

Typically, I cool fruit pies for 2 to 4 hours before slicing. I think a fruit pie tastes best when it's still slightly warm or almost room temperature. When you cut into a hot fruit pie, the juice tends to run out all over the place. It needs a little time to cool and develop body.

Of course, circumstances don't always lend themselves to eating a pie at the ideal moment, but we do the best we can. If you're eating the pie the same day, don't bother to cover it after it's cooled, especially with anything like plastic wrap that will trap moisture and make the crust soggy. I usually put the pie under a screen dome to keep away any flying invaders while allowing moisture to escape. A wicker picnic basket also works.

Beyond 24 hours, it's time to think about refrigerating the fruit pie. A refrigerator is a humid environment, so it's not kind to pies, especially those with a top pastry crust. Crumb-topped pies fare better; the cold sort of seizes the crumb topping and does a half-decent job of preserving it. But top-crust pies soon start to lose their flakiness and appeal, thereby giving you permission to polish off the pie more quickly. To serve a refrigerated pie, cut it cold, then let it come to room temperature before serving. Or reheat it in a low oven — say 300°F (150°C) — for 10 to 15 minutes first.

As for freezing baked fruit pies, whole or in slices, it's essentially a lost cause if you place any value on texture. (Crumb-topped pies fare slightly better than top-crust pies.) I've tried it dozens of times over the years, and the result is always a limp disappointment. I don't recommend it. Nor do I recommend reheating fruit pie in the microwave; it's terribly unkind to the crust. A few minutes in a 300°F (150°C) oven, uncovered, is a much better option.

The Learning Is in the Doing

And there you have it: how to make a great pie from start to finish. You've gotten to know the ingredients and how to handle and mix them; you've learned to shape and roll the dough, get it into the pan, and form the edge of the pie; and you've picked up tips for baking the pie and so much more. Now it's time to jump into the recipes and put theoretical learning into practice.

Before you do, however, let me leave you with this: as much as possible, enjoy the process of making a pie without stressing too much about the outcome. Just show up, put in the effort, and become an observer and practitioner of what works and what doesn't.

Trust me when I tell you that nobody on the receiving end of your pies will think they are anything but fabulous. You'll be their pie hero, someone who can turn a few basic ingredients into a delectable dessert. Good luck, and have fun!

Dealing with Dampness

Many pies — and, it seems, custard pies in particular — shed a lot of moisture as they cool. They might feel completely cool, but even after they go into the fridge, moisture in the filling continues to evaporate. That's why I typically don't immediately cover my pies with foil when I refrigerate them; I wait a couple of hours. Even after covering them with foil, I remove the foil every few hours and wipe the dampness off the inside of the foil with a paper towel. This helps prevent moisture from dripping off the foil and onto the top of the pie, lest the filling end up with unappetizing moisture pockets.

Fruit Pie Doneness Checklist

- Use the total elapsed baking time as a guide, not an absolute.

- A double-crust fruit pie will have thick, bubbling fruit juice visible somewhere; it could be coming up through the crust, between lattice strips, or out along the edge.

- The top crust will often push up slightly from steam building within the filling.

- Even if you can't see the juice under the top crust, you can often hear the fruit bubbling vigorously when the pie is done. Try it. Learn to be a pie listener, which is like a pie whisperer but with your ears instead of your lips.

- Thick, bubbling juice will be visible on crumb-topped pies, too, typically around the edge but sometimes in the middle as well. The filling and topping will often heave upward when the juices come to a boil.

How to Make a Lattice-Top Pie

A lattice top can give your pie an especially attractive and folksy appeal. Lattice tops can be quite fancy, with multiple strips running in all directions, but a good place to start, if you're a lattice beginner, is with the basic lattice here.

Start with a double-crust dough recipe and divide the dough into equal pieces. Or make two single-crust dough recipes. Either way, roll out one of the disks and line the pie pan with it, letting the excess dough drape over the edge of the pan.

CUT THE STRIPS

A Roll the other dough half into the best rectangle you can manage, roughly 12 inches long and 11 inches wide. Using a pastry wheel, a pizza cutter, or a paring knife, and a ruler for a guide, cut the dough into lengthwise strips 1¼ inches wide. (Each strip, in other words, will be about 12 inches long and 1¼ inches wide.)

B Turn the pie filling into the pie shell, taking care to smooth over any pieces of fruit that jut up, like apples and other larger pieces of sliced fruit; the fruit's edges could tear the lattice. If you're dotting the top of the fruit with butter, do it now.

C Lay five of the pastry strips vertically across the pie. Fold back strips 2 and 4 a little more than halfway, then lay another strip horizontally across the center of the pie.

D Unfold the folded dough strips, then fold back strips 1, 3, and 5.

E Lay another perpendicular strip across the pie.

F Unfold strips 1, 3, and 5 over the second strip. Fold the other ends up over the perpendicular strip and lay another strip across the pie.

G Unfold strips 1, 3, and 5 to form the final lattice.

H Trim the strips and overhang evenly all around the pie, leaving a ½- to ¾-inch overhang, then pinch the excess dough into an upstanding ridge. Flute or crimp the edge as desired, then proceed to bake the pie according to the recipe instructions.

Experiment with strips of different widths,
even alternating wide and narrow ones to
change up the look.

FANCY CRUST SAMPLER

Pie is usually great no matter what it looks like, but for a special occasion, or whenever you're feeling fancy, you can impress your guests with pie-crust artistry. Here are just a few examples.

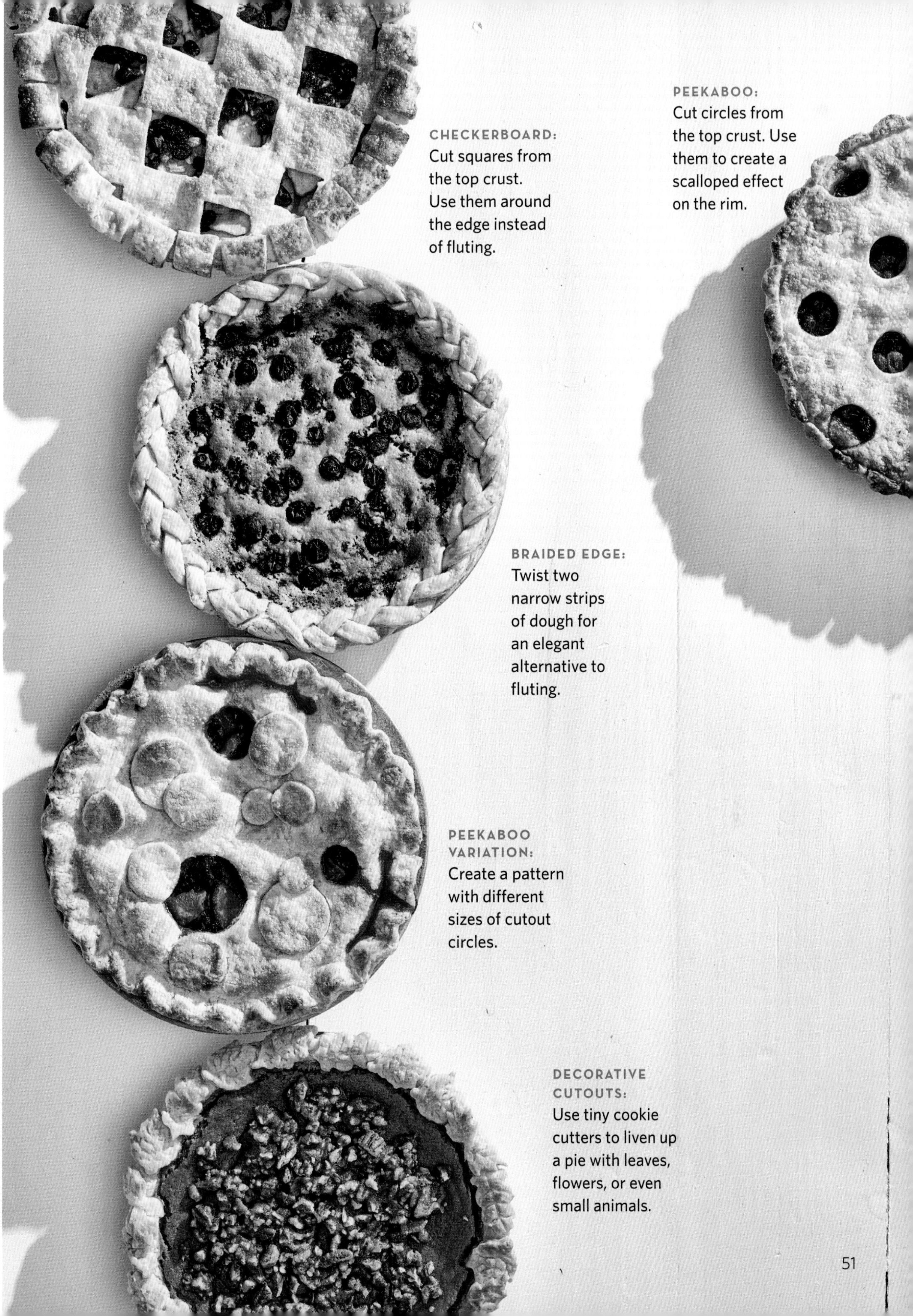

CHECKERBOARD:
Cut squares from
the top crust.
Use them around
the edge instead
of fluting.

PEEKABOO:
Cut circles from
the top crust. Use
them to create a
scalloped effect
on the rim.

BRAIDED EDGE:
Twist two
narrow strips
of dough for
an elegant
alternative to
fluting.

**PEEKABOO
VARIATION:**
Create a pattern
with different
sizes of cutout
circles.

**DECORATIVE
CUTOUTS:**
Use tiny cookie
cutters to liven up
a pie with leaves,
flowers, or even
small animals.

PART TWO

The Wonderful World of Pie

4

A Panoply of Pie Doughs:
ALL THE DOUGH YOU'LL EVER NEED

Twenty-five different pie doughs in a single collection might seem a bit excessive, but it's really not. For one thing, it's striking how much a small difference in the proportions of fat, or type of fat, can alter the flavor and texture of the crust. (To clarify, it's a dough before you bake it, and a crust after. One way you'll know you're getting good is when they no longer taste the same.) But we live in a day and age when folks expect to have choices.

So it's choices you have.

The first handful of recipes in the chapter are my go-to recipes, the ones I make most often. But there's also a whole-wheat crust I adore, a multigrain crust I've been making for decades, and a gluten-free version that's captured my fancy more recently.

You'll find an all-butter dough, an all-shortening dough, one sort of in between, and a lard-and-butter dough, too. Last but not least, I included a nice little collection of crumb-style crusts for cream pies, using a variety of crumbs, from the familiar graham cracker to the more unusual saltine.

I can't say that one is better than the next; they're all wonderful, and my hope is that you'll find a few you simply fall head over heels for. Good luck and let me know which ones turn out to be your favorites.

Perfect Pie Dough by Hand

If you're new to pie making, begin with this dough. This is the streamlined version of the tutorial recipe explained in detail in chapter 3. That illustrated recipe will help you read between the lines and understand the finer points of making this or nearly any other pie dough recipe you come across.

One 9- to 9½-inch standard or deep-dish pie shell

- 1½ cups all-purpose flour
- 1½ teaspoons cornstarch
- ½ teaspoon salt
- 10 tablespoons (1¼ sticks) cold unsalted butter, cut into ½-inch cubes, or 8 tablespoons (1 stick) cold, cubed unsalted butter plus 2 tablespoons vegetable shortening or lard in small pieces
- 2 teaspoons white vinegar
- ¼–⅓ cup cold water

DOUBLE-CRUST VERSION

To make this a double-crust recipe, simply double all of the ingredients and proceed as above. When you turn the dough out onto your work surface, divide it in two, making one part — for the bottom crust — a little larger than the other. Wrap the pieces separately in plastic wrap and refrigerate for at least 1 hour before rolling.

1. Combine the flour, cornstarch, and salt in a large bowl. Scatter the fat on a large flour-dusted plate. Measure the vinegar into a 1-cup glass measuring cup. Add just enough cold water to equal ⅓ cup. Refrigerate everything for 10 to 15 minutes.

2. Add all of the fat to the dry mixture, tossing the fat with the flour to coat it well. Using your fingers, squeeze the fat to flatten out the butter and smear it with the flour. When the cubes are flattened, switch to a pastry blender and continue to cut the fat into the flour until the largest pieces are about the size of small peas and everything looks like it has been touched by the fat. At that point, rub everything between your fingers for 30 to 45 seconds to make sure no dry pockets remain.

3. Mound the ingredients in the center of the bowl. Drizzle about half of the water down the sides of the bowl, turning the bowl as you pour so the water doesn't end up all in one place. Using a large fork, lightly mix the dough, tossing it from the perimeter toward the center of the bowl. Don't compress the dough at this point; you're trying to spread the moisture around. Sprinkle half of the remaining water over the dough and toss again. Finally, sprinkle all but the last tablespoon of liquid over the dough and stir vigorously. The dough should start to gather in large clumps, but if it is dry in places, add the last bit of water.

4. Turn the dough out onto your work surface and pack it into a ball, then knead it several times to smooth it out. Put the dough on a sheet of plastic wrap and flatten it into a ¾-inch-thick disk. If the edges crack, don't worry; just pinch them back together. Wrap the disk and refrigerate for at least 1 hour before rolling.

Single-Crust Food Processor Pie Dough

This pie dough is wonderfully versatile: I use it for at least 75 percent of the sweet and savory pies I make. It has great flavor and a flaky texture, it is easy to handle, and it freezes well (see page 29). Once you're comfortable making this dough with all butter, I encourage you to try the variation with 2 tablespoons shortening or lard. Those two fats will make the dough more tender and less prone to shrinkage.

One 9- to 9½-inch standard or deep-dish pie shell

1½ cups all-purpose flour

1½ teaspoons cornstarch

½ teaspoon salt

10 tablespoons (1¼ sticks) cold unsalted butter, cut into ½-inch cubes, or 8 tablespoons (1 stick) cold, cubed unsalted butter plus 2 tablespoons vegetable shortening or lard in small pieces

2 teaspoons white vinegar

Scant ⅓ cup cold water

1. Combine the flour, cornstarch, and salt in a large bowl. Scatter the fat on a large flour-dusted plate. Measure the vinegar into a 1-cup glass measuring cup. Add just enough cold water to equal a scant ⅓ cup. Refrigerate everything for 10 to 15 minutes.

2. Transfer the dry ingredients to a food processor. Add all of the fat, then pulse the machine six or seven times, until the pieces of fat are roughly the size of small peas.

3. Pour the vinegar-water mixture through the feed tube in a 7- or 8-second stream, pulsing the machine as you add it. Stop pulsing when the mixture is just starting to form larger clumps.

4. Turn the dough out onto your work surface and pack it into a ball. Put the dough on a sheet of plastic wrap and flatten it into a ¾-inch-thick disk. Wrap the disk and refrigerate for at least 1 hour before rolling.

Double-Crust Food Processor Pie Dough

Generally speaking, I think most food processors do a better job with single-crust recipes than with double-crust ones: because there's less bulk in the machine, single crusts mix up more evenly. However, it's quite possible to make a double-crust batch successfully, especially if you take care to read all the notes.

One 9- to 9½-inch standard or deep-dish double-crust piecrust with top or two pie shells

2¾ cups all-purpose flour

1 tablespoon cornstarch

1 teaspoon salt

1 cup (2 sticks) plus 2 tablespoons cold unsalted butter, cut into ½-inch cubes, or ½ cup (1 stick) plus 6 tablespoons cold, cubed unsalted butter plus 4 tablespoons cold shortening or lard in small pieces

½ cup cold water

1 tablespoon white vinegar

1. Combine the flour, cornstarch, and salt in a medium bowl. Scatter the butter on a large flour-dusted plate. Combine the water and vinegar in a 1-cup glass measuring cup. Refrigerate everything for 10 to 15 minutes.

2. Transfer the dry mixture to a food processor. Scatter the butter over the dry mixture. Pulse the machine seven or eight times, until the pieces of fat are roughly the size of small peas. Remove the lid and fluff the mixture with a fork, loosening it up from the bottom of the bowl.

3. Replace the lid. Pour the water-vinegar mixture through the feed tube in a 8- to 10-second stream, pulsing the machine repeatedly as you pour. Continue to pulse, briefly, until the dough just starts to form larger clumps. The dough should not ball up around the blade.

4. Turn the dough out onto your work surface or into a large bowl, then divide in two. Remember to make one portion — for the bottom crust — slightly larger than the other. If you're making two pie shells instead of a shell and top crust, divide the dough equally.

5. Shape the dough into balls, then put the balls on separate sheets of plastic wrap and flatten each one into a ¾-inch-thick disk. Wrap each disk and refrigerate for at least 1 hour before rolling.

Recipe for Success

You need a food processor with at least a 12-cup capacity to handle a double-crust recipe.

   Don't start pulsing the machine until you have the measuring cup of water poised above the feed tube. Start pulsing as soon as you start pouring.

Working with Shortening Pie Dough

These next couple of pie dough recipes, whose exclusive or primary fat is vegetable shortening, almost belong in a category by themselves. Why? Because shortening doesn't behave like butter in the dough.

For starters, shortening has no taste. Butter, on the other hand, contributes delicious, delicate flavor. Butter is also firm when cold, and that's one main reasons butter pie pastry is relatively easy to roll out and handle. It firms up the dough.

Shortening, on the other hand, doesn't do that. Even when shortening is cold, it stays pretty soft, so it won't add much durability, making the pie dough trickier to roll out. Refrigerating a shortening pie dough helps some, but not much.

Not to worry. Shortening is a staple ingredient in the American pie-making tradition, and millions of home bakers have used it for generations. You can, too. If you're new to pie making, the following tips will help you roll your shortening pie dough successfully.

KEEP IT COLD. This means both the shortening itself and the pie dough after you mix it. Like I said, cold shortening won't stabilize pie dough the way butter will, but it helps a little. Once you shape the dough into a disk, wrap it in plastic wrap and refrigerate for 1 hour before rolling.

DON'T SKIMP ON THE FLOUR. Put a generous dusting of flour on your rolling surface, dust the top of the dough, and dust the pin, too. Repeat as necessary.

EASE UP ON THE PRESSURE. You've probably seen videos of bakers whacking their pie dough with a rolling pin to loosen it up. You can't do that with a delicate shortening dough. Use gentle passes of the rolling pin. Too much pressure will cause the dough to stick.

KEEP THE DOUGH MOVING. With every few pin strokes, gently slide your fingers under the dough to make sure it isn't sticking. Give it a quarter turn before continuing. Slide the dough off to one side and reflour underneath when necessary.

USE PLASTIC WRAP. A foolproof way to roll out a shortening dough is to put it between sheets of plastic wrap. The dough won't stick to the plastic, but the plastic can be a little finicky. It tends to bunch up against the top of the dough, so you may have to stop occasionally and straighten it out. But it will do the job.

GET IT IN THE PAN. With the plastic-wrap technique, you can simply peel off the top sheet, slide your hand under the bottom sheet, and invert the rolled dough into the pan. Peel off the remaining plastic and work the dough into the pan. If you've rolled onto another surface, you can slide your hands under the dough and lift it into the pan. Or you can slide a floured, rimless baking sheet under the dough and slide the dough into the pan.

Old-Fashioned Shortening Pie Dough

This is a pretty standard all-shortening piecrust, like the one my dad used when I was a youngster. A shortening piecrust won't have the delicate flavor of a butter crust, and the texture is typically more crumbly, less flaky. Still, this yields a delicious, tender crust that many bakers believe makes the best pies.

One 9- to 9½-inch standard or deep-dish pie shell

- 1½ cups all-purpose flour
- 1 tablespoon confectioners' sugar (optional for a sweet pie; omit for a savory pie)
- ½ teaspoon salt
- ½ cup cold vegetable shortening
- ¼–⅓ cup cold water

DOUBLE-CRUST VERSION

The softness of the shortening makes this an easy recipe to double. Simply double all of the ingredients and proceed as above. Divide the dough in two when it comes out of the bowl, making one part slightly larger than the other if you're using it for a top and bottom crust.

1. Combine the flour, sugar (if using), and salt in a large bowl; refrigerate for 15 minutes.

2. Add the shortening to the dry ingredients and toss it with your hands to coat, then break it up into smaller pieces. Using a pastry blender, cut the shortening into the dry ingredients until the pieces of fat are roughly the size of small peas and everything looks like it has been touched by the fat. There should be no dry, floury areas.

3. Mound the ingredients in the center of the bowl. Drizzle about half of the water down the sides of the bowl, turning the bowl as you pour so the water doesn't end up in one spot. Using a large fork, lightly mix the dough, tossing it from the perimeter toward the center of the bowl. Drizzle most of the remaining water here and there over the dough and toss again.

4. Mix the dough vigorously now. The dough should start to gather in large clumps, but if it is dry in places, stir in the rest of the water.

5. Turn the dough out onto a lightly floured work surface and pack it into a ball, then knead it several times to smooth it out. Put the dough on a sheet of plastic wrap and flatten it into a ¾-inch-thick disk. Wrap the disk and refrigerate for about 1 hour before rolling.

"Pies Like Mom Used to Make"

When I started out as a young pie maker, the Crisco crust was the gold standard. Butter was never considered, and lard was a thing of the past. The recipe on the back of the can was all you needed for a great crust. Just flour, Crisco, salt, and water. The flake made using these basic ingredients is changed by adding anything. The best compliment we receive at our pie shop is that our pies taste just like the ones Mom made. We have had a great success using the most basic ingredients and have passed pie making on to our children and grandchildren.

— Connie Thayer, owner, Portage Pies, Westfield, New York

Shortening and Butter Dough *with* Egg

This dough makes a deliciously tender crust with some good butter flavor. The butter makes it a little easier to handle than most traditional shortening dough recipes. It's more supple and a dream to roll out. Because the dough has a high proportion of fat, set the pies on a rimmed, parchment-lined baking sheet to catch any fat that melts out of the crust during baking. I sometimes mix a large quantity of dough like this in my stand mixer (see page 71).

One 9- to 9½-inch standard or deep-dish double-crust pie-crust with top or two pie shells

- 3 cups all-purpose flour
- 1 tablespoon cornstarch
- 1¼ teaspoons salt
- 1 cup cold vegetable shortening
- 6 tablespoons cold unsalted butter, cut into ½-inch cubes
- 6 tablespoons cold milk
- 1 large egg, lightly beaten

1. Combine the flour, cornstarch, and salt in a large bowl. Divide the shortening into several pieces and place them on one side of a large floured-dusted plate. Put the butter pieces on the other side. Measure the milk into a 1-cup glass measuring cup. Stir in the egg. Refrigerate everything for 10 to 15 minutes.

2. Add the butter to the dry ingredients and toss to coat with the flour, then rub the cubes into the flour to flatten them. If the butter is too cold to squeeze, let the mixture sit for 5 minutes. When the butter is flattened, use a pastry blender to cut the butter into the dry mixture until it is broken into lima bean–size pieces. Add the shortening, toss it with the flour, and use your hands to break it into smaller pieces. Using the pastry blender, cut all of the fat into the dry mixture until everything looks like it has been touched by the fat.

3. Mound the ingredients in the center of the bowl. Drizzle about half of the egg-and-milk liquid down the sides of the bowl, turning the bowl as you pour. Using a large fork, lightly mix the dough, tossing it from the perimeter toward the center of the bowl. Drizzle the rest of the liquid here and there over the mixture, and mix again.

4. Now start mixing the dough more vigorously, until it balls together. If the mixture seems a bit dry and floury, drizzle on another teaspoon or two of milk. Don't worry if the dough feels more damp or is shaggier than other doughs you may be used to. It probably will be.

5. Turn the dough out onto a lightly floured work surface. (If your hands are messy from handing the dough, wipe them off with paper towels and flour your hands before continuing.) Divide the dough in two, then gently knead each part until the dough is smooth, 20 to 30 seconds. Round off the portions, place on sheets of plastic wrap, and flatten into ¾-inch-thick disks. Wrap each disk and refrigerate for at least 1 hour before rolling.

Lard *and* Butter Pie Dough

There's no point in making a lard crust, the flakiest of all, if you're not going to use it on top of the pie also, so this is a double-crust recipe. (Though I have used a single-crust recipe of lard pie dough with a different kind of bottom crust more than a few times.) This is the crust to showcase your favorite summer and fall pies.

One 9- to 9½-inch standard or deep-dish double-crust piecrust or two pie shells

- 3 cups all-purpose flour
- 1 teaspoon salt
- ½ cup cold lard
- 10 tablespoons (1¼ sticks) cold unsalted butter, cut into ½-inch cubes
- 6-7 tablespoons cold water

1. Combine the flour and salt in a medium bowl. Break up the lard and spread it out on one side of a large flour-dusted plate. Put the butter cubes on the other side. Measure the water into in a 1-cup glass measuring cup. Refrigerate everything for 10 to 15 minutes.

2. Transfer the dry ingredients to a food processor. Pulse several times to mix. Remove the lid and scatter the butter over the dry mixture. Replace the lid and pulse the machine six or seven times, until the butter pieces are roughly the size of small peas. Remove the lid and scatter the lard over the mixture. Replace the lid and pulse five or six times, until all of the fat is broken into very small pieces.

3. Pour the water through the feed tube in a gradual 8- to 10-second stream, pulsing the machine as you add it. Continue to pulse, briefly, until the dough just starts to form large clumps. The dough should not ball up around the blade.

4. Turn the dough out onto a work surface or into a large bowl, then divide it in two. Remember to make one portion — for the bottom crust — slightly larger than the other. If you're making two pie shells instead of a shell and top crust, divide the dough equally.

5. Pack the dough into balls, then put the balls on separate sheets of plastic wrap and flatten each into a ¾-inch-thick disk. Wrap the disks and refrigerate for at least 1 hour before rolling.

Dough *for* Fried Pies

My fried-pie dough is a shortening dough with a little less fat and an added egg, both of which help make the dough sturdier, an important consideration when you are frying rather than baking pies.

Enough dough for at least 8 hand pies

- 2¾ cups all-purpose flour
- ¾ teaspoon salt
- ¾ cup cold vegetable shortening
- 1 large egg

1. Combine the flour and salt in a large bowl. Scatter the shortening on a large flour-dusted plate. Crack the egg into a 1-cup glass measuring cup and beat it with a fork. Add just enough cold water to equal ½ cup. Refrigerate everything for 10 to 15 minutes.

2. Add the shortening to the dry ingredients and toss it with your hands to coat, then break it up into smaller pieces. Using a pastry blender, cut in the shortening until the largest pieces of fat are roughly the size of small peas and everything looks like it has been touched by the fat. There should be no dry, floury areas.

3. Mound the ingredients in the center of the bowl. Drizzle about half the egg-and-water liquid down the sides of the bowl, turning the bowl as you pour. Using a large fork, lightly mix the dough, tossing it from the perimeter toward the center of the bowl. Drizzle most of the remaining liquid over the dough and toss again.

4. Mix vigorously now. The dough should start to gather in large clumps, but if it is dry in places, stir in the rest of the liquid.

5. Turn the dough out onto a lightly floured work surface and pack it into a ball, then knead it several times to smooth it out. Put the dough on a sheet of plastic wrap and flatten it into a 1-inch-thick disk. Wrap the disk and refrigerate for at least 30 minutes before rolling.

Whole-Wheat Pie Dough

This excellent crust partners beautifully with just about any fruit or savory pie. Be advised that the recipe calls for whole-wheat pastry flour, which is not the same thing as regular whole-wheat flour. It's made from a softer type of wheat and has less protein, so it yields a more tender crust. Whole-grain flours can be a little coarse; if yours is, I suggest sifting or sieving it before measuring to remove some of the larger particles.

One 9- to 9½-inch standard or deep-dish pie shell

- ¾ cup all-purpose flour
- ¾ cup whole-wheat pastry flour
- 2 teaspoons cornstarch
- ½ teaspoon salt
- 10 tablespoons (1¼ sticks) cold unsalted butter, cut into ½-inch cubes, or 8 tablespoons (1 stick) cold, cubed unsalted butter plus 2 table-spoons cold shortening or lard, in small pieces
- ⅓ cup cold water

DOUBLE-CRUST VERSION

Double all of the ingredients and refrigerate them as above prior to mixing the dough. Add a total of ½ cup water when you add the liquid. Stop the machine, remove the lid, and determine as best you can how much more water you will need. Replace the lid, then pulse again two or three times while you add the extra water. Shape and refrigerate the dough as usual.

1. Combine the flours, cornstarch, and salt in a large bowl. Scatter the fat on a large flour-dusted plate. Measure the water into a 1-cup glass measuring cup. Refrigerate everything for 10 to 15 minutes.

2. Transfer the dry mixture to a food processor. Pulse the machine several times to mix. Remove the lid and scatter all of the fat over the dry mixture. Replace the lid. Pulse the machine six or seven times, until the largest pieces of fat are roughly the size of small peas.

3. Pour the water through the feed tube in a 7- to 8-second stream, pulsing as you add it. Continue to pulse until the dough is still fairly crumbly but starts to gather in large clumps. If it is dry in places, stir in another tablespoon or two of water.

4. Turn the dough out onto a work surface and pack it into a ball, then knead it several times to smooth it out. Put the dough on a sheet of plastic wrap and flatten it into a ¾-inch-thick disk. Wrap the disk and refrigerate for 45 minutes to 1 hour before rolling.

TO MAKE THIS DOUGH BY HAND

Combine the flours, cornstarch, and salt in a large bowl. Add all of the fat; toss to coat with the flour. Using your fingers, rub and squeeze the butter cubes to flatten them out. (To make it easier, push the butter against the bottom of the bowl with your thumbs; you'll get more leverage this way.) Using a pastry blender, cut in the fat until you have pea-size clods and everything looks like it has been touched by the fat.

Mound the dry ingredients in the center of the bowl. Drizzle half of the water down the sides of the bowl. Using a fork, mix well to distribute the water. Sprinkle on the remaining water and continue to mix until the dough pulls together.

Turn the dough out onto your work surface and pack it into a ball, then knead it gently two or three times. Put the dough on a sheet of plastic wrap and flatten it into a ¾-inch-thick disk. Wrap and refrigerate for 45 minutes to 1 hour before rolling.

Variation: Whole-Wheat Hand Pie Dough

When I use this dough to make any sort of sweet hand pie, I make the following changes to the single-crust recipe: Add 1½ tablespoons sugar to the dry ingredients. Instead of ⅓ cup water, whisk 1 large egg in a 1-cup glass measuring cup. Add just enough cold milk to equal ⅓ cup. Use this egg-and-milk liquid in place of the water.

Buttermilk Pie Dough

You've probably heard of buttermilk pie — it's a Southern staple and one of my absolute favorites. But did you know that you could make a delicate piecrust using buttermilk? It's delicious, and once you've made this, I know you'll become a fan as well. I can't think of any sweet or savory pie that this crust wouldn't go with. The buttermilk can make it just a touch stickier than doughs made with water, so don't dawdle when you're rolling it. One-half cup may seem like a lot of liquid for a single-crust batch of dough, but that's what it takes.

One 9- to 9½-inch standard or deep-dish pie shell

1½ cups all-purpose flour

½ teaspoon salt

1 teaspoon cornstarch

10 tablespoons (1¼ sticks) cold unsalted butter, cut into ½-inch cubes

½ cup cold buttermilk

DOUBLE-CRUST VERSION

Double all of the ingredients and refrigerate them for 15 minutes prior to mixing the dough. Pulse the machine seven to eight times, adding the buttermilk in an 8- to 10-second stream, until the dough just starts to gather in large clumps. Proceed with step 4.

1. Combine the flour, salt, and cornstarch in a large bowl. Scatter the butter on a large flour-dusted plate. Measure the buttermilk into a 1-cup glass measuring cup. Refrigerate everything for 10 to 15 minutes.

2. Transfer the dry ingredients to a food processor. Pulse several times to mix. Remove the lid and scatter the butter over the dry mixture. Replace the lid. Pulse the machine six or seven times, until the butter is roughly the size of small peas.

3. Pour the buttermilk through the feed tube in a 7- to 8-second stream, pulsing as you add it. Stop pulsing when the mixture is still crumbly but starting to gather in larger clumps.

4. Turn the mixture out onto your work surface and pack it into a ball, then knead it once or twice to smooth it out. Put the dough on a sheet of plastic wrap and flatten it into a ¾-inch-thick disk. Wrap the disk and refrigerate for about 1 hour before rolling.

TO MAKE THIS DOUGH BY HAND

Combine the flours, cornstarch, and salt in a large bowl. Add all of the fat; toss to coat with the flour. Using your fingers, rub and squeeze the butter pieces to flatten them out. (To make it easier, push the butter against the bottom of the bowl with your thumbs; you'll get more leverage this way.) Using a pastry blender, cut in the fat until you have pea-size clods and everything looks like it has been touched by the fat.

Drizzle half of the buttermilk over the mixture. Using a fork, mix well to distribute the buttermilk. Sprinkle on the remaining buttermilk and continue to mix until the dough pulls together.

Turn the dough out onto your work surface and pack it into a ball, then knead it gently two or three times. Put the dough on a sheet of plastic wrap and flatten it into a ¾-inch-thick disk. Wrap and refrigerate for 45 minutes to 1 hour before rolling.

Variation: Sour Cream Dough

Sour cream can be substituted for buttermilk. After step 2, spoon ½ cup plus 1 tablespoon cold sour cream into the processor, dolloping it here and there in big spoonfuls. Pulse the machine again, seven or eight times, until the dough starts to form good-size clumps. Gather and shape the dough into a disk, as above.

Cornmeal Pie Dough

This dough is similar to the following Oat and Cornmeal Pie Dough (page 69), but with more cornmeal crunch. I like to use it for Hominy Grill Buttermilk Pie (page 292), North Carolina Sweet Potato Pie (page 228), and just about any blueberry pie. It's particularly well suited for savory pies, too. Be sure to use fine cornmeal here. Coarse-ground cornmeal will not give the crust the correct texture.

One 9- to 9½-inch standard or deep-dish pie shell

1⅓ cups all-purpose flour

¼ cup fine yellow cornmeal

½ teaspoon salt

7 tablespoons cold unsalted butter, cut into ½-inch cubes

3 tablespoons cold shortening or lard, cut into several small pieces

¼ cup cold water

2 teaspoons white vinegar

DOUBLE-CRUST VERSION
Double all of the ingredients and refrigerate them for 15 minutes prior to mixing the dough. Pulse the machine seven to eight times to cut in the fat. Add the liquid in a 8- to 10- second stream, until the dough just starts to gather in large clumps. Proceed with step 4.

1. Combine the flour, cornmeal, and salt in a large bowl. Scatter all of the fat on a large flour-dusted plate. Measure the water and vinegar into a 1-cup glass measuring cup. Refrigerate everything for 10 to 15 minutes.

2. Transfer the dry ingredients to a food processor. Pulse several times to mix. Remove the lid and scatter all of the fat over the dry mixture. Replace the lid. Pulse the machine six or seven times, until the pieces of fat are roughly the size of small peas.

3. Pour the water-and-vinegar liquid through the feed tube in a 7- to 8-second stream, pulsing the machine as you add it. Once all the liquid has been added, you'll only need to process for another few seconds. The dough should come gather into large clumps but not ball up around the blade. It will probably seem a bit moister than other food processor doughs you may have made, and that's fine. The cornmeal will gradually absorb the liquid.

4. Turn the dough out onto your work surface and pack it into a ball, then knead it gently several times to smooth it out. Put the dough on a sheet of plastic wrap and flatten it into a ¾-inch-thick disk. Wrap the disk and refrigerate for about 1 hour before rolling. If you chill the dough longer, you may have to leave it at room temperature for 10 to 15 minutes before you start rolling to prevent it from cracking; cornmeal can make the dough a little brittle.

TO MAKE THIS DOUGH BY HAND

Combine the flours, cornstarch, and salt in a large bowl. Add all of the fat; toss to coat with the flour. Using your fingers, rub and squeeze the butter pieces to flatten them out. (To make it easier, push the butter against the bottom of the bowl with your thumbs; you'll get more leverage this way.) Using a pastry blender, cut in the fat until you have pea-size clods and everything looks like it has been touched by the fat.

Mound the dry ingredients in the center of the bowl. Drizzle half of the water-and-vinegar liquid down the sides of the bowl. Using a fork, mix well to distribute the liquid. Sprinkle on the remaining liquid and continue to mix until the dough pulls together.

Turn the dough out onto your work surface and pack it into a ball, then knead it gently two or three times. Put the dough on a sheet of plastic wrap and flatten it into a ¾-inch-thick disk. Wrap the disk and refrigerate for 45 minutes to 1 hour before rolling.

Oat *and* Cornmeal Pie Dough

About 25 years after this recipe first appeared in one of my earlier cookbooks, I got a message, through LinkedIn of all places, from a woman who had purchased my book way back when, telling me this was her favorite crust recipe of all time. It's certainly one of mine, too — wholesome, grainy, and delicious. The graininess of the dough can make it a little crumbly, but you can minimize this tendency by not chilling the dough too long, and by not skimping on the amount of water you add.

One 9- to 9½-inch standard or deep-dish pie shell

- ¼ cup old-fashioned or quick-cooking rolled oats
- ¼ cup fine yellow cornmeal
- 2 teaspoons sugar (optional; omit for a savory pie)
- ½ teaspoon salt
- 1 cup all-purpose flour
- ½ cup (1 stick) plus 1 tablespoon cold unsalted butter, cut into ½-inch cubes
- 1 large egg yolk

1. Combine the oats, cornmeal, sugar (if using), and salt in a large bowl. Measure the flour into a separate bowl. Scatter the butter on a large flour-dusted plate. Put the egg yolk in a 1-cup glass measuring cup, add just enough water to equal ⅓ cup, and mix well with a fork. Refrigerate everything for 10 to 15 minutes.

2. Transfer the oat and cornmeal mixture to a food processor. Pulse the machine until the oats are finely ground. It will look more like a coarse meal than a fine flour. Still, make it as fine as you can. Add the flour and pulse again several times to mix.

3. Remove the lid and scatter the butter over the dry ingredients. Replace the lid. Pulse the machine six to seven times, until the pieces of butter are roughly the size of small peas.

4. Pour the egg-and-water liquid through the feed tube in a 7- to 8-second stream, pulsing the machine as you add it. Once all the liquid has been added, you'll only need to process for a few more seconds. The dough should gather in loose clumps but not ball up around the blade. It will probably seem a bit moister than other food processor doughs you may have made, and that's fine.

5. Turn the dough out onto your work surface and pack it into a ball, then knead it gently several times to smooth it out. Put the dough on a sheet of plastic wrap and flatten it into a ¾-inch-thick disk. Wrap the disk and refrigerate for about 1 hour before rolling. If you chill the dough longer, you may have to leave it at room temperature for 10 to 15 minutes before rolling to prevent it from cracking.

DOUBLE-CRUST VERSION

Double all of the ingredients. Process the oat and cornmeal mixture as above. Add all of the butter (18 tablespoons) at once, and pulse until the pieces of butter are roughly the size of small peas. Add both egg yolks to the measuring cup, then add enough cold water to equal ⅔ cup; mix with a fork. Pour the liquid through the feed tube, in an 8- to 10-second stream, pulsing the machine. After turning the dough out, divide it in two, making one part slightly larger than the other if you're making a double-crust pie. Shape into disks and refrigerate.

Cheddar Cheese Pie Dough

Every true New Englander knows that nothing goes better with apples than sharp Cheddar cheese. My favorite way of combining these two is by baking the cheese right in the crust. The baked-in Cheddar flavor is out of this world, and it's one of the prettiest crusts you'll find, all golden and covered with crispy cheese freckles. It makes a great crust for savory pies, too, like quiches and pot pies.

One 9- to 9½-inch standard or deep-dish double-crust piecrust or two pie shells

- 2½ cups all-purpose flour
- ⅓ cup fine yellow cornmeal
- 2 teaspoons cornstarch
- ¾ teaspoon salt
- 1 cup (2 sticks) cold unsalted butter, cut into ½-inch cubes
- 1¼ cups cold grated sharp Cheddar cheese (white or yellow)*
- ½ cup plus 2 tablespoons cold water

*ALTERNATIVE:
Sharp and flavorful cheeses like Gouda or Gruyére work best.

1. Combine the flour, cornmeal, cornstarch, and salt in a large bowl. Scatter the butter around on a large flour-dusted plate. Measure the water into a 1-cup glass measuring cup. Refrigerate everything for 10 to 15 minutes.

2. Transfer the dry ingredients to a food processor. Pulse several times to mix. Scatter the butter over the dry mixture. Pulse the machine seven or eight times, until the pieces of butter are roughly the size of small peas. Remove the lid and scatter the cheese over the mixture. Replace the lid. Pulse three or four times, just long enough to mix in the cheese thoroughly.

3. Pour the water through the feed tube in a 8- to 10-second stream, pulsing the machine as you add it. Stop pulsing when the mixture begins to form large clumps.

4. Turn the dough out onto your work surface and divide it in two, making one part — for the bottom crust — slightly larger than the other. Pack the dough into balls, place on separate sheets of plastic wrap, and flatten into ¾-inch-thick disks. Wrap the disks and refrigerate for about 1 hour before rolling.

TO MAKE THIS DOUGH BY HAND

Combine the chilled dry ingredients in a large bowl. Add the butter and cut it in thoroughly. Mix in the cheese by hand. Mound the ingredients in the center of the bowl. Drizzle half of the water down the sides of the bowl, rotating the bowl as you pour. Mix well with a fork. Sprinkle half of the remaining water over the mixture; mix again. Pour most of the remaining water over the mixture; mix vigorously until the dough gathers in large clumps. If there are dry, floury areas remaining, stir in the last spoonfuls of water. Turn the dough out onto your work surface and proceed as in step 4.

Mixing Pie Dough in a Stand Mixer

A stand mixer is a useful tool for mixing larger double-crust pie dough recipes. It works particularly well with shortening pie doughs. It's easier to regulate the slow, smearing motion of the mixer than it is to control the hyper-cutting action of the food processor, so you feel like you're more in charge of the mixing process.

There may be slight variations in technique from recipe to recipe, but if you want to give it a try, the process goes something like this.

1. Attach the flat paddle, not the whisk attachment. Combine the dry ingredients in the bowl of a stand mixer and give them a quick stir.

2. If you're using just butter, add it to the dry ingredients all at once. Toss it with the flour to coat it.

   If you're using both butter and shortening, as in the Shortening and Butter Dough with Egg recipe (page 63), add the butter first, "cut" it in for a minute or two on low speed, then add the shortening.

3. With the machine on the lowest speed — you'll never raise it above low speed — mix the butter and flour for 1 to 2 minutes, until it's roughly the size of small peas. (If you're using butter and shortening, add the shortening just before it gets to this stage. Mix for another 30 seconds.)

4. When everything looks like it has been touched by the fat, add all but about 1 tablespoon of the liquid in a 7- to 8-second stream. Continue to mix for a few seconds. Then, if the dough seems to need it, add the remaining liquid. Mix for a few more seconds, then stop the machine. Turn the dough out onto a lightly floured surface and proceed as usual, dividing and wrapping the dough as instructed.

And that's all there is to it. This is an enjoyable way to make pie dough, so I hope you'll give it a try. You'll be an expert in short order.

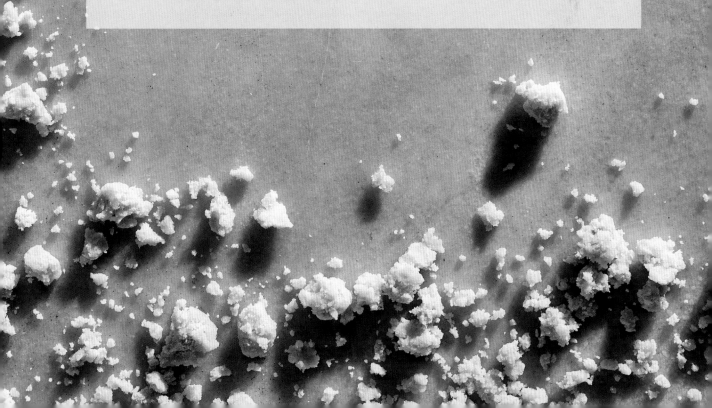

Flaky Cream Cheese Pie Dough

This tender pastry works wonderfully for fruit pies and fruit hand pies. Unlike most doughs, it's made with softened ingredients, and the fats are creamed before the dry ingredients are added. Because of the cream cheese, the dough can soften up and turn a little sticky if it stays at room temperature for too long. But if you roll the dough on parchment or waxed paper, you can easily slide it onto a baking sheet and refrigerate it for 10 or 15 minutes to firm it back up.

One 9- to 9½-inch standard or deep-dish pie shell

1½ cups all-purpose flour

2 tablespoons confectioners' sugar

½ teaspoon salt

½ cup (1 stick) unsalted butter, at room temperature

4 ounces full-fat cream cheese, at room temperature

¼ cup heavy cream

DOUBLE-CRUST VERSION

Due to the large volume of ingredients and the dense nature of the dough, I suggest making the single dough twice, but that's just me. If you'd like to give the larger batch a go, double all of the ingredients and proceed as for the single crust.

1. Combine the flour, sugar, and salt in a medium bowl and mix briefly with a whisk.

2. Combine the butter, cream cheese, and heavy cream in a food processor. Process for 6 or 7 seconds to blend. Add the dry ingredients and pulse the machine eight or nine times, until it forms a shaggy mass. Don't overdo it.

3. Turn the dough out onto a lightly floured surface and knead it gently into a smooth ball, 15 to 20 seconds. Put the dough on a sheet of plastic wrap and flatten it into a ¾-inch-thick disk. Wrap the disk and refrigerate for about 1 hour before rolling.

Recipe for Success

The butter and cream cheese should not be squishy soft when you mix the dough. Rather, they should yield to medium finger pressure.

If you like to make smaller pies — like the Downsized Apple Pie (page 198) — there's enough dough in the single-crust recipe to make a double-crust 7- or 8-inch standard pie.

Simple Press-In Pie Dough

This dough is sort of at odds with one of the aims of this book — to help make you a confident and proficient pie dough roller — but it's such a useful recipe that I can't resist including it here. The ingredients and proportions are virtually identical to other basic pie dough recipes; it's the way they're handled that sets the recipe apart. Instead of rolling it, you simply press the dough into the pie pan. And here's the really neat trick: if you use a standard pie pan instead of a deep-dish pie pan, there's enough dough mixture left to make a crumb topping with it.

One 9- to 9½-inch standard or deep-dish pie shell

1¾ cups all-purpose flour

2 tablespoons sugar

½ teaspoon salt

½ cup (1 stick) plus 3 tablespoons cold unsalted butter, cut into ½-inch cubes

2½ tablespoons cold water

1. Combine the flour, sugar, and salt in a large bowl. Scatter the butter on a large flour-dusted plate. Refrigerate everything for 10 to 15 minutes.

2. Transfer the dry mixture to a food processor. Pulse several times to mix. Scatter the butter over the dry ingredients. Pulse the machine six or seven times, until the pieces of butter are roughly the size of small peas. Remove the lid and sprinkle all of the water evenly over the mixture. Replace the lid. Continue to pulse the machine as many times as necessary, until the mixture has the consistency of coarse sand. It won't feel damp, but if you — carefully! — reach in and pick up some of the mixture, it should hold together when you press it between your fingers. If it doesn't, pulse it a few more times instead of adding more water. The mixture should remain crumbly and not start to form clumps.

3. If you're making a deep-dish pie, lightly butter the pie pan. Transfer all of the crumbs to the pan, spreading them around evenly before you begin to press. Spread them heavily near the sides, so there's plenty of crumbs for the sides of the pan as well. (If you're making a fruit pie in a standard pie pan, not a deep-dish one, see the box below.)

4. When the crumbs are evenly spread, start pressing them into the bottom and up the sides of the pan; the dough should come to the top of the pan. At some point, it helps to drape a piece of plastic wrap over the crumbs as you push. The plastic will keep the crumbs from sticking to your fingers, and you'll be able to press on them firmly. When you've pressed out a nice even shell, refrigerate for at least 1 hour before using.

How to Get a Pie Shell and Crumb Topping from One Recipe

Transfer 1 cup of the pie dough crumbs to a medium bowl; don't pack them when you measure. Add 3 tablespoons sugar and gently rub with the crumbs until evenly incorporated. Refrigerate.

Transfer the remaining crumbs to a 9- to 9½-inch buttered pie pan and press them in as described in step 4 above. Refrigerate for at least 1 hour before using. If you're not using the extra dough to make crumb topping, there's a lot of dough here, so use it for a deep-dish pie.

Slab Pie Dough *and* Shell

Slab pies, which can be sweet or savory, have caught on in popularity over the last few years. I don't know who first coined the term slab pie, but it's a fitting description for a pie that looks more like a plank than a wheel. If there's a bit of a challenge to assembling a slab pie, it's getting the oversized dough rolled out and into the pan without incident (see Recipe for Success). It's important to use the right jelly-roll pan here, one that measures 15- by 10- by 1-inch. Unless the sides are a full 1 inch high, your fillings will likely spill over the sides.

One large slab pie shell

- **3** cups all-purpose flour
- **2** tablespoons confectioners' sugar (for sweet pies) or 2 tablespoons cornstarch (for savory pies)
- **1** teaspoon salt
- **1¼** cups (2½ sticks) cold unsalted butter, cut into ½-inch cubes
- **½–⅔** cup cold water

1. Combine the flour, sugar or cornstarch, and salt in a large bowl. Scatter the butter on a large flour-dusted plate. Measure the water into a 1-cup glass measuring cup. Refrigerate everything for 10 to 15 minutes. Set out a 15- by 10- by 1-inch jelly-roll pan. Butter it lightly with soft butter, unless it is a non-stick pan.

2. Transfer the dry ingredients to a food processor. Pulse several times to mix. Remove the lid and scatter all of the butter over the dry ingredients. Replace the lid. Pulse the machine seven to eight times, or until the pieces of butter are roughly the size of small peas.

3. Pour half of the water through the feed tube in a 5- to 6-second stream, pulsing the machine as you pour. Remove the lid and fluff the mixture with a fork, loosening it up from the bottom of the bowl. Replace the lid and pour in most of the remaining liquid, pulsing as you add it. When you still have a couple of tablespoons of water left, remove the lid and check the dough; it should hold together easily when you press it between your fingers. If it's still quite crumbly, add the remaining water and pulse a few more times. The dough should start to form larger clumps.

4. Turn the dough out onto a lightly floured work surface. Shape and compact the dough into a rectangle roughly 1¼ inches thick. Lightly flour a 24-inch-long sheet of plastic wrap. Put the dough in the center of it. Dust the top of the dough with flour and gently — because the dough will be soft — roll it out a bit to increase the size of the rectangle. It should still be pretty thick — perhaps ¾ inch thick. Square up the sides and corners as best you can. Wrap the dough, slide it onto a small baking sheet, and refrigerate for at least 1 hour before rolling; longer is fine.

5. When you're ready to roll the dough, unwrap it and dust the top lightly with flour. Put the dough on a 24-inch-long sheet of waxed paper or fresh piece of plastic wrap. Roll out the dough into an 18- by 13-inch rectangle and invert or slide it into the jelly-roll pan. Center the dough, then tuck it down into the creases of the pan so it fits like a glove. If excess dough hangs over the edges, fold it over and press it against the sides to beef up the edge of the pastry. Refrigerate the shell for at least 30 minutes before filling and baking. Keep it cold until right before filling.

TO USE THIS AS A DOUBLE CRUST FOR A 9- TO 9½-INCH DEEP-DISH PIE: Chill the ingredients as described in step 1, but do not prepare the jelly roll pan. Then follow the recipe through step 3. Turn out the dough onto your work surface and shape into two thick disks, one of them — for the bottom crust — slightly larger than the other. Wrap in plastic wrap and refrigerate for at least 1 hour before rolling.

TO MAKE THIS DOUGH BY HAND
Refrigerate the ingredients as described in step 1. Then, using a pastry blender, cut the butter into the flour mixture until it is broken into pieces roughly the size of small peas. Mound the ingredients in the center of the bowl. Drizzle half of the water down the sides, rotating the bowl as you pour. Mix and toss lightly with a fork. Sprinkle half of the remaining water over the dough and mix again. Repeat with most of the remaining water, until the dough gathers in large clumps. Shape, refrigerate, and roll as above, starting at step 4.

Recipe for Success

If you'd rather not work with such a big piece of dough all at once, divide the dough in half and shape each half into a thick rectangle. Using the same approach as above, lightly roll the dough into two rectangles and refrigerate them. Then roll each one into an 11- by 8½-inch rectangle, overlapping them slightly in the middle of the pan; press to seal the pieces together, and proceed as described in step 5.

Gluten-Free Pie Dough

You may have heard stories that gluten-free pie dough is difficult to make, but this recipe is a charm. It mixes up easily in the food processor and rolls easily, too (see the notes on opposite page). The dough may seem more moist than traditional pie dough, but don't be alarmed. Because gluten-free flours are a little grittier than all-purpose flour, the moisture in the dough takes a little longer to absorb, but it will.

One 9- to 9½-inch standard or deep-dish pie shell

1⅓ cups gluten-free flour mix (see box)

1 tablespoon sugar (optional; omit for a savory pie)

Scant ½ teaspoon salt

½ cup (1 stick) cold unsalted butter, cut into ½-inch cubes

1 large egg

Cold water

DOUBLE-CRUST VERSION

Double all of the ingredients and proceed as for the single-crust recipe. There will be just enough of the gluten-free flour mix for a double-crust recipe, plus a little for dusting your work surface. For the liquid, use a total of 2 eggs plus enough water to equal ⅔ cup, plus 2 teaspoons.

1. Combine the flour mix, sugar (if using), and salt in a medium bowl. Scatter the butter on a large plate dusted with flour mix. Break the egg into a 1-cup glass measuring cup and whisk briefly, then add enough water to equal ⅓ cup. Add 1 additional teaspoon of water to the cup. Refrigerate everything for 10 to 15 minutes.

2. Transfer the dry ingredients to a food processor. Pulse several times to mix. Scatter the butter over the dry mixture. Pulse the machine six or seven times, until the butter is broken into small pieces and the mixture resembles coarse crumbs.

3. Pour the egg-and-water liquid through the feed tube in a 7- to 8-second stream, pulsing the machine as you add it. Continue to pulse until the dough just starts to form large clumps, but don't let it ball up around the blade.

4. Turn the dough out onto a lightly floured work surface. Knead it once or twice to smooth, then shape it into a ball. Put the ball on a sheet of plastic wrap and flatten it into a ¾-inch-thick disk. Wrap the disk and refrigerate for about 1 hour before rolling. It's fine if the dough chills longer than that, but you'll have to leave it at room temperature for 10 to 15 minutes before rolling.

Recipe for Success

Process the dough somewhat longer than usual, both when you're cutting the butter into the dry mixture and when you add the liquid. This helps bind the ingredients and make the dough easier to roll.

Because gluten-free flours tend to be grittier than all-purpose flour, the dough may crack when you roll it. Don't panic. Just roll the dough between two large sheets of plastic wrap. That will help hold it together and minimize breaking. Peel off the top sheet of plastic, slide your hand under the bottom sheet of plastic, then lift and invert the dough into the pan. Peel off the plastic, nudge the dough into the pan, and shape the edge of the dough as you would for any other pie.

TO MAKE THIS DOUGH BY HAND

Whether you're making the single- or double-crust recipe, briefly chill all the ingredients as described in step 1. Add the butter to the dry ingredients; mix with your hands to coat the fat. Using a pastry blender, thoroughly cut in the butter until it is broken into fine pieces and the mixture looks like coarse crumbs.

Drizzle half of the egg-and-water liquid down the sides of the bowl, turning the bowl as you add it. Using a large fork, mix the dough to spread the moisture around.

Sprinkle half of the remaining liquid over the dough and mix again. Add the remaining liquid and mix briskly until the dough comes together.

Gather the dough and divide it in two. If you're making a double-crust pie, make one part — for the bottom crust — a little larger than the other. Shape the dough into balls, put them on sheets of plastic wrap, and flatten into ¾-inch-thick disks. Wrap the disks and refrigerate before rolling.

Gluten-Free Flour Mix

2 cups white rice flour
⅔ cup potato starch
⅓ cup tapioca flour (tapioca starch)
1 teaspoon xanthan gum

Combine the rice flour, potato starch, tapioca flour, and xanthan gum in a medium bowl. Mix well.

This makes enough dough for two pie shells or a double-crust pie, with some left over for flouring your work area. Store the unused portion in a tightly sealed container. If you can't find these ingredients at your local supermarket, look at a natural foods store or online.

Oil Pie Dough

Here's a pie dough for those, who for dietary or other reasons, prefer not to use butter, shortening, or other solid fats in their piecrust. While it's a cinch to mix up — there's no fat cutting or dough chilling required — you should roll it between sheets of waxed paper for the best results; it rolls out like a charm that way. This dough makes a satisfying crust, albeit without the butter flavor, but with more flakiness than you might expect.

One 9- to 9½-inch double-crust standard or deep-dish piecrust or two pie shells

- 2⅔ cups all-purpose flour
- ¾ teaspoon salt
- ½ cup vegetable oil or other oil
- ½ cup whole or reduced-fat milk

1. Combine the flour and salt in a large bowl. Measure the oil and milk into a glass measuring cup. Make a well in the dry mixture and add the liquids. Mix well with a large fork until the dough pulls together into a single mass.

2. Turn the dough out onto your work surface. Divide the mixture in two, making one part — for the bottom crust — a little larger than the other. Pack each part into a ball, then knead several times to smooth them out. If you're not using the dough right away (it doesn't need to be refrigerated), place the balls on separate sheets of plastic wrap and shape into ¾-inch-thick disks. Wrap the disks and leave at room temperature. Note that if you're making two pie shells with this dough instead of a top and bottom crust, divide the dough into equal halves.

Cottage Cheese Pie Dough

This recipe is from my friend Patsy Jamieson, the former food editor and test kitchen director of *Eating Well* magazine. Patsy — an expert in healthy recipe makeovers — uses it for all of her open-face pies. The crust doesn't have the buttery richness and flakiness of a traditional piecrust, but it's wholesome and satisfying and the perfect way to wrap up the juicy filling in her Mixed-Berry Free-Form Pie on page 115.

One large open-face pie or crostata

- 2 cups all-purpose flour
- 2 teaspoons baking powder
- ½ teaspoon salt
- 1½ tablespoons cold unsalted butter, cut into small pieces
- ¾ cup low-fat cottage cheese
- ½ cup sugar
- ¼ cup canola or other vegetable oil
- 2 tablespoons low-fat milk
- ½ teaspoon vanilla extract

1. Mix the flour, baking powder, and salt together in a medium bowl. Add the butter and rub it into the dry ingredients until it is well incorporated. Set aside.

2. Combine the cottage cheese, sugar, oil, milk, and vanilla in a food processor. Process until smooth, scraping down the sides once or twice if needed.

3. Add the dry ingredients to the food processor. Pulse several times to mix, until the dough just starts to form large clumps. It won't take long. Do not overmix.

4. Turn the dough out onto a lightly floured work surface and pack it into a ball, then knead it several times to smooth it out. Put the dough on a sheet of plastic wrap and flatten it into a ¾-inch thick disk. Sprinkle the dough with flour, then wrap the disk and refrigerate for at least 1 hour before rolling. You can make the dough up to 1 day ahead.

Recipe for Success

Patsy prefers to use low-fat dairy products in her cooking, but feel free to substitute full-fat products if that's what you have.

If you want a slightly less sweet crust, reduce the sugar to ⅓ cup.

Crostata Dough

This type of dough is what Italian cooks use to make a variety of pielike tarts — crostatas or crostate — traditionally filled with fruits, fruit preserves, and other good things. By design, this recipe isn't as sweet as many of its kind, allowing its use for a variety of baked goods beyond jam-filled ones (such as the Apple and Gingered Pear Crostata on page 200). This dough is a pleasure to handle and blessedly simple to make in the food processor.

One large open-face pie or crostata

- 2 cups all-purpose flour
- 3 tablespoons confectioners' sugar
- ¾ teaspoon salt
- 1 cup (2 sticks) cold unsalted butter, cut into ½-inch cubes
- 1 large egg
- ¼ cup cold water

1. Combine the flour, sugar, and salt in a medium bowl. Scatter the butter on a large flour-dusted plate. Combine the egg and water in a 1-cup glass measuring cup, and mix well with a fork. Refrigerate everything for 10 to 15 minutes.

2. Transfer the dry ingredients to a food processor. Pulse the machine once or twice to mix. Scatter the butter over the dry mixture. Pulse the machine six to seven times, until the butter is finely chopped and the mixture has a sandy consistency.

3. Pour the egg-and-water liquid through the feed tube in a 7- or 8-second stream, pulsing as you add it. Continue to pulse the dough until it just starts to form large clumps.

4. Turn the dough out onto a lightly floured work surface and pack it into a ball, then knead it once or twice to smooth it out. Put the dough on a piece of plastic wrap and flatten it into a ¾-inch-thick disk. Wrap the disk and refrigerate for at least 1 hour before rolling, preferably a little longer. It's fine if it chills for several hours or overnight, though it may have to sit at room temperature for 10 to 15 minutes to soften enough to roll.

Almond Pie Dough

Adding finely ground almonds to a buttery pie dough does wonderful things to a crust. It takes on a nutty almond flavor and crunchiness, naturally, but the nuts also relax the dough and make it a pleasure to roll. Use this dough under any nut pies, chess pies, or custard pies. It's a real standout with the Open-Face Plum Pie on page 000.

One 9- to 9½-inch standard or deep-dish pie shell

⅓ cup whole almonds, toasted (page 453) or not, cooled and coarsely chopped

2½ tablespoons sugar

1½ cups all-purpose flour

½ teaspoon salt

½ cup (1 stick) unsalted butter, cut into ½-inch cubes

1 large egg yolk

Cold water

¼ teaspoon almond extract or vanilla extract

1. Put the nuts in a small bowl and chill in the refrigerator for 15 minutes; they should be cold when you make the dough.

2. Combine the almonds and sugar in a food processor. Pulse the machine until the nuts are finely ground. Don't overdo it or you'll turn them into a paste. Add the flour and salt. Pulse several times to mix.

3. Scatter the butter over the dry ingredients. Pulse the machine six or seven times, until the pieces of butter are roughly the size of small peas.

4. Put the egg yolk in a 1-cup glass measuring cup and add just enough cold water to equal ¼ cup liquid. Add the almond extract, then beat the liquid with a fork to blend.

5. Pour the egg liquid through the feed tube in a 7- to 8-second stream, pulsing the machine as you add it. Continue to pulse until the dough just starts to form large clumps, but don't let it ball up around the blade.

6. Turn the dough out onto your work surface and pack it into a ball, then knead it gently two or three times to smooth it out. Put the dough on a large sheet of plastic wrap and flatten it into a ¾-inch-thick disk. Wrap the disk and refrigerate for at least 1 hour before rolling.

Recipe for Success

Like any pie dough, this should not be hard when you roll it. The ground nuts will make it prone to cracking if the dough is too cold.

Graham Cracker Crust

It's tempting to use packaged crumb crusts from the supermarket. They're convenient, and the quality is fine. But if you're going to the trouble of making a pie from scratch, why cut corners with something that only takes 5 minutes to assemble and tastes so much better? This master crumb crust recipe has many variations, a few of which appear here. Mix up several batches at a time and keep a couple of spares in the freezer.

One 9- to 9½-inch standard or deep-dish pie shell

- **3 cups coarsely crumbled graham crackers or 2 cups packaged graham cracker crumbs**
- **3 tablespoons sugar**
- **Scant ¼ teaspoon salt**
- **¼ teaspoon ground cinnamon**
- **5 tablespoons unsalted butter, melted**
- **1-2 teaspoons milk (if needed)**

Nut Crumb Crust
Finely grind ¾ cup almond, pecan, or walnut halves in a food processor and mix them into the crumb mixture before adding the butter. Roasted peanuts and cashews will also work.

Vanilla or Chocolate Wafer Crust
Replace the graham crackers with 3 cups small vanilla or chocolate wafers.

Shortbread Cookie Crust
Replace the graham crackers with 3 cups crumbled shortbread cookies, like Keebler Sandies. Reduce the butter to 4 tablespoons. Add ⅛ teaspoon ground nutmeg, if desired.

1. If you are using graham crackers, combine the crumbled crackers, sugar, salt, and cinnamon in a food processor. Using long pulses, grind the ingredients thoroughly, until they have the texture of coarse whole-grain flour or fine bread crumbs. Transfer to a large bowl. If you are using packaged crumbs, combine the crumbs, sugar, salt, and cinnamon in a large bowl. Mix well by hand.

2. Add the butter to the dry mixture. Stir well with a large fork, then switch to your hands and rub the crumbs thoroughly to work in the butter. When you can press the mixture together firmly in your palm and it doesn't crumble apart, it's ready. If the mixture still seems a bit crumbly, drizzle in 1 to 2 teaspoons of the milk and mix again.

3. Transfer the crumbs to the pie pan. Spread them around loosely in the pan and up the sides. When they're evenly distributed, start pressing them into place. Drape a piece of plastic wrap over the crust for the final pressing. (This will help you do a cleaner job of getting the shell even.) Refrigerate for about 10 minutes.

4. Preheat the oven to 350°F (180°C) while the shell chills. Bake the pie shell on the center oven rack for 8 to 10 minutes. It should barely brown, if at all. Transfer to a rack and cool thoroughly.

Recipe for Success
There's enough crumb crust mixture here for a 9- to 9½-inch deep-dish pie. If you're making a standard pie, you can use all of it to make a thicker crust, or freeze the remainder for crumb topping on muffins and quick breads. Or make a couple of mini pies as sidekicks to the larger one.

Pretzel Crust

Pretzel crusts have become quite popular in the last few years. Their saltiness is a good counterpoint to certain chocolate pies and cream pies, like the Peanut Butter Cup Cream Pie on page 388. The pretzels need to be finely chopped, like they are for any crumb crust.

One 9- to 9½-inch standard or deep-dish pie shell

- 3½ **cups small plain traditional pretzels (not sticks or flavored), whole, not crumbled**
- ¼ **teaspoon ground cinnamon (optional)**
- ½ **cup (1 stick) unsalted butter**
- ¼ **cup packed light brown sugar**
- ¼ **teaspoon ground cinnamon (optional)**

1. Put the pretzels in a food processor. Pulse the machine repeatedly until the pieces have the approximate consistency of fine dry bread crumbs. Transfer to a large bowl; add the cinnamon, if using.

2. Gently heat the butter and sugar in a small saucepan until the butter melts. Scrape the mixture over the pretzel crumbs. Mix well with a fork. Cool briefly, then work the crumbs by hand. The crumbs should hold together easily when you press the mixture in your palm.

3. Transfer the crumbs to the pie pan and spread them around loosely in the pan and up the sides. When they're evenly distributed, start pressing them into place. Drape a piece of plastic wrap over the crust for the final pressing. (This will help you do a cleaner job of getting the shell even.) Refrigerate the pie shell for about 10 minutes.

4. Preheat the oven to 350°F (180°C) while the shell chills. Bake the pie shell on the center oven rack for 8 to 10 minutes. It should barely brown, if at all. Transfer to a rack and cool thoroughly.

Erin Chapman on American Pie Abroad

After living abroad in Denmark for nearly 20 years, I began to bake pies to ward off homesickness. In 2014, I met Dorte, an American-loving Dane who also had strong connections to the USA. We shared a simple vision to create what we had both been missing in Denmark — a home away from home.

In 2015, The American Pie Company opened its doors as Denmark's first American pie shop. Since then, so many different types of people have walked through our front door, from Danes who had spent time in the USA and wanted to relive memories, to others who had family "over there" and wanted to feel a connection.

There were also curious Danes who had only seen pie in old Hollywood movies or Bugs Bunny cartoons, or who had whistled along with Don McLean's "American Pie" and wanted to finally try a slice.

And then there were the homesick American expats like me. I remember one expat from Texas who fell to her knees and bowed to our neon PIE sign on her first visit, thanking us for opening a real pie shop.

The list of stories and memories that visitors bring to us about pie goes on and on and has been the wind beneath our wings. Pie has a way of bringing all of us together.

— Erin Chapman, partner/creative director, The American Pie Co., Copenhagen, Denmark

Saltine Cracker Crust

Here is the crust used for Atlantic Beach Pie on page 432. It will also work with cream pies and others requiring a crumb crust. It can best described as plain, which one has to believe is the way it was intended. I mean no disrespect by that comment, because the crust works perfectly with the appropriate filling.

1. Crush the crackers by hand or in a food processor, or crumble them into a gallon-size freezer bag, seal partially, then finish the job with a rolling pin. Transfer to a bowl and mix in the sugar.

2. Add the butter to the crumbs. Vigorously rub the butter into the dry ingredients by hand, until evenly mixed. When you squeeze some of the mixture in your palm, it will feel clumpy and just hold together.

3. Transfer the crumbs to the pie pan and spread them around loosely and evenly over the bottom and up the sides. When they're evenly distributed, start pressing them into place. Drape a piece of plastic wrap over the crust for the final pressing. (This will help you do a cleaner job of getting the shell even.) Refrigerate the pie shell for about 10 minutes.

4. Preheat the oven to 350°F (180°C) while the shell chills. Bake the pie shell on the center oven rack for 18 to 20 minutes, just until it starts to turn golden brown. Transfer to a rack and cool thoroughly.

Amaretti Crumb Crust

Amaretti are dry little Italian cookies made with almonds. They make a perfect crust for the Amaretto-Amaretti Chocolate Fudge Pie (page 419), but this crust would also work nicely with brownie pies.

One 9- to 9½-inch standard or deep-dish pie shell

2½–3   cups amaretti cookies

6   tablespoons unsalted butter

1   ounce unsweetened chocolate, coarsely chopped

2   tablespoons sugar

⅛   teaspoon salt

1. Crush the cookies by hand or in a food processor, or crumble them into a gallon-size freezer bag, seal partially, then finish the job with a rolling pin. You need 1⅓ cups of crumbs.

2. Combine the butter and chocolate in a small saucepan over very low heat, stirring slowly, until melted and smooth. Remove from the heat and cool to room temperature.

3. Combine the amaretti crumbs, sugar, and salt in a medium bowl. Add the chocolate mixture and mix well. Transfer the crumbs to a 9- to 9½-inch standard or deep-dish pie pan, pressing the crumbs into the bottom and up the sides. Refrigerate until needed.

Recipe for Success

If you can't find amaretti cookies at your supermarket, try an Italian market.

Oreo Crumb Crust

This is the crust to use with the Chocolate Coffee Cream Pie (page 391), among others. It's great with butterscotch pies or any filling with a coffee flavor. Use the traditional cookies, not one of the fancy flavors or overstuffed versions. Other brands probably work fine, but I've always used these as the standard.

One 9- to 9½-inch standard or deep-dish pie shell

3   cups coarsely crumbled Oreo cookies

2–3   tablespoons sugar

  Scant ¼ teaspoon salt

4   tablespoons unsalted butter, melted

1. Combine the cookies, sugar to taste, and salt in a food processor. Pulse the machine repeatedly to make fine crumbs. Transfer to a large bowl.

2. Pour the butter over the crumbs. Mix well with a fork, then use your fingers to rub the mixture together thoroughly. If you press some of the mixture between your fingers, it should hold together without immediately crumbling apart. (The cookie filling gives it extra holding power.)

3. Transfer the crumbs to the pie pan and spread them around loosely in the pan and up the sides. When they're evenly distributed, start pressing them into place. Drape a piece of plastic wrap over the crust for the final pressing. (This will help you do a cleaner job of getting the shell even.) Refrigerate the pie shell for about 10 minutes.

4. Preheat the oven to 350°F (180°C) while the shell chills. Bake the pie shell on the center oven rack for 8 minutes. Transfer to a rack and cool thoroughly.

5
Berry Pies:
SUMMER'S JEWELS
IN A CRUST

Fresh summer berries are so irresistible in homemade pies that it's only right to give them their own showcase. This chapter is precisely that. You might stumble upon an errant fig, peach, or slice of rhubarb here as well, but these recipes are connected by a single purpose: to celebrate those fresh black, red, and blue summer jewels that steal the show in some of our most memorable pies.

This is not to say that you can't use frozen or canned berries in some of these pies; there are times when that's the only thing in the house, or they're the logical alternative to the jet-lagged fruit on the supermarket shelves. For the most part, however, strive to bake your pies with the best berries you can find in season.

I've tried to make this chapter as inclusive as possible, but I make no apologies for the fact that a personal bias or two may have crept in. For instance, I love blueberries and have plenty for the pickin' at my nearby sister's home. So you'll find a lot of blueberry pie recipes here. When you love pie and pie making as much as I do, it's hard not to be transparent in a recipe collection this big.

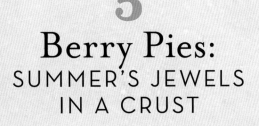

Tips for Baking Beautiful Berry Pies

• Don't jump on the berry-pie bandwagon too early; the early crop is often a little underripe. The best berries come to market midseason. If you can, support local farmers by purchasing the fruit at farmers' markets.

• Inspect baskets of berries carefully. Fresh berries are fragile and easily damaged by their own weight or other bad berries. Give them a sniff and make sure there's no moldy smell.

• Store berries in the refrigerator. Spread them in a shallow dish so they're not crushed by their own weight.

• Don't rinse berries until you're ready to use them. Because raspberries have a cavity, they need to be inverted on paper towels to drain the cavity of excess moisture.

• Mix berry fillings gently so you don't mash the fruit any more than is necessary. A few crushed berries are fine, but you want most of them to be whole.

• Don't overfill a berry pie. Berries are so juicy that if you're too lavish with them, you'll end up with berry juice all over the baking sheet.

• This goes for any fruit pie, but don't underbake a berry pie or it won't thicken properly. The juices must bubble thickly before you remove the pie from the oven.

• To keep the filling from oozing everywhere, be sure to let the pie cool for at least 1½ to 2 hours before slicing and serving — longer if the pie is very juicy.

All-Strawberry Pie

Some folks think strawberries are unsuitable for pies because they bake up so soft. It's true, but so what? That doesn't mean you should eliminate them from your pie repertoire. With fresh, in-season berries, your pie will be fabulous. Mint adds a seasonal accent mark to this pie. Minced fresh mint is good, but it turns a little dark in the baking. Instead, you might consider a drop or two of mint oil or use white crème de menthe, as I do here.

Makes 8–10 servings

Old-Fashioned Shortening Pie Dough, double-crust version (page 62) or another double-crust dough

FILLING

- 4 **cups hulled and thickly sliced fresh strawberries**
- ⅓ **cup plus 2 tablespoons sugar, plus a little for sprinkling**
- 1 **tablespoon white crème de menthe (optional)**
- 1 **tablespoon lemon juice**
- ¼ **teaspoon ground nutmeg**
- 2 **tablespoons cornstarch**
- 1 **tablespoon cold unsalted butter, cut into small pieces**

  Milk or half-and-half, for glaze

1. Prepare and refrigerate the pie dough. Roll the larger dough portion into a 12-inch circle and line a 9- to 9½-inch standard pie pan with it, letting the excess dough drape over the edge. Refrigerate the shell until needed.

2. Adjust the oven racks so one is in the lower position and another is in the middle of the oven. Preheat the oven to 400°F (200°C). Line a baking sheet with parchment paper.

3. Mix the strawberries and the ⅓ cup sugar in a large bowl. Add the crème de menthe (if using), lemon juice, and nutmeg, and mix again. Let stand for 10 minutes. Combine the 2 tablespoons sugar and cornstarch in a small bowl and stir into the fruit.

4. Roll the other dough half into an 11-inch circle. Turn the filling into the pie shell and smooth it out to even the top. Dot the filling with the butter. Lightly moisten the rim of the pie shell. Drape the top pastry over the filling, pressing along the edge to seal. Trim the overhang with scissors, leaving an even ½ to ¾ inch all around, then sculpt the edge into an upstanding ridge. Flute or crimp the edge, as desired. Poke several steam vents in the top of the pie with a large fork or paring knife. Put a couple of the vents near the edge so you can check the juices. Lightly brush the pie with milk and sprinkle with sugar.

5. Put the pie on the prepared baking sheet and bake on the lower rack for 30 minutes. Reduce the heat to 375°F (190°C) and move the pie up to the middle rack, rotating it 180 degrees. Bake for 25 to 35 minutes longer, until the juices bubble thickly at the steam vents and the top is golden brown.

6. Transfer the pie to a rack and cool for at least 1½ to 2 hours before serving. Cover and refrigerate leftovers after 24 hours.

Recipe for Success

This is meant to be an all-strawberry pie, with the purest strawberry flavor. But if you just can't resist adding a handful of leftover raspberries or cherries, I understand.

If the strawberries are a little lackluster, add 2 tablespoons strawberry preserves to the filling to enhance the flavor.

Strawberry-Rhubarb Crumb Pie

Spring should never pass without baking at least one or two rhubarb pies: rhubarb pie is a rite of spring, after all. When strawberries come along a little later in the season, the rhubarb and berries make perfect pie partners. Their flavors are so bright and agreeable that you need little more than sugar and lemon to accent them. This recipe makes a handsome lattice-top pie, so try it that way, too. But I love the way it tastes with the Cornmeal Streusel topping.

Makes 8–10 servings

Cornmeal Pie Dough (page 68) or another single-crust dough

FILLING

3 **cups sliced fresh rhubarb stalks, cut crosswise into ½-inch-thick pieces**

¾ **cup sugar**

1 **tablespoon lemon juice**

Finely grated zest of 1 lemon

3 **cups hulled and halved strawberries (quartered if very large)**

3 **tablespoons quick-cooking tapioca**

Cornmeal Streusel (page 450)

1. Prepare and refrigerate the pie dough. Roll the dough into a 12½- to 13-inch circle and line a 9- to 9½-inch deep-dish pie pan with it, shaping the edge into an upstanding ridge. Flute or crimp the edge, then refrigerate the shell until needed.

2. Adjust the oven racks so one is in the lower position and another is in the middle of the oven. Preheat the oven to 400°F (200°C). Line a baking sheet with parchment paper.

3. Combine the rhubarb, sugar, lemon juice, and lemon zest in a large bowl. Add the strawberries and tapioca and mix. Let stand for 10 minutes.

4. Turn the filling into the pie shell and smooth it with a spoon to level off the fruit. Put the pie on the prepared baking sheet and spread a generous layer of the streusel over the pie; you may not need all of it. Tamp the streusel down lightly.

5. Put the pie, on the sheet, on the lower oven rack and bake for 30 minutes. Reduce the heat to 375°F (190°C) and move the pie up to the middle rack, rotating it 180 degrees. Bake for 25 to 30 minutes longer, until the juices bubble thickly around the edge. If the top of the pie starts to get too dark, cover it with aluminum foil.

6. Transfer the pie to a rack and cool for at least 1½ to 2 hours before serving. Cover and refrigerate leftovers after 24 hours.

Recipe for Success

When you're shopping for rhubarb, buy solid, crisp, bright red stalks. If the stalks seem too wide, halve them lengthwise before slicing them crosswise to make the filling. Get rid of any leaves that happen to be attached; they'll make you sick if you eat them.

Two-Berry Mint Pie

When fresh, local, in-season berries aren't available, frozen ones offer a perfectly acceptable alternative. A bag of strawberries and another of raspberries makes a terrific pie in a tender crust. A little mint gives the pie a summery sparkle even in the dead of winter.

Makes 8–10 servings

Shortening and Butter Dough with Egg (page 63) or another double-crust dough

FILLING

- 1 **(1-pound) bag frozen strawberries, partially thawed**
- 1 **(1-pound) bag raspberries, partially thawed**
- ½ **cup plus 3 tablespoons granulated sugar**
- 2 **tablespoons orange liqueur or ½ teaspoon orange extract**
- 1 **tablespoon lemon juice**
- ¼ **teaspoon ground cinnamon**
- ¼ **teaspoon ground nutmeg**
- 1–2 **tablespoons fresh mint leaves or ½ teaspoon crumbled dried**
- ¼ **cup cornstarch**
- 2 **tablespoons cold unsalted butter, cut into small pieces**

  Confectioners' sugar, for garnish

1. Prepare and refrigerate the pie dough. Roll the larger dough portion into a 12½- to 13-inch circle and line a 9- to 9½-inch deep-dish pie pan with it, letting the excess dough drape over the edge. Refrigerate the shell until needed.

2. Adjust the oven racks so one is in the lower position and another is in the middle of the oven. Preheat the oven to 400°F (200°C). Line a baking sheet with parchment paper.

3. If the strawberries are whole or in large pieces, use a sharp knife to cut them in half. Combine the strawberries, raspberries, and the ½ cup granulated sugar in a large bowl. Add the liqueur, lemon juice, cinnamon, nutmeg, and mint, and mix well. Let stand for 10 minutes. Mix the 3 tablespoons sugar and cornstarch in a small bowl; stir into the fruit.

4. Roll the other dough half into an 11-inch circle. Turn the filling into the pie shell and smooth out the fruit with the back of a spoon. Dot the filling with the butter. Lightly moisten the rim of the pie shell. Drape the top pastry over the filling, pressing along the edge to seal. Trim the overhang with scissors, leaving an even ½ to ¾ inch all around, then sculpt the edge into an upstanding ridge. Flute or crimp the edge, as desired. Poke several steam vents in the top of the pie with a large fork or paring knife. Put a couple of the vents near the edge so you can check the juices.

5. Put the pie on the prepared baking sheet and bake on the lower oven rack for 30 minutes. Reduce the heat to 375°F (190°C) and move the pie up to the middle rack, rotating the pie 180 degrees. Bake for 25 to 35 minutes longer, until the juices bubble thickly at the steam vents.

6. Transfer the pie to a rack and cool for 15 to 20 minutes. While it is still quite warm, dust the top lightly with confectioners' sugar. Once the pie has cooled, dust it again. Let the pie cool for a total of 1½ to 2 hours before serving. Cover and refrigerate leftovers after 24 hours.

Recipe for Success

This filling is pretty soft and tends to settle low in the pan, leaving the top somewhat domed. To shrink the distance between crust and filling, drape a clean tea towel over the pie as soon as it comes out of the oven. Let it sit there for 30 or 40 seconds, steam softening the crust, then gently press down on the towel to collapse the pastry a little. There's no guarantee that the pastry won't shatter or break slightly, but it's usually not a disaster. The more pronounced the pastry dome is, the more difficult it is to press it without serious breakage.

Breitbach's Raspberry Pie

The raspberry pie at Breitbach's Country Dining in Balltown, Iowa — the state's oldest bar and restaurant — has a stellar reputation. Cindy Breitbach, who's been making pies since the age of ten, told me that this customer favorite could not be easier — just raspberries, blackberries, sugar, and tapioca. Lemon juice? Nope. She thinks there is enough acidity in the fruit itself. She uses frozen fruit, and as for the crust, it's a shortening double crust. "Nothing fancy about that, either," she says.

Makes 8–10 servings

Old-Fashioned Shortening Pie Dough, double-crust version (page 62)

FILLING

- 3 cups frozen raspberries, partially thawed
- 1 cup frozen blackberries, partially thawed
- 1¼ cups sugar, plus a little for sprinkling
- 3 tablespoons quick-cooking tapioca

1. Prepare and refrigerate the pie dough. Roll the larger dough portion into a 12-inch circle and line a 9- to 9½-inch standard pie pan with it, letting the excess dough drape over the edge. Refrigerate the shell until needed.

2. Preheat the oven to 375°F (190°C). Line a baking sheet with parchment paper.

3. Combine the berries, sugar, and tapioca in a large bowl. Toss gently to mix. Let stand for 10 minutes.

4. Roll the other dough half into an 11-inch circle. Turn the filling into the pie shell and smooth out the fruit with the back of a spoon. Lightly moisten the rim of the pie shell. Drape the top pastry over the filling, pressing along the edge to seal. Trim the overhang with scissors, leaving an even ½ to ¾ inch all around, then sculpt the edge into an upstanding ridge. Flute or crimp the edge, as desired. Poke several steam vents in the top of the pie with a large fork or paring knife. Put a couple of the vents near the edge so you can check the juices. Sprinkle the top of the pie with sugar.

5. Put the pie on the prepared baking sheet and bake on the middle rack for 55 to 65 minutes, rotating the pie 180 degrees midway through the baking. When the pie is done, the juices will bubble thickly at the steam vents.

6. Transfer the pie to a rack and cool for at least 1½ to 2 hours before serving. Cover and refrigerate leftovers after 24 hours.

Recipe for Success

Cindy uses the same trick I do to prepare frozen fruit for baking. She microwaves the fruit in a bowl just until it is nearly thawed. Of course, you can simply let it sit in a bowl for 45 to 60 minutes, if you prefer.

Cindy says it is important to bake the pie thoroughly "so the beads of tapioca disappear."

Vid *and* Annie's Fresh Raspberry Crumb Pie

When my New Hampshire neighbors Vid and Annie Valdmanis used to give me boxes of fresh raspberries from their garden, I would quickly turn around and bake the fragile berries into pies before they slid past their prime. I still make this pie two or three times each summer.

Makes 8–10 servings

Single-Crust Food Processor Pie Dough (page 58) or another single-crust dough

FILLING

- 4 cups fresh raspberries
- ½ cup plus 3 tablespoons sugar
- 2 teaspoons lemon juice
- 1½ tablespoons cornstarch
- ¼ teaspoon ground nutmeg
- 2–3 tablespoons seedless raspberry jam

  Traditional German Streusel (page 450) or another crumb topping

  Vanilla, peach, or strawberry ice cream, for serving

1. Prepare and refrigerate the pie dough. Roll the dough into a 12-inch circle and line a 9- to 9½-inch standard pie pan with it, shaping the edge into an upstanding ridge. Flute or crimp the edge, then refrigerate the shell until needed.

2. Adjust the oven racks so one is in the lower position and another is in the middle of the oven. Preheat the oven to 400°F (200°C). Line a baking sheet with parchment paper.

3. Combine the raspberries, the ½ cup sugar, and lemon juice in a large bowl, mixing carefully so you don't break up the fruit too much. Let stand for 10 minutes. Mix the 3 tablespoons sugar, cornstarch, and nutmeg in a small bowl; stir into the fruit.

4. Spread the jam over the bottom of the pie shell. Turn the filling into the shell, smoothing the fruit with a spoon. Put the pie on the prepared baking sheet and cover with a generous amount of the streusel; you may not need all of it. Tamp the streusel down lightly.

5. Put the pie, on the sheet, on the lower oven rack and bake for 30 minutes. Reduce the heat to 375°F (190°C) and move the pie up to the middle rack, rotating the pie 180 degrees. Bake for 25 to 35 minutes longer, until the juices bubble thickly around the edge of the pie. If the top of the pie starts to get too dark, cover it with aluminum foil.

6. Transfer the pie to a rack and cool for at least 1½ to 2 hours before serving , garnished with ice cream. Cover and refrigerate leftovers after 24 hours.

Recipe for Success

Because of their fragile constitution, raspberries are prone to mold. Always give them the sniff test before purchasing. If you detect any smell of mold — which is often difficult to see — pass them up. Even the smallest amount of mold can taint the flavor of a pie.

New England Raspberry–Red Currant Pie

Right about the time my secret red currant picking spot would bear fruit, the first of the raspberries would find their way to me from nearby gardener friends. How could I resist taking advantage of this microseason to make a double-crust pie with roughly equal amounts of fruit? Nowadays I buy red currants, when I'm lucky enough to find them at all. These tart, translucent red jewels team up beautifully with raspberries.

Makes 8–10 servings

Old-Fashioned Shortening Pie Dough, double-crust version (page 62) or another double-crust dough

FILLING

2½ cups fresh raspberries

2 cups fresh red currants

½ cup plus 3 tablespoons sugar, plus a little for sprinkling

2 tablespoons red currant jelly

1 teaspoon lemon juice

2½ tablespoons cornstarch

1 tablespoon cold unsalted butter, cut into small pieces

1 egg beaten with 1 tablespoon milk, for glaze

1. Prepare and refrigerate the pie dough. Roll the larger dough portion into a 12-inch circle and line a 9- to 9½-inch standard pie pan with it, letting the excess dough drape over the edge. Refrigerate the shell until needed.

2. Adjust the oven racks so one is in the lower position and another is in the middle of the oven. Preheat the oven to 400°F (200°C). Line a baking sheet with parchment paper.

3. Combine the raspberries, currants, and the ½ cup sugar in a large bowl. Warm the jelly in a small microwavable container, then add to the fruit along with the lemon juice. Mix gently, then let stand for 10 minutes. Mix the 3 tablespoons sugar and cornstarch in a small bowl; stir into the fruit.

4. Roll the other dough half into an 11-inch circle. Turn the filling into the pie shell and smooth it out with the back of a spoon. Dot the filling with the butter. Lightly moisten the rim of the pie shell. Drape the top pastry over the filling, pressing along the edge to seal. Trim the overhang with scissors, leaving an even ½ to ¾ inch all around, then sculpt the edge into an upstanding ridge. Flute or crimp the edge, as desired. Poke several steam vents in the top of the pie with a large fork or paring knife. Put a couple of the vents near the edge so you can check the juices. Brush the pie lightly with the egg wash glaze and sprinkle with sugar.

5. Put the pie on the prepared baking sheet and bake on the lower rack for 30 minutes. Reduce the oven temperature to 375°F (190°C) and move the pie up to the middle rack, rotating the pie 180 degrees. Bake for 25 to 35 minutes longer, until the juice bubbles thickly at the steam vents and the top is a rich golden brown.

6. Transfer the pie to a rack and cool for at least 1½ to 2 hours before serving. Cover and refrigerate leftovers after 24 hours.

Recipe for Success

If you happen to taste the uncooked filling and find the currants quite tart — they are — don't be tempted to add more sugar. Hiding their tartness behind too much sugar detracts from their unique flavor.

Raspberry *and* Fresh Fig Free-Form Pie

Jeanne Kelley is a California-based cookbook author and former contributing editor at *Bon Appétit* magazine whom I know from my years of freelance work. When I told her I was working on a book of pies and asked her if she had any stylish, California-inspired pies in her files, she thought of this one. I'm glad, because the combination of fresh figs and raspberries is one I'd never considered. Jeanne tops off this delicious pie with an unusual honey-anise whipped cream that's out of this world.

Makes 8 servings

Crostata Dough (page 80)

FILLING

¼ cup granulated sugar

¼ cup packed light brown sugar

1 tablespoon all-purpose flour

2–2½ cups fresh raspberries

2 cups small, fresh black figs, stemmed and quartered

4 tablespoons honey

1 cup cold heavy cream

2 tablespoons anisette or other anise-flavored liqueur

Recipe for Success

Keep in mind that the season for making this pie is limited, especially if you live in a place where fresh figs are hard to find. Look for them in late summer.

1. Prepare the pie dough and refrigerate for about 1 hour.

2. Mix the sugars and flour together in a large bowl. Add three-quarters of the raspberries and all the figs. Toss gently to combine, then set aside.

3. Adjust the oven racks so one is in the higher position and another is in the middle of the oven. Preheat the oven to 400°F (200°C). Chill a medium bowl and a set of mixer beaters.

4. The best way to assemble this is to roll the dough onto a large sheet of parchment paper, assemble the pie, then lift the pie onto a rimmed baking sheet with the paper. Alternatively, roll the dough onto a piece of floured waxed paper, invert it onto the baking sheet, peel off the paper, then assemble the pie on the baking sheet. In either case, roll the dough into a 12-inch circle. Imagine an 8-inch circle in the center of the dough, then spoon the fruit onto that area. Using a metal spatula or the paper itself to help lift the pastry, fold the overhanging dough over the filling. The dough will sort of self-pleat as

you do so, leaving uncovered filling in the center.

5. Bake the pie on the middle oven rack for 30 minutes. Move the pie up to the higher rack, rotating it 180 degrees. Bake for about 10 minutes longer, until the crust is golden brown and the juice bubbles thickly in the center of the pie. (Note that if the pastry is browning nicely at 30 minutes, you may not have to move the pie up to the higher rack.)

6. Transfer the baking sheet to a rack and drizzle 2 tablespoons of the honey over the pie. Cool on the sheet. If the pie has leaked juice, loosen it in those areas with a spatula while the pie is still quite warm, to minimize sticking when it cools.

7. While the pie is still warm, make the whipped cream. Using the chilled bowl and beaters, beat the cream, anisette, and the remaining 2 tablespoons honey until soft peaks form. Scatter the remaining raspberries over the pie and serve garnished with the whipped cream.

Elizabeth's Pie

Elizabeth is the granddaughter of Louise Piper, one of the stellar pie bakers and consistent winners at the Iowa State Fair. This particular pie, a mixed-fruit affair, earned Louise a ribbon at the 2003 fair. The combination of fruit and other filling ingredients was first suggested years earlier by her then six-year-old granddaughter. Since that time, the pie has become a family tradition. Louise bakes the pie in an oil crust, a recipe she's been using for years.

Makes 8–10 servings

Oil Pie Dough (page 78)

FILLING

- 1 **cup sugar, plus a little for sprinkling**
- ¼ **cup all-purpose flour**
- 2 **tablespoons quick-cooking tapioca**
- ½ **teaspoon ground cinnamon**
- ¼ **cup honey**
- 1 **cup diced tart apple (Louise likes Jonathans or Red Romes)**
- 1 **cup fresh red raspberries**
- 1 **cup hulled and sliced fresh strawberries**
- 1 **cup diced fresh rhubarb stalks**
- 2 **tablespoons cold unsalted butter, cut into small pieces**
  Milk or half-and-half, for glaze

1. Prepare the pie dough, wrap in plastic, and set it aside.

2. Combine the sugar, flour, tapioca, and cinnamon in a large bowl. Toss well to mix. Add the honey, apple, berries, and rhubarb, and mix gently but thoroughly. Let stand for 10 minutes.

3. Preheat the oven to 375°F (190°C). Line a baking sheet with parchment paper.

4. Put the larger dough half between two sheets of waxed paper and roll the dough into a 12-inch circle. Peel off the top sheet of paper. Invert the pastry over a 9-inch standard pie pan, center, and peel off the paper. Gently tuck the pastry into the pan, without stretching it, and let the overhang drape over the edge. Using the same sheets of waxed paper, roll the other dough half into an 11-inch circle. Remove the top sheet of paper.

5. Turn the filling into the pie shell and smooth the top with a spoon. Dot the fruit with the butter. Dampen the edge of the pie shell with a pastry brush. Invert the top pastry over the filling, center, and slowly peel off the paper, pressing down along the edge to seal. Sculpt the overhanging dough into an upstanding ridge. Sprinkle the top of the pie generously with sugar, then drizzle with milk. Using a fork or paring knife, poke several steam vents in the top of the pie. Put a couple of them along the edge so you can check the juices.

6. Put the pie on the prepared baking sheet and bake on the center rack for 30 minutes, then rotate the pie 180 degrees. Bake for 25 to 30 minutes longer, until the top is a rich golden brown and the juices bubble thickly at the vents.

7. Transfer the pie to a rack and cool. Serve just barely warm or at room temperature. Cover and refrigerate leftovers after 24 hours.

Recipe for Success

I find that oil dough works best if rolled shortly after making it. That's why I don't refrigerate it the way I typically do other pastries.

The dough will need to be rolled very thin to make a 12-inch circle. Don't be surprised if it is a little crumbly at the edge. Just handle it delicately.

I usually glaze my pies with milk first, then with sugar, but Louise does it just the opposite. It makes a slight difference in that the sugar sort of gathers into crunchy waves rather than being uniformly crunchy. I like it. Try it yourself and see.

Blackberry Silk Pie

When my kids were young, we spent a good deal of time picking wild blackberries on the old logging roads near our home. I used to say I did it for the kids, but in fact I liked trudging through the thorny bushes as much as they did. This blackberry custard pie is a holdover from those days. It's a bit of a production because you make blackberry purée from scratch. But the gorgeous dark berry color and silky texture of the filling make it all worthwhile. You don't even need a patch of wild berries; frozen fruit will do.

Makes 8–10 servings

Single-Crust Food Processor Pie Dough (page 80)

FILLING

- 1 **pint fresh blackberries or 1 (1-pound) bag frozen blackberries, partially thawed**
- 1 **cup sugar**
- 3 **large eggs, at room temperature**
- 1 **tablespoon all-purpose flour**
- 1½ **cups heavy cream**
- ½ **cup half-and-half**
- 1 **teaspoon vanilla extract**

1. Prepare and refrigerate the pie dough. Roll the dough into a 12½- to 13-inch circle and line a 9- to 9½-inch deep-dish pie pan with it, shaping the edge into an upstanding ridge. Flute or crimp the edge, chill the shell, and partially prebake it according to the instructions on page 36.

2. Preheat the oven to 300°F (150°C). Combine the blackberries and ¼ cup of the sugar in a food processor. Process long enough to make a smooth purée, about 30 seconds. Put a fine-mesh strainer over a bowl and pour the purée into it. Using a rubber spatula, press the purée through the mesh, leaving just the seeds. Discard the seeds.

3. Whisk the eggs until frothy in a large bowl. Combine the remaining ¾ cup sugar and the flour in a small bowl; whisk into the eggs. Whisk in the cream, half-and-half, vanilla, and 1 cup of the purée, mixing until evenly blended. Place the pie shell on a baking sheet, near the oven, and carefully pour the filling into the shell.

4. Bake the pie, on the sheet, on the middle oven rack for 50 to 60 minutes, rotating the pie 180 degrees midway through the baking. When done, the filling will likely have puffed somewhat. The center may seem a bit jiggly; that's fine. If after the allotted time the pie seems quite puffy but the center is a little underdone, turn off the oven and leave the pie in it for 10 to 15 minutes longer.

5. Transfer the pie to a rack and cool thoroughly. Refrigerate for at least 3 to 4 hours before serving. To serve, spoon some of the leftover purée onto each plate and over each slice, and garnish with extra blackberries, if you have any. Loosely cover leftovers with foil and refrigerate.

Recipe for Success

Since this is essentially a custard pie, you should observe the "low and slow" rule of baking. If you rush this pie by raising the oven temperature, the custard will "break" and result in a watery filling.

Save any leftover purée for another use. It's great on pancakes, with fresh berries, or with cheesecake or crêpes.

Sour Cream–Blackberry Pie

The pie couldn't be more deliciously simple: put a layer of blackberries in a pie shell, pour a sweetened sour cream mixture on top, cover with streusel, and bake. The creamy filling bakes up to something like a moist, spongy cake, covering the fruit below. I've also made this recipe with raspberries. The same formula could be adapted to other berries as well.

Makes 8–10 servings

Single-Crust Food Processor Pie Dough (page 58)

FILLING

- 2 **large eggs, at room temperature**
- 2 **cups full-fat sour cream, at room temperature**
- ¾ **cup sugar**
- ⅓ **cup all-purpose flour**
- ½ **teaspoon vanilla extract**
- ½ **teaspoon grated orange zest**
  Big pinch of salt
- 3 **cups fresh blackberries, raspberries, or other berries**
- 1 **cup Traditional German Streusel (page 450)**

1. Prepare and refrigerate the pie dough. Roll the dough into a 12½- to 13-inch circle and line a 9- to 9½-inch deep-dish pie pan with it, shaping the edge into an upstanding ridge. Flute or crimp the edge, chill the shell, and partially prebake it according to the instructions on page 36. Let the shell cool.

2. Preheat the oven to 350°F (180°C). Whisk the eggs in a large bowl until frothy. Add the sour cream, sugar, flour, vanilla, orange zest, and salt, and whisk until evenly combined. Spread the berries in the pie shell, then ladle the sour cream mixture over them; smooth with a spoon. Cover the sour cream layer with the streusel.

3. Put the pie on the middle oven rack and bake for 35 to 40 minutes, until the filling is set. When done, the filling will likely have puffed slightly and will no longer seem liquidy or loose. Don't expect the top of the pie to brown much.

4. Transfer the pie to a rack and cool thoroughly. Serve at room temperature, or — the way I prefer it — well chilled. Refrigerate leftovers.

Recipe for Success

If you rinse the berries in a colander before using them — you probably should unless you grow them or are certain of the source — be sure to drain them well on paper towels to keep the pie filling from getting watery. Line a baking sheet with a double layer of paper towels. Quickly rinse the berries with cold water and shake the colander to knock off excess water. Upend them onto the paper towels, spread them out, and give them time to air-dry. If I'm rinsing raspberries, I turn them stem end down so that any water trapped in the cavities can drain.

Patsy's Blackberry-Rhubarb Free-Form Pie

Makes 10 servings

Cottage Cheese Pie Dough (page 79)

TOPPING

⅔ cup all-purpose flour

¼ cup packed light brown sugar

½ teaspoon ground cinnamon

2 teaspoons cold unsalted butter, cut into ¼-inch pieces

1 tablespoon canola or other vegetable oil

1 tablespoon frozen orange juice concentrate, thawed

¼ cup sliced almonds

FILLING

3 cups sliced fresh rhubarb stalks, cut crosswise into ½-inch-thick pieces

1 cup frozen blackberries, partially thawed

¾ cup plus 1 teaspoon granulated sugar

1 large egg white

1 tablespoon water

My friend and colleague Patsy Jamieson, who knows her way around pies, calls this pie a celebration of spring — spring being something to celebrate when you live and work in northern Vermont. In addition to fresh rhubarb, Patsy uses frozen blackberries, a great complementary flavor and color enhancer. (You can, of course, use fresh blackberries when they're in season and frozen rhubarb.) Patsy specializes in developing reduced-fat recipes, so you'll be delighted how much great flavor there is in this pie with a relatively small amount of butter. Her crumb topping, made with orange juice concentrate, is delicious.

1. Prepare the pie dough and refrigerate until firm enough to roll, about 1 hour.

2. To make the topping, combine the flour, brown sugar, and cinnamon in a medium bowl. Reserve 2 tablespoons of this mixture in a small bowl; set aside. Add the butter to the larger portion and rub it into the dry mixture with your fingers until crumbly. Add the oil and orange juice concentrate, tossing lightly with a fork to blend. Add the almonds, then rub the mixture gently between your fingers to form evenly mixed crumbs. Refrigerate until ready to use.

3. To make the filling, combine the rhubarb, blackberries, and the ¾ cup granulated sugar in a medium bowl; place in the refrigerator.

4. Preheat the oven to 425°F (220°C). Line a large baking sheet with lightly oiled parchment paper or aluminum foil.

5. On a sheet of lightly floured waxed paper, roll the dough into a 13-inch circle. Invert the dough over the prepared baking sheet, center, and peel off the paper. Without upsetting the overhanging dough, put the entire baking sheet in the refrigerator for 5 minutes to refirm dough.

6. Imagine an 8-inch circle in the center of the pastry. Sprinkle the reserved flour-sugar mixture over this area. Pour the fruit filling over the same area, then even it out with your hands or a fork. Sprinkle the topping evenly over the fruit. Using a spatula to help you lift the pastry, fold the uncovered portion of dough over the filling. The pastry will sort of self-pleat as you do so, leaving uncovered filling in the center. Whisk together the egg white and water in a small bowl and brush the mixture over the exposed pastry. Sprinkle with the 1 teaspoon sugar.

7. Place the pie, on the sheet, on the center oven rack and bake for 15 minutes. Reduce the oven temperature to 350°F (180°C) and bake for another 15 minutes, then rotate the pie 180 degrees. Bake for 10 to 20 minutes longer, until the crust is golden brown and the fruit bubbly. If the pie starts to get a little too dark, cover with aluminum foil.

8. Transfer the pie, on the sheet, to a rack. Cool for 10 minutes, then slide the pie, with the foil or parchment, onto the rack to finish cooling. Serve warm.

Recipe for Success

It's always best to line the baking sheet with aluminum foil or parchment paper when you're baking a juicy free-form pie such as this one. (I almost always use parchment.) Often, hot juice will seep through a thin spot in the pastry. There's really no way to stop the leak, and the best thing to do is nothing because the leaking juice will eventually harden and plug the hole. If your pie springs a leak, run a spatula between the pie and the parchment or foil as soon as the pie comes out of the oven to keep the pie from getting stuck to the hardened juice.

Deep-Dish Blackberry-Peach Pie

It's hard to beat this generously proportioned summer fruit pie, especially if you take yours with a double crust.

Makes 8–10 servings

Shortening and Butter Dough with Egg (page 62) or another double-crust dough

FILLING

4	cups blackberries, fresh or frozen and partially thawed
2½–3	cups peeled and sliced ripe peaches
½	cup plus 3 tablespoons sugar, plus a little for sprinkling
3½	tablespoons cornstarch
¼	teaspoon ground nutmeg
1	tablespoon lemon juice
1	teaspoon finely grated lemon zest
2	tablespoons cold unsalted butter, cut into small pieces
	Milk or half-and-half, for glaze
	Vanilla ice cream, for serving

1. Prepare and refrigerate the pie dough. Roll the larger dough portion into a 12½- to 13-inch circle and line a 9- to 9½-inch deep-dish pie pan with it, letting the excess dough drape over the edge. Refrigerate the shell until needed.

2. Adjust the oven racks so one is in the lower position and another is in the middle of the oven. Preheat the oven to 400°F (200°C). Line a baking sheet with parchment paper.

3. Combine the blackberries, peaches, and the ½ cup sugar in a large bowl. Mix well and let stand for 10 minutes. Mix the 3 tablespoons sugar and cornstarch in a small bowl; stir into the fruit along with the nutmeg, lemon juice, and lemon zest.

4. Roll the other dough half into an 11-inch circle. Turn the filling into the pie shell and smooth the fruit with a spoon to even it out. Dot the fruit with the butter. Lightly moisten the rim of the pie shell.

Drape the top pastry over the filling, pressing along the edge to seal. Trim the overhang with scissors, leaving an even ½ to ¾ inch all around, then sculpt the edge into an upstanding ridge. Flute or crimp the edge, as desired. Poke several steam vents in the top of the pie with a large fork or paring knife. Put a couple of the vents near the edge so you can check the juices. Lightly brush the pie with milk and sprinkle with sugar.

5. Put the pie on the prepared baking sheet and bake on the lower oven rack for 30 minutes. Reduce the heat to 375°F (190°C) and move the pie up to the middle rack, rotating the pie 180 degrees. Bake for 35 to 45 minutes longer, until the juices bubble thickly at the steam vents.

6. Transfer the pie to a rack and cool for at least 2 hours before serving, garnished with ice cream. Cover and refrigerate leftovers after 24 hours.

Recipe for Success

This is a very juicy pie. Use a deep pie pan and leave at least ½ to ¾ inch of headroom between the top of the filling and the rim of the pan to minimize the chance of a spillover.

Marionberry Pie
with Hazelnut Crumb Topping

This pie features two of Oregon's premier agricultural products, marion-berries — considered by some to be the best-tasting type of blackberries — and hazelnuts, toasted and incorporated into the crumb topping. The hazelnuts, whose flavor notes hint of wine and Brie cheese, add a sharp toasted flavor to the sweet fruit. Don't miss this one.

Makes 8–10 servings

Single-Crust Food Processor Pie Dough (page 58)

FILLING

4½ cups marionberries or blackberries, fresh or frozen and partially thawed

½ cup plus 2 tablespoons sugar

1½ tablespoons cornstarch

1 tablespoon lemon juice

1 teaspoon finely grated lemon zest

Big pinch of salt

Melted Butter Crumb Topping (page 449) made with toasted hazelnuts (page 453)

Coffee or vanilla ice cream, for serving (optional)

1. Prepare and refrigerate the pie dough. Roll the dough into a 12-inch circle and line a 9- to 9½-inch standard pie pan with it, shaping the edge into an upstanding ridge. Flute or crimp the edge, then refrigerate the shell until needed.

2. Adjust the oven racks so one is in the lower position and another is in the middle of the oven. Preheat the oven to 400°F (200°C). Line a baking sheet with parchment paper.

3. Combine the marionberries and the ½ cup sugar in a large bowl. Mix gently, then let stand for 10 minutes. Mix the 2 tablespoons sugar and cornstarch in a small bowl; stir into the fruit along with the lemon juice, lemon zest, and salt. Turn the filling into the pie shell and smooth the top with a spoon. Cover with a generous layer of the crumb topping; you may not need all of it. Tamp the crumb down lightly.

4. Put the pie on the prepared baking sheet and bake on the lower oven rack for 30 minutes. Reduce the heat to 375°F (190°C) and move the pie up to the middle rack, rotating it 180 degrees. Bake for 25 to 35 minutes longer, until the juices bubble thickly around the edge and perhaps up through the topping. Cover the pie with aluminum foil if the topping starts to get too dark.

5. Transfer the pie to a rack and cool for at least 1½ to 2 hours before serving, garnished with ice cream, if desired. Cover and refrigerate leftovers after 24 hours.

Recipe for Success
Much as I love the hazelnut's distinctive flavor here, if you'd rather not bother with peeling them, other nuts, such as pecans or walnuts, will work, too.

Loganberry Pie
with Sour Cream Topping

My favorite book on American Northwest cooking is Janie Hibler's *Dungeness Crabs and Blackberry Cobblers*. I've not spent much time in the Northwest, but I armchair travel there when I can with Hibler's book, tasting my way through wild mushroom pizzas, salmon and caper spreads, and irresistible berry desserts. Loganberries, writes Hibler, are a variety of blackberries grown commercially in the Pacific Northwest. Their intense berry flavor and slight tartness, she says, make them the perfect candidate for pies like this one. I think you'll agree.

Makes 8–10 servings

Old-Fashioned Shortening Pie Dough (page 62)

FILLING

- 4 cups loganberries, fresh or frozen and partially thawed
- ¾ cup plus 2 tablespoons granulated sugar
- 1 tablespoon lemon juice
- 2 tablespoons cornstarch

TOPPING

- 1¼ cups full-fat sour cream
- 3 tablespoons packed brown sugar
- ½ teaspoon lemon extract

1. Prepare and refrigerate the pie dough. Roll the dough into a 12-inch circle and line a 9- to 9½-inch standard pie pan with it, shaping the edge into an upstanding ridge. Flute or crimp the edge, then refrigerate the shell until needed.

2. Adjust the oven racks so one is in the lower position and another is in the middle of the oven. Preheat the oven to 400°F (200°C).

3. To make the filling, combine the loganberries, the ¾ cup granulated sugar, and lemon juice in a large bowl. Mix well and let stand for 10 minutes. Mix the 2 tablespoons sugar and cornstarch in a small bowl; stir into the fruit. Turn the filling into the pie shell and smooth the top of the fruit with a spoon.

4. Place the pie on the lower oven rack and bake for 30 minutes. Reduce the heat to 375°F (190°C) and move the pie up to the middle rack, rotating it 180 degrees. Bake for 15 to 25 minutes longer, until the juices bubble thickly around the edge and in the center of the pie. Transfer the pie to a rack and cool for 30 minutes.

5. To make the topping, combine the sour cream and brown sugar in a small saucepan over low heat. Gently heat the mixture, stirring virtually nonstop, until it is warm and thin enough to pour, 2 to 3 minutes. Stir in the lemon extract. Slowly pour the sour cream mixture over the center of the pie filling, then tilt and jiggle the pie to spread out the topping.

6. Put the pie back on the rack and cool thoroughly. Serve at room temperature or refrigerate several hours before serving; I prefer it slightly chilled. Cover and refrigerate leftovers.

Recipe for Success

Be careful not to overheat the sour cream mixture or it will curdle and become unusable.

Don't worry if the sour cream and pie juices bleed together when you add the topping. It's bound to happen a bit, and a little berry color in the topping will only whet the appetite.

Blueberry–Sour Cream Pie

This is one of the easiest pies in this collection, made with a stovetop blueberry filling. Once that cools, a coat of sweetened cream cheese and sour cream gets spooned on top. It looks and tastes almost like an upside-down blueberry cheesecake, but with a lot less effort. If fresh blueberries are in season, I recommend folding a handful of them into the cooked berries when you spoon the filling into the pie shell.

Makes 8–10 servings

Graham Cracker Crust
(page 82)

FILLING

- 1 (1-pound) bag frozen blueberries
- 1½ tablespoons lemon juice
- ⅓ cup granulated sugar
- 2 tablespoons cornstarch
- ½ teaspoon vanilla extract
- 1 cup fresh blueberries (optional)

TOPPING

- 8 ounces full-fat cream cheese
- ⅓ cup confectioners' sugar
- 2 tablespoons granulated sugar
- 1 teaspoon finely grated lemon zest
- ½ cup full-fat sour cream
- ¼ teaspoon vanilla extract

1. Prepare the crust and press it into the bottom and up the sides of a 9½-inch standard pie pan. Refrigerate, prebake, and cool as directed. Refrigerate until needed.

2. To make the filling, combine the frozen blueberries and lemon juice in a medium nonreactive saucepan. Cover and cook over medium to low heat until the blueberries are quite juicy, 7 to 10 minutes.

3. Mix the granulated sugar and cornstarch together in a small bowl; stir into the blueberries. Bring the fruit to a boil, stirring. Once the fruit starts to boil, reduce the heat slightly and cook, stirring nonstop, for 1½ minutes. Remove from the heat and stir in the vanilla. Transfer the fruit to a large bowl and cool for 30 minutes.

4. If you're adding the fresh blueberries to the filling, fold them in now. Either way, spoon the filling into the pie shell and smooth with a spoon. Refrigerate for about 1 hour.

5. To make the topping, place the cream cheese, sugars, and lemon zest in a medium bowl. Beat with an electric mixer (handheld is fine) until smooth and creamy. Add the sour cream and vanilla, and beat until smooth. Spoon all of the topping over the chilled pie and smooth with the back of a spoon. Refrigerate for at least 3 hours before serving. Cover and refrigerate leftovers.

Recipe for Success

The pie is great just like this, but a sprinkling of crushed vanilla wafers or shortbread cookies makes a tasty, crunchy finish.

Note that the creamy layer doesn't set up firm like a cheesecake. It stays softish, like thick yogurt, so your slices will probably slump a little.

Maine Wild Blueberry–Maple Pie *with* Cornmeal Crust

Without apology, here is yet another blueberry pie that I simply love, inspired by any number of excellent Maine wild blueberry pies I've eaten in that state. In this version, small, sweet-tart wild berries are sweetened with real maple syrup. The cornmeal crust is a nod to earlier times, when cornmeal was a staple in American kitchens. It's both crunchy and tender, perfect when you want a rustic pie for a casual gathering.

Makes 8–10 servings

Cornmeal Pie Dough, double-crust version (page 68)

FILLING

4½ cups frozen Maine wild blueberries, partially thawed, or other blueberries

⅓ cup maple syrup

2 tablespoons sugar, plus a little for sprinkling

2 tablespoons cornstarch

1 tablespoon lemon juice

1 teaspoon finely grated lemon zest

⅛ teaspoon ground cinnamon

Heavy cream, for glaze

1. Prepare and refrigerate the pie dough. Roll the larger dough portion into a 12-inch circle and line a 9- to 9½-inch standard pie pan with it, letting the excess dough drape over the edge. Refrigerate the shell until needed.

2. Adjust the oven racks so one is in the lower position and another is in the middle of the oven. Preheat the oven to 400°F (200°C). Line a baking sheet with parchment paper.

3. Combine the blueberries and maple syrup in a medium bowl. Mix the sugar and cornstarch together in a small bowl, then stir into the blueberries along with the lemon juice, lemon zest, and cinnamon. Let stand for 5 minutes.

4. Roll the other dough half into an 11-inch circle. Turn the filling into the pie shell and smooth out the fruit with a spoon. Lightly moisten the rim of the pie shell. Drape the top pastry over the filling, pressing along the edge to seal. Trim the overhang with scissors, leaving an even ½ to ¾ inch all around, then sculpt the edge into an upstanding ridge. Flute or crimp the edge, as desired. (Alternatively, instead of sculpting the dough into an upstanding ridge, simply trim the dough flush with the sides of the pan.) Poke several steam vents in the top of the pie with a large fork or paring knife. Put a couple of the vents near the edge so you can check the juices. Brush the pie with heavy cream and sprinkle generously with sugar.

5. Set the pie on the prepared baking sheet and bake on the lower oven rack for 30 minutes. Reduce the heat to 375°F (190°C) and move the pie up to the middle rack, rotating it 180 degrees. Bake for 25 to 35 minutes longer, until the juices bubble thickly at the steam vents.

6. Transfer the pie to a rack and cool for at least 1½ to 2 hours before serving. Cover and refrigerate leftovers after 24 hours.

Wild Blueberry Lattice-Top Pie

Wild blueberries — most of which come from Maine and the eastern provinces of Canada — are smaller than their cultivated counterparts, with a more distinctive, sweet-tangy flavor. They're also a bit firmer, so they hold their shape in baked goods. If you've never tried them, you should! This lattice-top pie showcases their rich flavor and deep blue color.

Makes 8–10 servings

Double-Crust Food Processor Pie Dough (page 60) or another double-crust dough

FILLING

5 **cups wild blueberries, fresh or frozen and partially thawed**

½ **cup plus 2 tablespoons sugar, plus a little for sprinkling**

2½ **tablespoons cornstarch**

2 **teaspoons lemon juice**

1 **teaspoon finely grated lemon zest**

¼ **teaspoon ground cinnamon**

Big pinch of salt

Milk or half-and-half, for glaze

1. Prepare the dough, shaping half of it into a disk and the other half into a square; both should be about ¾ inch thick. Wrap and refrigerate until firm enough to roll, about 1 hour. Roll the round portion of dough into a 12½- to 13-inch circle and line a 9- to 9½-inch deep-dish pie pan with it. Refrigerate the shell until needed.

2. Adjust the oven racks so one is in the lower position and another is in the middle of the oven. Preheat the oven to 400°F (200°C). Line a baking sheet with parchment paper.

3. Combine the blueberries and the ½ cup sugar in a large bowl. Mix gently, then let stand for 10 minutes. Mix the 2 tablespoons sugar and cornstarch in a small bowl; stir into the fruit along with the lemon juice, lemon zest, cinnamon, and salt.

4. Roll the other dough half and cut it into lattice strips as described on page 46.

5. Turn the filling into the pie shell, smoothing out the fruit. Weave a lattice top with the dough strips as described on page 47. Brush the lattice strips lightly with milk and sprinkle with sugar.

6. Put the pie on the prepared baking sheet and bake on the lower oven rack for 30 minutes. Reduce the heat to 375°F (190°C) and move the pie up to the middle rack, rotating the pie 180 degrees. Bake for 30 to 40 minutes longer, until the pie is golden brown and you can see the juices bubble thickly through the lattice.

7. Transfer the pie to a rack and cool for at least 1½ to 2 hours before serving. Cover and refrigerate leftovers after 24 hours.

Recipe for Success

Especially with a blue filling like this, you are better off brushing the lattice strips with milk before you put the lattice on the pie. Otherwise, you may leave blue streaks on the lattice. No tragedy, but perhaps not what you want.

Blueberry-Lime Pie

Here's an approachable blueberry pie with a tangy lime taste. It calls for grated lime zest plus frozen limeade concentrate, a convenient product that means you need less sugar in the filling. Let this cool well before slicing or it will be pretty runny.

Makes 8–10 servings

Double-Crust Food Processor Pie Dough (page 60) or another double-crust dough

FILLING

- 1 (1-pound) bag frozen blueberries, partially thawed
- ⅓ cup frozen limeade concentrate, thawed
- 3 tablespoons sugar, plus a little for sprinkling
- 3 tablespoons quick-cooking tapioca
- 1 teaspoon finely grated lime zest
- 1 teaspoon finely grated orange zest
- Heavy cream, for glaze

1. Prepare and refrigerate the pie dough. Roll the larger dough portion into a 12-inch circle and line a 9- to 9½-inch standard pie pan with it, letting the excess dough drape over the edge. Refrigerate the shell until needed.

2. Adjust the oven racks so one is in the lower position and another is in the middle of the oven. Preheat the oven to 400°F (200°C). Line a baking sheet with parchment paper.

3. Combine the blueberries, limeade concentrate, sugar, tapioca, lime zest, and orange zest in a large bowl. Mix well. Let stand for 10 minutes.

4. Roll the other dough half into an 11-inch circle. Turn the filling into the pie shell and smooth it with a spoon to even the top. Lightly moisten the rim of the pie shell. Drape the top pastry over the filling, pressing along the edge to seal. Trim the overhang with scissors, leaving an even ½ to ¾ inch all around, then sculpt the edge into an upstanding ridge. Flute or crimp the edge, as desired. Poke several steam vents in the top of the pie with a large fork or paring knife. Put a couple of the vents near the edge so you can check the juices. Brush the pie with cream and sprinkle with sugar.

5. Put the pie on the prepared baking sheet and bake on the lower rack for 30 minutes. Reduce the temperature to 375°F (190°C) and move the pie up to the center rack, rotating it 180 degrees. Bake for 25 to 35 minutes, until the top of the pie is golden brown and any juices bubble thickly.

6. Transfer the pie to a rack and cool for at least 2 hours before serving. Cover and refrigerate leftovers after 24 hours.

Blueberry-Peach Pie
with Pecan Crumb Topping

If I had to choose one mixed-fruit pie to eat for the rest of my life, it would probably be this one made with blueberries and peaches, covered with a pecan crumb topping. My idea of a perfect summer afternoon is some free-ranging conversation with friends or family on the patio, with fat slices of this pie standing by as the ice cream maker hums in the background churning up a batch of fresh peach or vanilla ice cream.

Makes 8–10 servings

Single-Crust Food Processor Pie Dough (page 58) or another single-crust dough

FILLING

3 **cups wild or regular blueberries, fresh or frozen and partially thawed**

3 **cups peeled and sliced ripe peaches or frozen sliced peaches, partially thawed**

½ **cup plus 3 tablespoons sugar**

1 **tablespoon lemon juice**

2 **teaspoons finely grated lemon zest**

3 **tablespoons cornstarch**

Melted Butter Crumb Topping (page 449) made with pecans

Vanilla or peach ice cream, for serving

1. Prepare and refrigerate the pie dough. Roll the dough into a 12½- to 13-inch circle and line a 9- to 9½-inch deep-dish pie pan with it, shaping the edge into an upstanding ridge. Flute or crimp the edge, then refrigerate the shell until needed.

2. Adjust the oven racks so one is in the lower position and another is in the middle of the oven. Preheat the oven to 400°F (200°C). Line a baking sheet with parchment paper.

3. Combine the blueberries, peaches, the ½ cup sugar, lemon juice, and lemon zest in a large bowl. Mix well, then let stand for 10 minutes. Mix the 3 tablespoons sugar and cornstarch in a small bowl; stir into the fruit.

4. Turn the filling into the pie shell and smooth the fruit with a spoon. Put the pie on the prepared baking sheet and cover it with a generous layer of the topping; you may not need all of it. Press down gently on the topping.

5. Bake the pie, on the sheet, on the lower oven rack for 30 minutes. Reduce the heat to 375°F (190°C) and move the pie up to the middle rack, rotating it 180 degrees. Bake for 30 to 40 minutes longer, until the juices bubble thickly around the edge. If the topping starts to get too brown, cover the pie with aluminum foil.

6. Transfer the pie to a rack and cool for at least 2 hours before serving, garnished with ice cream. Cover and refrigerate leftovers after 24 hours.

Spoken like a True-Blue Curmudgeonly Yankee

Cherry pie was never as important in New England as in other parts of the United States. Yankees prefer blueberry pie, which, when properly baked, is a glorious thing. Unfortunately, it is often made badly. Restaurant and store-bought blueberry pies usually have more flour or cornstarch in them than blueberries, and many home-baked blueberry pies are too runny.

— Jonathan Norton Leonard, American Cooking: New England

Blueberry-Pineapple Piña Colada Pie

This pie is absolutely delicious, with a tropical island flair that makes it the perfect dessert for a tailgate or island theme party, even if you never leave home. The secret ingredient? Frozen piña colada concentrate.

Makes 8–10 servings

Buttermilk Pie Dough (page 67) or another single-crust dough

FILLING

3   **cups blueberries, fresh or frozen and partially thawed**

1   **cup canned crushed pineapple, well drained**

⅓   **cup frozen piña colada concentrate, thawed**

¼   **cup sugar**

2½ **tablespoons cornstarch**

1   **tablespoon light or dark rum (optional)**

½   **teaspoon coconut extract or vanilla extract**

   Big pinch of salt

   Coconut-Almond Crumb Topping (page 451)

1. Prepare and refrigerate the pie dough. Roll the dough into a 12-inch circle and line a 9- to 9½-inch standard pie pan with it, shaping the edge into an upstanding ridge. Flute or crimp the edge, then refrigerate the shell until needed.

2. Adjust the oven racks so one is in the lower position and another is in the middle of the oven. Preheat the oven to 400°F (200°C). Line a baking sheet with parchment paper.

3. Combine the blueberries, pineapple, and piña colada concentrate in a large bowl. Let stand for 10 minutes. Mix the sugar and cornstarch together in a small bowl; stir into the fruit. Stir in the rum (if using), coconut extract, and salt. Scrape the filling into the pie shell and smooth the top with a spoon.

4. Set the pie on the prepared baking sheet and spread a generous amount of topping over the pie; you probably won't need all of it. Press down gently on the topping.

5. Bake the pie, on the sheet, on the lower oven rack for 30 minutes. Reduce the heat to 375°F (190°C) and move the pie up to the middle rack, rotating it 180 degrees. Bake for 25 to 35 minutes longer, until the juices bubble thickly around the edge of the pie and perhaps through cracks in the topping. Cover the pie with aluminum foil if the topping starts to get too dark.

6. Transfer the pie to a rack and cool for at least 1½ to 2 hours before serving. Cover and refrigerate leftovers after 24 hours.

Blueberries, 20 Cents a Quart

Wild blueberries are best for pie. Picking them is still a considerable industry in Maine, where great areas of barren land are covered with low bushes that in season are covered with small, somewhat acid berries. In the rest of New England the bushes do best on burned-over forest-land. This was the ravaged condition of much of Cape Cod's interior when I was a boy. Sometimes I picked as many as 20 quarts a day, which I divided between my family, gratis, and the grocery store across Main Street from our house, at 20 cents a quart. . . . The large cultivated berries that grow on big bushes in marshy areas are apt to be too sweet to make perfect pies. Yet even the sweetest can be remedied with a touch of lemon juice.

—Jonathan Norton Leonard, American Cooking: New England

Jumble Berry Pie

Do jumble berries grow near you? They appear every summer around my place: first a few leftover blueberries from making pancakes, then some strawberries or a pint of raspberries dropped off by a friend. Before you know it, you have a jumble of berries in the fridge. When that happens, I like to make this pie, tossing in some frozen cranberries for tartness and good measure. It's a delicious way to cap off any summer meal.

Makes 8–10 servings

Shortening and Butter Dough with Egg (page 63), Flaky Cream Cheese Pie Dough, double-crust version (page 72), or another double-crust dough

FILLING

1¼ cups fresh blueberries

1¼ cups hulled and sliced fresh strawberries

1 cup fresh raspberries

1 cup fresh blackberries

1 cup frozen cranberries, partially thawed

½ cup plus 2 tablespoons sugar, plus a little for sprinkling

3 tablespoons cornstarch

¼ teaspoon ground nutmeg

Pinch of salt

1 tablespoon lemon juice

1 teaspoon grated lemon zest

Heavy cream or milk, for glaze

1. Prepare and refrigerate the pie dough. Roll the larger dough portion into a 12½- to 13-inch circle and line a 9- to 9½-inch deep-dish pie pan with it, letting the excess dough drape over the edge. Refrigerate the shell until needed.

2. Adjust the oven racks so one is in the lower position and another is in the middle of the oven. Preheat the oven to 400°F (200°C). Line a baking sheet with parchment paper.

3. Mix all of the fruit and the ½ cup sugar in a large bowl. Let stand for 10 minutes. Mix the 2 tablespoons sugar and cornstarch together in a small bowl; stir into the fruit along with the nutmeg, salt, lemon juice, and lemon zest.

4. Roll the other dough half into an 11-inch circle. Turn the filling into the pie shell and smooth the fruit with a spoon. Lightly moisten the rim of the pie shell. Drape the top pastry over the filling, pressing along the edge to seal. Trim the overhang with scissors, leaving an even ½ to ¾ inch all around, then sculpt the edge into an upstanding ridge. Flute or crimp the edge, as desired. Poke several steam vents in the top of the pie with a large fork or paring knife. Put a couple of the vents near the edge so you can check the juices. Brush the pie with cream and sprinkle with sugar.

5. Set the pie on the prepared baking sheet and bake on the lower rack for 30 minutes. Reduce the heat to 375°F (190°C) and move the pie up to the middle rack, rotating it 180 degrees. Bake for 30 to 40 minutes longer, until the juices bubble thickly at the vents.

6. Transfer the pie to a rack and cool for at least 2 hours before serving. Cover and refrigerate leftovers after 24 hours.

Recipe for Success

The quantities of the various fruits here are somewhat arbitrary. Adjust as appropriate.
Using heavy cream, rather than milk or light cream, creates a thin, brittle glaze on top of the pie, something like a thin sheet of phyllo. It adds another dimension of flavor and interest to any double-crust pie.

Three-Berry Crostata

Here's a blueprint for a simple summer berry crostata, or open-face berry pie. Roll the crostata dough into a big circle, then start piling on the berries. There's just enough sugar to sweeten the berries, and a little cornstarch to thicken the fruit juice, but little else to complicate the fresh flavors of this colorful dessert. Try to serve this soon after baking, or at least the same day it is made.

Makes 8–10 servings

Crostata Dough (page 80)

FILLING

1½ cups fresh blueberries

1½ cup fresh blackberries

1½ cups halved or sliced fresh strawberries

⅓ cup sugar, plus a little for sprinkling

2 tablespoons cornstarch

⅛ teaspoon ground nutmeg

1 tablespoon lemon juice

1 teaspoon finely grated orange zest or lemon zest

Heavy cream, for glaze

1. Prepare the pie dough and refrigerate it for at least 1 hour before rolling.

2. Preheat the oven to 400°F (200°C). The best way to assemble this pie is to roll the dough onto a large sheet of parchment paper, assemble the crostata, then lift it onto a baking sheet with the paper. Alternatively, roll the dough onto a piece of waxed paper, invert it onto the baking sheet, peel off the paper, then assemble the crostata on the baking sheet. In either case, roll the dough into a 13-inch circle.

3. Put the berries in a medium bowl. Mix the sugar, cornstarch, and nutmeg in a small bowl; gently stir into the fruit along with the lemon juice and orange zest.

4. Imagine a 9-inch circle in the center of the dough. Turn the filling out onto that area; leave a generous 2-inch border all around. Using your hands, a metal spatula, or the parchment paper, fold the dough border up and over the outer 2 inches of filling. As you make your way around the crostata, the border will self-pleat, leaving uncovered filling in the center. Lightly brush the border with cream and sprinkle it with sugar.

5. Bake the pie, on the sheet, on the middle oven rack for 20 minutes. Reduce the heat to 375°F (190°C). Bake for about 30 minutes longer, rotating the crostata after 15 minutes, until the crostata is golden brown and the fruit is bubbly.

6. Transfer the crostata to a rack and cool on the sheet. Serve warm or at room temperature. Cover and refrigerate leftovers after 24 hours.

Recipe for Success

If you don't have enough fresh berries on hand, don't worry — some of them can come from the freezer. To thaw, microwave the fruit in a bowl just until it is nearly thawed. Of course, you can simply let it sit in a bowl for 45 to 60 minutes, if you prefer.

Mixed-Berry Free-Form Pie

Here's a recipe from Patsy Jamieson, the former food editor of *EatingWell* magazine. Like her, I will often combine berries in a summer pie. Here she does just that, but in a free-form pie with a bottom layer of cheesecakelike custard that provides a creamy contrast to the berries on top.

Makes 8–10 servings

Cottage Cheese Pie Dough (page 79)

FILLING

4   ounces reduced-fat cream cheese, softened

¼   cup plus 2 tablespoons sugar

1   teaspoon cornstarch

1   large egg yolk

2   teaspoons finely grated lemon zest

1   teaspoon vanilla extract

4   cups fresh mixed berries, such as blackberries, raspberries, blueberries, or others

1   egg white beaten with 1 tablespoon water, for glaze

1. Prepare the pie dough and refrigerate it for at least 1 hour.

2. Preheat the oven to 400°F (200°C). Line a large baking sheet with lightly oiled parchment paper or aluminum foil.

3. Using an electric mixer, beat the cream cheese, the ¼ cup sugar, and cornstarch together in a medium bowl until smooth. Beat in the egg yolk, lemon zest, and vanilla until smooth. Set aside.

4. The best way to assemble this is to roll the dough on a large sheet of lightly oiled parchment paper or aluminum foil, assemble the pie, then lift the entire thing onto the prepared baking sheet. Alternatively, roll the dough onto a long sheet of waxed paper, invert it onto the baking sheet, then peel off the paper, letting the pastry drape slightly over the edges if necessary. Either way, roll the dough into a 13-inch circle.

5. Imagine a circle 8 or 8½ inches in diameter in the center of the dough. Spread the cream cheese mixture over that area, leaving a wide border all around. Pile the berries evenly over the mixture. Using a metal spatula to help you lift it, fold the uncovered perimeter of dough over the filling. The dough will sort of self-pleat as you do so, leaving uncovered filling in the center. Lightly brush the egg wash glaze over the exposed portion of dough. Sprinkle the berries and dough with the 2 tablespoons sugar.

6. Bake the pie, on the sheet, on the center oven rack for 35 to 40 minutes, until the crust is deep golden brown. When the pie is done, the fruit will probably be bubbling.

7. Transfer the pie to a rack and cool on the sheet. Serve slightly warm or at room temperature.

Recipe for Success

This dough is more moist than some, so if it starts to get sticky and you need to firm it up, slide the parchment or waxed paper and pastry onto a large rimless baking sheet and refrigerate for 10 to 15 minutes before rolling it out.

6
More Summer Delights:
A PROFUSION OF FRUIT PIES

Fall may be peak pie-making season, but summer is the
pie maker's sweet spot. How could it not be, with such an
embarrassment of riches to work with? The season begins
modestly enough, with strawberries and rhubarb, but then
the floodgates open and the challenge becomes keeping
up with the parade of peaches, nectarines, cherries — sweet
and tart — and so much more.

In this section, let's imagine that you have a long, leisurely
summer to devote to daily pie baking and consider as many
options as space allows. You probably won't make a pie
a day, but you can dream about having the time to bake
enough double-crust peach pies, crumb-topped blueberry
pies, tempting plum tarts, and scrumptious cherry pies
to fill a small book of their own.

All-Rhubarb Pie

Alaskan Eskimos and Afghans eat rhubarb raw, according to Waverley Root in *Food*. The rest of us, when we eat it at all, like it baked in a pie. (Rhubarb is, after all, also known as *pie plant*.) Here's a recipe for those who like their rhubarb straight up, without any help from strawberries or raspberries, two common companions. There's a fair amount of sugar in the pie to counter rhubarb's tart flavor, plus a little orange juice and zest for citrus zing.

Makes 8 servings

Old-Fashioned Shortening Pie Dough, double-crust version (page 62) or another double-crust dough

FILLING

- 5 **cups sliced fresh rhubarb stalks, cut crosswise into ½-inch-thick pieces**
- 1¼ **cups plus 2 tablespoons sugar, plus a little for sprinkling**
- 2 **tablespoons orange juice**
- **Finely grated zest of ½ orange**
- **Big pinch of salt**
- ¼ **teaspoon ground nutmeg**
- 3 **tablespoons cornstarch**
- 2 **tablespoons cold unsalted butter, cut into small pieces**
- **Milk or half-and-half, for glaze**

1. Prepare and refrigerate the pie dough. Roll the larger dough portion into a 12-inch circle and line a 9- to 9½-inch standard pie pan with it, letting the excess dough drape over the edge. Refrigerate the shell until needed.

2. Adjust the oven racks so one is in the lower position and another is in the middle of the oven. Preheat the oven to 400°F (200°C). Line a baking sheet with parchment paper.

3. Combine the rhubarb, the 1¼ cups sugar, orange juice, orange zest, salt, and nutmeg in a large bowl. Mix well. Let stand for 10 minutes. Mix the 2 tablespoons sugar and cornstarch in a small bowl; stir into the fruit. Turn the filling into the chilled pie shell and smooth the top of the fruit to even it out. Dot the filling with the butter.

4. Roll the other dough half into an 11-inch circle. Lightly moisten the rim of the pie shell. Drape the top pastry over the filling, pressing along the edge to seal. Trim the overhang with scissors, leaving an even ½ to ¾ inch all around, then sculpt the edge into an upstanding ridge. Flute or crimp the edge, as desired. Poke several steam vents in the top of the pie with a large fork or paring knife. Put a couple of the vents near the edge so you can check the juices. Lightly brush the pie with milk and sprinkle with sugar.

5. Put the pie on the prepared baking sheet and bake on the lower oven rack for 30 minutes. Reduce the heat to 375°F (190°C) and move the pie up to the middle rack, rotating it 180 degrees. Bake for 25 to 30 minutes longer, until the juices bubble thickly at the vents.

6. Transfer the pie to a rack and cool for at least 1½ to 2 hours before serving. Cover and refrigerate leftovers after 24 hours.

Recipe for Success

Because of its red color, rhubarb makes an attractive lattice-top pie. Follow the lattice weaving instruction on page 46.

Even though this is an all-rhubarb pie, feel free to substitute a cup or two of raspberries for an equal amount of sliced rhubarb.

If the rhubarb comes with leaves attached, do not eat them. They contain oxalic acid, which can cause sickness or even death.

Tips for Baking Sensational Summer Fruit Pies

- Whenever possible, buy fruit as close as possible to when you plan to bake the pie. Peaches and apricots might need to ripen on your counter, but cherries don't improve by sitting around. Peaches will ripen faster if you put them in a loosely sealed paper bag and leave them at room temperature. If they're already ripe or you want to slow the ripening, store them in the fridge. Scrutinize all of your produce carefully for signs of spoilage or mold.

- Don't hesitate to take a bite out of a piece of fruit to check the flavor and texture. I frequently do this (always offering to pay for the bitten fruit). I'd rather buy one lousy peach than eight.

- Store stone fruit out of the bag so it doesn't bruise.

- Summer fruit can be very juicy, so I almost always bake my fruit pies on a parchment-lined baking sheet to catch spills.

- Don't underbake juicy summer fruit pies. Unless the juices in the pie come to a boil and stay there for a little bit, the thickener won't "take" and the pie may end up with a raw-thickener flavor.

- Don't forget the lemon juice in summer fruit pies. Rare is the fruit pie that doesn't benefit from the acidic tang of lemon.

- No matter the season, allow all your fruit pies to cool for at least 1½ hours, preferably 2, before slicing. Otherwise, the juices may be too thin, the filling won't have the proper body, and the fruit will ooze all over when you serve a slice.

Rhubarb Custard Pie

This recipe originally came to me from Barbara Skinner, former mayor of Sumner, Washington, which calls itself the rhubarb pie capital of the world. When I asked for her favorite rhubarb pie recipe, she sent me this one from the local St. Andrew's Church cookbook, adding that "Everyone in the church is a good cook." They must be, because the pie is excellent — a thick layer of rhubarb on top of a very light custard.

Makes 8 servings

Old-Fashioned Shortening Pie Dough (page 62)

FILLING

3 cups diced fresh rhubarb stalks

1½ cups sugar

3 tablespoons all-purpose flour

Big pinch of salt

½ teaspoon ground nutmeg

2 large eggs

2 tablespoons milk

1 tablespoon cold unsalted butter, cut into small pieces

Whipped Cream (page 447), for garnish

1. Prepare and refrigerate the pie dough. Roll the dough into a 12-inch circle and line a 9- to 9½-inch standard pie pan with it, shaping the edge into an upstanding ridge. Flute or crimp the edge, then refrigerate the shell until needed.

2. Preheat the oven to 350°F (180°C). Combine the rhubarb, sugar, flour, salt, and nutmeg in a large bowl. Toss well. Let stand for 10 minutes. Whisk the eggs and milk together in a small bowl. Add to the fruit, stirring well to combine. Scrape the filling into the pie shell, smoothing the top of the fruit with a spoon. Dot the filling with the butter.

3. Put the pie directly on the center oven rack and bake for about 50 minutes, until the top is crusted over and the filling is set, rotating the pie 180 degrees midway through the baking.

4. Transfer the pie to a rack and cool. Serve barely warm, at room temperature, or chilled, with a dollop of whipped cream. Cover and refrigerate leftovers.

Recipe for Success

I didn't try this, but Barbara mentioned adding a couple of drops of red food coloring to the filling to give it more color.

Don't expect this to bake up like other custard pies. The "custard" is more of a translucent jelly that settles on the bottom of the pie, not a traditional creamy custard surrounding the fruit.

Fresh Sweet Cherry Pie *with* Coconut-Almond Crunch Topping

Making a cherry pie is serious business. Fresh cherries are pricey, and then there are the pits, which need to be removed one by one (see Recipe for Success). With so much at stake, there's a bit of pressure to make a great pie, but this version nails it.

Makes 8 servings

Single-Crust Food Processor Pie Dough (page 58) or another single-crust dough

FILLING

4½ cups pitted fresh sweet cherries

½ cup plus 2 tablespoons sugar

2 tablespoons cherry liqueur or peach schnapps

1 tablespoon lemon juice

¼ teaspoon vanilla extract

2 tablespoons cornstarch

Coconut-Almond Crumb Topping (page 451)

Vanilla ice cream, for serving (optional)

1. Prepare and refrigerate the pie dough. Roll the dough into a 12-inch circle and line a 9- to 9½-inch standard pie pan with it, shaping the edge into an upstanding ridge. Flute or crimp the edge, then refrigerate the shell until needed.

2. Adjust the oven racks so one is in the lower position and another is in the middle of the oven. Preheat the oven to 400°F (200°C). Line a baking sheet with parchment paper.

3. Combine the cherries, the ½ cup sugar, liqueur, lemon juice, and vanilla in a large bowl. Stir well. Let stand for 10 minutes. Combine the 2 tablespoons sugar and cornstarch in a small bowl; stir into the fruit.

4. Turn the filling into the pie shell, smoothing the top with a spoon. Put the pie on the prepared baking sheet and cover with a generous layer of the topping; you may not need all of it. Tamp the topping down lightly.

5. Bake the pie, on the sheet, on the lower oven rack for 30 minutes. Reduce the heat to 375°F (190°C) and move the pie up to the middle rack, rotating the pie 180 degrees. Bake for 30 to 35 minutes longer, until the juices bubble thickly around the edge and perhaps between the topping. If the top starts to get too brown, cover the pie with aluminum foil.

6. Transfer the pie to a rack and cool. Serve barely warm, with a scoop of ice cream, if desired. Cover and refrigerate leftovers after 24 hours.

Recipe for Success

Pitting cherries takes a little time, but fortunately there are any number of good gadgets for the job. To pit by hand, score around the circumference with a small serrated knife and give the cherry a little squeeze to pop out the pit. To mitigate the mess of the accompanying juice spatter, I often take this task outside to the picnic table.

Rainier Cherry Pie
with Grated Top Crust

How could you *not* like a cherry that tastes something like a peach? Unlike other cherries, Rainier cherries have peach-yellow skin and flesh, with a blush of red and a hint of vanilla flavor. And they don't squirt red juice all over the place when you pit them. This exquisite pie is excellent with peach or vanilla ice cream. The top crust is a neat trick: instead of rolling dough, you grate the block of pastry onto the fruit.

FILLING

- 5 **cups pitted and halved Rainier cherries**
- ½ **cup plus 1½ tablespoons granulated sugar**
- 1 **tablespoon lemon juice**
- ¼ **teaspoon vanilla extract**
- 2½ **tablespoons cornstarch**
- 1 **tablespoon coarse sugar (see box) or granulated sugar**

  Vanilla or peach ice cream, for serving

Coarse Sugar

Granulated sugar is fine for sprinkling on pie pastry. It gives the top crust a golden finish and sandy-sugary texture. When you want more crunch, however, use coarse sugar, also known as sanding sugar. The crunchy texture is especially welcome with a soft fruit filling. Store it in a jar or other tightly sealed container in the pantry.

1. Prepare the pie dough. Shape the smaller piece into a square block rather than a disk; place in the freezer until good and firm but not frozen solid, up to 1¼ hours. Refrigerate the larger piece until firm enough to roll, about 1 hour.

2. Roll the disk of dough into a 13-inch circle and line a 9- to 9½-inch deep-dish pie pan with it, shaping the edge into an upstanding ridge. Flute or crimp the edge, then refrigerate the shell until needed.

3. Adjust the oven racks so one is in the lower position and another is in the middle of the oven. Preheat the oven to 400°F (200°C). Line a baking sheet with parchment paper.

4. Combine the cherries, the ½ cup granulated sugar, lemon juice, and vanilla in a large bowl. Mix well. Let stand for 10 minutes. Combine the 1½ tablespoons granulated sugar and cornstarch in a small bowl; stir into the fruit. Turn the filling into the pie shell and smooth the fruit to level it off.

5. Using the large holes of a box grater, grate the pastry block over the top of the fruit as if it was a block of cheese, covering the filling more or less evenly. At some point, you'll need to move the topping around with a fork to evenly distribute it. Sprinkle the coarse sugar over the pastry.

6. Set the pie on the prepared baking sheet and bake on the lower oven rack for 30 minutes. Reduce the oven temperature to 375°F (190°C) and move the pie up to the middle rack, rotating it 180 degrees. Bake for 25 to 35 minutes longer, until the top is golden brown and the juices bubble thickly around the edge.

7. Transfer the pie to a rack and cool for at least 1½ to 2 hours before serving. Garnish slices with ice cream. Cover and refrigerate leftovers after 24 hours.

Recipe for Success

Rainier cherries lack the tartness of some cherries, so consider adding an additional ½ tablespoon lemon juice for a little citrus zing.

   The pastry block should be firm but not frozen solid.

Lattice-Top Deep-Dish Sour Cherry Pie

The key to making a good sour cherry pie, I believe, is adding just enough sugar to tame the tartness without smothering it. The other trick is to use enough thickening to gel the prodigious amount of juice. Other than that, I like to keep the filling simple with a little lemon juice and zest, a dab of butter, and a pretty lattice top so the bright red cherries can peek through. Sour cherries can be difficult to find in many parts of the country, so ask around if your market doesn't carry them.

Makes 8–10 servings

Shortening and Butter Dough with Egg (page 63) or another double-crust dough

FILLING

- 6 **cups pitted fresh sour cherries**
- 1¼ **cups plus 3 tablespoons sugar, plus a little for sprinkling**
- ¼ **cup cornstarch**
- 2 **teaspoons lemon juice**
- **Finely grated zest of 1 lemon**
- 2 **tablespoons cold unsalted butter, cut into small pieces**
- **Milk or half-and-half, for glaze**
- **Vanilla ice cream, for serving (optional)**

1. Prepare and refrigerate the pie dough. Shape the larger dough piece into a disk and the other piece — for the lattice strips — into more of a rectangle. Roll the larger dough portion into a 13-inch circle and line a 9- to 9½-inch deep-dish pie pan with it, letting the excess dough drape over the edge. Refrigerate the shell until needed.

2. Adjust the oven racks so one is in the lower position and another is in the middle of the oven. Preheat the oven to 400°F (200°C). Line a baking sheet with parchment paper.

3. Mix the cherries and the 1¼ cups sugar in a large bowl; let stand for 10 minutes. Mix the 3 tablespoons sugar and cornstarch together in a small bowl; stir into the fruit along with the lemon juice and zest.

4. Roll the other dough half and cut it into lattice strips as described on page 46.

5. Turn the filling into the pie shell, smoothing out the fruit with a spoon. Dot with little bits of butter here and there. Weave a lattice top with the dough strips as described on page 47. Using a small pastry brush, carefully brush the lattice strips with milk. Try to avoid touching the filling with the brush so you don't paint the strips red. Sprinkle the pie generously with sugar.

6. Put the pie on the prepared baking sheet and bake on the lower oven rack for 30 minutes. Reduce the heat to 375°F (190°C) and move the pie up to the middle rack, rotating it 180 degrees. Bake for 30 to 40 minutes longer, until the juices bubble thickly through the lattice strips.

7. Transfer the pie to a rack and cool for at least 1½ to 2 hours before serving. Garnish slices with ice cream, if desired. Cover and refrigerate leftovers after 24 hours.

Recipe for Success

Don't use anything less than a large deep-dish pie pan because this pie is very juicy.

Ripe sour cherries are easy to pit. After you pull off the stem, you can simply squeeze the pit out of the stem end.

Don't omit the lemon juice and zest, thinking the cherries will be tart enough. The lemon flavor is wonderful with the cherries.

Dense Cherry-Almond Coffeecake Pie

I love a good almond cake so much that I started spinning almond cake-pie hybrids; this is a particularly good one. Simply scatter a single layer of cherries in the pie shell, then pour a rich sour cream–almond filling over them. A deliciously moist, cakey filling with a golden crust forms around the cherries as they bake.

Makes 10 servings

Almond Pie Dough (page 81) or Simple Press-In Pie Dough (page 73)

FILLING

- 2 **cups pitted sweet cherries, fresh or frozen and thawed**
- 1 **cup whole almonds, toasted (page 453)**
- ⅓ **cup all-purpose flour**
- 1⅓ **cups granulated sugar**
- ¼ **teaspoon salt**
- 3 **large eggs plus 2 large egg yolks, at room temperature**
- 1 **cup sour cream**
- 2 **tablespoons packed light brown sugar**
- 2 **tablespoons unsalted butter, melted**
- 1 **teaspoon vanilla extract**
- ¼ **teaspoon almond extract**

1. Prepare and refrigerate the pie dough. Roll the dough into a 13-inch circle and line a 9- to 9½-inch deep-dish pie pan with it, shaping the edge into an upstanding ridge. Flute or crimp the edge, chill the shell, and partially pre-bake it according to the instructions on page 36. (If you're using the press-in pie dough, follow the recipe on page 73.)

2. Preheat the oven to 350°F (180°C). Put the cherries on a double layer of paper towels and set them aside for 10 minutes. Meanwhile, combine the almonds, flour, ⅓ cup of the granulated sugar, and the salt in a food processor and pulse until the mixture resembles a coarse meal.

3. Using an electric mixer (handheld is fine), beat the eggs, egg yolks, sour cream, brown sugar, and the remaining 1 cup granulated sugar in a large bowl until smooth. Blend in the butter, vanilla, and almond extract. Stir the dry mixture into the liquid, blending until smooth.

4. Arrange the cherries in a single layer in the pie shell. Ladle the filling over the cherries.

5. Place the pie directly on the middle oven rack and bake for 30 minutes. Rotate the pie 180 degrees, then bake for 20 to 25 minutes longer, until the filling is set in the center and the surface of the pie is a rich, uniform golden brown.

6. Transfer the pie to a rack and cool. Serve slightly warm or at room temperature. Refrigerate leftovers.

Recipe for Success

You wouldn't normally want to drain or blot away any juice when you're making a cherry pie, but this recipe is a little different. If too much cherry juice bleeds into the filling, it will lose some of its cakelike texture. That's why you drain them on paper towels first.

Refrigerate leftovers, but gently rewarm the pie before serving, especially if you're serving it with ice cream.

Floating-Top Cherry-Vanilla Pie

A floating-top pie is pretty much what it sounds like: a pie whose crust just sits on top of the filling. It's a fashion statement more than anything, a neat little trick that creates a pretty fruit-colored ring around the edge of the pie where the juices have bubbled up. The darker the fruit (think blackberries or cherries), the more striking the effect, but you can achieve this look with almost any fruit.

Makes 8–10 servings

Double-Crust Food Processor Pie Dough (page 60)

FILLING

- **4 cups pitted fresh sweet cherries**
- **⅓ cup plus 2 tablespoons sugar, plus a little for sprinkling**
- **2 teaspoons lemon juice**
- **2 tablespoons cornstarch**
- **Pinch of ground nutmeg**
- **¾ teaspoon vanilla extract**
- **Milk or half-and-half, for glaze**

1. Prepare and refrigerate the pie dough. Roll the larger dough portion into a 12-inch circle and line a 9- to 9½-inch standard pie pan with it, shaping the edge into an upstanding ridge. Flute the edge, then refrigerate the shell until needed.

2. Adjust the oven racks so one is in the lower position and another is in the middle of the oven. Preheat the oven to 400°F (200°C). Line a baking sheet with parchment paper.

3. Combine the cherries, the ⅓ cup sugar, and lemon juice in a medium bowl. Mix well. Let stand for 10 minutes. Mix together the 2 tablespoons sugar and cornstarch in a small bowl; stir into the fruit along with the nutmeg and vanilla.

4. Roll the other dough portion into a 10- to 10½-inch circle. Use a bowl or another template for this next step. Cut out a 7-inch round from the middle of the circle with a paring knife or pastry wheel. Remove the outer scraps and save for another use; keep the circle of dough nearby.

5. Turn the filling into the pie shell, smoothing the top with a spoon. Carefully place the top pastry over the center of the filling. Brush the top dough with milk and sprinkle with sugar.

6. Set the pie on the prepared baking sheet and bake on the lower oven rack for 30 minutes. Reduce the heat to 375°F (190°C) and move the pie up to the middle rack, rotating the pie 180 degrees. Bake for 25 to 30 minutes longer, until the juices bubble thickly all around the edge.

7. Transfer the pie to a rack and cool for at least 1½ to 2 hours before serving. Cover and refrigerate leftovers after 24 hours.

Recipe for Success

An attractive variation on a floating top is to use decorative pastry cutouts, like diamonds or circles, to "attach" the floating crust to the pie shell. Lay six or eight cutouts evenly around the perimeter, placing them partly on the floating pastry and partly on the shell, spanning the fruit filling.

Double Cherry Pie

I found this recipe years ago on a cherry marketing website. The recipe is no longer there, but it should be. With two kinds of sour cherries — fresh and dried — along with sugar and a bit of butter, nutmeg, and almond extract to highlight the flavor of the fruit, it's a cherry pie for cherry purists.

Makes 8–10 servings

Old-Fashioned Shortening Pie Dough, double-crust version (page 62) or another double-crust dough

FILLING

- 4½ cups pitted sour cherries, frozen and partially thawed, or canned and drained
- 1 cup dried sour cherries
- 1 cup sugar, plus a little for sprinkling
- 2 tablespoons quick-cooking tapioca
- ½ teaspoon almond extract
- ¼ teaspoon ground nutmeg
- 1 tablespoon cold unsalted butter, cut into small pieces

  Milk or half-and-half, for glaze

1. Prepare and refrigerate the pie dough. Roll the larger dough portion into a 13-inch circle and line a 9- to 9½-inch deep-dish pie pan with it, letting the excess dough drape over the edge. Refrigerate the shell until needed.

2. Adjust the oven racks so one is in the lower position and another is in the middle of the oven. Preheat the oven to 375°F (190°C). Line a baking sheet with parchment paper.

3. Combine all the cherries, the sugar, tapioca, and almond extract in a large bowl. Mix well. Let stand for 10 to 15 minutes.

4. Roll the other dough half into an 11-inch circle. Turn the filling into the pie shell, smoothing out the fruit with a spoon. Sprinkle the nutmeg over the fruit and dot the filling with the butter. Lightly moisten the rim of the pie shell. Drape the top pastry over the filling, pressing along the edge to seal. Trim the overhang with scissors, leaving an even ½ to ¾ inch all around, then sculpt the edge into an upstanding ridge. Flute or crimp the edge, as desired. Poke several steam vents in the top of the pie with a large fork or paring knife. Put a couple of the vents near the edge so you can check the juices. Lightly brush the pie with milk and sprinkle with sugar.

5. Put the pie on the prepared baking sheet and bake on the lower oven rack for 30 minutes. Move the pie up to the middle rack, rotating it 180 degrees. Bake for 30 to 35 minutes longer, until the juices bubble thickly up through the steam vents.

6. Transfer the pie to a rack and cool for at least 1½ to 2 hours. This pie is best eaten slightly warm or at room temperature. Cover and refrigerate leftovers after 24 hours.

Recipe for Success

Do try to find sour cherries to make this pie, but don't despair if all you can find are sweet ones. Just reduce the sugar by about half and add 1 tablespoon lemon juice to the filling.

At the very least, you should be able to find dried sour cherries, most likely at Whole Foods Market or some place like that. They're a little pricey, but worth it to make this great pie.

The Ultimate Four-Cherry Pie

I'm the proverbial kid in the candy store when it comes to cherries, a situation that sometimes finds me with an assortment of pie cherries on hand: sweet, sour, and the Rainier cherries I like so much for pies. Since I almost always have at least a partial bag of dried cherries hanging around, I've been known to combine all of them in a pie and make one heck of a good four-cherry pie.

Makes 8–10 servings

Buttermilk Pie Dough (page 67) or another single-crust dough

FILLING

- 2 **cups pitted fresh sour cherries**
- 2 **cups pitted fresh Rainier cherries**
- 1 **cup pitted fresh sweet cherries**
- ½ **cup dried sour or sweet cherries**
- ½ **cup plus 2 tablespoons sugar**
- 1 **tablespoon lemon or orange juice**
- **Finely grated zest of ½ orange**
- ½ **teaspoon vanilla extract (optional)**
- 3 **tablespoons cornstarch**
- **Traditional German Streusel (page 450)**

1. Prepare and refrigerate the pie dough. Roll the dough into a 13-inch circle and line a 9- to 9½-inch deep-dish pie pan with it, shaping the edge into an upstanding ridge. Flute or crimp the edge, then refrigerate the shell until needed.

2. Adjust the oven racks so one is in the lower position and another is in the middle of the oven. Preheat the oven to 400°F (200°C). Line a baking sheet with parchment paper.

3. Combine all the cherries, the ½ cup sugar, lemon juice, orange zest, and vanilla (if using) in a large bowl. Mix well. Let stand for 5 to 10 minutes. Mix the 2 tablespoons granulated sugar and cornstarch together in a small bowl; stir into the fruit.

4. Turn the filling into the pie shell and smooth the fruit out with a spoon. Put the pie on the prepared baking sheet and cover with a generous amount of the streusel; you may not need all of it. Tamp the streusel down gently.

5. Bake the pie, on the sheet, on the lower oven rack for 30 minutes. Reduce the heat to 375°F (190°C) and move the pie up to the middle rack, rotating it 180 degrees. Bake for 30 to 35 minutes longer, until the juices bubble thickly around the edge. If the top of the pie starts to get too dark, cover it with aluminum foil.

6. Transfer the pie to a rack and cool for at least 1½ to 2 hours before serving. Cover and refrigerate leftovers after 24 hours.

Recipe for Success

You'll flatten the subtle cherry notes if you oversweeten this pie, so resist the temptation to add more sugar to the filling.

Cherry-Blueberry Slab Pie

You could make this pie with fresh summer fruit, but I rarely do. I use frozen cherries and blueberries, which are economical and available year-round. Take the extra step of precooking the filling and allowing it to cool before you fill the slab pie shell. For this extra bit of trouble, you get a perfectly even layer of filling throughout the pie. The top dough is cut into squares and gives a charming sort of cobblestone look that's lovely with the confectioners' sugar glaze. A real crowd-pleaser.

Makes 12 or more pieces

Slab Pie Dough and Shell (page 74)

Single-Crust Food Processor Pie Dough, (page 58)

FILLING

- **5 cups frozen cherries**
- **3½ cups frozen blueberries**
- **1 cup plus 2 tablespoons sugar, plus a little for sprinkling**
- **2 tablespoons lemon juice**
- **⅔ cup cranberry juice or apple juice**
- **4½ tablespoons cornstarch**
- **Milk or half-and-half, for glaze**
- **Confectioners' Sugar Glaze (page 452)**

1. Prepare both pie doughs and refrigerate for at least 1 hour.

2. Roll out the slab pie dough and line the pan with it according to the instructions; be sure to use the correct pan. Don't trim off extra dough around the edges: let it run up the sides of the pan or hang over it because you will need it when you assemble the pie. Refrigerate the shell.

3. Roll the food processor dough into an approximately 10- by 15-inch rectangle. Using a pastry wheel or paring knife, cut the dough into 12 more-or-less-equal pieces, making three equally spaced cuts crosswise and two lengthwise. Spread these sections on a baking sheet, cover with plastic wrap, and refrigerate.

4. Combine the cherries and blueberries in a large, heavy, nonreactive pot. Slowly heat the fruit, partially covered, until it is juicy and mostly thawed. Stir in the 1 cup sugar and the lemon juice. Raise the heat a bit and continue to cook until the fruit is very juicy.

5. Pour the cranberry juice into a small bowl. Add 3 tablespoons of the cornstarch and mix well. Stir into the fruit and bring to a boil, stirring nonstop. When the fruit comes to a boil, lower the heat slightly and boil for 1½ minutes, stirring continually. Remove from the heat, cool briefly, then transfer the fruit to a shallow casserole dish and cool completely. When the fruit has cooled, mix the 2 tablespoons sugar with the remaining 1½ tablespoons cornstarch in a small bowl. Shake this mixture over the fruit and stir it in thoroughly.

Recipe continues on next page

6. Adjust the oven racks so one is in the lower position and another is in the middle of the oven. Preheat the oven to 400°F (200°C).

7. Transfer the filling to the pie shell and smooth it out with a spoon. Working with one piece of dough at a time, brush one side lightly with milk and place it in a corner of the pie, butting against the sides, milked side up. Repeat for another section, overlapping it slightly — by about ⅛ inch — with the previous one. Continue with the pieces, overlapping them in rows until the pie is covered. Fold down any excess dough along the edge and pinch it against the top sections to form a seal. You will have three rows of four sections each. Sprinkle the pie with sugar.

8. Bake the pie on the lower oven rack for 25 minutes. Reduce the heat to 375°F (190°C) and move the pie up to the middle rack, rotating it 180 degrees. Bake for 25 to 35 minutes until the top of the pie is golden and you see fruit juice bubbling up thickly through some of the seams.

9. Transfer the pie to a rack and cool. When the pie is barely lukewarm or cool, drizzle some of the glaze over the top. Cut into slices and serve.

Recipe for Success

This is something of a project pie, so don't feel like you have to make it all in one session. Maybe make the doughs and shell one day, and save the filling and baking for the next.

If You Get Bored Waiting for Your Cherry Pie to Bake . . .

You can always try knotting cherry stems with your tongue. But you'll have to be fast to break the record, set in 1999 in Orlando, Florida. Al Gliniecki of Gulf Breeze, Florida, managed to do 39 of them in 3 minutes, enough to twist, turn, and ultimately tongue-tie his way into the Guinness Book of World Records.

All-Peach Crumb Pie

The season for truly good, ripe peaches is short — far shorter than the length you'll find them in the supermarkets come summer. When the quality isn't what it should be, I don't hesitate to use frozen peaches. Not only are bagged frozen peach slices a relative bargain compared to fresh or canned, but the quality is high.

Makes 8–10 servings

Perfect Pie Dough by Hand (page 56) or another single-crust dough

FILLING

- 2 **pounds frozen sliced peaches, partially thawed**
- 1½ **tablespoons lemon juice**
  Finely grated zest of lemon
- ⅓ **cup plus 3 tablespoons sugar**
- 3 **tablespoons cornstarch**
- ½ **teaspoon vanilla extract**
- ¼ **teaspoon ground nutmeg**
  Traditional German Streusel (page 450)

1. Prepare and refrigerate the pie dough. Roll the dough into a 13-inch circle and line a 9- to 9½-inch deep-dish pie pan with it, shaping the edge into an upstanding ridge. Flute or crimp the edge, then refrigerate the shell until needed.

2. Adjust the oven racks so one is in the lower position and another is in the middle of the oven. Preheat the oven to 400°F (200°C). Line a baking sheet with parchment paper.

3. Combine the peaches, lemon juice, lemon zest, and the ⅓ cup sugar in a large bowl. Mix well. Let stand for 10 minutes. Combine the 3 tablespoons sugar and cornstarch in a small bowl; stir into the fruit. Stir in the vanilla and nutmeg.

4. Turn the filling into the pie shell and smooth out the filling. Put the pie on the prepared baking sheet and cover the filling with a generous layer of the streusel; you may not need all of it. Gently press down on the streusel.

5. Bake the pie, on the sheet, on the lower oven rack for 35 minutes. Reduce the heat to 375°F (190°C) and move the pie up to the middle rack, rotating it 180 degrees. Bake for 25 to 35 minutes longer, until the juices bubble thickly around the edge of the pie and perhaps up through the streusel. Be patient; because the fruit was cold when the pie went in the oven, this might take longer to bake, so wait for those bubbling juices. If the top starts to look too brown near the end of the baking, cover the pie with aluminum foil.

6. Transfer the pie to a rack and cool for at least 1½ to 2 hours before serving. Cover and refrigerate leftovers after 24 hours.

Recipe for Success

Really juicy pies like this one need a thick layer of crumb topping. If you use too little topping, it tends to just soak into the juice, and you end up with sludge on top rather than crumbs.

Peach-Blueberry Slab Pie

For some slab pies — especially juicy ones like this with a crumb topping — I precook the filling ahead to thicken it up. Otherwise, the crumbs can settle into the juicy fruit and lose their crunch. We can't have that. This is the ideal pie to serve at a big summer get-together because it makes ample servings. I've also made this with frozen fruit in the cold months and have had zero complaints.

Makes 12–15 servings

Slab Pie Dough and Shell (page 74)

FILLING

- ⅔ cup plus 2 tablespoons sugar
- 3½ tablespoons cornstarch
- ⅓ cup water or fruit juice (such as cranberry, apple, white grape)
- 4½ cups peeled and sliced ripe peaches
- 2½ cups blueberries
- 1 tablespoon lemon juice
- 1–2 teaspoons finely grated lemon zest

  Oatmeal Crumb Topping (page 449) or Melted Butter Crumb Topping (page 449)

1. Prepare the slab pie dough and make the slab shell in a jelly-roll pan. Refrigerate for at least 1 hour.

2. Adjust the oven racks so one is in the lower position and another is in the middle of the oven. Preheat the oven to 400°F (200°C).

3. Combine the ⅔ cup sugar and 2½ tablespoons of the cornstarch in a large heavy pot. Whisk to mix. Add the water and whisk again. Add the peaches and blueberries, then slowly begin heating the fruit, stirring occasionally. Go easy; you don't want to break up the fruit too much.

4. After several minutes, when the fruit is very juicy, increase the heat and bring the fruit to a boil. Cook at a low boil, stirring, until the juice is thick, about 1½ minutes. Remove from the heat and transfer to a large bowl. Stir in the lemon juice and zest. Cool. Mix the 2 tablespoons sugar and the remaining 1½ tablespoons cornstarch in a small bowl. Sprinkle over the fruit and stir it in. Turn the fruit filling into the slab pie shell, smoothing it out with a spoon. Spread the crumb topping evenly over the fruit, tamping it down lightly.

5. Bake the pie on the lower oven rack for 25 minutes. Reduce the heat to 375°F (190°C) and move the pie up to the middle rack, rotating it 180 degrees. Bake for 20 to 25 minutes longer, until the juices bubble thickly and the topping is golden brown. Cover the pie with foil if it starts to get too brown.

6. Transfer the pie to a rack and cool for at least 1 hour before serving; it's best served lukewarm or at room temperature. Cover and refrigerate leftovers after 24 hours.

Recipe for Success

You'll notice that I add a second measure of cornstarch to the filling after I cook the fruit on the stovetop. That's because cornstarch can sometimes break down and lose its oomph if it is cooked more than once. This second addition of cornstarch acts as an insurance policy and helps keep the fruit nice and "tight" during the baking.

Minimalist Peach Crumb Galette

I'm always game to make a pie from scratch, but even I have a desire to keep things simple and minimalist at times. That's what this galette — or open-face pie — is about. Galettes are typically baked free form, on a baking sheet, but with this pan method there are no concerns about the crust splitting and the filling leaking out.

I make it in my largest pie pan, which is nearly 12 inches in diameter, but yours doesn't need to be that big. If you want to keep things really simple, you can forgo the topping altogether, but this is a good opportunity to use up that leftover topping lurking in the freezer.

Makes 8–10 servings

Almond Pie Dough (page 81), Single-Crust Food Processor Pie Dough (page 58), or another single-crust dough

FILLING

4-4½ cups peeled and sliced ripe peaches or about 1½ pounds frozen sliced peaches, partially thawed

1 tablespoon lemon juice

⅓ cup sugar

1½ tablespoons cornstarch

Oatmeal Crumb Topping (page 449) or another crumb topping or streusel

1. Prepare and refrigerate the pie dough. Adjust the oven racks so one is in the lower position and another is in the middle of the oven. Preheat the oven to 400°F (200°C).

2. Roll the dough into a large circle, about 12½ inches wide for a 10-inch diameter pan and about 1 inch bigger for larger pans. Line the pan with the dough so there's an even overhang all around.

3. Combine the peaches and lemon juice in a large bowl. Mix the sugar and cornstarch in a small bowl; stir into the fruit.

4. Turn the filling into the pie shell, distributing the fruit evenly. Fold the overhanging dough over the fruit and press down gently on the resulting dough border so the top of the galette is more or less level. Cover everything — the filling and exposed dough — with a generous layer of the crumb topping. If you're working with a full recipe of topping, you may not need all of it. Press the crumbs down gently.

5. Bake the galette on the lower oven rack for 30 minutes. Lower the heat to 375°F (190°C) and move the galette up to the middle rack, rotating the pie 180 degrees. Bake for 20 to 30 minutes longer, until the juices bubble thickly through the topping. If the galette starts to get too dark, cover it with foil.

6. Transfer the galette to a rack and cool. Serve warm or at room temperature. Cover and refrigerate after 24 hours.

Peach-Mango Pie *with* Coconut-Almond Crumb Topping

Here's the perfect armchair vacation pie when you need to escape to someplace warm and inviting, but a real getaway isn't in the cards. With one bite of this mango, coconut, and almond trio, you'll think you've been transported to the tropics. A great way to conclude a shrimp meal.

Makes 8–10 servings

Single-Crust Food Processor Pie Dough (page 58) or another single-crust dough

FILLING

3 cups frozen sliced peaches, partially thawed

2 cups frozen mango chunks, partially thawed

½ cup plus 2 tablespoons sugar

1½ tablespoons cornstarch

1 tablespoon lemon juice

1 tablespoon finely grated lemon zest or orange zest

Coconut-Almond Crumb Topping (page 451)

1. Prepare and refrigerate the pie dough. Roll the dough into a 13-inch circle and line a 9- to 9½-inch deep-dish pie pan with it, shaping the edge into an upstanding ridge. Flute or crimp the edge, then refrigerate the shell until needed.

2. Adjust the oven racks so one is in the lower position and another is in the middle of the oven. Preheat the oven to 400°F (200°C). Line a baking sheet with parchment paper.

3. Combine the fruit and the ½ cup sugar in a large bowl; it should be about half frozen. Let stand for 10 minutes. Mix the 2 tablespoons sugar and cornstarch in a small bowl; stir into the fruit. Mix in the lemon juice and lemon zest.

4. Turn the filling into the pie shell and smooth it out. Put the pie on the prepared baking sheet and cover the filling with a generous layer of the crumb topping. Tamp the crumbs down lightly.

5. Bake the pie, on the sheet, on the lower oven rack for 30 minutes. Reduce the heat to 375°F (190°C) and move the pie up to the middle rack, rotating it 180 degrees. Bake for 30 to 35 minutes longer, until the juices bubble thickly around the edge of the pie and perhaps up through the filling. If the top starts to get too brown, cover the pie with aluminum foil.

6. Transfer the pie to a rack and cool for at least 1½ to 2 hours before serving. Cover and refrigerate leftovers after 24 hours.

Recipe for Success

When I use frozen fruit in a pie, I typically measure it into my large mixing bowl and let it sit at room temperature for 30 to 45 minutes before I mix up the filling. If it's frozen solid, and you're using a good deal of fruit, the crust or crumb topping is likely to overbake before the filling is done. To help the fruit along, I will sometimes microwave it for 30 to 60 seconds.

Lemonade Peach Pie

Everyone loves this streamlined peach pie, where the lemonade concentrate acts as both sweetener and flavoring. I'm sure you will enjoy it, too.

Makes 8–10 servings

Simple Press-In Pie Dough (page 73)

FILLING

- 4 cups peeled and thinly sliced ripe peaches
- ⅓ cup frozen lemonade concentrate, thawed
- ¼ cup sugar
- 2½ tablespoons quick-cooking tapioca or 2 tablespoons cornstarch
- 1-2 teaspoons finely grated lemon zest
- Oatmeal Crumb Topping (page 000)

1. Prepare the pie dough and press it into a 9- to 9½-inch deep-dish pie pan according to the recipe on page 73.

2. Combine the peaches, lemonade concentrate, sugar, tapioca, and lemon zest in a large bowl. Let stand for 10 minutes.

3. Adjust the oven racks so one is in the lower position and another is in the middle of the oven. Preheat the oven to 400°F (200°C). Line a baking sheet with parchment paper.

4. Turn the filling into the pie shell and smooth out the fruit. Put the pie on the prepared baking sheet and cover the filling with a generous layer of the crumb topping; you may not need all of it. Tamp the crumbs down lightly.

5. Bake the pie, on the sheet, on the lower oven rack for 30 minutes. Reduce the heat to 375°F (190°C) and move the pie up to the middle rack, rotating it 180 degrees. Bake for 25 to 35 minutes longer, until the juices bubble thickly around the edge of the pie and perhaps through cracks in the topping. If the top of the pie starts to get too dark, cover it with aluminum foil.

6. Transfer the pie to a rack and cool for at least 1½ to 2 hours before serving. Cover and refrigerate leftovers after 24 hours.

Recipe for Success

I've mentioned this doneness indicator elsewhere, but in case you missed it: When a juicy crumb-top pie is fully baked, the bubbly filling will "lift" or push up the topping — as if someone is inflating it — just a little bit. When you see this happen, you can be sure the pie is done.

Peachy Peach Butter Pie *with* Sour Cream Topping

One of the best ways to make a really peachy peach pie is with peach butter, often available at farmers markets. If you've never tried it, peach butter is like apple butter — a thick fruit spread made primarily from the fruit itself. I combine it with sliced peaches, sugar, spices, and flour — all baked until bubbly and thick. Once the pie cools, I spread brown sugar–sweetened sour cream over the top for a smooth and creamy contrast to the chunky fruit filling.

Makes 8–10 servings

Old-Fashioned Shortening Pie Dough (page 62)

FILLING

- 4 cups peeled and sliced ripe peaches
- 1 cup peach butter
- ½ cup granulated sugar
- 1½ tablespoons lemon juice
- Finely grated zest of 1 lemon
- 2 tablespoons all-purpose flour
- ½ teaspoon ground cinnamon
- ¼ teaspoon ground nutmeg

TOPPING

- 1¼ cups full-fat sour cream
- ¼ cup packed light brown sugar
- ½ teaspoon vanilla extract

1. Prepare and refrigerate the pie dough. Roll the dough into a 13-inch circle and line a 9- to 9½-inch deep-dish pie pan with it, shaping the edge into an upstanding ridge. Flute or crimp the edge, then refrigerate the shell until needed.

2. Adjust the oven racks so one is in the lower position and another is in the middle of the oven. Preheat the oven to 400°F (200°C).

3. Combine the peaches, peach butter, granulated sugar, lemon juice, lemon zest, flour, cinnamon, and nutmeg in a large bowl. Mix well. Let stand for 10 minutes.

4. Turn the filling into the pie shell and smooth the top of the fruit with a spoon. Put the pie on the lower oven rack and bake for 30 minutes. Reduce the heat to 375°F (190°C) and move the pie up to the middle rack, rotating it 180 degrees. Bake for about 30 minutes longer, until the filling bubbles thickly.

5. Transfer the pie to a rack and cool for 2 hours, then refrigerate for at least 2 more hours.

6. About 30 minutes before serving the pie, make the topping. Combine the sour cream and brown sugar in a small saucepan over low heat. Heat, stirring nonstop, until the sour cream is runny, 2 to 3 minutes; do not boil. Remove from the heat and stir in the vanilla. Slowly pour the sour cream mixture over the center of the pie, then quickly tilt the pie this way and that so the topping runs up to the edge. Refrigerate for 30 minutes before serving. Refrigerate leftovers.

Recipe for Success

Many brands of peach butter already contain spices. Taste yours to see how spicy it is. If the spices are bold, reduce the amount of cinnamon and nutmeg added to the filling here.

This filling may appear to have thickened after 30 to 40 minutes, but don't be tempted to remove the pie from the oven before you see it bubble. It won't be as juicy as a traditional fruit pie, but it should be bubbly thick in several locations.

Vanilla Bean–Scented All-Peach Pie

When I'm feeling extravagant and in the thrall of the summer peach harvest, I'll slit open a vanilla bean, scrape out the seeds, and grind them with a cup of sugar. I use this vanilla sugar three ways: to sweeten the filling, to sprinkle over the piecrust when it comes out of the oven, and to flavor the whipped cream I serve with it. It's all quite indulgent — vanilla beans costing what they do — but worth it once a year when peaches are at their best.

Makes 8–10 servings

Double-Crust Food Processor Pie Dough (page 60) or another double-crust dough

FILLING

- 1 **cup sugar**
- 1 **plump vanilla bean**
- 2½ **tablespoons cornstarch**
- 5 **cups peeled and thickly sliced ripe peaches**
- 1 **tablespoon lemon juice**
- 2 **tablespoons cold unsalted butter, cut into small pieces**
- 1 **cup cold heavy cream**

1. Prepare and refrigerate the pie dough. Roll the larger dough portion into a 12-inch circle and line a 9- to 9½-inch standard pie pan with it, letting the excess dough drape over the edge. Refrigerate the shell until needed.

2. Adjust the oven racks so one is in the lower position and another is in the middle of the oven. Preheat the oven to 400°F (200°C). Line a baking sheet with parchment paper.

3. Put the sugar in a food processor. Slit the vanilla bean lengthwise. With the blade of a paring knife, scrape the seeds out of the bean and into the processor; process for about 1 minute. (The machine might send a cloud of sugar dust up through the feed tube; just cover the tube with your hand.) Mix ½ cup of the vanilla sugar with the cornstarch in a small bowl. Set the remaining the vanilla sugar aside.

4. Combine the peaches, sugar-cornstarch mixture, and lemon juice in a large bowl. Let stand for 10 minutes.

5. Roll the other dough half into an 11-inch circle. Turn the filling into the pie shell and smooth it out to even the top. Dot the filling with the butter. Lightly moisten the rim of the pie shell. Drape the top pastry over the filling, pressing along the edge to seal. Using a paring knife, trim the dough so it's even with the edge of the pan, then crimp the edge with a fork. Poke several steam vents in the top of the pie with a large fork or paring knife. Put a couple of the vents near the edge so you can check the juices.

6. Set the pie on the prepared baking sheet and bake on the lower oven rack for 30 minutes. Reduce the heat to 375°F (190°C) and move the pie up to the middle rack, rotating it 180 degrees. Bake for 30 minutes longer, until the juices bubble thickly at the vents.

7. Transfer the pie to a rack and immediately sprinkle 2 to 3 tablespoons of the reserved vanilla sugar over the top. Cool for at least 1½ to 2 hours. At the same time, chill a medium bowl and a set of mixer beaters.

8. Shortly before serving, beat the cream in the chilled bowl with an electric mixer (handheld is fine) until it holds soft peaks. Add the remaining vanilla sugar, or to taste, and continue to beat until stiff but not grainy. Serve a large dollop with each slice of pie.

Recipe for Success

Choose a fat, supple vanilla bean about 8 inches long, meaning it's fully mature.

Be sure to sprinkle the vanilla sugar on the pie as soon as it comes out of the oven so some of it melts into the top crust. Expect much of it to remain crunchy, however.

Peach Pointers

- Use your nose when choosing peaches. They should have a sweet, peachy aroma.

- Ripe peaches will yield to gentle finger pressure. They shouldn't be rock hard.

- Avoid greenish peaches. They were picked too early and won't ripen or make a good pie.

- Buy only enough peaches for your immediate needs. Once they're ripe, they won't keep more than a day or two.

- Refrigerate fully ripe peaches, in a single layer. Use within a day or two. Store underripe fruit at room temperature, again in a single layer. Turn frequently to minimize bruising.

Peach Custard Pie

This has everything I like in a pie: peaches, custard, and a crumb topping.
As the pie bakes, the various elements almost melt into one, forming a sort of
peach custard. Use only very ripe, juicy summer peaches.

Makes 8–10 servings

*Simple Press-In Pie Dough
(page 73)*

FILLING

¾ cup sugar

3 tablespoons all-
    purpose flour

¼ teaspoon ground
    nutmeg

1 cup full-fat sour cream

⅓ cup heavy cream

4 large egg yolks

1 teaspoon vanilla
    extract

3½ cups peeled and sliced
    ripe peaches

    **Traditional German
    Streusel (page 450)**

1. Prepare the pie dough and press it into a 9- to 9½-inch pie pan according to the recipe on page 73. Refrigerate the shell until needed.

2. Adjust the oven racks so one is in the lower position and another is in the middle of the oven. Preheat the oven to 400°F (200°C). Line a baking sheet with parchment paper.

3. Whisk the sugar, flour, and nutmeg in a large bowl. Add the sour cream, heavy cream, egg yolks, and vanilla. Whisk again until evenly blended.

4. Arrange the sliced peaches in a single layer in the pie shell. Slowly pour the custard over them. Using a fork, gently nudge the peaches this way and that so the custard surrounds them. Put the pie on the center oven rack and bake for 15 minutes. Reduce the heat to 350°F (180°C) and bake for 10 minutes longer.

5. When the 10 minutes are up, remove the pie from the oven and set it on the prepared baking sheet. Cover the filling with a thick layer of the streusel; you probably won't need all of it. Tamp lightly to compress the streusel.

6. Continue to bake the pie, on the sheet, on the middle oven rack for 25 to 30 minutes longer, until the filling is wobbly and shows no signs of soupiness in the middle. When the pie is done, turn off the oven, slide out the rack, and leave the pie in the oven for about 10 minutes with the door halfway open.

7. Transfer the pie to a rack and cool for at least 2 hours. Serve at room temperature, if desired. However, I much prefer this pie served cold. Cover and refrigerate leftovers.

Recipe for Success

**The denseness of this pie makes it hard to judge when it is done. If in doubt, insert
a thin knife blade into the center of the pie. It should come out clean, not covered
in custard.**

Pennsylvania Dutch Market Peach *and* Sour Cherry Pie

Makes 8–10 servings

Perfect Pie Dough by Hand (page 56)

FILLING

- 4 cups peeled and sliced ripe peaches
- 2 cups pitted fresh sour cherries
- ⅔ cup granulated sugar
- 1 tablespoon lemon juice
- ¼ cup packed light brown sugar
- 3 tablespoons cornstarch
- ⅛ teaspoon ground nutmeg

  Oatmeal Crumb Topping (page 449)

Recipe for Success

If you can't find fresh sour cherries, use frozen. Drained canned sour cherries will also do in a pinch.

Either peel the peaches by hand or use the blanching method described here.

One of my favorite places to shop when my wife and I lived in Annapolis, Maryland, was the Amish market. The market attracted shoppers from miles around because the food and selection were always good, the portions large, and the prices fair. Come summer, I could find sour cherries there and fresh Lancaster County, Pennsylvania, peaches, too — the stars of this pie. I love the way the tartness and color of the cherries contrast with the sweetness of the peaches. It's a summer classic.

1. Prepare and refrigerate the pie dough. Roll the dough into a 12½- to 13-inch circle and line a 9- to 9½-inch deep-dish pie pan with it, shaping the edge into an upstanding ridge. Flute or crimp the edge, then refrigerate the shell until needed.

2. Adjust the oven racks so one is in the lower position and another is in the middle of the oven. Preheat the oven to 400°F (200°C). Line a baking sheet with parchment paper.

3. Combine the peaches, cherries, granulated sugar, and lemon juice in a large bowl. Mix well. Let stand for 10 minutes. Mix the brown sugar, cornstarch, and nutmeg in a small bowl; stir into the fruit.

4. Turn the filling into the pie shell and smooth over the fruit with a spoon. Put the pie on the prepared baking sheet. Cover the filling with a generous layer of the crumb topping; you may not need all of it. Press the crumbs down lightly.

5. Bake the pie, on the sheet, on the lower oven rack for 30 minutes. Reduce the heat to 375°F (190°C) and move the pie up to the middle rack, rotating it 180 degrees. Bake for 30 to 40 minutes, until the fruit bubbles thickly around the edge and the topping is dark golden brown. If the topping starts to get too dark, cover the pie with aluminum foil.

6. Transfer the pie to a rack and cool for at least 1½ to 2 hours before serving. Cover and refrigerate leftovers after 24 hours.

Blanching Peaches

Peeling peaches by hand can result in a lot of wasted flesh that gets removed with the peels. Blanching is often a better option, because you can easily slip off the skins. Bring a large saucepan of water to a boil. Using a long-handled strainer, lower the peaches into the boiling water, one or two at a time. Leave them in for 30 seconds, then lift them right out. Cool briefly, then pinch the skins and peel them off.

Fresh Peach *and* Red Currant Pie

When I lived in New Hampshire, I had a secret spot along an old logging road where if I would patiently pick the fragile red currants one by one, I could gather just enough fresh berries for one or two pies each summer. These days I have to search for them in the market, no easy task. If you've never had fresh currants, they're extremely tart, almost too tart to eat out of hand. But that very tartness makes them such a good addition to this peach pie.

Makes 8–10 servings

Flaky Cream Cheese Pie Dough, double-crust version (page 72) or another double-crust dough

FILLING

4½–5 cups peeled and sliced ripe peaches

1 cup sugar, plus a little for sprinkling

2½–3 tablespoons cornstarch

1 tablespoon lemon juice

1 teaspoon finely grated lemon zest

¼ teaspoon ground cinnamon

2 cups fresh red currants, picked over for stems

Milk or half-and-half, for glaze

1. Prepare and refrigerate the pie dough. Roll the larger dough portion into a 12½- to 13-inch circle and line a 9- to 9½-inch deep-dish pie pan with it, letting the excess dough drape over the edge. Refrigerate the shell until needed.

2. Adjust the oven racks so one is in the lower position and another is in the middle of the oven. Preheat the oven to 400°F (200°C). Line a baking sheet with parchment paper.

3. Put the peaches in a large bowl. Mix together the sugar and cornstarch in a small bowl, using the larger amount of cornstarch if the peaches seem very juicy. Add to the peaches and mix well. Stir in the lemon juice, lemon zest, and cinnamon. Add the currants and toss once or twice, but don't overdo it; you don't want to crush the fragile currants.

4. Roll the other dough piece into an 11-inch circle. Turn the filling into the pie shell and smooth it out to even the top. Lightly moisten the rim of the pie shell. Drape the top pastry over the filling, pressing along the edge to seal. Trim the overhang with scissors, leaving an even ½ to ¾ inch all around, then sculpt the edge into an upstanding ridge. Flute or crimp the edge, as desired. Poke several steam vents in the top of the pie with a large fork or paring knife. Put a couple of the vents near the edge so you can check the juices. Brush the pie with milk and sprinkle with sugar.

5. Place the pie on the prepared baking sheet and bake on the lower oven rack for 30 minutes. Reduce the heat to 375°F (190°C) and move the pie up to the middle rack, rotating it 180 degrees. Bake for 30 to 40 minutes longer, until the juices bubble up thickly through the vents.

6. Transfer the pie to a rack and cool for at least 1½ to 2 hours before serving. Cover and refrigerate leftovers after 24 hours.

Recipe for Success

If the asking price for 2 cups of currants seems exorbitant, simply buy fewer and add another cup of sliced peaches. Reduce the sugar by about ¼ cup if you do. The pie will still be wonderful.

Deep-Dish Nectarine Pie
with Almond Crumb Topping

All stone fruits — peaches, nectarines, apricots, and plums — have an affinity for almonds, a pairing that can be used to your advantage. Here, for instance, summer-fresh nectarines are flavored with almond extract and topped with almond crumb topping in one of the summer pies I most look forward to making. Choose your nectarines carefully. Like peaches, they should yield to gentle finger pressure but not feel mushy. There's no need to peel the skins; they soften up nicely as the pie bakes.

Makes 8–10 servings

Almond Pie Dough (page 81) or another single-crust dough

FILLING

6 cups sliced ripe nectarines, unpeeled

Scant ½ cup plus 2 tablespoons sugar

1½ tablespoons lemon juice

2 teaspoons finely grated lemon zest

2½ tablespoons cornstarch

¼ teaspoon almond extract

Melted Butter Crumb Topping (page 449) made with almonds

Vanilla ice cream (optional)

1. Prepare and refrigerate the pie dough. Roll the dough into a 12½- to 13-inch circle and line a 9- to 9½-inch deep-dish pie pan with it, shaping the edge into an upstanding ridge. Flute or crimp the edge, then refrigerate the shell until needed.

2. Adjust the oven racks so one is in the lower position and another is in the middle of the oven. Preheat the oven to 400°F (200°C). Line a baking sheet with parchment paper.

3. Combine the nectarines, the ½ cup sugar, lemon juice, and lemon zest in a large bowl. Mix well. Let set for 10 minutes. Mix the 2 tablespoons sugar and cornstarch in a small bowl; stir into the fruit along with the almond extract.

4. Turn the filling into the pie shell and smooth over the fruit with a spoon. Put the pie on the prepared baking sheet and cover the filling with a generous layer of the crumb topping; you may not need all of it. Tamp the crumbs down gently.

5. Bake the pie, on the sheet, on the lower oven rack for 30 minutes. Reduce the heat to 375°F (190°C) and move the pie up to the middle rack, rotating it 180 degrees. Bake for 30 to 40 minutes longer, until the juice bubbles thickly around the edge. If the topping starts to get too dark, cover the pie with aluminum foil.

6. Transfer the pie to a rack and cool for at least 1½ to 2 hours before serving. Garnish pieces with vanilla ice cream, if desired. Cover and refrigerate leftovers after 24 hours.

Recipe for Success
The same filling can be used in a double-crust pie or with a different crumb topping. The Coconut-Almond Crumb Topping (page 451) is an excellent choice.

Nectarine *and* Blueberry-Lime Pie

You can shift the balance of fruit here if you want, increasing the amount of blueberries and cutting back on the nectarines. But no matter how you balance them, I think you'll be delighted with this summer pie fruit combo.

Makes 8 servings

Simple Press-In Pie Dough (page 73)

FILLING

4 cups sliced ripe nectarines, unpeeled

1½ cups blueberries

½ cup plus 2 table-spoons sugar

1 tablespoon lime juice

1 teaspoon grated lime zest

2–2½ tablespoons cornstarch

Pinch of ground nutmeg

Oatmeal Crumb Topping (page 449)

1. Prepare the pie dough and press it into a 9- to 9½-inch standard pie pan according to the recipe on page 73. Refrigerate the shell until needed.

2. Adjust the oven racks so one is in the lower position and another is in the middle of the oven. Preheat the oven to 400°F (200°C). Line a baking sheet with parchment paper.

3. Combine the nectarines, blueberries, the ½ cup sugar, lime juice, and lime zest in a large bowl. Mix well. Let stand for 10 minutes.

4. After 10 minutes, check the accumulated juice. If the nectarines are pretty much covered with juice, use 2½ tablespoons of the cornstarch. If not, use 2 tablespoons. Mix the cornstarch with the 2 tablespoons sugar in a small bowl; stir into the fruit along with the nutmeg.

5. Turn the filling into the pie shell, smoothing the top with a spoon. Put the pie on the prepared baking sheet and cover it with a thick layer of the crumb topping; you may not need all of it. Tamp the crumbs down gently.

6. Bake the pie, on the sheet, on the lower oven rack for 30 minutes. Reduce the heat to 375°F (190°C) and move the pie up to the middle rack, rotating the pie 180 degrees. Bake for 25 to 35 minutes longer, until the juice bubbles thickly around the edge of the pie and the top is golden brown. If the topping starts to get too dark, cover the pie with aluminum foil.

7. Transfer the pie to a rack and cool for at least 1½ to 2 hours before serving.

Recipe for Success

Use only fresh, ripe nectarines and be selective about the ones you choose. Like peaches, they should yield to gentle finger pressure — not feel hard or too soft. Each nectarine should have a faint but distinct fruity fragrance and feel weighty (meaning juicy) in proportion to its size.

Apricot-Strawberry Pie

This might sound like an unlikely combination, but it works well. The sweet strawberries gently soften and — in my opinion — enhance the more forward flavor of the apricots. Let me know what you think.

Makes 8–10 servings

Buttermilk Pie Dough, double-crust version (page 67) or another double-crust dough

FILLING

2½ **cups sliced fresh apricots, unpeeled**

⅓ **cup plus 3 tablespoons sugar, plus a little for sprinkling**

1 **tablespoon lemon juice**

2 **tablespoons cornstarch**

2 **cups hulled and thickly sliced fresh strawberries**

1 **egg beaten with 1 tablespoon milk, for glaze**

Vanilla, peach, or strawberry ice cream, for serving (optional)

1. Prepare and refrigerate the pie dough. Roll the larger dough portion into a 12-inch circle and line a 9- to 9½-inch standard pie pan with it, letting the excess dough drape over the edge. Refrigerate the shell until needed.

2. Adjust the oven racks so one is in the lower position and another is in the middle of the oven. Preheat the oven to 400°F (200°C). Line a baking sheet with parchment paper.

3. Combine the apricots, the ⅓ cup sugar, and lemon juice in a large bowl. Mix well. Let stand for 20 minutes. Mix the 3 tablespoons sugar and cornstarch in a small bowl; stir into the apricots. Add the strawberries and mix gently.

4. Roll the other dough portion into an 11-inch circle. Turn the filling into the pie shell and smooth over the fruit with a spoon. Lightly moisten the rim of the pie shell. Drape the top pastry over the filling, pressing along the edge to seal. Trim the overhang with scissors, leaving an even ½ to ¾ inch all around, then sculpt the edge into an upstanding ridge. Flute or crimp the edge, as desired. Poke several steam vents in the top of the pie with a large fork or paring knife. Put a couple of the vents near the edge so you can check the juices. Brush the pie lightly with the egg wash glaze and sprinkle with sugar.

5. Put the pie on the prepared baking sheet and bake on the lower oven rack for 30 minutes. Reduce the heat to 375°F (190°C) and move the pie up to the middle rack, rotating it 180 degrees. Bake for 25 to 35 minutes longer, until the juices bubble thickly through the steam vents.

6. Transfer the pie to a rack and cool for at least 1½ to 2 hours before serving. Garnish slices with ice cream, if desired. Cover and refrigerate leftovers after 24 hours.

Catoctin Mountain Three-Fruit Pie

When you think of Maryland, you probably think of blue crab; everyone does. But out in the western part of the state, far from the Chesapeake Bay, Maryland has beautiful farm country and orchards. My wife, Bev, and I stumbled upon several of these farm stands and orchards in Catoctin Mountain Park. At Catoctin Mountain Orchard in Thurmont, run by the Black family for more than 50 years, we found excellent fresh apricots, blueberries, plums, and sour cherries alongside the family's own orchard-baked pies. One of their mixed-fruit pies was the inspiration for this recipe, which we made with the orchard's fruit. It was a top pie of that summer.

Makes 8–10 servings

Old-Fashioned Shortening Pie Dough (page 62) or another single-crust dough

FILLING

- **2 cups sliced fresh apricots, unpeeled**
- **2 cups fresh blueberries**
- **2 cups sliced ripe plums**
- **⅔ cup plus 2 tablespoons sugar**
- **1 tablespoon lemon juice**
- **1-2 teaspoons finely grated lemon or orange zest**
- **3 tablespoons cornstarch**
- **¼ teaspoon ground nutmeg**
- **Traditional German Streusel (page 450)**

1. Prepare and refrigerate the pie dough. Roll the dough into a 12½- to 13-inch circle and line a 9- to 9½-inch deep-dish pie pan with it, shaping the edge into an upstanding ridge. Flute or crimp the edge, then refrigerate the shell until needed.

2. Adjust the oven racks so one is in the lower position and another is in the middle of the oven. Preheat the oven to 400°F (200°C). Line a baking sheet with parchment paper.

3. Combine the apricots, blueberries, plums, the ⅔ cup sugar, lemon juice, and lemon zest in a large bowl. Mix well. Let stand for 10 minutes. Mix the 2 tablespoons sugar and cornstarch in a small bowl; stir into the fruit along with the nutmeg.

4. Turn the filling into the pie shell and smooth the top of the filling with a spoon. Put the pie on the prepared baking sheet and cover with a generous layer of the streusel; you may not need all of it. Tamp the streusel down gently.

5. Bake the pie, on the sheet, on the lower oven rack for 30 minutes. Reduce the heat to 375°F (190°C) and move the pie up to the middle rack, rotating it 180 degrees. Bake for 30 to 40 minutes longer, until the juices bubble thickly around the edge. If the topping starts to get too dark, cover the pie with aluminum foil.

6. Transfer the pie to a rack and cool for at least 1½ to 2 hours before serving. Cover and refrigerate leftovers after 24 hours.

Recipe for Success

This also makes a gorgeous double-crust pie. I've also made it with a lattice top (page 46), which is perhaps the most attractive option of all.

Quick *and* Easy Apricot Pie

If you've given up on rolling pie dough, especially during the warm and humid summer months, or you just don't want to bother rolling, then you'll like this pie. The shortcut dough is simply scattered around the pie pan and pressed into it. The same blueprint for this quick-to-assemble pie can be used for all sorts of summer fruit pies. To keep things really simple, some of the press-in dough is used to make the topping.

Makes 8–10 servings

Simple Press-In Pie Dough (page 73)

FILLING

4	**cups sliced fresh apricots, unpeeled**
½	**cup plus 2 table-spoons sugar**
1	**tablespoon lemon juice**
1	**teaspoon finely grated lemon zest**
1½–2	**tablespoons cornstarch**

1. Prepare the pie dough as instructed, setting aside one-third of the crumbs as described in the box How to Get a Pie Shell and Crumb Topping from One Recipe (page 73). Press the larger portion evenly into a 9- to 9½-inch standard pie pan, and refrigerate the shell until needed.

2. Combine the apricots, the ½ cup sugar, lemon juice, and zest in a large bowl. Mix well. Let stand for 10 to 15 minutes.

3. Adjust the oven racks so one is in the lower position and another is in the middle of the oven. Preheat the oven to 400°F (200°C). Line a baking sheet with parchment paper.

4. Mix the 2 tablespoons sugar and cornstarch in a small bowl; stir into the fruit. Turn the filling into the pie shell and smooth the top of the fruit with a spoon.

5. Put the pie on the prepared baking sheet. Spread the reserved crumb topping — the one you made with the pie dough — evenly over the filling.

6. Bake the pie, on the sheet, on the lower oven rack for 30 minutes. Reduce the heat to 375°F (190°C) and move the pie up to the middle rack, rotating it 180 degrees. Bake for 20 to 25 minutes longer, until the juices bubble thickly around the edge and the topping is golden brown. If the topping starts to get too dark, cover the pie with aluminum foil.

7. Transfer the pie to a rack and cool for at least 1½ to 2 hours before serving. Cover and refrigerate leftovers after 24 hours.

Recipe for Success

Fresh apricots can be a little dry. If the apricots aren't all that juicy after 15 minutes of sitting in the sugar and lemon juice, moisten them with 2 to 4 tablespoons orange juice, lemonade, or another fruit juice.

Some people find an all-apricot pie to be too much of a good thing. You can soften the flavor of the apricots by substituting peaches, sliced apples, or even raspberries or blueberries for an equal amount of sliced apricots.

Double-Crust Apricot-Mango Pie

Given the unreliability of out-of-season fresh apricots, this is really a summer pie, though I have had pretty good results with drained canned apricots. For the mango, you can use fresh fruit, of course. But for convenience, you can't beat those jars of long mango slices found in the produce section of the grocery store, or frozen mango chunks.

Makes 8–10 servings

Shortening and Butter Dough with Egg (page 63) or another double-crust dough

FILLING

4 **cups sliced fresh apricots, unpeeled**

2 **cups mango chunks from a jar, drained, or frozen and partially thawed chunks**

½ **cup plus 2 tablespoons sugar, plus a little for sprinkling**

1 **tablespoon lemon juice**

1 **teaspoon grated lemon zest**

2½ **tablespoons cornstarch**

Milk or half-and-half, for glaze

1. Prepare and refrigerate the pie dough. Roll the larger dough portion into a 12½- to 13-inch circle and line a 9- to 9½-inch deep-dish pie pan with it, letting the excess dough drape over the edge. Refrigerate the shell until needed.

2. Adjust the oven racks so one is in the lower position and another is in the middle of the oven. Preheat the oven to 400°F (200°C). Line a baking sheet with parchment paper.

3. Combine the apricots, mango, the ½ cup sugar, lemon juice, and lemon zest in a large bowl. Mix well. Let stand for 10 minutes. Mix the 2 tablespoons sugar and cornstarch in a small bowl; stir into the fruit.

4. Roll the other dough portion into an 11-inch circle. Turn the filling into the pie shell and smooth over the filling with a spoon. Lightly moisten the rim of the pie shell. Drape the top pastry over the filling, pressing along the edge to

seal. Trim the overhang with scissors, leaving an even ½ to ¾ inch all around, then sculpt the edge into an upstanding ridge. Flute or crimp the edge, as desired. Poke several steam vents in the top of the pie with a large fork or paring knife. Put a couple of the vents near the edge so you can check the juices. Lightly brush the pie with milk and sprinkle with sugar.

5. Place the pie on the prepared baking sheet and bake on the lower oven rack for 30 minutes. Reduce the heat to 375°F (190°C) and move the pie up to the middle rack, rotating the pie 180 degrees. Bake for 30 to 40 minutes longer, until the juices bubble thickly through the steam vents.

6. Transfer the pie to a rack and cool for at least 1½ to 2 hours before serving. Cover and refrigerate leftovers after 24 hours.

Recipe for Success
To prepare a fresh mango, slice the skin lengthwise and remove the peel. Cutting lengthwise and avoiding the large pit in the center, cut off a large slab of flesh on either side. Cut the remaining flesh off the pit in chunks.

Fresh Plum *and* Port Pie

Sweet-tart and refreshing, juicy ripe plums are one of the best summer fruits to eat out of hand. But a lot of people don't realize what a fine pie plums make. Indeed, the French adore their fresh plum tarts. Here's an American plum pie made with reduced port, which adds a fruity accent to the plums and provides extra juice for the plums to bake in and become meltingly soft. Use a top crust if you'd prefer it to this crumb top.

Makes 8–10 servings

Whole-Wheat Pie Dough (page 66) or another single-crust dough

FILLING

½ cup ruby port

6 cups sliced ripe plums, unpeeled

½ cup sugar

3 tablespoons quick-cooking tapioca

2 tablespoons raspberry preserves (optional)

1 tablespoon lemon juice

1 teaspoon grated lemon zest

Coconut-Almond Crumb Topping (page 451)

1. Prepare and refrigerate the pie dough. Roll the dough into a 12½- to 13-inch circle and line a 9- to 9½-inch deep-dish pie pan with it, shaping the edge into an upstanding ridge. Flute or crimp the edge, then refrigerate the shell until needed.

2. Adjust the oven racks so one is in the lower position and another is in the middle of the oven. Preheat the oven to 400°F (200°C). Line a baking sheet with parchment paper.

3. Bring the port to a boil in a medium nonreactive saucepan. Continue to boil until reduced by roughly one-half; check by pouring it into a 1-cup glass measuring cup. Combine the plums, sugar, and reduced port in a large bowl. Stir in the tapioca, preserves (if using), lemon juice, and lemon zest. Let stand for 10 to 15 minutes.

4. Turn the filling into the chilled pie shell and smooth the fruit with a spoon. Put the pie on the prepared baking sheet and cover with a thick layer of the topping; you may not need all of it. Press down lightly on the topping.

5. Bake the pie, on the sheet, on the lower oven rack for 30 minutes. Lower the heat to 375°F (190°C) and move the pie up to the middle rack, rotating it 180 degrees. Bake for 30 to 40 minutes longer, until the juices bubble thickly around the edge. If the topping starts to get too dark, cover the pie with aluminum foil.

6. Transfer the pie to a rack and cool for at least 1½ to 2 hours before serving. Cover and refrigerate leftovers after 24 hours.

Recipe for Success

Remember that it's important to soften quick-cooking tapioca by letting it stand in the fruit filling for 10 to 15 minutes. If you don't, the tapioca may not fully dissolve in the pie.

The best advice I can give for making plum pie is this: wait for the really good summer plums. It's true about other fruits, but it bears repeating. Plums are the trickiest of fruits to buy because even though the skins look dark, ripe, and inviting, the flesh can be mushy and disappointing. Even the finger-pressure test will often fail because yielding flesh is not necessarily an indicator of peak ripeness.

Open-Face Plum Pie *with* Almond Crust

This elegant, free-form summer pie requires the best juicy summer plums. Take a little extra time to make it look pretty, arranging overlapping rows of sliced plums. The plum juices concentrate the fruit's flavor in my favorite nut pastry. Vanilla Custard Sauce is my first choice for garnish.

Makes 8–10 servings

Almond Pie Dough (page 81)

FILLING

7 or 8 good-size ripe plums (not small prune plums or extralarge ones)

2 teaspoons lemon juice

¾ cup sugar

1½ tablespoons cornstarch

2 teaspoons balsamic vinegar

1 tablespoon fine yellow cornmeal

Vanilla Custard Sauce (page 446)

2–3 tablespoons red currant or raspberry jelly (optional)

1. Prepare the pie dough and refrigerate for at least 1 hour.

2. Using a sharp knife, score the plums lengthwise all around, down to the pit. Twist the halves apart and remove the pits. Cut the halves into ¼- to ⅓-inch-thick lengthwise slices. Put the slices in a bowl and add the lemon juice and all but about 2 tablespoons of the sugar. Mix well. Let stand for 1 to 1½ hours for the fruit to juice.

3. Put a colander over a bowl to catch the juice, then pour the fruit into the colander. Drain for 5 to 10 minutes. Reserve the juice. Place the plum slices back in the original bowl. Mix the cornstarch with the reserved sugar, then add it to the fruit. Set aside.

4. Pour the reserved plum juice into a 2-cup glass measuring cup. Add the vinegar and take note of how much total liquid you have. Pour the juice into a small nonreactive saucepan. Bring to a boil and reduce by half. Pour the reduced liquid back into the measuring cup if you want to check the quantity of reduced juice. Set aside.

5. Adjust the oven racks so one is in the lower position and another is in the middle of the oven. Preheat the oven to 375°F (190°C). Remove the pastry from the fridge 5 to 10 minutes before you start rolling.

6. The best way to assemble this is to roll the dough onto a large sheet of parchment paper, assemble the pie, then lift the pie onto a rimmed baking sheet with the paper. Alternatively, you can roll the dough onto a piece of floured waxed paper, invert it onto the baking sheet, peel off the paper, then assemble the pie on the sheet. Either way, roll the dough into a 12½- to 13-inch circle. Sprinkle the cornmeal in the middle of the dough and spread it around with your fingers, leaving a border of 2 to 2½ inches all around the perimeter. Cover the cornmeal area with overlapping plum slices, following the curve of the dough. Cover all the dough with slices except for the border area.

7. Using a metal spatula or the parchment paper to help you lift, carefully fold the uncovered border of dough over the fruit; the dough will self-pleat, leaving uncovered filling in the center. Spoon the reserved reduced juice over the fruit.

8. Bake the pie on the middle oven rack for 40 to 45 minutes, until the filling is bubbly and the crust is golden brown. Transfer the pie to a rack and cool on the baking sheet. Serve warm or at room temperature, with the custard sauce. If you wish to give the fruit a lacquered finish, warm the jelly in a microwavable bowl to thin it, then brush it over the plum slices.

Italian Prune Plum Pie

Little Italian prune plums aren't good only for turning into prunes. They're excellent fresh — compact, tasty, easy to handle — and even better baked in a pie. With a couple of pounds of plums and a basic double-crust dough, you can work some pie magic with these pint-size prunes.

Makes 8 servings

Double-Crust Food Processor Pie Dough (page 60) or another double-crust dough

FILLING

- 4 cups halved (lengthwise) and pitted fresh prune plums
- ⅓ cup plus 2 tablespoons sugar
- 1 tablespoon lemon juice
- 1½ tablespoons cornstarch
- 1 egg beaten with 1 tablespoon milk, for glaze

1. Prepare and refrigerate the pie dough. Roll the larger dough portion into a 12-inch circle and line a 9- to 9½-inch standard pie pan with it, letting the excess dough drape over the edge. Refrigerate the shell until needed.

2. Adjust the oven racks so one is in the lower position and another is in the middle of the oven. Preheat the oven to 400°F (200°C). Line a baking sheet with parchment paper.

3. Combine the plums, the ⅓ cup sugar, and lemon juice in a large bowl. Mix well. Let stand for 10 minutes. Mix the 2 tablespoons of sugar and cornstarch in a small bowl; stir into the fruit.

4. Roll the other dough portion into an 11-inch circle. Turn the filling into the pie shell and smooth out the fruit with a spoon. Lightly moisten the rim of the pie shell. Drape the top pastry over the filling, pressing along the edge to seal. Using a paring knife, trim the overhanging dough flush with the edge of the pan; crimp the edge with a fork. Poke several steam vents in the top of the pie with a large fork or paring knife. Put a couple of the vents near the edge so you can check the juices. Brush the pie sparingly with the egg wash glaze.

5. Place the pie on the prepared baking sheet and bake on the lower oven rack for 30 minutes. Reduce the heat to 375°F (190°C) and move the pie up to the middle rack, rotating it 180 degrees. Bake for 25 to 35 minutes longer, until the juices bubble thickly through the vents.

6. Transfer the pie to a rack and cool for at least 1½ to 2 hours before serving. Cover and refrigerate leftovers after 24 hours.

Recipe for Success

Choose prune plums that are uniformly dark and yielding without being overly so. Avoid fruit with soft, mushy spots.

Buy extra plums if you have kids or grandkids. They love the scaled-down size, which fits perfectly into their little hands.

Deep-Dish Pluot Pie
with Oatmeal Crumb Topping

Pluots, also sold as plumcots, are a cross between a plum and an apricot. The first time I tasted one, I knew it would make a great pie because it was sweeter than any plum I'd ever had and juicier than an apricot, with the delicate flavor of both.

Makes 8–10 servings

Perfect Pie Dough by Hand (page 56)

FILLING

5½ cups sliced pluots

½ cup plus 2 tablespoons sugar

1 tablespoon lemon juice

1–2 teaspoons freshly grated lemon zest

⅛ teaspoon ground nutmeg

3 tablespoons cornstarch

Oatmeal Crumb Topping (page 449)

1. Prepare and refrigerate the pie dough. Roll the dough into a 13-inch circle and line a 9- to 9½-inch deep-dish pie pan with it, shaping the edge into an upstanding ridge. Flute or crimp the edge, then refrigerate the shell until needed.

2. Adjust the oven racks so one is in the lower position and another is in the middle of the oven. Preheat the oven to 400°F (200°C). Line a baking sheet with parchment paper.

3. Combine the pluots, the ½ cup sugar, lemon juice, lemon zest, and nutmeg in a large bowl. Mix well. Let stand for 10 minutes. Mix the 2 tablespoons sugar and cornstarch in a small bowl; stir into the fruit.

4. Turn the filling into the pie shell and smooth the fruit with a spoon. Put the pie on the prepared baking sheet and cover the filling with a generous layer of the crumb topping; you may not need all of it. Tamp the crumbs down lightly.

5. Bake the pie, on the sheet, on the lower oven rack for 30 minutes. Reduce the heat to 375°F (190°C) and move the pie up to the middle rack, rotating it 180 degrees. Bake for 30 to 40 minutes longer, until the juices bubble thickly around the edge and the topping is golden brown. If the topping starts to get too dark, cover the pie with aluminum foil.

6. Transfer the pie to a rack and cool for at least 1½ to 2 hours before serving. Cover and refrigerate leftovers after 24 hours.

Recipe for Success

Pluots tend to be very juicy, which is why it's important to use a deep-dish pie pan. If the pan is very deep, you could use a full 6 cups of fruit.

You can blanch pluots like you do peaches (see page 144) to remove the skins, but pluot skins bake up quite soft, so I don't think it's necessary. Besides, a lot of the deep burgundy color is in the skin, so you'll lose some of that attractive color if you peel them.

Crumb-Topped Zapple Pie

I borrowed this idea from *The Classic Zucchini Cookbook* (Storey Publishing). Zapple pie is a sweet zucchini pie that tastes like apple pie, sort of. The theory goes that because zucchini doesn't taste like anything, if you throw enough spice, apple juice concentrate, lemon juice, and crumb topping at it, you'll have a decent approximation of real apple pie. I was intrigued by the whole idea of a sweet zucchini pie, so with the authors' recipe as my blueprint, I played around with variations of my own. It's not apple, but you'll like it.

Makes 8–10 servings

Single-Crust Food Processor Pie Dough (page 58) or another single-crust pie

FILLING

- 6 cups peeled, halved lengthwise, then thinly sliced zucchini
- ⅔ cup sugar
- 3 tablespoons thawed apple juice concentrate
- 1 teaspoon ground cinnamon
- ¼ teaspoon ground nutmeg
- ¼ teaspoon salt
- 2 tablespoons cornstarch
- ⅓ cup lemon juice
- 1 tablespoon apple cider vinegar
- Oatmeal Crumb Topping (page 449)

1. Prepare and refrigerate the pie dough. Roll the dough into a 12½ to 13-inch circle and line a 9- to 9½-inch deep-dish pie pan with it, shaping the edge into an upstanding ridge. Flute or crimp the edge, then refrigerate the shell until needed.

2. Preheat the oven to 375°F (190°C). Line a baking sheet with parchment paper.

3. In a large, heavy stovetop casserole dish, combine the zucchini, sugar, apple juice concentrate, cinnamon, nutmeg, and salt. Heat gradually over medium-high heat, stirring occasionally, until the liquid starts to boil. Reduce the heat slightly and simmer until the zucchini is tender but not mushy, about 10 minutes.

4. Blend the cornstarch and lemon juice in a small bowl, stirring until smooth. When the zucchini is tender, stir the cornstarch slurry into the pot and cook, stirring nonstop to prevent sticking, for 1 to 1½ minutes. The juice will thicken noticeably. Remove the pot from the heat and stir in the vinegar. Cool for 10 minutes.

5. Spoon the filling into the pie shell, smoothing the top with a spoon. Put the pie on the prepared baking sheet and cover with a generous layer of the crumb topping; you probably won't need all of it. Tamp the crumbs lightly.

6. Bake the pie, on the sheet, on the lower oven rack for about 45 minutes, rotating the pie 180 degrees midway through the baking. When done, you may or may not see thick juice bubbling around the edge. The best indication of doneness is total elapsed time and a golden-brown topping.

7. Transfer the pie to a rack and cool. Serve slightly warm, at room temperature, or chilled. This is best served the same day it is made. Cover and refrigerate leftovers after serving.

Recipe for Success

Choose small to medium zucchini for the filling. The flesh will be firmer, more applelike, and better able to hold its shape.

The pie can be made with a top crust instead of the crumb topping.

Watermelon Rind Pie

When you eat a piece of watermelon, you take that last juicy bite and toss out the rind. But wait! You can make a delicious pie with that rind. A holdover from the days when thrifty farm wives wouldn't waste a scrap of food, this pie gets its primary ingredient not from the flesh of the melon but from the peeled rind. Does the pie taste anything like watermelon? Not really; it's more like mock mincemeat. See if your family and friends can guess what's in it.

Makes 8–10 servings

Old-Fashioned Shortening Pie Dough (page 62) or another double-crust dough

FILLING

- 3½ **cups peeled and finely diced watermelon rind**
- ¾ **cup granulated sugar, plus a little for sprinkling**
- ½ **cup dark raisins**
- ½ **cup chopped walnuts or pecans**
- 2 **tablespoons apple cider vinegar**
- 1 **tablespoon lemon juice**
- 3 **tablespoons packed light brown sugar**
- 2 **tablespoons finely chopped crystallized ginger**
- 1 **tablespoon all-purpose flour**
- ½ **teaspoon ground cinnamon**
- ¼ **teaspoon ground cloves**
- ¼ **teaspoon ground nutmeg**
- ¼ **teaspoon salt**
- 1 **large egg beaten with 1 tablespoon milk, for glaze**

1. Prepare and refrigerate the pie dough. Roll the larger dough portion into a 12-inch circle and line a 9- to 9½-inch standard pie pan with it, letting the excess dough drape over the edge. Refrigerate the shell until needed.

2. Combine the watermelon rind and ¼ cup of the granulated sugar in a large saucepan. Add enough water to barely cover. Bring to a boil, partially covered, and continue to boil until the rind is tender and translucent, 20 to 25 minutes. Drain well, then transfer the rind to a large bowl and cool thoroughly.

3. Adjust the oven racks so one is in the lower position and another is in the middle of the oven. Preheat the oven to 400°F (200°C).

4. Stir the remaining ½ cup granulated sugar into the cooled rind. Stir in the raisins, nuts, vinegar, lemon juice, and brown sugar. Add the ginger, flour, cinnamon, cloves, nutmeg, and salt; mix well.

5. Roll the other dough portion into an 11-inch circle. Turn the filling into the pie shell and smooth it out to even the top. Lightly moisten the rim of the pie shell. Drape the top pastry over the filling, pressing along the edge to seal. Trim the

overhang with scissors, leaving an even ½ to ¾ inch all around, then sculpt the edge into an upstanding ridge. Flute or crimp the edge, as desired. Poke several steam vents in the top of the pie with a large fork or paring knife. Put a couple of the vents near the edge; you may (or may not) see some juice there later. Brush the pie sparingly with the egg wash glaze and sprinkle with sugar.

6. Bake the pie on the lower oven rack for 30 minutes. Reduce the heat to 375°F (190°C) and move the pie up to the middle rack, rotating it 180 degrees. Bake for 25 to 35 minutes longer, until the topping is a rich golden brown. This is not a particularly juicy pie, so you may or may not see juices bubbling up through the steam vents. The best clue to doneness is the total elapsed time. You can also poke the filling with a skewer as you would with apples (see box on page 190) to make sure the filling is soft.

7. Transfer the pie to a rack and cool for at least 1½ to 2 hours. Serve slightly warm or at room temperature. Cover and refrigerate leftovers after 24 hours.

Recipe for Success

When you peel the watermelon rind, be sure to remove all the outermost green skin with a sharp peeler, since it's the toughest part of the skin. Don't undercook the rind in step 2; it will soften only marginally more as the pie bakes.

Grape *and* Fig Pie

Black grapes and dried figs create a fragrant, deep purple filling that's like a ticket to the sunny Mediterranean. Instead of poaching the figs, as I sometimes do when I use them in pies, I simply steam them for a few minutes so they soften enough to absorb the copious grape juices. Garnished with Mascarpone Whipped Cream, this is a wonderful pie to follow a light Mediterranean meal.

Makes 8–10 servings

Whole-Wheat Pie Dough, double-crust version (page 66) or another double-crust dough

FILLING

- 1½ cups stemmed and diced dried Black Mission figs
- 3½ cups halved seedless black grapes
- ⅓ cup plus 2 tablespoons sugar, plus a little for sprinkling
- 1 tablespoon lemon juice
- 1 teaspoon finely grated lemon zest
- 1½ tablespoons Frangelico or hazelnut liqueur (optional)
- 1½ tablespoons cornstarch
- 1 tablespoon cold unsalted butter, cut into small pieces
- Milk or half-and-half, for glaze
- Mascarpone Whipped Cream (page 448), for garnish

1. Prepare and refrigerate the pie dough. Roll the larger dough portion into a 12-inch circle and line a 9- to 9½-inch standard pie pan with it, letting the excess dough drape over the edge. Refrigerate the shell until needed.

2. Adjust the oven racks so one is in the lower position and another is in the middle of the oven. Preheat the oven to 400°F (200°C). Line a baking sheet with parchment paper.

3. Put the figs in a steamer basket set in a saucepan — or directly in the saucepan — and add about ½ inch of water to the pan. Cover tightly and bring the water to a boil. Reduce the heat slightly and simmer-steam the figs for 5 minutes. Drain in a colander or sieve.

4. Combine the grapes, figs, the ⅓ cup sugar, lemon juice, lemon zest, and liqueur (if using) in a large bowl. Mix well. Let stand for 10 minutes. Mix the 2 tablespoons sugar and cornstarch in a small bowl; stir into the fruit.

5. Roll the other dough portion into an 11-inch circle. Turn the filling into the pie shell and smooth it out to even the top. Lightly moisten the rim of the pie shell. Drape the top pastry over the filling, pressing along the edge to seal. Trim the overhang with scissors, leaving an even ½ to ¾ inch all around, then sculpt the edge into an upstanding ridge. Flute or crimp the edge, as desired. Poke several steam vents in the top of the pie with a large fork or paring knife. Put a couple of the vents near the edge so you can check the juices. Brush the pie with milk and sprinkle with sugar.

6. Place the pie on the prepared baking sheet and bake on the lower oven rack for 30 minutes. Reduce the heat to 375°F (190°C) and move the pie up to the middle rack, rotating it 180 degrees. Bake for 25 to 35 minutes longer, until the juices bubble thickly at the vents.

7. Transfer the pie to a rack and cool for at least 1½ to 2 hours before serving. Cover and refrigerate leftovers after 24 hours.

Recipe for Success

Other types of dried figs will work, too, including Turkish figs. Lacking figs altogether, you can substitute pitted prunes.

   If the figs are pleasantly moist, skip the steaming.

Fruits *of the* Forest Pie *(Fruit Version)*

Fruits of the forest pies — at least the recipes I've seen — fall into two distinct categories: nut fillings (see page 273) and fruit fillings. I'm guessing the nut versions came first, since one could well consider them forest fruits. Someone probably appropriated the name and applied it to a mixed-fruit pie, giving the fruit version some traction. This recipe obviously falls into the latter category. The blueberries might be the only thing here that grow anywhere near the forest, but we'll overlook those liberties because the pie is so appealing.

Makes 8–10 servings

Buttermilk Pie Dough, double-crust version (page 67) or another double-crust dough

FILLING

- 2 **medium-size ripe peaches, peeled and sliced**
- 1 **large Granny Smith or other tart apple, peeled, cored, and sliced**
- 1 **cup fresh blueberries**
- 1 **cup hulled and sliced fresh strawberries**
- ½ **cup chopped pineapple, fresh or canned and drained**
- ½ **cup plus 3 tablespoons granulated sugar**
- ½ **teaspoon ground ginger**
- ¼ **teaspoon ground nutmeg**
- 1 **tablespoon lemon juice**
- 3 **tablespoons cornstarch**
  Milk or half-and-half, for glaze
  Coarse sugar (see page 122) or granulated sugar, for sprinkling

1. Prepare and refrigerate the pie dough. Roll the larger dough portion into a 12½- to 13-inch circle and line a 9- to 9½-inch deep-dish pie pan with it, letting the excess dough drape over the edge. Refrigerate the shell until needed.

2. Adjust the oven racks so one is in the lower position and another is in the middle of the oven. Preheat the oven to 400°F (200°C). Line a baking sheet with parchment paper.

3. Combine the fruits, the ½ cup granulated sugar, ginger, nutmeg, and lemon juice in a large bowl. Mix well. Let stand for 10 minutes. Mix the 3 tablespoons granulated sugar and cornstarch in a small bowl; stir into the fruit.

4. Roll the other dough portion into an 11-inch circle. Turn the filling into the pie shell and smooth it out with a spoon. Lightly moisten the rim of the pie shell. Drape the top pastry over the filling, pressing along the edge to seal. Trim the overhang with scissors, leaving an even ½ to ¾ inch all around, then sculpt the edge into an upstanding ridge. Flute or crimp the edge, as desired. Poke several steam vents in the top of the pie with a large fork or paring knife. Put a couple of the vents near the edge so you can check the juices. Lightly brush the pie with milk, then sprinkle generously with coarse sugar.

5. Put the pie on the prepared baking sheet and bake on the lower oven rack for 30 minutes. Reduce the heat to 375°F (190°C) and move the pie up to the middle rack, rotating it 180 degrees. Bake for 30 to 40 minutes longer, until the juices bubble thickly at the steam vents.

6. Transfer the pie to a rack and cool for at least 1½ to 2 hours before serving. Cover and refrigerate leftovers after 24 hours.

Recipe for Success

There is a lot of room here for substitutions. You can use blackberries or raspberries in place of the strawberries or nectarines in place of the peaches.

If you happen to have fruit cookie cutters, especially small ones, an arrangement of fruit pastry cutouts on top is very pretty and hints at what's to come.

7
Make Mine Apple:
VARIATIONS ON A CLASSIC

Apple is America's signature pie: not just something we love to eat, but a universal symbol of things we hold dear. Is it any wonder, then, that making an apple pie is one of fall's enduring rituals? To some degree, whether it is store-bought or homemade, or even how it tastes, is irrelevant: apple pie enjoys iconic status in this country, and we cherish it all the same.

You may have a single, irrefutable memory of what constitutes a true apple pie — maybe it was the one your grandmother or mother baked. For me, it was the one my mom and dad made, with a Crisco crust and McIntosh apples. But perhaps the most surprising thing about apple pie is just how varied it can be. You'll find plenty of proof in the following pages: double-crust apple pies, crumb-topped ones, custard apple pies, some made with grated apples, even one baked in a paper bag. (And this chapter could have been longer still, by far.)

One of the things I love most about apple pie is that it marks the unofficial start of the fall baking season. Relief from the oppressive summer heat arrives, bringing with it a renewed interest in dusting off favorite recipes and baking almost every weekend. There are family outings to farm markets and orchards to procure the best local apples. Warm, fresh pies are delivered to friends and family, strengthening ties loosened by months of vacations and far-flung endeavors. Apple pie brings us home, in a very real sense, and envelops us in the warmth of domestic well-being.

Here's hoping all your apple pies are memorable.

Tips for Baking Delicious Apple Pies

- Start with the best fruit you can find. The box on page 169 will point you in the right direction. If you have access to local orchards, talk to the people who grow the apples. They can give you guidance on regional apple varieties that may be perfect for pies.

- You can work miracles on lackluster apples with the addition of lemon juice or a little apple butter, apple jelly, or boiled cider (see What Is Boiled Cider?, page 313) to the filling.

- To make a more compact pie with a dense filling, cut some of the fruit into slices and some into small chunks. You'll get more fruit into the filling that way.

- Don't go overboard with sugar in apple pies. Sweetness is appropriate, but you don't want to obscure the pleasant, understated flavor notes of good apples.

- Don't underbake apple pies (or any fruit pie, for that matter) or the thickening will not "take," leaving you with a runny filling. In most cases, you want to see thick fruit juice bubbling up somewhere: through the vents, around the edge of the pie, from cracks in the crumb topping.

- Always cool the pie for at least 1½ hours — and preferably 2 — so the juice can develop body and has a chance to reabsorb into the fruit.

My Mom and Dad's Brown Sugar–Apple Pie

This is the way my parents always made apple pie, told in my dad's voice. If anything inspired me to become a pie baker and happy home cook, it was the sight of the two of them purposefully engaged in the simple art of making an apple pie.

"I always started with a basic crust — just flour, butter, and Crisco, plus a tin cup filled with cold water and a few ice cubes to keep it cold. I liked working on a large maple board, which I floured so all was ready when I mixed the butter — cut into little squares with several tablespoons of Crisco — into the flour with a wire pastry blender. I would mix this combination with enough cold water to easily handle everything, then make up two balls for chilling in the refrigerator.

After that, I would help your mother core, peel, and slice the apples — New York State McIntosh. Some people think they get too mushy in a pie, but we liked them. I don't remember how many we would cut up. I do remember that there were a lot of sliced apples, maybe 7 or 8 cups in all, and we never thought we could get that many in a 9-inch pie plate. We used a glass pie plate at one time, but at some point shifted to a shiny metal one. Those who ate the pie never seemed to mind.

The apples got a coating of nutmeg (just a small amount) and some cinnamon (a larger amount), a heavy dusting of brown sugar, and the rest of the stick of butter I didn't use for the crust. We didn't use any flour or cornstarch to thicken it; we liked a juicy filling. Then I got busy rolling out the dough using waxed paper until it looked right but was thick enough to handle. I lined the pie plate with the dough, with an extra inch hanging over the edge, then we poured the apples onto the dough.

We would put the top layer on, slit the top dough, brush it with milk, dust it with a small amount of sugar, and put it in the oven at 375°F (190°C) until it was done. We learned to put foil under the pie rack to catch the drippings. It smelled wonderful and tasted even better."

Washington State Granny Smith Apple Pie

Many home cooks like Granny Smith apples for their tartness, juiciness, and complex flavor. Bakers in the know will often use a minimum of sugar to make a Granny Smith pie, to help preserve the apples' best qualities and grace notes. Here's a novel layering technique that uses little sugar and works great for Granny Smith pies. I like a crumb topping for this one, but a top crust would work just as well.

Makes 8–10 servings

Single-Crust Food Processor Pie Dough (page 58) or another single-crust dough

FILLING

- ⅓ cup sugar
- 1½ tablespoons cornstarch
- ⅛ teaspoon salt
- 6½–7 cups peeled, cored, and sliced Granny Smith apples
- 1 tablespoon lemon juice
- **Oatmeal Crumb Topping (page 449)**

1. Prepare and refrigerate the pie dough. Roll the dough into a 12½- to 13-inch circle and line a 9- to 9½-inch deep-dish pie pan with it, shaping the edge into an upstanding ridge. Flute or crimp the edge, then refrigerate the shell until needed.

2. Adjust the oven racks so one is in the lower position and another is in the middle of the oven. Preheat the oven to 400°F (200°C). Line a baking sheet with parchment paper.

3. Mix the sugar, cornstarch, and salt together in a small bowl. Combine the apples and lemon juice in a large bowl. Sprinkle about 1 tablespoon of the sugar mixture evenly over the pie shell. Arrange a single, compact layer of apples in the shell, flat side down. Sprinkle with 1 tablespoon of the sugar mixture. Arrange a second layer of apples on top of the first, and sprinkle with another tablespoon of the sugar mixture. Continue layering until all the apples and sugar mixture have been used.

4. Set the pie on the prepared baking sheet and cover with a generous amount of the crumb topping; you may not need all of it. Tamp the crumbs down lightly.

5. Bake the pie, on the sheet, on the lower oven rack for 30 minutes. Reduce the heat to 375°F (190°C) and move the pie up to the middle rack, rotating it 180 degrees. Bake for 30 to 40 minutes longer, until you see thick juices bubbling up around the edge of the pie. If the top of the pie starts to get too dark, cover it with foil.

6. Transfer the pie to a rack and cool for at least 1½ to 2 hours before serving. Cover and refrigerate leftovers after 24 hours.

Recipe for Success

You can, of course, use this layering technique for other apple pies. It gives the slices a nicely layered look and compact consistency.

Pie Apples at a Glance

There is no best apple for making pies; most of them will do nicely, as long as they're fresh and juicy. A certain amount of tartness helps, too, as well as complexity of flavor.

Many excellent apples can be found right in your supermarket, but I encourage you to have fun researching and experimenting with apples available in your area. Talk to the farmers and growers who know about the local gems. Seek out heirloom varieties.

Here are some of the more common varieties you're likely to find.

- **Baldwin.** This aromatic, all-purpose red-skinned apple has a mild, sweet-tart flavor and crisp texture. It stores well and makes a commendable pie.

- **Braeburn.** The skin varies in color from greenish gold to red with yellow markings. The flesh is smooth, juicy, and crisp, with a good flavor.

- **Cortland.** Common in the Northeast, it's one of Vermont's leading apples. The early ones are more tart and generally better than the later ones, which tend to be fairly sweet.

- **Fuji.** One of the best-selling apples in Japan, it's a cross between Red Delicious and Ralls Janet. More prized for eating out of hand than for baking, it has a spicy flavor and juiciness that I quite like in pies.

- **Golden Delicious.** A reliable, all-purpose apple, it has legions of both fans and detractors, the latter who don't care for its sometimes bland flavor. The skin is soft enough to leave on, and the slices hold their shape well. When fresh and juicy, this is a fine pie apple.

- **Gravenstein.** Thought to be one of the best early apples, this one ripens in late August. It has a creamy, sweet-tart flesh and makes a delicious pie.

- **Honeycrisp.** It's crisp, like the name says, and has just the right balance of sweetness and tanginess.

- **Jonagold.** A cross between a Jonathan and a Golden Delicious, it doesn't store well, but it has a sweet, creamy, juicy flesh that tastes great in a pie.

- **Jonathan.** Some think it ranks as one of the best pie apples; others are less effusive. It has a soft, fine-textured flesh with a spicy flavor that translates well into pies.

- **Macoun.** Developed in New York State, the Macoun is a cross between a McIntosh and a Jersey Black. Generally considered to be a dessert apple, some say it makes a much better pie than the McIntosh.

- **McIntosh.** Some love, others despise the McIntosh's fine-textured flesh, which tends to turn very soft when baked. I prefer the early Macs to the later ones, as they're generally sweeter, firmer, and more distinctive in flavor.

- **Northern Spy.** "Spies are for pies," the saying goes, and this is perhaps the quintessential pie apple: tart, tangy, juicy, and firm. Sometimes hard to find, the Northern Spy is an excellent storage apple.

- **Red Delicious.** This is the one apple that, unequivocally, does not make a decent pie. Bred more for good looks than flavor or texture, it lacks the personality for a successful apple pie.

- **Winesap.** A superior, late-ripening apple with sweet-tart, winey, juicy flesh. The complex flavor has made it a favorite of cider makers for hundreds of years. Though hard to find, it's worth the hunt.

Grated Apple Pie

I've always liked adding grated apples or pears to my fall pies, so I took note when I came across a Pennsylvania Dutch recipe for something called Griene Ebbelkuche, or green apple pie, in which all of the fruit is grated. The recipe called for eggs, but I didn't want this to be a custard pie. So I skipped the eggs, added cornstarch, and kept it simple. The grated apples more or less disintegrate while the pie bakes, leaving something like a thick layer of applesauce. I love the way it tastes. The original recipe calls for Winesap apples, but any firm, juicy, tart apple will do.

Makes 8–10 servings

Shortening and Butter Dough with Egg (page 63) or another double-crust dough

FILLING

- 5 **large apples, peeled**
- 1½ **tablespoons lemon juice**
- ½ **cup sugar, plus a little for sprinkling**
- 2 **tablespoons cornstarch**
- ½ **teaspoon ground cinnamon**
- ⅛ **teaspoon salt**
- ½ **cup raisins**
- **Milk, for glaze**

1. Prepare and refrigerate the pie dough. Roll the larger dough portion into a 12½- to 13-inch circle and line a 9- to 9½-inch deep-dish pie pan with it, letting the overhang drape over the edge. Place in the refrigerator for 10 to 15 minutes.

2. Adjust the oven racks so one is in the lower position and another is in the middle of the oven. Preheat the oven to 400°F (200°C). Line a baking sheet with parchment paper.

3. Grate the apples, right into a large bowl, on the large holes of a box grater, making sure to capture all of the juice. Stir in the lemon juice. Mix the sugar, cornstarch, cinnamon, and salt in a small bowl; stir into the fruit. The simplest way to do a thorough job of this is with your hands. Mix in the raisins, then set aside.

4. Roll the other dough portion into an 11-inch circle. Turn the filling into the pie shell and smooth the filling with a spoon. Lightly moisten the rim of the pie shell.

Drape the top pastry over the filling, pressing along the edge to seal. Trim the overhang with scissors, leaving an even ½ to ¾ inch all around, then sculpt the edge into an upstanding ridge. Flute or crimp the edge, as desired. Poke several steam vents in the top of the pie with a large fork or paring knife. Put a couple of the vents near the edge so you can check the juices. Brush the pie lightly with milk and sprinkle with sugar.

5. Put the pie on the prepared baking sheet and bake on the lower rack for 30 minutes. Reduce the heat to 375°F (190°C) and move the pie up to the middle rack, rotating the pie 180 degrees. Bake for 30 to 35 minutes. This pie doesn't put off juice the way most apple pies do, so there may not be thick juice bubbling up through the vents. The best indicator of doneness is total elapsed baking time.

6. Transfer the pie to a rack and cool for at least 1½ to 2 hours before serving. Cover and refrigerate leftovers after 24 hours.

Green Tomato *and* Apple Mock Mincemeat Pie

Old-fashioned mincemeat pie isn't something you hear much about anymore. One glance at my vintage copy of *Joy of Cooking* and it's easy to understand why: beef suet and chopped ox heart aren't exactly in vogue these days, not even when combined with copious amounts of sugar, dried fruit, candied citrus peels, and a heavy hand with the baking spices. This kinder, gentler version of mincemeat is made with equal parts green tomatoes and apples, a ground orange, dried fruit, lots of spices, and a snort of rum and cider. I think you'll be pleased.

Makes 8–10 servings

Double-Crust Food Processor Pie Dough (page 60) or another double-crust dough

FILLING

- 1 **navel orange, washed**
- ⅔ **cup sugar, plus a little for sprinkling**
- 2 **large tart apples, peeled, cored, and finely chopped**
- 2 **green tomatoes, cored and finely chopped**
- ½ **cup dried currants**
- ¼ **cup dried cranberries**
- ¼ **cup rum or brandy**
- ¼ **cup apple cider**
- 1 **tablespoon unsulphured molasses**
- 2 **tablespoons all-purpose flour**
- ½ **teaspoon ground cinnamon**
- ¼ **teaspoon ground nutmeg**
- ¼ **teaspoon ground cloves**
- ⅛ **teaspoon salt**
- 1 **egg beaten with 1 tablespoon milk, for glaze**

1. Prepare and refrigerate the pie dough. Roll the larger dough portion into a 12½- to 13-inch circle and line a 9- to 9½-inch deep-dish pie pan with it, letting the overhang drape over the edge. Refrigerate the shell until needed.

2. Cut the orange into large chunks and combine in a food processor with the ⅔ cup sugar; process to a roughly textured purée. Scrape the purée into a large bowl and add the apples, green tomatoes, currants, cranberries, rum, cider, molasses, flour, cinnamon, nutmeg, cloves, and salt. Let stand for 1 hour, stirring occasionally.

3. Adjust the oven racks so one is in the lower position and another is in the middle of the oven. Preheat the oven to 400°F (200°C). Line a baking sheet with parchment paper.

4. Roll the other dough portion into an 11-inch circle. Turn the filling into the pie shell and smooth it out to even the top. Lightly moisten the rim of the pie shell. Drape the top pastry over the filling, pressing along the edge to seal. Trim the overhang with scissors, leaving an even ½ to ¾ inch all around, then sculpt the edge into an upstanding ridge. Flute or crimp the edge, as desired. Poke several steam vents in the top of the pie with a large fork or paring knife. Put a couple of the vents near the edge; you may be able to check the juices. Brush the pie lightly with the egg wash glaze and sprinkle with sugar.

5. Put the pie on the prepared baking sheet and bake on the lower rack for 30 minutes. Reduce the heat to 375°F (190°C) and move the pie up to the middle rack, rotating the pie 180 degrees. Bake for 30 minutes longer. This pie doesn't put off juice the way most apple pies do, so there may not be thick juice bubbling up through the vents. The best indicator of doneness is total elapsed baking time.

6. Transfer the pie to a rack and cool for at least 1½- to 2 hours before slicing. Cover and refrigerate leftovers after 24 hours.

Caramel Apple Slab Pie
with Melted Butter Crumb Topping

This is a popular recipe from my book *The Harvest Baker*, so I'm including it here with a couple of slight changes. I'm a big fan of slab pies; I'm glad they're finally getting the love they deserve. Among other things, you'll like the way the cream and brown sugar form a thick, caramel-like coating around the apples.

Makes 12–15 servings

Slab Pie Dough and Shell (page 74)

FILLING

7 **cups peeled, cored, and sliced baking apples**

½ **cup raisins**

⅔ **cup packed dark brown sugar**

1 **tablespoon plus 1 teaspoon cornstarch**

½ **teaspoon ground cinnamon**

Big pinch of salt

¼ **cup heavy cream**

1 **tablespoon lemon juice**

Melted Butter Crumb Topping (page 449) or another crumb topping

1. Prepare the slab pie dough and make the slab shell in a jelly-roll pan. Refrigerate the shell until needed.

2. Adjust the oven racks so one is in the lower position and another is in the middle of the oven. Preheat the oven to 400°F (200°C).

3. Combine the apples, raisins, sugar, cornstarch, cinnamon, salt, cream, and lemon juice in a large bowl. Mix well; with so much filling, I like to mix with my hands. Spread everything out evenly in the shell, taking care to smooth over any apple tips, which have a tendency to scorch in the oven. Spread the crumb topping evenly over the apples; you'll probably need all of it.

4. Put the pie on the lower oven rack and bake for 25 minutes. Lower the heat to 375°F (190°C) and move the pie up to the middle rack, rotating it 180 degrees. Bake for 30 to 35 minutes longer, until the juices are bubbly and the topping is golden brown. If the crumb topping starts to get too brown, cover it with aluminum foil.

5. Transfer the pie to a rack and cool for at least 1 hour before serving. I prefer it lukewarm or at room temperature. Cover and refrigerate leftovers after 24 hours.

Recipe for Success

It bears repeating that you really have to use a proper jelly-roll pan. If the pan has sides shorter than 1 inch, the pie might bubble over.

Use light brown sugar in the filling if that's all you have, but the dark does give it an extra caramel flavor.

No-Roll Apple Crumble Pie

Here's an apple pie for anyone with a dough-rolling phobia. Instead of the traditional bottom crust, there's an oat crumb crust that's pressed in the pan. Sautéed apple chunks and dates are spooned into the shell, then the topping — the same oat mixture — is scattered over the apples. You end up with a delicious, compact, barlike apple pie that's sturdy enough to pack in brown-bag lunches and eat out of hand. With the press-in crust and fewer than usual apples to cut, this is a good recipe to make with kids.

Makes 8–10 servings

CRUST

- 1 **cup all-purpose flour**
- 1 **cup old-fashioned rolled oats**
- ¾ **cup packed light brown sugar**
- ⅓ **cup sweetened flaked coconut**
- ½ **teaspoon ground cinnamon**
- ¼ **teaspoon salt**
- 10 **tablespoons (1¼ sticks) cold unsalted butter, cut into ½-inch cubes**

FILLING

- 3 **tablespoons unsalted butter**
- 4 **cups peeled, cored, and diced apples**
- ¼ **cup packed light brown sugar**
- ½ **cup chopped pitted dates**
- 1 **tablespoon lemon juice**
- **Big pinch of salt**

1. To make the crust, put the flour, oats, sugar, coconut, cinnamon, and salt in a food processor. Pulse the machine five or six times to mix. Scatter the butter over the dry mixture. Pulse again until the mixture forms loose, coarse crumbs that begin to clump together. Transfer the mixture to a bowl and rub it between your fingers until it all feels buttery and no dry areas remain.

2. Spread a little more than half of the crumbs evenly in the bottom and two-thirds of the way up the sides of a lightly buttered 9- to 9½-inch deep-dish pie pan, pressing them into the pan. Refrigerate the crust and the remaining crumbs while you prepare the filling.

3. Preheat the oven to 375°F (190°C). To make the filling, melt the butter in a large nonreactive skillet over medium heat. Add the apples and cook for 3 minutes. Stir in the sugar, dates, lemon juice, and salt, and cook 2 minutes longer. Remove from the heat and cool for 10 minutes.

4. Turn the filling and all the juice into the pie shell and spread it evenly. Scatter the remaining crumbs evenly over the top of the pie, pressing them gently into the apples.

5. Bake the pie on the center oven rack for 25 minutes, then rotate the pie 180 degrees. Bake for 20 to 25 minutes longer, until the top of the pie is golden brown and the apples are tender.

6. Transfer the pie to a rack and cool to room temperature before serving. Cover and refrigerate leftovers after 24 hours.

Apple Upside-Down-Pan Pie

Here's a rustic, top-crust-only pie with a thin profile. It's baked in a skillet, giving it an informality that's perfect for casual get-togethers. You can serve it hot from the pan, or — if you're more daring — invert the whole thing onto a plate, exposing the caramelized apple filling. You'll need a cast-iron pan for this.

Makes 8–10 servings

Single-Crust Food Processor Pie Dough (page 58) or another single-crust dough

FILLING

- 4 **tablespoons unsalted butter**
- ⅓ **cup packed light brown sugar**
- 4 **Golden Delicious apples, peeled, quartered, and cored**
- 1 **tablespoon lemon juice**

1. Prepare the pie dough and refrigerate it until firm enough to roll, about 1 hour.

2. Get out an ovenproof skillet or shallow sauté pan that measures roughly 9 inches across the bottom and 11 to 12 inches across the top. Melt the butter in the skillet over medium heat; stir in the sugar. Heat, stirring, until the mixture spreads across the skillet more or less evenly. Remove from the heat.

3. Preheat the oven to 400°F (200°C). Cut 2 of the apples into thick slices and lay them in the pan. Don't bother to arrange them in perfect rows; just lay them flat and somewhat even. Dice the remaining 2 apples and scatter the pieces evenly over the sliced apples. Sprinkle the lemon juice over all the apples.

4. Roll the dough into a 12-inch circle, and drape it over the apples. Tuck the edge of the dough down next to the apples inside the skillet; the residual warmth will allow the pastry to relax, so you can push it down gently with a butter knife. Using a large fork or paring knife, poke several steam vents in the dough.

5. Bake the pie on the center oven rack for 20 minutes. Reduce the temperature to 375°F (190°C) and bake for 20 to 25 minutes longer, until the top pastry is golden brown.

6. Transfer the pie to a rack. To remove the pie from the skillet, wear long sleeves and oven mitts to protect your arms and hands. Gently place a plate, as large as the pastry, on top of the pie. Quickly invert the pie onto the plate; it should come right out. Let the pie cool for at least 10 minutes, then slice and serve.

Recipe for Success

I recommend Golden Delicious apples because they'll hold their shape and look better if you serve this apple-side-up.

If you like this skillet apple pie idea and would like to try an excellent variation of it, I recommend the Cast-Iron-Skillet Diced-Apple Pie on page 182.

Andy's Cranberry-Apple Pie *with* Oatmeal Crumb Topping

My friend Andy Johnson is a frugal New Englander, first-rate fiddler, and latter-day Euell Gibbons who forages for at least some of his diet when the opportunity arises. One year Andy arrived at my place with a paper sack full of cranberries he'd gathered from the bogs near his home on the New Hampshire seacoast. I "re-pied" him with this delicacy, named in his honor, which I make several times a year. Sometimes I use a pear in place of the apple or add a top crust instead of a crumb topping. It would be very un-Andy-like to be too rigid about any of this.

Makes 8–10 servings

Single-Crust Food Processor Pie Dough (page 58) or another single-crust dough

FILLING

5–5½   **cups peeled, cored, and sliced apples**

2   **cups fresh or frozen cranberries**

½   **cup chopped walnuts**

⅓   **cup plus 2 tablespoons sugar**

¼   **cup maple syrup**

1½   **tablespoons lemon juice**

Finely grated zest of 1 orange

½   **teaspoon ground cinnamon**

½   **teaspoon ground cloves**

2   **tablespoons cornstarch**

Oatmeal Crumb Topping (page 449)

1. Prepare and refrigerate the pie dough. Roll the dough into a 12½- to 13-inch circle and line a 9- to 9½-inch deep-dish pie pan with it, shaping the edge into an upstanding ridge. Flute or crimp the edge, then refrigerate the shell until needed.

2. Adjust the oven racks so one is in the lower position and another is in the middle of the oven. Preheat the oven to 400°F (200°C). Line a baking sheet with parchment paper.

3. Mix the apples, cranberries, walnuts, and the ⅓ cup sugar together in a large bowl. Let stand for 10 minutes.

4. Stir the maple syrup, lemon juice, grated orange zest, cinnamon, and cloves into the apples. Mix the 2 tablespoons sugar and cornstarch in a small bowl; stir into the fruit.

5. Put the pie shell on the prepared baking sheet and turn the filling into the shell. Smooth out the filling. Cover with a generous layer of the crumb topping; you may not need all of it. Press the crumbs down gently.

6. Bake the pie, on the sheet, on the lower oven rack for 30 minutes. Reduce the heat to 375°F (190°C) and move the pie up to the middle rack, rotating it 180 degrees. Bake for 30 to 40 minutes longer, until the juices bubble thickly around the edge. If the top of the pie starts to get too dark, cover the pie with foil.

7. Transfer the pie to a rack and cool for at least 1½ to 2 hours before slicing. Cover and refrigerate leftovers after 24 hours.

Recipe for Success

Like most fresh picked berries, cranberries sometimes have little sticks, stems, and the occasional leaf mixed in with them. It takes just a moment to pick them over and remove these little bits and pieces before you use the cranberries.

Apple Butter Pie

This recipe is from my wife Bev's late Aunt Marge who, within five minutes of my meeting her, took me aside and plainly asked: *Just when are you going to make my niece an honest woman?* I assured her it wouldn't be long. (It wasn't.) Marge was a member of the Fairview Methodist Church in Charleston, West Virginia, where the ladies of the church made and sold delicious apple butter every fall. I came up with this pie in Marge's honor. The texture is something like a rich pumpkin pie, smooth and well spiced. A good choice for Thanksgiving season.

Makes 8–10 servings

Old-Fashioned Shortening Pie Dough (page 62) or another single-crust dough

FILLING

- 3 **large eggs, at room temperature**
- ½ **cup sugar**
- 1¾ **cups spiced apple butter (for homemade, see page 451)**
- ⅓ **cup half-and-half**
- ¼ **teaspoon salt**
- 1 **tablespoon lemon juice**
- 1 **teaspoon finely grated lemon zest**
- ½ **teaspoon vanilla extract**
- 4 **tablespoons unsalted butter, melted**
- **Whipped Cream (page 447), for garnish**

1. Prepare and refrigerate the pie dough. Roll the dough into a 12-inch circle and line a 9- to 9½-inch standard pie pan with it, shaping the edge into an upstanding ridge. Flute or crimp the edge, chill the shell, and partially pre-bake it according to the instructions on page 36.

2. Preheat the oven to 375°F (190°C). Combine the eggs and sugar in a large bowl. Using an electric mixer (handheld is fine), beat on medium speed until thoroughly blended, 30 to 45 seconds. Add the apple butter, half-and-half, salt, lemon juice, and lemon zest. Beat again until smooth. Mix in the vanilla and butter. Put the pie shell on a baking sheet, near the oven, then carefully pour the filling into the shell.

3. Bake the pie, on the sheet, on the middle oven rack for 15 minutes. Lower the heat to 350°F (180°C) and rotate the pie 180 degrees. Bake for 25 to 30 minutes longer, until the sides start to puff and the filling is set. When the pie is done, the very center will probably look a little glossy compared to most of the perimeter.

4. Transfer the pie to a rack and cool completely. Refrigerate for at least 2 hours before serving, dolloping slices with whipped cream. Cover and refrigerate leftovers.

Recipe for Success

Apple butter brands vary in sweetness and spiciness. So give yours a taste, and taste the filling, too, before it goes into the pan. You may decide that the filling needs more sugar or spices. Just whisk them right in, as needed.

Cheddar-Crusted Apple Pie

New Englanders have known the pleasures of combining apple pie and Cheddar cheese for a very long time — long enough to be quite opinionated about how the two should be eaten together. Some cooks include grated Cheddar in the filling itself. Others grate the cheese over the top of the pie, which is fine when the pie is warm but less so when it is cool and the cheese hardens. Old-timers lay a slab of Cheddar right on top of their pie slice and dig in. I wanted to integrate the cheese into the pie itself, so I baked grated cheese into the crust, which keeps the snappy Cheddar flavor front and center. This is one good pie.

Makes 8 servings

Cheddar Cheese Pie Dough (page 70)

FILLING

- 8 cups peeled, cored, and sliced Granny Smith or other apples
- ½ cup sugar
- 2 tablespoons lemon juice
- ¾ cup chopped walnut halves, preferably toasted (page 453)
- 2½–3 tablespoons all-purpose flour
- 1 egg beaten with 1 tablespoon milk, for glaze

1. Prepare and refrigerate the pie dough. Roll the larger dough portion into a 12½- to 13-inch circle and line a 9- to 9½-inch deep-dish pie pan with it, letting the overhang drape over the edge. Refrigerate the shell until needed.

2. Combine the apples, sugar, lemon juice, and walnuts in a large bowl. Mix well. Let stand for 5 to 10 minutes.

3. Adjust the oven racks so one is in the lower position and another is in the middle of the oven. Preheat the oven to 400°F (200°C). Line a baking sheet with parchment paper.

4. Sprinkle the flour over the apples, using the larger amount of flour if the apples seem very juicy. Mix well.

5. Roll the other dough portion into an 11-inch circle. Turn the filling into the pie shell and smooth it over to level out the fruit. Lightly moisten the rim of the pie shell. Drape the top pastry over the filling, pressing along the edge to seal. Trim the overhang with scissors, leaving an even ½ to ¾ inch all around, then sculpt the edge into an upstanding ridge. Flute or crimp the edge, as desired. Poke several steam vents in the top of the pie with a large fork or paring knife. Put a couple of the vents near the edge so you can check the juices. Brush the pie lightly with the egg wash glaze.

6. Put the pie on the prepared baking sheet and bake on the lower oven rack for 30 minutes. Reduce the oven temperature to 375°F (190°C) and move the pie up to the middle rack, rotating the pie 180 degrees. Bake for 30 to 40 minutes longer, until the pie is a rich, golden brown and juices bubble thickly up through the vents.

7. Transfer the pie to a rack and cool for about 1 hour before serving. Longer is fine, but you'll bring out the flavor of the cheese if you serve this pie warmer than most.

Oatmeal Raisin–Apple
and Apple Butter Pie

Here's my advice for would-be blue ribbon pie bakers: apple butter. This thick reduction of apples, sweetener, and spices, processed to a smooth purée, makes an unmistakable flavor statement in an apple pie. I use it with a heavy hand here, adding less sugar than usual since most apple butter is already sweetened. No additional spice is needed, either, for the same reason. Try one of your locally made or regional brands; I buy it at local church bazaars whenever possible (see also Apple Butter Pie on page 177).

Makes 8–10 servings

Buttermilk Pie Dough (page 67) or another single-crust dough

FILLING

8 cups peeled, cored, and sliced apples

¼ cup sugar

1½ tablespoons lemon juice

   Finely grated zest of 1 lemon

1½ tablespoons all-purpose flour

1 cup spiced apple butter (for homemade, see page 451) or store-bought

¾ cup raisins

   Oatmeal Crumb Topping (page 449)

1. Prepare and refrigerate the pie dough. Roll the dough into a 12½- to 13-inch circle and line a 9- to 9½-inch deep-dish pie pan with it, shaping the edge into an upstanding ridge. Flute or crimp the edge, then refrigerate the shell until needed.

2. Adjust the oven racks so one is in the lower position and another is in the middle of the oven. Preheat the oven to 400°F (200°C). Line a baking sheet with parchment paper.

3. Combine the apples, sugar, lemon juice, and lemon zest in a large bowl. Mix well. Let stand for 10 minutes. Sprinkle the flour over the apples and mix well. Stir in the apple butter and raisins. Turn the filling into the pie shell, smoothing the filling with your hands to even out the fruit. Set the pie on the prepared baking sheet, then cover the pie with a generous layer of the topping; you probably won't need all of it. Tamp the topping down gently.

4. Bake the pie, on the sheet, on the lower oven rack for 30 minutes. Reduce the heat to 375°F (190°C) and move the pie up to the middle rack, rotating the pie 180 degrees. Bake for 30 to 40 minutes longer, until the juices bubble thickly around the edge. If the topping starts to get too dark, cover the pie with aluminum foil.

5. Transfer the pie to a rack and cool for at least 1½ to 2 hours before serving. Cover and refrigerate leftovers after 24 hours.

When you can make a good pie, you will have a special gift to give others that money can't buy.

— *Marion Cunningham,* Cooking with Children

Apple and Pear Pie *with* Hot Pepper Jelly

If there was ever a gimmicky-sounding apple pie, this would be it. Fortunately, this is the real deal: a delicious fruit filling flavored with hot pepper jelly and topped with a cornmeal streusel. I started making this during our Navy football tailgating days in Annapolis, and it remains one of my favorite pies of all time. I think you'll love the warm and spicy exotic flavor of the filling and the crunch of the cornmeal topping, all in the same bite.

Makes 8–10 servings

Whole-Wheat Pie Dough (page 66) or another single-crust dough

FILLING

- 6 **cups peeled, cored, and sliced apples**
- 2 **cups peeled, cored and sliced ripe pears**
- 2 **tablespoons sugar**
- 1½ **tablespoons cornstarch**
- ¼ **teaspoon ground cinnamon**
- ¾ **cup jalapeño jelly**
- 2 **tablespoons minced pickled jalapeños (optional)**
- 1 **tablespoon lemon juice**

  Cornmeal Streusel (page 450)

1. Prepare and refrigerate the pie dough. Roll the dough into a 12½- to 13-inch circle and line a 9- to 9½-inch deep-dish pie pan with it, shaping the edge into an upstanding ridge. Flute or crimp the edge, then refrigerate the shell until needed.

2. Preheat the oven to 400°F (200°C). Line a large baking sheet with parchment paper.

3. Mix the apples and pears in a large bowl. Mix the sugar, cornstarch, and cinnamon in a small bowl; stir into the fruit. Put the pepper jelly in a small glass measuring cup and warm it in the microwave for 15 seconds, to thin. Stir into the fruit along with the minced jalapeños, if using, and lemon juice.

4. Transfer the filling to the pie shell. Smooth the fruit with your hands to even it out. Place the pie on the prepared baking sheet and cover with a generous amount of the streusel; you may not need all of it. Press the streusel down gently.

5. Bake the pie, on the sheet, on the lower oven rack for 30 minutes. Reduce the heat to 375°F (190°C) and move the pie up to the middle rack, rotating it 180 degrees. Bake for 30 to 40 minutes longer, until the juices bubble thickly around the edge. If the top of the pie starts to get too dark, cover it with the pie with aluminum foil.

6. Transfer the pie to a rack and cool for at least 1½ to 2 hours before serving. Cover and refrigerate leftovers after 24 hours.

An A-peeling Tradition

There are any number of old traditions whereby a young lady would enlist the help of an apple peel for a glimpse into her future love life. A long-standing Scottish and Irish tradition holds that a girl might learn the identity of her beloved by peeling the apple in one long continuous piece and tossing it over her left shoulder: the profile of the peel would reveal the profile of her future love. In another variation, the peel would reveal his initials. And if the peel broke, the young lady would, alas, remain unmarried.

Cast-Iron-Skillet Diced-Apple Pie

A new generation of cooks seem to have discovered the utility of cast-iron cookware, because the stuff is getting an awful lot of attention these days. And why not? Cast iron is a bargain compared to a lot of cookware, it conducts heat beautifully, and it lasts forever. A cast-iron skillet will double as a deep-dish pie pan if that's all you have, and even if it isn't, I urge you to try this pie and see for yourself what a great job that skillet can do with a good old apple pie. Among other things, you're going to like the brown sugar–glazed bottom crust and the caramel-like sauciness of the pie.

Makes 8–10 servings

Double-Crust Food Processor Pie Dough (page 60) or another double-crust dough

FILLING

- 3 **tablespoons unsalted butter**
- ¼ **cup plus 3 tablespoons packed light brown sugar**
- 6 **cups peeled, cored, and diced apples**
- 1½ **tablespoons lemon juice**
- ¼ **teaspoon ground nutmeg**
- ¼ **cup plus 1 tablespoon granulated sugar**
- 2 **tablespoons cornstarch**
- 2 **tablespoons heavy cream, plus some for glaze**
- ¼ **teaspoon ground cinnamon, for glaze**

1. Prepare and refrigerate the pie dough for at least 1 hour.

2. Heat the butter and the 3 tablespoons brown sugar in a 9½- to 10-inch cast-iron skillet over medium-high heat, stirring, until the mixture bubbles across the pan. Set aside to cool briefly, then refrigerate the skillet for at least 10 minutes.

3. Adjust the oven racks so one is in the lower position and another is in the middle of the oven. Preheat the oven to 400°F (200°C).

4. Combine the apples, lemon juice, nutmeg, and the ¼ cup brown sugar in a large bowl. Mix well. Let stand for 5 minutes. Mix the ¼ cup granulated sugar and cornstarch in a small bowl; stir into the fruit.

5. Roll the larger dough portion into a 13-inch circle and line the chilled sugar-glazed skillet with it. Turn the filling into the pie shell, smoothing out the fruit with a spoon. Drizzle the cream over the apples. Moisten the upper portion of the pie shell with water. Roll the other dough portion into an 11-inch circle. Drape the dough over the filling, pressing around the edge to seal. If you have excess dough sticking up above the rim of the skillet, trim it away with a paring knife.

6. Brush the top of the pie with cream. Mix the 1 tablespoon granulated sugar with the cinnamon in a small bowl and sprinkle over the pie. Using a paring knife or large fork, poke several steam vents in the top of the pie.

7. Bake the pie on the lower oven rack for 30 minutes (don't put it on a baking sheet). Reduce the heat to 375°F (190°C) and move the pie up to the middle rack, rotating it 180 degrees. Bake for about 30 minutes longer, until the top is a dark golden brown and you (most likely) see thick juice bubbling up around the edge of the pie or through the vents.

8. Transfer the pie to a rack and cool for at least 1½ to 2 hours before serving. Refrigerate leftovers after 24 hours.

Farm-Style Buttermilk Pie
with Fried Apple Rings

Here's a pie that might have been served on farms of an earlier day, when buttermilk was the everyday by-product of churning butter and fried apples were served with great country breakfasts or with a supper of ham. The thick apple rings go into a prebaked pie shell and rise to the top when you pour in the filling. Unlike many pies, this one is meant to be chilled before serving. You could serve it warm, but I think the custard tastes so much better when it's cold.

Makes 8–10 servings

Perfect Pie Dough by Hand (page 56) or another single-crust dough

FILLING

- 2 **large Golden Delicious apples**
- 1½ **tablespoons unsalted butter**
- 2 **tablespoons granulated sugar**
- 1 **cup packed light brown sugar**
- 3 **tablespoons all-purpose flour**
- 3 **large eggs plus 1 large egg yolk**
- 1 **teaspoon vanilla extract**
- 1½ **cups buttermilk**
- 3 **tablespoons unsalted butter, melted**

1. Prepare and refrigerate the pie dough. Roll the dough into a 12½- to 13-inch circle and line a 9- to 9½-inch deep-dish pie pan with it, shaping the edge into an upstanding ridge. Flute or crimp the edge, chill the shell, and partially prebake it according to the instructions on page 34.

2. Preheat the oven to 350°F (180°C). Leaving the skins on, cut the apples into crosswise slices about ¾ inch thick. Core each slice and select six of the best-looking ones. Melt the 1½ tablespoons butter in a large skillet and add the apple slices, sprinkling 1 tablespoon of the granulated sugar over them. Fry over medium heat for about 4 minutes, then flip the slices and fry them on the other side for another few minutes, until not quite tender. Sprinkle the remaining 1 tablespoon granulated sugar over the apples and flip once more. Cook for another minute or two, until the slices are tender.

3. Meanwhile, combine the brown sugar and flour in the bowl of a food processor. Pulse to mix. Add the eggs, egg yolk, and vanilla; process until smooth. Add the buttermilk and melted butter, and process just until blended.

4. Put one apple ring in the center of the pie shell and arrange the others around it. Very slowly pour the buttermilk custard over the apples; if the slices don't rise, gently nudge them with a fork.

5. Bake the pie on the center oven rack for about 45 minutes, until the center is set. To check, give the pie a little nudge; the custard should not move in waves. Don't overbake or the custard won't be nice and creamy.

6. Transfer the pie to a rack and cool thoroughly. Cover with aluminum foil or plastic wrap and refrigerate for at least several hours before serving.

How to Store Apples

A bag of fresh apples will keep in the refrigerator for several weeks, and apples are available year-round at the grocery store, of course. But what if you want to store a bushel of local apples for making pies all winter?

First, know that some apples keep better than others; those picked at their prime will keep best. Among the best storage apples are Northern Spy, Winesap, and Rome Beauty. Ask your local apple grower which apples he or she recommends for storage.

For long-term storage, choose a cool location with relatively high humidity. The ideal storage temperature is 32 to 34°F (0 to 1°C). Below that, apples will freeze, causing the cell structure to break down and ruin the apples.

Storage apples must be unblemished. Use up any with bruises or soft spots as soon as possible. Wrap the fruit individually in black-and-white newsprint or packing paper. Don't use paper with color photos, as the ink may contaminate the apples. Place the apples in a box, and store it in a dark place. Check weekly to see how they're faring. Damp spots on the newsprint are an indication that an apple is rotting.

Finally, don't store apples next to potatoes: those spuds put off a gas that will hasten the demise of stored apples. Apples stored under ideal conditions can keep for 4 to 5 months.

Marion Cunningham on Apples and Apple Pie

If we're talking about supermarket apples — and let's face it, that's where most of us buy them — I like the flavor and juiciness of both the Fuji apple and Gravenstein. I think they hold up better than some when they're baked in a pie. In general, though, I don't think apples are as juicy as they used to be because so many of them spend so much time in cold storage. They aren't as bad as the stone fruits we get today, however. I feel sorry for the newest generation of cooks. Most of them have never tasted a good fresh peach or plum or nectarine. As for the top of the pie, I prefer a crumb crust to a top crust.

— Marion Cunningham, author, among many other books, of The Fannie Farmer Baking Book

Lauren's Salted Caramel–Apple Streusel Pie

My friend Lauren Bolden is head baker and co-owner of Pie Bar, a popular Woodstock, Georgia, pie shop. Like all accomplished pie bakers, she's a keen observer of the countless small details that go into making a truly memorable pie, like Pie Bar's famed salted caramel apple pie. You can't go more than a few clicks on most recipe websites without bumping into a salted caramel pie, but you won't run across one this tasty very often — layer upon layer of pie goodness.

Makes 8–10 servings

Single-Crust Food Processor Pie Dough (page 58) or another single-crust dough

FILLING

- 9 **cups peeled, cored, and thinly sliced apples**
- 1 **cup granulated sugar**
- 1¾ **teaspoon ground cinnamon**
- ½ **teaspoon ground nutmeg**
- 2 **tablespoons all-purpose flour**

STREUSEL TOPPING

- 1 **cup all-purpose flour**
- ¼ **cup granulated sugar**
- 3 **tablespoons packed light brown sugar**
- **Pinch of coarse kosher salt**
- 6 **tablespoons cold unsalted butter, cut into pieces**
- **Lauren's Salted Caramel Sauce (page 444)**

1. Prepare and refrigerate the pie dough. Roll the dough into a 12½- to 13-inch circle and line a 9- to 9½-inch deep-dish pie pan with it, shaping the edge into an upstanding ridge. Flute the edge, then refrigerate the shell until needed. (Because the apples have to macerate overnight, you can, if you prefer, make the pie shell on the day you assemble and bake the pie.)

2. To make the filling, put the apples in a large bowl. Add the granulated sugar, cinnamon, nutmeg, and flour. Mix well by hand. Cover the bowl with plastic wrap and refrigerate overnight.

3. The next day, mix the apples with their juice. Transfer the contents of the bowl to a colander placed over a large bowl and drain off the juice. Pour the juice into a small saucepan and bring to a boil. Boil until thickened and somewhat reduced, but don't let it get too thick and syrupy. Remove from the heat and set aside to cool.

4. Preheat the oven to 375°F (190°C). Line a large baking sheet with parchment paper or aluminum foil.

5. To make the streusel topping, combine the flour, sugars, and salt in a food processor. Pulse the machine several times to mix. Scatter the butter over the dry mixture and pulse until the butter is cut into very small pieces. Refrigerate until using.

6. Transfer the drained apple slices to the pie shell. Press down gently on the apples to level them off. The apple level should be almost the same height as the flutes of the pie shell. Pour ⅓ cup of the reduced apple juice evenly over the pie. Cover the apples evenly with all of the streusel.

7. Place the pie on the prepared baking sheet and bake for 15 minutes. Reduce the temperature to 350°F (180°C) and bake 20 minutes longer. Rotate the pie 180 degrees and bake for another 20 to 25 minutes, until the topping has browned and the juices bubble thickly. (The total baking time is 1 hour to 1 hour 10 minutes.)

8. Transfer the pie to a rack and cool for about 30 minutes. Pour ⅓ to ½ cup Lauren's Salted Caramel over the top of the pie, first in vertical lines and then horizontal ones; serve. Cover and refrigerate leftovers after 24 hours.

The Farm-to-Oven Goodness of Apple Pie

Every week during fall, an apple farmer from Ellijay, Georgia, loads up his flatbed truck with hundreds of Honeycrisps, Galas, Pink Ladies, and Jonagolds, delivering apples fresh from the trees. They — the apples — are the lucky ones. These apples are going to receive the highest honor possible: they were chosen to become apple pie.

Bushels of apples are dropped at our pie shop's back door, and that is when the prep work begins. We peel, core, and slice each apple. After hours of this work, apples begin to pile higher and higher. We sprinkle them with a little bit of sugar, cinnamon, and nutmeg. When you are working with fresh, crisp apples, there is no reason to mask that fresh fruit taste.

We assemble our pies and into the oven they go. As they bake, they transform into something amazing. The crust turns golden brown and flaky. The filling bubbles over. The shop smells like the world's largest apple pie candle; it is pie heaven. We carefully remove the bubbling pies from the oven and place them on the cooling rack. This is the hardest part of being a baker . . . the waiting. Cut into the pie too soon, and you have an apple puddle. We wait until the pie cools just enough to keep its shape but is still warm enough to slowly melt a scoop of vanilla ice cream on top.

— Lauren Bolden, founder and co-owner of Pie Bar, Woodstock, Georgia

Apple-Oatmeal Breakfast Pie
with Checkerboard Lattice

Most of the time bakers use cornstarch or flour to thicken fruit pies; this one uses oatmeal. Consequently, the filling isn't uniformly thickened — you get some pockets of thin juice here and there — but the upside is you've cooked your oatmeal right into the filling, making this fair game for breakfast. The top crust is a checkerboard lattice — a solid top pastry cut into squares, checkerboard-style. It's fun to make a very attractive pie. Use a good juicy apple here.

Makes 8–10 servings

Double-Crust Food Processor Pie Dough (page 60)

FILLING

- 7 **cups peeled, cored, and sliced apples**
- ½ **cup packed light brown sugar**
- 1½ **tablespoons lemon juice**
- **Finely grated zest of 1 lemon**
- ½ **cup raisins**
- ⅓ **cup old-fashioned rolled oats**
- ½ **teaspoon ground cinnamon**
- **Milk, for glaze**
- **Granulated sugar, for sprinkling**

1. Prepare and refrigerate the pie dough. Roll the larger dough portion into a 12½- to 13-inch circle and line a 9- to 9½-inch deep-dish pie pan with it, letting the excess dough drape over the edge. Refrigerate the shell until needed.

2. Roll the other dough portion into an 11½-inch circle on a large sheet of lightly floured waxed paper or parchment paper. Slide it onto a baking sheet and refrigerate for 15 minutes.

3. Combine the apples, brown sugar, lemon juice, and lemon zest in a large bowl. Mix well. Let stand for 10 minutes.

4. Remove the top pastry from the refrigerator. Using a ruler or very thin straight edge, gently press the edge into the dough to barely score it, making the score marks about 1 inch apart. Score the pastry one way, then the other, checkerboard fashion. You won't be cutting precisely on these marks; they're only a guide. Using a sharp paring knife or razor blade, cut out squares of dough — a little smaller than the squares you see — in an alternating checkerboard arrangement. (In other words, if this were a real checkerboard, you'd be cutting out only the black squares, or the red ones.) Leave a continuous border of pastry at the edge. The reason you're making the cutouts a little smaller than the squares you see is to make sure the pastry holds together. (If necessary, put the dough back in the fridge to refirm it.) Remove the pastry squares, but reserve them for step 6.

5. Preheat the oven to 400°F (200°C). Line a large baking sheet with parchment paper or aluminum foil.

Recipe continues on next page

6. Stir the raisins, oats, and cinnamon into the apples. Turn the filling into the pie shell, smoothing the top of the filling with your hands. Make it nice and flat. Moisten the edge of the pie shell, then invert or slide the checkerboard top dough over the filling. Press the pastries together along the dampened edge, then trim the overhang with scissors or a paring knife, leaving an even ½ to ¾ inch all around. Use the cut-out squares to decorate the rim. Brush the top dough lightly with milk and sprinkle with granulated sugar.

7. Place the pie on the prepared baking sheet and bake for 30 minutes on the lower oven rack. Reduce the heat to 375°F (190°C) and move the pie up to the middle rack, rotating it 180 degrees. Bake for 30 to 40 minutes longer, until the juices bubble vigorously inside the pie — you'll be able to look right in through the lattice to see.

8. Transfer the pie to a rack and cool for at least 1½ to 2 hours before serving. Cover and refrigerate leftovers after 24 hours.

Skewer Those Apples

A good way to check a pie to see if the apples are done is to poke the apples. Wooden kabob skewers make excellent testers because they are long and pointy, and unlike an ordinary toothpick, you can insert a skewer into the center of the pie without burning your fingers. Poke the skewer into one or two places, including near the center. If the pie has a top pastry, aim to insert it through one of the steam vents; you should encounter no apple resistance. Be discreet about this testing and try not leave the pastry looking like Swiss cheese.

Skins-On Apple-Honey Pie

Apples are healthy, with fiber and antioxidants galore. A case could be made for leaving the skins on when you make a pie. But many people find the skins chewy and intrusive. The solution? Cut the apples into small dice. You'll end up with an acceptable level of chewiness, without the intrusion. A few other touches here for the healthy-eating crowd: walnuts, a whole-wheat crust, and honey (I prefer a mild clover honey). As for the apples, Golden Delicious have soft skins so they're a good choice.

Makes 8–10 servings

Whole-Wheat Pie Dough, double-crust version (page 62)

FILLING

7½ cups quartered, cored, and diced apples (about ½ inch dice)

½ cup honey

⅓ cup chopped walnuts

1½ tablespoons lemon juice

Finely grated zest of 1 lemon

2½ tablespoons cornstarch

½ teaspoon ground cinnamon

1 egg beaten with 1 tablespoon milk, for glaze

Sugar, for sprinkling

1. Prepare and refrigerate the pie dough. Roll the larger dough portion into a 13-inch circle and line a 9- to 9½-inch deep-dish pie pan with it, letting the excess dough drape over the edge. Refrigerate the shell until needed.

2. Adjust the oven racks so one is in the lower position and another is in the middle of the oven. Preheat the oven to 400°F (200°C). Line a large baking sheet with parchment paper.

3. Combine the apples, honey, walnuts, lemon juice, and lemon zest in a large bowl. Mix well. Add the cornstarch and cinnamon, and mix again.

4. Roll the other dough portion into an 11-inch circle. Turn the filling into the pie shell and smooth it out to even the top. Lightly moisten the rim of the pie shell. Drape the top pastry over the filling, pressing along the edge to seal. Trim the overhang with scissors, leaving an even ½ to ¾ inch all around, then sculpt the edge into an upstanding ridge. Flute or crimp the edge, as desired. Poke several steam vents in the top of the pie with a large fork or paring knife. Put a couple of the vents near the edge so you can check the juices. Brush the pie lightly with the egg wash glaze and sprinkle with sugar.

5. Put the pie on the prepared baking sheet and bake the lower oven rack for 30 minutes. Reduce the temperature to 375°F (190°C) and move the pie to the middle rack, rotating it 180 degrees. Bake for 30 to 40 minutes longer, until the top of the pie is a dark golden brown and you see thick juices bubbling up through the vents.

6. Transfer the pie to a rack and cool for at least 1½ to 2 hours before serving. Cover and refrigerate leftovers after 24 hours.

Marlborough Pie

Marlborough pie is an old British recipe that's also known as Deerfield pie in New England. I've seen a number of such recipes in cookbooks and, save some minor differences, it's always an apple custard pie usually served for Thanksgiving. Typically, the apples are grated and then cooked, which yields a pie with a fine custard filling with just a bit of apple texture. I use Grand Marnier or triple sec to cook the apples. This isn't traditional: brandy and applejack are more common. I just like the orange flavoring. This pie is best served chilled.

Makes 8–10 servings

Shortening and Butter Dough with Egg (page 63) or another double-crust dough

FILLING

4 **large apples, peeled (McIntosh or another soft-cooking apple will work)**

3 **tablespoons unsalted butter**

¼ **cup Grand Marnier, triple sec, or brandy**

⅓ **cup plus ¼ cup sugar**

Big pinch of salt

3 **large eggs**

1 **cup heavy cream**

1 **tablespoon all-purpose flour**

½ **teaspoon vanilla extract**

Several pinches of ground nutmeg, for garnish

1. Prepare and refrigerate the pie dough. You can either halve the recipe to make one crust or freeze the second crust for later use. Roll the dough into a 12-inch circle and line a 9- to 9½-inch standard pie pan with it, shaping the edge into an upstanding ridge. Flute or crimp the edge, chill the shell, and partially prebake it according to the instructions on page 36.

2. Preheat the oven to 350°F (180°C). Grate the apples down to their cores on the large holes of a box grater. Melt the butter in a large nonreactive skillet — nonstick is best. Add the apples, Grand Marnier, the ¼ cup sugar, and salt. Bring the apple mixture to a boil, stirring often. Reduce the heat slightly and continue to simmer actively until the apples are very soft and much of the liquid has evaporated, 8 to 10 minutes. Remove from the heat and cool briefly.

3. Whisk the eggs in a large bowl until frothy. Whisk in the cream, flour, vanilla, and the ⅓ cup sugar. Stir the apples, about one-third at a time, into the custard.

4. Put the pie shell on a baking sheet, near the oven, and slowly pour the filling into the shell; smooth the filling with a spoon. Bake the pie, on the sheet, on the center oven rack for 35 to 40 minutes. When the pie is done, the center will be set, not runny, and the pie may puff slightly. The custard isn't likely to brown, so don't wait for that or you may overcook the filling.

5. Transfer the pie to a rack and dust with nutmeg. Eat warm, or cool thoroughly and refrigerate for several hours before slicing. Refrigerate leftovers loosely covered with aluminum foil.

James Beard on Apple Pie

In early America and well up into the nineteenth century, pie was a standard breakfast dish. Since the men of rural families rose early and had an hour or more of outside chores before breakfast, there was time to make such treats. So common has apple pie always been in this country — although it did not originate here — that many old American cookbooks did not bother to give a recipe. It was taken for granted that every housewife had her own favorite.

— James Beard, James Beard's American Cookery

Baked Apple Dumpling Pie

A cross between baked apples and apple dumplings, this pie has as a top crust only, which molds itself around the apples as the pie bakes. I prefer Golden Delicious apples here because they hold their shape well. They're halved and baked in a pool of melted butter, brown sugar, and raspberry preserves, with a raisin-sugar-nut mixture stuffed in the hollowed cores. Excellent on its own, but even better with chilled Vanilla Custard Sauce (page 446).

Makes 7 servings

Single-Crust Food Processor Pie Dough (page 58) or another single-crust dough

FILLING

- ½ **cup raisins**
- ½ **cup walnut pieces**
- ½ **cup packed light brown sugar**
- ¼ **teaspoon ground cinnamon**
- 3 **tablespoons unsalted butter**
- 3 **tablespoons raspberry preserves**
- 4 **large Golden Delicious apples, cored**
- **Milk or half-and-half, for glaze**
- **Granulated sugar, for sprinkling**

1. Prepare the pie dough and refrigerate it until firm enough to roll, about 1 hour.

2. Combine the raisins, walnuts, ¼ cup of the brown sugar, and the cinnamon in a food processor. Pulse the machine until the mixture is finely ground. Transfer to a small bowl.

3. Melt the butter over medium heat in an ovenproof skillet (cast-iron is perfect) that measures 9 inches across the bottom and 11 to 12 inches across the top. Stir in the preserves and the remaining ¼ cup brown sugar. When the mixture is bubbling evenly over the surface of the skillet, remove from the heat.

4. Do not peel the apples; the peels will help them hold together. Cut the apples in half crosswise, not from top to bottom, so they have a hole in the middle. Place the apple halves in the skillet, cut side down. You should be able to get 6 around the outside and 1 in the center. Finely dice the remaining apple half and scatter the pieces between the apples. Preheat the oven to 400°F (200°C).

5. Spoon some of the raisin-walnut mixture into the hole of each apple half, pressing it in with a finger. Sprinkle any leftover mixture between the apples.

6. Roll the dough into a 12-inch circle and drape it over the apples. Tuck the edge of the pastry down along the inside of the pan. Poke several holes in the dough with a paring knife or large fork. Lightly brush the pie with milk and sprinkle with granulated sugar.

7. Bake the pie on the center oven rack for 20 minutes. Reduce the heat to 375°F (190°C) and bake for another 25 minutes, until the top crust is golden brown.

8. Transfer the pie to a rack and cool for at least 20 minutes before serving. Cover and refrigerate leftovers.

Paper Bag Apple Pie

Remember the last time you jumped out of bed and said to yourself, "Now this is a great day to bake an apple pie in a paper bag!"? I didn't think so. But that doesn't mean it's not a really cool idea (this coming from a fellow who never gets behind an idea just because it's novel). I was skeptical at first; I thought the bag might catch fire, especially at the relatively high recommended heat. But it won't if you follow the directions. The bag keeps all the mess off the baking sheet, like parchment paper, but this method seems more fun. Make this pie when you have company, so you have someone to impress.

Makes 8 servings

Old-Fashioned Shortening Pie Dough (page 62) or another single-crust dough

FILLING

7-8 **cups peeled, cored, and sliced apples**

½ **cup packed light brown sugar**

2 **tablespoons granulated sugar**

2 **tablespoons cornstarch**

1 **teaspoon ground cinnamon**

¼ **teaspoon ground nutmeg**

⅛ **teaspoon salt**

1½ **tablespoons lemon juice**

½ **cup dark raisins**

Melted Butter Crumb Topping (page 449)

1. Prepare and refrigerate the pie dough. Roll the dough into a 13-inch circle and line a 9- to 9½-inch deep-dish pie pan with it, shaping the edge into an upstanding ridge. Flute or crimp the edge, then refrigerate the shell until needed.

2. Position one of the oven racks in the second-to-lowest position. Remove any other racks above that one. Preheat the oven to 425°F (220°C). Set out a brown paper grocery bag and a large baking sheet.

3. Mix the apples and brown sugar in a large bowl. Let stand for 10 minutes. Mix the granulated sugar, cornstarch, cinnamon, nutmeg, and salt in a small bowl; stir into the fruit along with the lemon juice and raisins.

4. Turn the filling into the pie shell, mounding it toward the center. Spread a generous layer of topping over the filling; you may not need all of it. Pack the topping down gently.

5. Put the pie in the brown paper bag, fold over the end and tuck it under the pie. (You may need to staple a smaller bag.) Put the pie and bag on the baking sheet and place in the oven. Make sure the bag isn't touching the oven walls, a heating element, or any other part of the oven.

6. Bake for 1 hour to 1 hour 20 minutes. To check the pie, open the bag carefully; the interior will be hot, so use oven mitts, and don't put your face right near the opening or the steam will burn you. If you see plenty of thick apple juice bubbling up around the pie, and perhaps some juice that spilled over and into the bag, the pie is done. If not, close the bag and bake for 15 to 20 minutes longer. To cool the pie, place the baking sheet, bag, and pie on a rack. Cut away most of the bag to ventilate the pie. Serve warm or at room temperature. Cover and refrigerate leftovers after 24 hours.

Recipe continues on next page

Paper Bag Apple Pie *continued*

Recipe for Success

Because the filling in this pie is likely to spill over and make a mess under and around the pie pan, I typically use a disposable aluminum pie pan when I make it. You can use any pan you like, but just know that it will probably need some soaking and a good cleaning.

Love Apple Pie

The story goes that sometime in the mid-1970s, the Heinz test kitchen developed a recipe for Love Apple Pie, "love apple" being another name for the tomato. The idea didn't exactly take off, but Heinz reintroduced the recipe in the 1990s, hoping it would catch on with a new generation of pie makers. Maybe it's time: the pie is actually quite good. It has a certain spicy sweetness, but the ketchup itself is virtually undetectable. I added brown sugar to the original recipe and found the pie more to my taste.

Makes 8–10 servings

Old-Fashioned Shortening Pie Dough (page 66) or another single-crust dough

FILLING

- ⅓ cup ketchup
- 2 teaspoons lemon juice
- 6 cups peeled, cored, and sliced tart apples
- ⅓ cup granulated sugar
- 2 tablespoons packed light brown sugar
- Traditional German Streusel (page 450) or other crumb topping

1. Prepare and refrigerate the pie dough. Roll the dough into a 12½- to 13-inch circle and line a 9- to 9½-inch deep-dish pie pan with it, shaping the edge into an upstanding ridge. Flute or crimp the edge, then refrigerate the shell until needed.

2. Adjust the oven racks so one is in the lower position and another is in the middle of the oven. Preheat the oven to 400°F (200°C). Line a baking sheet with parchment paper.

3. Combine the ketchup and lemon juice in a large bowl. Add the apples and sugars, and stir well. Turn the filling into the pie shell, smoothing over the fruit. Put the pie on the prepared baking sheet and cover with a generous layer of the streusel; you may not need all of it.

4. Bake the pie, on the sheet, on the lower oven rack for 25 minutes. Reduce the heat to 375°F (190°C) and move the pie up to the middle rack, rotating it 180 degrees. Bake for 25 to 35 minutes longer, until the pie is juicy.

5. Transfer the pie to a rack and cool. Serve slightly warm or at room temperature. Cover and refrigerate leftovers after 24 hours.

Recipe for Success

Good as this is, I wouldn't reveal the secret ingredient until dessert is over. You'll run into less resistance that way.

Note that in keeping with the original recipe, there is no thickener added to the filling. Use a few teaspoons flour or cornstarch, if you like.

Downsized Apple Pie

Over the last few years I've started making a lot of smaller pies, both individual ones and the 7- and 8-inch size. Especially when you bake them in disposable aluminum pie pans, they're the perfect size for gifting because, frankly, a 9-inch pie is more than many people need. I make this classic favorite in a standard (not deep-dish) aluminum pan that measures 8 inches from outside rim to outside rim. It holds roughly half the amount of filling of a typical apple pie, and yields six pretty decent-size pieces.

Makes 6 servings

Flaky Cream Cheese Pie Dough, double-crust version (page 72)

FILLING

- 4 **cups peeled, cored, and diced apples**
- ½ **cup packed light brown sugar**
- 4 **teaspoons cornstarch**
- 1 **tablespoon granulated sugar, plus a little for sprinkling**
- ¼ **teaspoon ground cinnamon**
- **Pinch of salt**
- 1 **tablespoon lemon juice**
- 1 **teaspoon finely grated lemon zest**
- ¼ **teaspoon vanilla extract (optional)**
- **Milk, for glaze**

1. Prepare and refrigerate the pie dough. This is typically a single-crust batch of dough, but since we're making a smaller pie, there's enough dough for a double-crust pie. So before you make the disks, divide the dough in two, making one portion — for the bottom crust — slightly larger than the other. Once it has chilled, roll the larger portion of dough into an 11-inch circle and line an 8-inch standard pie pan with it, letting the excess dough drape over the edge. Refrigerate the shell until needed.

2. Adjust the oven racks so one is in the lower position and another is in the middle of the oven. Preheat the oven to 400°F (200°C). Line a baking sheet with parchment paper.

3. Mix the apples and brown sugar in a large bowl. Let stand for 10 minutes. Mix the cornstarch, granulated sugar, cinnamon, and salt in a small bowl; stir into the apples. Add the lemon juice, zest, and vanilla, if using, and mix again.

4. Roll the other dough portion into a 9- to 9½-inch circle. Turn the filling into the pie shell and smooth it out to even the top. Lightly moisten the rim of the pie shell with water. Drape the top pastry over the filling, pressing along the edge to seal. Trim the overhang with scissors, if necessary, leaving an even ½ inch all around, then sculpt the edge into an upstanding ridge. Flute or crimp the edge, as desired. (Alternatively, trim the dough flush with the edge of the pan, then crimp with a fork.) Poke several steam vents in the top of the pie with a large fork or paring knife. Put a couple of the vents near the edge so you can check the juices. Lightly brush the pie with milk and sprinkle with granulated sugar.

Recipe for Success

When you're making a scaled-down fruit pie like this one, cut the apples (pears, peaches, whatever) into smallish dice of about ½ inch. Small pieces pack tighter than big ones, and you'll be able to get more fruit filling into your pies.

5. Put the pie on the prepared baking sheet and bake on the lower rack for 25 minutes. Reduce the heat to 375°F (190°C) and move the pie up to the middle rack, rotating the pie 180 degrees. Bake for 25 to 30 minutes longer, until the crust is a rich golden brown and you can see thick juices bubbling up through the vents.

6. Transfer the pie to a rack and cool for at least 1½ to 2 hours before slicing. Cover and refrigerate leftovers after 24 hours.

Apple and Gingered Pear Crostata

I love making crostatas, the Italian version of pie. While the two have much in common, a crostata is often baked open face or with a lattice top. And the pastry — which typically includes an egg or egg yolk and sometimes baking powder — is a bit more delicate and tender than most flaky pie dough. This is my favorite fall crostata, made with apples and pears and topped with streusel. I love it for breakfast with my coffee. If you like this one, try the jelly version on page 181.

Makes 6–8 servings

Crostata Dough (page 80)

FILLING

2 **large apples, peeled, cored, and diced**

2 **large pears, peeled, cored, and diced**

2 **teaspoons lemon juice**

⅓ **cup sugar**

1½ **tablespoons cornstarch**

¼ **teaspoon ground cinnamon or cardamom**

8 **ounces ginger preserves**

Traditional German Streusel (page 450) or another crumb topping

1. Prepare the pie dough and refrigerate it for at least 1 hour.

2. Preheat the oven to 400°F (220°C). Combine the apples, pears, and lemon juice in a large bowl. Mix the sugar, cornstarch, and cinnamon in a small bowl, but don't add it to the fruit yet.

3. The best way to assemble this is to roll the dough onto a large sheet of parchment paper, assemble the pie, then lift the crostata onto a large rimmed baking sheet with the paper. Alternatively, roll the dough onto a piece of floured wax paper, invert it onto the baking sheet, peel off the paper, then assemble the pie on the baking sheet. Either way, roll the dough into large oval approximately ⅛ inch thick.

4. Stir the preserves briskly to loosen them, then dot them on the surface of the dough, leaving a good 2½-inch border of uncovered dough all around. Spread the preserves with the back of a spoon.

Stir the sugar-cornstarch mixture into the fruit. Spoon the fruit evenly over the preserves. Using a spatula to help lift the dough, fold the pastry border over the fruit; the dough will self-pleat, leaving uncovered filling in the center. Spread a generous layer of the streusel over the fruit; you won't need all of it.

5. Put the baking sheet on the center oven rack and bake for 15 minutes. Reduce the heat to 375°F (190°C). Bake for 30 to 40 minutes longer, rotating the sheet 180 degrees midway through this baking time, until the crostata is golden brown and bubbly. Cover the crostata with aluminum foil if the topping starts to get too dark.

6. Transfer the crostata to a rack and cool for at least 20 minutes before serving. Cover and refrigerate leftovers after 24 hours.

The Original Ritz Mock Apple Pie

The original mock apple pie made with Ritz crackers is still the gold standard of the mock cracker pie genre and by far Nabisco's most requested recipe. But does it taste anything like apple pie? I was more than skeptical — how could wet crackers double as apples? — but ended up a believer. Even my wife guessed "apples" when I gave her a bite of this. It tastes most appley while it's still warm, so serve it thus, with a scoop of vanilla ice cream.

Makes 8–10 servings

Old-Fashioned Shortening Pie Dough, double-crust version (page 62) or another single-crust dough

FILLING

- 36 **Ritz crackers, coarsely broken (scant 2 cups)**
- 1¾ **cups water**
- 2 **cups sugar**
- 2 **teaspoons cream of tartar**
- 2 **tablespoons lemon juice**
  - **Grated zest of 1 lemon**
- 2 **tablespoons cold unsalted butter or margarine, cut into small pieces**
- ½ **teaspoon ground cinnamon**
  - **Vanilla ice cream, for serving**

1. Prepare and refrigerate the pie dough. Roll the larger dough portion into a 12-inch circle and line a 9- to 9½-inch standard pie pan with it, letting the excess dough drape over the edge. Scatter the cracker pieces evenly in the shell. Refrigerate the shell until needed.

2. Preheat the oven to 375°F (190°C). Bring the water, sugar, and cream of tartar to a boil in a medium saucepan over high heat. Reduce the heat to medium and simmer for 15 minutes. Remove from the heat and stir in the lemon juice and lemon zest. Cool.

3. Slowly pour the cooled syrup over the cracker crumbs in the pie shell. Dot the filling with the butter and sprinkle with the cinnamon. Roll the other dough portion into an 11-inch circle. Lightly moisten the rim of the pie shell. Drape the pastry over the filling, pressing along the edges to seal. Using the back of a butter knife or paring knife, trim the pastry flush with the edge of the pan. Make several steam vents in the top of the pie with the tip of a paring knife.

4. Place the pie on the middle oven rack and bake for 35 to 45 minutes, until the top crust is golden brown.

5. Transfer the pie to a rack and cool. Serve slightly warm with scoops of vanilla ice cream. Refrigerate leftovers.

8
The Other Fall Classics:
PEAR, PUMPKIN, CRANBERRY, AND MORE

To a lot of people, fall conjures up two kinds of pies: apple and pumpkin. That's a good start. But limiting your fall pie making to apple and pumpkin is like narrowing your choices to vanilla and chocolate at the ice cream parlor. There's a whole lot more going on here, and pie makers neglect the rich possibilities at their peril.

Pear pies are near the top of my list of favorite fall fruit pies; I like them as much as apple. Ripe pears tend to be very juicy, always an asset to fruit pies. And they have a soft, buttery flesh that makes for a meltingly tender slice of pie. I find their aroma intoxicating, and they're a team player: they go nicely with cranberries, among others.

An all-cranberry pie is a real treat, but more typically I use cranberries as an accent in a pie, not as the prevailing theme. Used judiciously, cranberries will not steal the show but instead will highlight the flavors of other fruit. They add tartness that's often lacking in other fruit and a splash of color that fits right in with the season.

Pumpkin and sweet potato pies are the other fall classics. Perhaps more so than any other pies in this collection, these have had to pass the most rigid scrutiny: having tasted too many blah versions of both, I have pretty high standards in this category. You can rest assured that the pumpkin and sweet potato pies in the following chapter are rich, exotic, or otherwise jazzed up to capture my fancy.

So take a minute to thumb through this section and see what looks good. Once you've baked a few of these pies, I doubt that you'll ever again think of fall pie baking as just apple and pumpkin.

All-Pear Pie *with* Maple and Candied Ginger

Pears have always been one of my favorite fruits. When I was a kid, my mom would open up several cans of pears for dessert for me and my six siblings, and I'd be in gourmet heaven. I still love pear desserts, especially this double-crust pie featuring pure maple syrup and candied ginger. As with the canned pears of my youth, I can't get enough of it. Make this in fall, when pears are juicy and abundant. I don't usually bother to peel pears because the skins of most varieties are very soft.

Makes 8–10 servings

Double-Crust Food Processor Pie Dough (page 60) or another double-crust dough

FILLING

- 7 **cups cored and sliced ripe pears, unpeeled**
- ⅓ **cup sugar, plus a little for sprinkling**
- ¼ **cup maple syrup**
- 2½ **tablespoons quick-cooking tapioca or cornstarch**
- ½ **teaspoon vanilla extract**
- 1½ **tablespoons lemon juice**

Finely grated zest of 1 lemon (optional)

- 1 **tablespoon minced crystallized ginger or ½ teaspoon ground ginger**
- 2 **tablespoons cold unsalted butter, cut into small pieces**

Milk, for glaze

1. Prepare and refrigerate the pie dough. Roll the larger dough portion into a 12½- to 13-inch circle and line a 9- to 9½-inch deep-dish pie pan with it, letting the excess dough drape over the edge. Refrigerate the shell until needed.

2. Adjust the oven racks so one is in the lower position and another is in the middle of the oven. Preheat the oven to 400°F (200°C). Line a baking sheet with parchment paper.

3. Combine the pears, sugar, maple syrup, tapioca, vanilla, lemon juice, lemon zest (if using), and ginger in a large bowl. Mix well. Let stand for 10 minutes.

4. Roll the other dough portion into an 11-inch circle. Turn the filling into the pie shell and smooth it out to even the top. Dot with butter. Lightly moisten the rim of the pie shell. Drape the top pastry over the filling, pressing along the edge to seal. Trim the overhang with scissors, leaving an even ½ to ¾ inch all around, then sculpt the edge into an upstanding ridge. Flute or crimp the edge, as desired. Poke several steam vents in the top of the pie with a large fork or paring knife. Put a couple of the vents near the edge so you can check the juices. Brush the top of the pie with milk and sprinkle with sugar.

5. Set the pie on the prepared baking sheet and bake on the lower oven rack for 30 minutes. Reduce the temperature to 375°F (190°C) and move the pie up to the middle rack, rotating it 180 degrees. Bake for 30 to 40 minutes longer, until the juices bubble thickly at the vents.

6. Transfer the pie to a rack and cool for at least 1½ to 2 hours before serving. Cover and refrigerate leftovers after 24 hours.

Pears for Your Pies

Provided they're fresh, juicy, and ripe, nearly all pears are excellent in pies. But their ripeness is sometimes difficult to judge, especially with the variety of skin colors available. Like peaches, pears are ripe when they yield to medium finger pressure. Keep in mind that pears do not ripen well on trees. They're harvested mature but unripe — which is often how you'll find them in the market — and must be ripened after harvest. When you get them home, place them in a paper bag and ripen them right on the counter. Check daily to see how they're progressing. Store ripe pears in the fridge for 2 to 3 days. Here are some varieties you'll want to try.

- **Bosc.** A highly aromatic pear with dense flesh; it makes for great pies.

- **Comice.** This is perhaps the sweetest, juiciest variety.

- **Red Bartlett.** This excellent pie pear is very sweet and juicy. The skin is bright red when fully ripe.

- **Yellow Bartlett.** It has the same flavor, texture, and qualities as the Red Bartlett, but ripens to bright yellow.

Pear Pie *with* Crumb Topping

I'm a big fan of pear pies, as you might have guessed from the number of them scattered throughout this collection. This one is topped with a crunchy melted butter crumb topping. Any good, juicy pear will do here. The pear brandy plays up that luscious pear flavor, but you can skip it.

Makes 8–10 servings

Whole-Wheat Pie Dough (page 66) or another single-crust dough

FILLING

5½ cups peeled, cored, and sliced ripe pears

½ cup sugar

2 tablespoons cornstarch

1 tablespoon lemon juice

2 tablespoons pear brandy (optional)

¼ teaspoon ground cinnamon

Pinch of ground nutmeg

Pinch of salt

Melted Butter Crumb Topping (page 449)

1. Prepare and refrigerate the pie dough. Roll the dough into a 12-inch circle and line a 9- to 9½-inch standard pie pan with it, shaping the edge into an upstanding ridge. Flute or crimp the edge, then refrigerate the shell until needed.

2. Adjust the oven racks so one is in the lower position and another is in the middle of the oven. Preheat the oven to 400°F (200°C). Line a baking sheet with parchment paper.

3. Place the pears in a large bowl. Mix the sugar and cornstarch together in a small bowl; stir into the fruit. Stir in the lemon juice, brandy to taste (if using), cinnamon, nutmeg, and salt.

4. Turn the filling into the pie shell, smoothing the top to even out the fruit. Put the pie on the prepared baking sheet and cover with a generous layer of the crumb topping; you may not need all of it. Press the crumbs down gently.

5. Bake the pie, on the sheet, on the lower oven rack for 30 minutes. Reduce the heat to 375°F (190°C) and move the pie up to the middle rack, rotating it 180 degrees. Bake for 30 to 35 minutes longer, until the top of the pie is golden brown and the juices bubble thickly around the edge of the pie and through the topping. Cover the pie with loosely tented aluminum foil during the last 15 minutes. If the topping starts to get too dark, cover the pie with aluminum foil.

6. Transfer the pie to a rack and cool for at least 1½ to 2 hours before serving. Cover and refrigerate leftovers after 24 hours.

Pear Pie *with* Almond Coffeecake Topping

Makes 8–10 servings

Almond Pie Dough (page 81) or Single-Crust Food Processor Pie Dough (page 58)

FILLING

5½ cups peeled, cored, and thinly sliced ripe pears

⅓ cup plus 2 tablespoons sugar

1 tablespoon lemon juice

1 teaspoon finely grated lemon zest

1½ tablespoons cornstarch

Big pinch of ground nutmeg or cardamom

ALMOND TOPPING

1 cup whole almonds, toasted (page 453) and coarsely chopped by hand

⅓ cup sugar

3 tablespoons all-purpose flour

¼ cup flaked sweetened coconut

1 teaspoon baking powder

¼ teaspoon salt

4 tablespoons unsalted butter, at room temperature but not soft, cut into ¼-inch pieces

1 large egg

½ teaspoon vanilla extract

¼ teaspoon almond extract (optional)

One of my favorite pies of all time, this has a layer of soft pears topped with a sort of buttery almond cake. It's no more difficult to make than a crumb-topped pie, since the almond topping is mixed right in the food processor. It's not your everyday pie, so it's a good one for company. It's delicious served with vanilla, butter pecan, or coffee ice cream.

1. Prepare and refrigerate the pie dough. Roll the dough into a 12½- to 13-inch circle and line a 9- to 9½-inch deep-dish pie pan with it, shaping the edge into an upstanding ridge. Flute or crimp the edge, then refrigerate the shell until needed.

2. Preheat the oven to 375°F (190°C). Line a baking sheet with parchment paper.

3. To make the filling, combine the pears, the ⅓ cup sugar, lemon juice, and lemon zest in a large bowl. Mix well. Let stand for 5 to 10 minutes. Mix the 2 tablespoons sugar, cornstarch, and nutmeg in a small bowl; stir into the fruit.

4. Turn the filling into the pie shell. Put the pie on the prepared baking sheet and bake on the center oven rack for 40 minutes.

5. As it bakes, prepare the almond topping: put the almonds, sugar, flour, coconut, baking powder, and salt in a food processor. Pulse the machine until the nuts are finely ground. Scatter the butter over the mixture. Pulse until the butter is well incorporated and the mixture is crumbly. Whisk the egg, vanilla, and almond extract (if using) together in a small bowl. Add to the processor and pulse again, just until the mixture starts to gather around the blade. Scrape the mixture into a bowl.

6. Remove the pie from the oven. Using a soup spoon, dollop the topping here and there over the fruit. Don't worry if it looks lumpy because it will settle as it bakes. Return the pie to the oven, rotating it 180 degrees. Bake for 22 to 25 minutes, until the top of the pie is golden brown and any juices bubble thickly.

7. Transfer the pie to a rack and cool for at least 1½ hours before serving. It's best served barely warm or at room temperature.

Recipe for Success

Typically I don't peel pears because their skins are so soft. But I recommend it here because this pie is a little more sophisticated than some, and I prefer the refined look of no skins.

If you plan to serve this pie for a party, make it the same day to preserve the wonderful texture of the cakelike almond topping, You want it to be a little on the dry side, and the longer it sits, the more moisture it will take on from below.

Warm Jalapeño-Pear Pie

Pears can take the heat, that's why you often see them teamed up with black pepper. My own forays into pear-pepper partnering led to this spicy pie, sweetened with jalapeño jelly and warmed even more with a little five-spice powder. The spices and jelly envelop the pears, leaving a subtly exotic aftertaste. If you like this one, there's a version with apples, too (see opposite page).

Makes 8–10 servings

Shortening and Butter Dough with Egg (page 63) or another double-crust dough

FILLING

5 **cups peeled, cored, and sliced ripe pears**

½ **cup jalapeño jelly**

2 **tablespoons unsalted butter**

¼ **cup sugar, plus a little for sprinkling**

2 **tablespoons cornstarch**

½ **teaspoon five-spice powder**

Big pinch of salt

Milk, for glaze

Vanilla or butter pecan ice cream, for serving (optional)

1. Prepare and refrigerate the pie dough. Roll the larger dough portion into a 12½-inch to 13-inch circle and line a 9- to 9½-inch deep-dish pie pan with it, letting the excess dough drape over the edge. Refrigerate the shell until needed.

2. Adjust the oven racks so one is in the lower position and another is in the middle of the oven. Preheat the oven to 400°F (200°C). Line a baking sheet with parchment paper.

3. Put the pears in a large bowl. Combine the jelly and butter in a small saucepan over medium heat (or in a heatproof bowl in the microwave). When the butter melts, whisk to smooth, then pour the mixture over the pears; stir. Mix the sugar, cornstarch, five-spice powder, and salt in a small bowl; stir into the fruit.

4. Roll the other dough portion into an 11-inch circle. Turn the filling into the pie shell and smooth it over to even out the fruit. Lightly moisten the rim of the pie shell. Drape the top pastry over the filling, pressing along the edge to seal. Trim the overhang with scissors, leaving an even ½ to ¾ inch all around, then sculpt the edge into an upstanding ridge. Flute or crimp the edge, as desired. Poke several steam vents in the top of the pie with a large fork or paring knife. Put a couple of them near the edge so you can check the juices. Brush the pie with milk and sprinkle with sugar.

5. Put the pie on the prepared baking sheet and bake on the lower rack for 30 minutes. Reduce the temperature to 375°F (190°C) and move the pie up to the middle rack, rotating it 180 degrees. Bake for 30 to 35 minutes longer, until the juices bubble thickly at the vents.

6. Transfer the pie to a rack and cool for at least 1½ to 2 hours before serving, topped with ice cream, if desired. Cover and refrigerate leftovers after 24 hours.

Five-Spice Apple-Pear Pie

Come winter, I love to make poached pears flavored with star anise, a flavor scheme I thought would adapt nicely to a pie. Anise is one of the more exotic spices in five-spice powder, and it stands out, giving this mixed-fruit pie a heady fragrance and warming flavor. I have made the same pie with a top crust, but I prefer the slight crunch of the cornmeal streusel.

Makes 8–10 servings

Whole-Wheat Pie Dough (page 66) or another single-crust dough

FILLING

3½ cups peeled, cored, and sliced apples

3½ cups cored and sliced ripe pears, peeled or unpeeled

Finely grated zest of 1 lemon

1 tablespoon lemon juice

2 tablespoons orange juice

¾ cup sugar

2 tablespoons cornstarch

2 teaspoons five-spice powder

Cornmeal Streusel (page 450)

1. Prepare and refrigerate the pie dough. Roll the dough into a 12½- to 13-inch circle and line a 9- to 9½-inch deep-dish pie pan with it, shaping the edge into an upstanding ridge. Flute or crimp the edge, then refrigerate the shell until needed.

2. Adjust the oven racks so one is in the lower position and another is in the middle of the oven. Preheat the oven to 400°F (200°C). Line a baking sheet with parchment paper.

3. Combine the apples, pears, lemon zest, lemon juice, orange juice, and ½ cup of the sugar in a large bowl. Mix well. Let stand for 5 to 10 minutes. Mix together the cornstarch, five-spice powder, and the remaining ¼ cup sugar in a small bowl; stir into the fruit. Turn the filling into the pie shell and smooth it over to even it out the fruit.

4. Put the pie on the prepared baking sheet and cover with a generous layer of the streusel; you may not need all of it. Gently tamp down the streusel.

5. Bake the pie, on the sheet, on the lower oven rack for 30 minutes. Reduce the heat to 375°F (190°C) and move the pie up to the middle rack, rotating it 180 degrees. Bake for 30 to 40 minutes longer, until the top of the pie is golden brown and the juices bubble thickly around the edge. If the top of the pie starts to get too dark, cover it with aluminum foil.

6. Transfer the pie to a rack and cool for at least 1½ to 2 hours before serving. Cover and refrigerate leftovers after 24 hours.

Recipe for Success

If you can't find five-spice powder, you can mix together roughly 1 teaspoon ground cinnamon, ¾ teaspoon ground anise seed, ½ teaspoon ground fennel seed, and ¼ teaspoon each ground cloves and ground white pepper.

Pear-Raspberry Lattice-Top Pie

My favorite pies for lattice tops are the ones with red fillings, like this one. Here you mix juicy sliced pears with fresh or frozen raspberries, which give the filling a deep, rosy blush. I've always loved the soft texture of pear fillings, and it's one of the things I like most about this pie.

Makes 8–10 servings

Double-Crust Food Processor Pie Dough (page 60) or another double-crust dough

FILLING

- 5 **cups cored and sliced ripe pears, peeled or unpeeled**
- 2 **cups raspberries, fresh or frozen and partially thawed**
- ⅔ **cup plus 2 tablespoons sugar, plus a little for sprinkling**
- 1 **tablespoon lemon juice**
- 1 **teaspoon finely grated lemon zest**
- ¼ **teaspoon ground cardamom or ginger**
- 2½ **tablespoons cornstarch**
- 2 **tablespoons cold unsalted butter, cut into small pieces**
- **Milk, for glaze**

1. Prepare and refrigerate the pie dough, but instead of making both portions round, shape one — the smaller portion — into a rectangle. (It will be easier to cut into lattice strips later.) Roll the larger dough portion into a 12½- to 13-circle and line a 9- to 9½-inch deep-dish pie pan with it, letting the excess dough drape over the edge. Place in the refrigerator for 10 to 15 minutes.

2. Adjust the oven racks so one is in the lower position and another is in the middle of the oven. Preheat the oven to 400°F (200°C). Line a baking sheet with parchment paper.

3. Combine the pears, raspberries, the ⅔ cup sugar, lemon juice, lemon zest, and cardamom in a large bowl. Mix well. Let stand for 5 to 10 minutes. Mix the 2 tablespoons sugar and cornstarch together in a small bowl; stir into the fruit.

4. Roll the other dough portion and cut the lattice strips as described on page 46. Have them standing by.

5. Turn the filling into the pie shell. Smooth over the fruit so that no pear slices jut up that could cut the lattice. Dot the top of the filling with bits of the butter. Weave the strips into a lattice top as described on page 47. Lightly brush the pastry strips with milk and sprinkle with sugar.

6. Set the pie on the prepared baking sheet and bake for 30 minutes. Reduce the temperature to 375°F (190°C) and move the pie up to the middle rack, rotating it 180 degrees. Bake for 25 to 35 minutes longer, until the juices bubble thickly at the vents.

7. Transfer the pie to a rack and cool for at least 1½ to 2 hours before serving. Cover and refrigerate leftovers after 24 hours.

Recipe for Success

If you're unfamiliar with cardamom, pick up a jar at the market. It tastes especially good with baked-pear goods. Don't overdo it, though; a little goes a long way. Blackberries are excellent in place of the raspberries.

Pear-Fig Pie *with* Hazelnut Crumb Topping

This is one of those pies that adds up to way more than the sum of its parts. Fresh figs can be difficult to find, so I use dried. I poach them in pear juice to add flavor and juiciness, then reduce the juice to sweeten the pie. The figs are mixed with ripe pear slices and baked with a toasted hazelnut topping. These flavors were made for one another.

Makes 8–10 servings

Perfect Pie Dough by Hand (page 56)

FILLING

2 cups stemmed dried Black Mission figs

About 2 cups pear juice

4 large ripe pears, peeled, cored, and sliced

⅓ cup plus 3 tablespoons sugar

2½ tablespoons cornstarch

1 tablespoon lemon juice

Finely grated zest of 1 orange

Melted Butter Crumb Topping (page 449) made with hazelnuts

1. Prepare and refrigerate the pie dough. Roll the dough into a 12½- to 13-inch circle and line a 9- to 9½-inch deep-dish pie pan with it, shaping the edge into an upstanding ridge. Flute or crimp the edge, then refrigerate the shell until needed.

2. Halve the figs or cut them into quarters if they're very large. Place them in a medium nonreactive saucepan and add enough pear juice to cover by about ½ inch. Bring to a boil, then lower the heat. Cover and gently simmer for 30 minutes. Remove from the heat.

3. Adjust the oven racks so one is in the lower position and another is in the middle of the oven. Preheat the oven to 400°F (200°C). Line a baking sheet with parchment paper.

4. Using a slotted spoon, transfer the figs to a large bowl. Put the poaching liquid back on the heat and boil any remaining liquid until it becomes thick and syrupy. You should have about ⅓ cup. Add to the figs and mix well. Add the pears and the ⅓ cup sugar, and toss well. Mix the 3 tablespoons sugar and cornstarch in a small bowl; stir into the fruit and mix again. Stir in the lemon juice and orange zest.

5. Turn the filling into the pie shell and smooth the top to even out the fruit. Set the pie on the prepared baking sheet and cover with a generous layer of the topping; you may not need all of it. Tamp down gently on the topping.

6. Bake the pie, on the sheet, on the lower oven rack for 30 minutes. Reduce the heat to 375°F (190°C) and move the pie up to the middle rack, rotating it 180 degrees. Bake for 30 to 35 minutes longer, until the juices bubble thickly around the edge and through the topping. If the top of the pie starts to get too dark, cover it with aluminum foil.

7. Transfer the pie to a rack and cool for at least 1½ to 2 hours before serving. Cover and refrigerate leftovers after 24 hours.

Recipe for Success

When I bake a pie like this that involves an extra step or two, like poaching the figs, I'll do that step beforehand. Here, for instance, the figs can be poached up to 2 days ahead and refrigerated. Bring them to room temperature the day you make the pie.

Very Cranberry Pear Pie

Cranberries are one of the most underused pie fruits, perhaps because they're so tart. But that tartness is easily balanced with the right amount of sugar, turning the tang into a real asset in this scrumptious, brightly colored pie. This is a superb holiday season pie.

Makes 8–10 servings

Buttermilk Pie Dough (page 67) or another single-crust dough

FILLING

3 **cups fresh or frozen cranberries**

½ **cup plus 2 tablespoons sugar**

2 **large unpeeled ripe pears, cored and coarsely chopped**

1 **tablespoon lemon juice**

Finely grated zest of 1 orange

1½ **tablespoons cornstarch**

¼ **teaspoon ground cinnamon**

¼ **teaspoon ground cardamom**

Melted Butter Crumb Topping (page 449) made with walnuts

1. Prepare and refrigerate the pie dough. Roll the dough into a 12½- to 13-inch circle and line a 9- to 9½-inch deep-dish pie pan with it, shaping the edge into an upstanding ridge. Flute or crimp the edge, then refrigerate the shell until needed.

2. Combine the cranberries and the ½ cup sugar in a food processor. Pulse the machine five or six times, until the cranberries are well chopped. Transfer to a large bowl and mix in the pears, lemon juice, and orange zest. Mix well. Let stand for 10 to 15 minutes.

3. Adjust the oven racks so one is in the lower position and another is in the middle of the oven. Preheat the oven to 400°F (200°C). Line a baking sheet with parchment paper.

4. Mix the 2 tablespoons sugar with the cornstarch, cinnamon, and cardamom in a small bowl; stir into the fruit. Turn the filling into the pie shell and smooth the top. Set the pie on the prepared baking sheet and cover with a generous layer of the topping; you may not need all of it. Tamp the topping down gently.

5. Bake the pie, on the sheet, on the lower oven rack for 30 minutes. Reduce the heat to 375°F (190°C) and move the pie up to the middle rack, rotating it 180 degrees. Bake for 30 to 35 minutes longer, until the top of the pie is golden brown and the juices bubble thickly around the edge and through the topping. If the pie starts to get too dark, cover it with aluminum foil.

6. Transfer the pie to a rack and cool for at least 1½ to 2 hours before serving. Cover and refrigerate leftovers after 24 hours.

Recipe for Success

If you like cranberry pies, buy a case of cranberries in the fall when they're on sale and freeze them. That way, you can make this and other cranberry pies throughout the year. If that's too many bags, split the cache with a pie-baking friend.

Cranberry-Cherry Peekaboo Pie

Here's a fun way to make a see-through pie by cutting a series of holes in the top crust. You'll need a small round cutter 1 to 1¼ inches in diameter. The holes make neat little windows for showing off the pretty red filling and give the pie an old-fashioned folk art vibe. Did I mention that this pie tastes as great as it looks? If holes aren't your thing, leave 'em out.

Makes 8–10 servings

Flaky Cream Cheese Pie Dough, double-crust version (page 72) or another double-crust dough

FILLING

- 3 **cups fresh or frozen cranberries**
- 3 **cups pitted sweet cherries, fresh or frozen and partially thawed**
- 1 **cup sugar, plus a little for sprinkling**
- 1 **tablespoon lemon or orange juice**
- **Finely grated zest of 1 orange**
- 2½ **tablespoons cornstarch**
- 1 **egg beaten with 1 tablespoon milk, for glaze**

1. Prepare and refrigerate the pie dough. Roll the larger dough portion into a 12½- to 13-inch circle and line a 9- to 9½-inch deep-dish pie pan with it, letting the excess dough drape over the edge. Refrigerate for at least 10 to 15 minutes.

2. Roll the other dough portion into an 11-inch circle on a sheet of parchment or waxed paper. Slide the paper and dough onto a small baking sheet. Place in the refrigerator for at least for 15 minutes.

3. Combine the cranberries, cherries, ¾ cup of the sugar, lemon juice, and orange zest in a large bowl. Mix well. Let stand for 10 minutes. Mix the cornstarch and the remaining ¼ cup sugar together in a small bowl; stir into the fruit.

4. Adjust the oven racks so one is in the lower position and another is in the middle of the oven. Preheat the oven to 400°F (200°C). Line a baking sheet with parchment paper.

5. Using a round 1- to 1¼- inch cutter, cut holes in the top pastry — randomly or in a pattern — but none of them closer than 1 inch from the edge. Remove the holes and reserve them.

6. Turn the filling into the pie shell and smooth the fruit to even it out. Lightly moisten the rim of the pie shell. Drape the top pastry over the filling, pressing along the edge to seal. Trim the overhang with scissors, leaving an even ½ to ¾ inch all around, then sculpt the edge into an upstanding ridge. Flute or crimp the edge, as desired. Brush the top lightly with the glaze and sprinkle with sugar. Take care not to drag the brush over the exposed fruit, or you'll streak the top pastry.

7. Put the pie on the prepared baking sheet and bake on the lower oven rack for 30 minutes. Reduce the temperature to 375°F (190°C) and move the pie up to the middle rack, rotating it 180 degrees, Bake for 25 to 35 minutes longer, until the top of the pie is golden brown and the juices bubble thickly.

8. Transfer the pie to a rack and cool for at least 1½ to 2 hours before serving. Cover and refrigerate leftovers after 24 hours.

Jellied Cranberry-Pecan Pie

Did you know that you can use *canned* cranberry sauce in pies? It makes a delicious and novel alternative to fresh cranberries. The cranberry sauce gives the filling a jellylike consistency and color; the pecans accentuate the autumn theme and add crunch to boot. Consider this one for your Thanksgiving holiday lineup.

Makes 8–10 servings

Whole-Wheat Pie Dough (page 66), Lard and Butter Pie Dough (page 64), or another double- or single-crust dough

FILLING

- ½ cup packed light brown sugar
- 3 tablespoons all-purpose flour
- ⅛ teaspoon ground cinnamon
- ⅛ teaspoon salt
- 3 large eggs
- 4 tablespoons unsalted butter, melted
- ½ cup light corn syrup
- 2 tablespoons maple syrup or honey
- ½ teaspoon vanilla extract
- 1 teaspoon finely grated lemon zest
- 1 cup pecan halves, toasted (page 453) and chopped by hand
- 1 cup whole-berry cranberry sauce

1. Prepare and refrigerate the pie dough. You can either halve the recipe to make one crust or freeze the second crust for later use. Roll the dough into a 12-inch circle and line a 9- to 9½-inch standard pie pan with it, shaping the edge into an upstanding ridge. Flute or crimp the edge, chill the shell, and partially prebake it according to the instructions on page 36.

2. Preheat the oven to 350°F (180°C). Combine the sugar, flour, cinnamon, and salt in a large bowl. Rub them together well, breaking up any clumps. Add the eggs, one at a time, whisking well after each addition. Whisk in the butter, corn syrup, maple syrup, vanilla, and lemon zest. Stir in the pecans and cranberry sauce until evenly combined.

3. Put the pie shell on a baking sheet, near the oven, and carefully pour the filling into the shell. Bake the pie, on the sheet, on the center oven rack for 40 to 45 minutes, until the filling is set, rotating the pie 180 degrees midway through the baking. When done, the filling should be wobbly, not soupy, in the center. Give the pie a little nudge to check.

4. Transfer the pie to a rack and cool. Serve at room temperature, or refrigerate for several hours before serving. Cover and refrigerate leftovers.

Recipe for Success

Don't measure the cranberry sauce directly from the can because the jellied part tends to settle to the bottom. Empty the entire can into a small bowl, stir well, then measure it.

Libby's Famous Pumpkin Pie

I don't lift recipes off boxes or cans — at least not without proper attribution — but when the recipe is as reliable and famous as this one, I make an exception. There are no real tricks or secrets here, just a straightforward approach to making a very pumpkiny pumpkin pie with a familiar taste and creamy texture. The liquid is evaporated milk, which — because it contains less water than fresh milk — contributes to the smooth texture.

Makes 8–10 servings

Old-Fashioned Shortening Pie Dough (page 62) or another single-crust dough

FILLING

- ¾ **cup sugar**
- ½ **teaspoon salt**
- 1 **teaspoon ground cinnamon**
- ½ **teaspoon ground ginger**
- ¼ **teaspoon ground cloves**
- 2 **large eggs**
- 1 **(15-ounce) can Libby's 100% pure pumpkin**
- 1 **(12-ounce) can Nestlé Carnation evaporated milk**
- **Whipped Cream (page 447) (optional)**

1. Prepare and refrigerate the pie dough. Roll the dough into a 12-inch circle and line a 9- to 9½-inch standard pie pan with it, shaping the edge into an upstanding ridge. Flute or crimp the edge, then refrigerate the shell until needed.

2. Preheat the oven to 425°F (220°C). Combine the sugar, salt, cinnamon, ginger, and cloves in a small bowl. Beat the eggs in a large bowl. Stir in the pumpkin and the sugar-spice mixture. Gradually stir in the evaporated milk. Pour the filling into the pie shell.

3. Place the pie on the center oven rack and bake for 15 minutes. Reduce the oven temperature to 350°F (180°C) and rotate the pie 180 degrees. Bake for 40 to 45 minutes longer, until a knife inserted near the center comes out clean.

4. Transfer the pie to a rack and cool for 2 hours. Serve immediately, or cover with loosely tented aluminum foil and refrigerate before serving. Garnish with whipped cream, if desired.

Recipe for Success

Where Libby's and I part ways is with the crust: I always prebake my pumpkin pie shells, and they don't necessarily recommend it.

Pie for Breakfast

I guess the one reason we eat pie for breakfast is because it's there from last night's supper. I can think of nothing more appealing than serving warm, plump pies laid out for the morning meal — there is something old-fashioned and homey about it. If you have a hard time arousing breakfast appetites, pies are a surefire way to get everyone to clean their plates.

— Marion Cunningham, The Breakfast Book

Maple-Pumpkin Pie

I've always had to work at loving pumpkin pie. I mean, I like it, but to really love it I've had to make special provisions over the years, such as sweetening it with maple syrup. One bite and you'll know I'm onto something here.

Makes 8–10 servings

Single-Crust Food Processor Pie Dough (page 58) or another single-crust dough

FILLING

- 3 **large eggs**
- 1 **cup half-and-half**
- ½ **cup maple syrup**
- 1 **teaspoon vanilla extract**
- ½ **cup packed dark brown sugar**
- 1½ **tablespoons all-purpose flour**
- 1 **teaspoon ground ginger**
- ½ **teaspoon ground cinnamon**
- ¼ **teaspoon ground cloves**
- ¼ **teaspoon ground nutmeg**
- ¾ **teaspoon salt**
- 1 **(15-ounce) can or 1¾ cups fresh pumpkin purée (see opposite page)**

  Whipped Cream (page 447), for garnish

1. Prepare and refrigerate the pie dough. Roll the dough into a 12½- to 13-inch circle and line a 9- to 9½-inch deep-dish pie pan with it, shaping the edge into an upstanding ridge. Flute or crimp the edge, chill the shell, and partially prebake it according to the instructions on page 36.

2. Preheat the oven to 350°F (180°C). Whisk the eggs in a medium bowl until frothy. Whisk in the half-and-half, maple syrup, and vanilla. Combine the sugar, flour, ginger, cinnamon, cloves, nutmeg, and salt in a small bowl. Add to the wet ingredients and whisk to combine. Whisk in the pumpkin.

3. Put the pie shell on a baking sheet, near the oven, and carefully pour the filling into the shell. Bake the pie, on the sheet, on the center oven rack for 25 minutes. Rotate the pie 180 degrees and bake for 25 minutes longer, until the filling is set. When the pie is done, the filling should not be soupy in the center. The perimeter of the pie will have puffed a little and the center section of the pie will have a slight sheen.

4. Transfer the pie to a rack and cool. Serve warm, at room temperature, or chilled, but always garnished with whipped cream.

Recipe for Success

Be sure to look for the subtle sheen differences on the surface of the pie, as described in step 3. If you can get the pie out of the oven while the center still has a shiny surface, it will be perfectly baked.

How to Make Winter Squash or Pumpkin Purée

Whether you need pumpkin purée for a pumpkin pie or winter squash purée for a quick bread or soup, the easiest way to get there is by roasting the item in question. Here's how to do it.

1. Especially if you're starting with homegrown produce, rinse and dry the squash first so you don't bring dirt into your work area.

2. Preheat the oven to 400°F (200°C). Line a large baking sheet with parchment paper or aluminum foil.

3. For pumpkin purée, start with a 4- to 6-pound pie pumpkin, not one of the big carving pumpkins. Break off the stem, if possible. Carefully slice the pumpkin or squash in half lengthwise (the line running from stem end to blossom end). This is where it comes in handy to have a really sharp kitchen knife or cleaver.

4. Scoop out the seeds from both halves; clean off the strings and goop and rinse well, if you want to roast the seeds later. Brush the flesh of the squash with a little olive oil, and salt the flesh lightly.

5. Place the halves on the prepared baking sheet, cut side down, and roast for 50 to 60 minutes. When the squash is done, you'll be able to pierce it with a paring knife and encounter no resistance. It will slide right through. If it's not done, bake for 15 minutes longer.

6. When the squash is done, turn it over on the sheet and let it cool for about 1 hour. Scoop out the flesh with a large spoon, transfer it to a food processor, and process to a smooth purée. Transfer the purée to a sealed container and refrigerate for 2 to 3 days, or freeze for several months.

Ben's Pumpkin Cheesecake Pie

I think the best pumpkin pies taste more like cheesecake than traditional pumpkin pie. Years ago, I started adding cream cheese to recipes I found too dry, and the creamy result was much to my liking. You can bake this in any pastry, but I like the earthiness of the cornmeal crust here; it's a good match for the pumpkin. The recipe is named for my oldest son, Ben, whose taste in pumpkin pie runs close to my own.

Makes 8–10 servings

Cornmeal Pie Dough (page 68)

FILLING

8 ounces cream cheese, softened

½ cup granulated sugar

½ cup packed light brown sugar

2 large eggs plus 1 large egg yolk, at room temperature

½ teaspoon vanilla extract

Finely grated zest of 1 lemon

½ teaspoon ground cinnamon

½ teaspoon ground nutmeg

¼ teaspoon ground ginger

¼ teaspoon salt

1 cup pumpkin purée, canned or fresh (see page 221)

⅔ cup half-and-half

Whipped Cream (page 447), for garnish

1. Prepare and refrigerate the pie dough. Roll the dough into a 12½- to 13-inch circle and line a 9- to 9½-inch deep-dish pie pan with it, shaping the edge into an upstanding ridge. Flute or crimp the edge, chill the shell, and partially prebake it according to the instructions on page 36.

2. Preheat the oven to 350°F (180°C). Using an electric mixer (handheld is fine), cream the cream cheese in a large bowl, gradually beating in the sugars. Blend in the eggs and egg yolk one at a time on medium speed. Blend in the vanilla, lemon zest, cinnamon, nutmeg, ginger, and salt. Add the pumpkin and half-and-half. Blend until smooth and evenly mixed.

3. Put the pie shell on a baking sheet near the oven. Carefully pour the filling into the shell and smooth the top. Bake the pie, on the sheet, on the center oven rack for 20 minutes. Rotate the pie 180 degrees and bake for about 20 minutes longer, until the top has puffed slightly and developed fine cracks around the perimeter. When done, the filling should be wobbly, but not soupy. Give the pie a little nudge to check.

4. Transfer the pie to a rack and cool to room temperature, then refrigerate for at least 4 hours before serving, garnished with whipped cream.

Recipe for Success

A chocolate glaze on top of this pie is a delicious touch. Prepare a batch of Chocolate Ganache (page 445) then let it cool until thickish but still warm and pourable. Drizzle the sauce lavishly over the pie, tilting it to spread the sauce evenly. Refrigerate for at least 30 minutes before serving.

Muirhead Pecan Pumpkin Butter Pie

I don't normally write a recipe around a product that isn't widely available in supermarkets, but I make an exception for Muirhead Pecan Pumpkin Butter. It's essentially puréed pumpkin cooked down to a thick, delicious paste, then combined with finely chopped pecans, sugar, lemon juice, and spices. It's mainly a spread for biscuits, toast, and English muffins, but one taste and you'll know why I love it in this perfectly spiced pie.

Makes 8–10 servings

Oat and Cornmeal Pie Dough (page 69) or another single-crust dough

FILLING

- 3 large eggs, at room temperature
- 1 (13.5-ounce) jar (about 1⅓ cups) Muirhead Pecan Pumpkin Butter
- ½ cup heavy cream
- ¼ cup half-and-half
- 3 tablespoons sugar
- ¼ teaspoon salt
- 1½ cups pecan halves, toasted (page 453) or not, coarsely chopped
- Whipped Cream (page 447), for garnish

1. Prepare and refrigerate the pie dough. Roll the dough into a 12-inch circle and line a 9- to 9½-inch standard pie pan with it, shaping the edge into an upstanding ridge. Flute or crimp the edge, chill the shell, and partially pre-bake it according to the instructions on page 36.

2. Preheat the oven to 350°F (180°C). Whisk the eggs in a large bowl until frothy. Add the pumpkin butter, cream, half-and-half, sugar, and salt; whisk well. Stir in the pecans. Put the pie shell on a baking sheet, near the oven, and carefully pour in the filling. Gently rake a fork through the filling to distribute the nuts evenly.

3. Bake the pie, on the sheet, on the center oven rack for 25 minutes. Rotate the pie 180 degrees and bake for 15 to 20 minutes longer, until the filling is barely set in the center. When done, the edge of the pie will probably puff up very slightly.

4. Transfer the pie to a rack and cool. The pie can be served slightly warm or at room temperature, garnished with whipped cream. Or it can be chilled and served cold.

Recipe for Success

Do not substitute canned pumpkin purée for the pumpkin butter. It just won't do the trick.

Triple-Layer Pumpkin-Chocolate Pie

If you never imagined chocolate and pumpkin as great pie partners, this pie will surprise and delight you. There's a "plain" pumpkin pie layer, a chocolate-pumpkin layer, and sweetened sour cream layer on top. It's the one pie my wife, Bev, must have every fall. You may feel the same once you've tried it.

Makes 8–10 servings

Perfect Pie Dough by Hand (page 56) or another single-crust dough

FILLING

- 2 tablespoons unsalted butter
- 4 ounces semisweet chocolate, coarsely chopped
- 12 ounces full-fat or reduced-fat cream cheese, softened
- 1½ cups sugar
- 2 large eggs, at room temperature
- 1 cup pumpkin purée, canned or fresh (see page 221)
- ½ teaspoon vanilla extract
- ¼ teaspoon ground cinnamon
- ¼ teaspoon ground nutmeg
- ¼ teaspoon ground cloves
- ¼ teaspoon salt
- 1 cup full-fat sour cream

1. Prepare and refrigerate the pie dough. Roll the dough into a 12½- to 13-inch circle and line a 9- to 9½-inch deep-dish pie pan with it, shaping the edge into an upstanding ridge. Flute or crimp the edge, chill the shell, and partially prebake it according to the instructions on page 36.

2. Preheat the oven to 350°F (180°C). Place the butter in the top insert of a double boiler set over, not in, barely simmering water. (Alternatively, use a heatproof bowl, suspended by the sides of a saucepan, over barely simmering water.) When the butter is partially melted, add the chocolate. Heat until the chocolate has melted, then whisk to smooth. Remove the insert. Let the chocolate partially cool.

3. Using an electric mixer (handheld is fine), cream the cream cheese on medium-high speed in a large bowl, gradually adding 1¼ cups of the sugar. Beat in the eggs, one at a time, beating well after each addition. Add the pumpkin, vanilla, cinnamon, nutmeg, cloves, and salt, and blend until evenly combined. Pour slightly less than half of the filling into a separate bowl and stir in the melted chocolate until evenly blended. Pour the chocolate filling into the cooled pie shell and gently shake the pan to settle the filling.

4. Place the pie on the center oven rack and bake for 20 minutes. Transfer the pie to a rack and cool for 15 minutes.

5. Carefully ladle the remaining plain pumpkin filling over the chocolate layer. Shake the pan gently to settle the filling. Bake for 35 to 40 minutes, until the pumpkin layer is set. When done, the perimeter of the filling will have puffed somewhat but not so much that it develops large cracks.

6. Transfer the pie to a rack and cool until the filling settles and flattens out, 30 to 45 minutes.

7. Combine the sour cream and the remaining ¼ cup sugar in a small saucepan over very low heat. Warm the mixture, stirring often, for 2 or 3 minutes. When the sour cream has thinned and is slightly warmer than body temperature, slowly pour it over the top of the pie. Immediately shake and tilt the pie so the topping spreads and fully covers the layer underneath. Cool thoroughly, then cover with loosely tented aluminum foil and refrigerate for at least 3 to 4 hours before serving. Cover and refrigerate leftovers right away.

Pumpkin-Praline Pie

There are pumpkin pies for purists and then there are over-the-top pumpkin pies for when you want a showstopper; this is the latter. The pumpkin filling would make a great pie on its own, but here it's topped off with a crunchy coating of brown sugar–pecan praline. The pie is a pleasure to slice, first cutting into the crunchy praline and then the soft pumpkin. Thanks to my colleague Diane Rossen Worthington for sharing her recipe.

Makes 8–10 servings

Single-Crust Food Processor Pie Dough (page 58) or another single-crust dough

FILLING

- 3 large eggs, at room temperature
- ⅔ cup granulated sugar
- 1 (15-ounce) can pumpkin purée or 1¾ cups fresh (see page 221)
- ¼ cup half-and-half
- ½ teaspoon salt
- ½ teaspoon ground ginger
- ½ teaspoon ground nutmeg
- ¼ teaspoon ground cinnamon
- ¼ teaspoon ground cloves
- 3 tablespoons bourbon or 1 teaspoon vanilla extract

PRALINE TOPPING

- 1¼ cups chopped pecans
- ¾ cup packed light brown sugar
- 4 tablespoons unsalted butter, melted
- 2 tablespoons heavy cream
- ¼ teaspoon ground cinnamon
- Whipped Cream (page 447), for garnish

1. Prepare and refrigerate the pie dough. Roll the dough into a 12½- to 13-inch circle and line a 9- to 9½-inch deep-dish pie pan with it, shaping the edge into an upstanding ridge. Flute or crimp the edge, chill the shell, and partially prebake it according to the instructions on page 36.

2. Preheat the oven to 350°F (180°C). To make the filling, combine the eggs and granulated sugar in a large bowl. Using a handheld electric mixer, beat on high speed until light and lemon-colored, about 3 minutes. Add the pumpkin, half-and-half, salt, ginger, nutmeg, cinnamon, cloves, and bourbon, and blend on low speed until evenly mixed.

3. Put the pie shell on a baking sheet, near the oven, and carefully pour the filling into the shell. Bake the pie, on the sheet, on the center rack for 20 minutes. Rotate the pie 180 degrees and bake for 40 to 45 minutes longer, until the filling is set. When done, the perimeter of the pie will have puffed slightly. The very center will look a little glossy compared to the perimeter, which will have a dull finish.

4. Transfer the pie to a rack and cool completely. The praline can be added once the pie has cooled, or the pie can be covered and refrigerated until you're ready to add the praline. The praline will need to stabilize for about 10 minutes before serving.

5. To add the praline topping, adjust one of the oven racks so that it is 6 to 8 inches from the broiler, and preheat the broiler. Combine the pecans, brown sugar, butter, heavy cream, and cinnamon in a medium bowl and stir well. Scrape the praline evenly over the pie and smooth with a spoon. Put the pie on a baking sheet and run it under the broiler until the topping is melted and bubbly. As it bubbles, move the baking sheet a couple of times, changing the position of the pie so it browns evenly. This entire process will happen quickly — in just a minute or two — so watch it like a hawk.

6. Transfer the pie to a rack and cool for at least 10 minutes before serving. Or cool thoroughly and refrigerate before serving. Garnish slices with whipped cream.

North Carolina Sweet Potato Pie

My adoptive North Carolina ranks first in the nation in the production of sweet potatoes: more than 60,000 acres of them, about half of the total US production. In light of that, I came up with this recipe as a tribute to the farmers and their lovely sweet potatoes. Sweet potatoes have a wonderfully dense flesh and deep color that are in their full glory in this tasty pie.

Makes 8–10 servings

Old-Fashioned Shortening Pie Dough (page 62) or another single-crust dough

FILLING

- 3 **medium-large sweet potatoes**
- 3 **large eggs plus 1 large egg yolk, at room temperature**
- ⅔ **cup packed light brown sugar**
- ⅓ **cup granulated sugar**
- 4 **tablespoons unsalted butter, melted**
- ½ **cup heavy cream**
- ½ **cup half-and-half**
- ¾ **teaspoon vanilla extract**
- 1 **tablespoon all-purpose flour**
- ½ **teaspoon ground cinnamon**
- ½ **teaspoon ground nutmeg**
- ¼ **teaspoon ground cloves**
- ½ **teaspoon salt**
- **Whipped Cream (page 447) (optional)**

1. Prepare and refrigerate the pie dough. Roll the dough into a 12½- to 13-inch circle and line a 9- to 9½-inch deep-dish pie pan with it, shaping the edge into an upstanding ridge. Flute or crimp the edge, chill the shell, and partially prebake it according to the instructions on page 000.

2. Preheat the oven to 400°F (200°C). Scrub the potatoes and place them on a baking sheet. Pierce them several times with a paring knife. Bake for 60 to 75 minutes, until they feel tender all the way through when pierced with a paring knife. Cut the potatoes open to help them cool faster.

3. When the potatoes have cooled, scoop the flesh into a food processor. Process to a smooth purée. Measure out 1½ cups purée. (Save any extra purée for another use.)

4. Preheat the oven to 375°F (190°C). Whisk the eggs and egg yolk in a large bowl until frothy. Add the potato purée, sugars, melted butter, heavy cream, half-and-half, and vanilla. Using a handheld electric mixer, beat on medium-low speed until evenly blended. Mix the flour, cinnamon, nutmeg, cloves, and salt in a small bowl. Sprinkle over the liquid and blend it in on low speed.

5. Put the pie shell on a baking sheet, near the oven, and carefully pour the filling into the shell. Bake the pie, on the sheet, on the middle oven rack for 20 minutes. Reduce the heat to 350°F (180°C) and rotate the pie 180 degrees. Bake for 30 to 40 minutes longer, until the filling is set. When the pie is done, the filling will be wobbly and puff slightly around the edges.

6. Transfer the pie to a rack. Serve slightly warm, at room temperature, or chilled, garnished with whipped cream, if desired.

Boil or Bake?

In my sweet potato pie trials, I both boiled and baked the potatoes and found that I preferred the baked results. Baking takes longer, but it concentrates the flavor without adding excess moisture to the pie. You get a creamier, fuller-bodied pie when the moisture comes from the cream and eggs. If you like, you can accelerate the pie-making process by baking the sweet potatoes the day before, perhaps when you have something else in the oven. Refrigerate them after they have cooled.

And by the way, since you're baking sweet potatoes anyway, why not bake a couple of extras and use them to thicken soups or stews, or in muffins and quick breads. Or serve them as a simple side dish, mixed with butter and a drizzle of maple syrup.

Sweet Carrot Custard Pie

This recipe originally appeared in my book *The Harvest Baker* and has made lots of new fans since then, so I'm including it here as well. Some have told me they prefer this to both pumpkin or sweet potato pie, so there you have it. Your guests will think you're serving them one of those, but wait till you see the reactions when they realize you had something else in mind.

Makes 8–10 servings

Single-Crust Food Processor Pie Dough (page 58) or another single-crust dough

FILLING

- 1 tablespoon butter, softened
- 1 pound medium carrots, trimmed and peeled
- 1 cup packed light brown sugar
- 1 tablespoon all-purpose flour
- 3 large eggs
- 1 teaspoon finely grated lemon zest
- ¼ teaspoon salt
- ¾ cup heavy cream
- ½ cup half-and-half
- ¾ teaspoon vanilla extract
- ½ teaspoon ground allspice
- ¼ teaspoon ground cinnamon

  Whipped Cream (page 447), for garnish

1. Prepare and refrigerate the pie dough. Roll the dough into a 12½- to 13-inch circle and line a 9- to 9½-inch deep-dish pie pan with it, shaping the edge into an upstanding ridge. Flute or crimp the edge, chill the shell, and partially prebake it according to the instructions on page 36.

2. Preheat the oven to 400°F (200°C). Tear off two long pieces of aluminum foil; butter the middle part of each portion with the soft butter. Cut the carrots into halves, or thirds, and place them in the middle of each sheet, dividing them up equally. Seal tightly in the foil and bake for about 50 minutes, until soft. Open the packets and let the carrots cool.

3. Preheat the oven to 350°F (180°C). When the carrots have cooled, cut them into slices and measure out 2 cups (save the extra for soups or stews). Put the carrots into a food processor with the sugar and flour. Process to a smooth purée, scraping down the sides once or twice. Add the eggs, lemon zest, and salt, and process until smooth. Transfer to a bowl and whisk in the heavy cream, half-and-half, vanilla, allspice, and cinnamon.

4. Put the pie shell on a baking sheet, near the oven, and carefully pour the filling into the shell. Bake the pie, on the sheet, on the middle oven rack for 45 to 55 minutes, until the filling is set, rotating the pie midway through the baking. There should be no sign of uncooked filling in the middle.

5. Transfer the pie to a rack and cool thoroughly. Refrigerate for at least 2 hours before serving, garnished with whipped cream, if desired. Refrigerate leftovers.

Recipe for Success

Buy the freshest carrots you can get. Late-summer, freshly dug carrots are the best and will make the sweetest, most flavorful pie.

This pie tastes extra nice with a honey or maple syrup accent. Substitute either for a little of the brown sugar in equal measure.

Spiced Parsnip Pie

This will not be everyone's idea of a dream pie, but some people, including gardeners and other earthy souls, may find it very appealing. Parsnips have a dense, meaty texture, so it takes a bit of finesse to elevate them to dessert pie status. In plain English, that means plenty of sugar, spices, and half-and-half. Try this around the holidays, although gardeners know that spring-dug parsnips are always the sweetest and best tasting.

Makes 8–10 servings

Whole-Wheat Pie Dough (page 66) or another single-crust dough

FILLING

- 4 **cups trimmed, peeled, and coarsely chopped parsnips (about 1¾ pounds)**
- 1¼ **cups half-and-half**
- 3 **large eggs**
- 1 **cup packed light brown sugar**
- ⅓ **cup granulated sugar**
- 4 **tablespoons unsalted butter, melted**
- 1 **tablespoon lemon juice**
- 2 **teaspoons finely grated lemon zest**
- 1 **teaspoon ground cinnamon**
- ½ **teaspoon ground cloves**
- ½ **teaspoon ground nutmeg**
- ½ **teaspoon ground ginger**
- ¾ **teaspoon salt**
- 1 **teaspoon vanilla extract**

Whipped Cream (page 447) (optional)

1. Prepare and refrigerate the pie dough. Roll the dough into a 12½- to 13-inch circle and line a 9- to 9½-inch deep-dish pie pan with it, shaping the edge into an upstanding ridge. Flute or crimp the edge, chill the shell, and partially prebake it according to the instructions on page 000.

2. Preheat the oven to 375°F (190°C). Put the parsnips in a large saucepan with just enough lightly salted water to cover. Bring to a boil, then continue to boil gently until tender, 15 to 18 minutes. Test a large chunk with a paring knife to be sure they are done. Drain in a colander and cool for 10 minutes.

3. Combine the parsnips and half-and-half in a food processor and process until smooth. Add the eggs, sugars, butter, lemon juice, and lemon zest, and process until smooth. Add the cinnamon, cloves, nutmeg, ginger, salt, and vanilla, and process again until smooth.

4. Put the pie shell on a baking sheet, near the oven, then carefully pour the filling into the shell, smoothing the top with a spoon. Bake the pie, on the sheet, on the middle oven rack for 30 minutes. Reduce the heat to 350°F (180°C), and rotate the pie 180 degrees. Bake for 20 to 25 minutes longer, until the edges have puffed and started to crack. When done, the center of the pie will be firmly set.

5. Transfer the pie to a rack and cool. Serve slightly warm, at room temperature, or — my favorite way — slightly chilled, garnished with whipped cream, if desired.

Recipe for Success

This may look done and appear set in the center after just 30 minutes. However, do continue to bake the pie as directed for an additional 20 to 25 minutes.

Judith and Evan Jones, in their informative *The L.L. Bean Book of New New England Cookery*, have a wonderful recipe for a parsnip pie sweetened with pure maple syrup, which would work well in this version. If you'd like to try it, substitute up to ½ cup maple syrup for an equal amount of the brown sugar.

Green Tomato Mincemeat Pie

I lived in New Hampshire for 20 years, so I know green tomatoes aren't just a bittersweet harbinger of fall; they're prime pie pickings, too. No frugal home gardener anywhere would let green tomatoes rot on the vine, not when there are delicious pies like this to be made. This one is sweet-tart and spicy, and tastes more like mincemeat than tomatoes, thus the pie's name. It's a good choice for any fall gathering.

Makes 8–10 servings

Cornmeal Pie Dough, double-crust version (page 68) or another double-crust dough

FILLING

- 4 cups quartered, cored, seeded, and very thinly sliced green tomatoes
- ½ cup raisins
- ½ cup chopped walnuts or pecans
- ½ cup chopped pitted dates
- ⅓ cup granulated sugar, plus a little for sprinkling
- ⅓ cup packed light brown sugar
- ¼ cup apple cider vinegar
- 3 tablespoons all-purpose flour
- ½ teaspoon ground cinnamon
- ½ teaspoon ground ginger
- ½ teaspoon ground cloves
  Scant ½ teaspoon salt
- 1 teaspoon finely grated lemon zest
- 2 tablespoons cold unsalted butter, cut into small pieces
- 1 egg beaten with 1 tablespoon milk, for glaze

1. Prepare and refrigerate the pie dough. Roll the larger dough portion into a 12½- to 13-inch circle and line a 9- to 9½-inch deep-dish pie pan with it, letting the excess dough drape over the edge. Refrigerate the shell until needed.

2. Adjust the oven racks so one is in the lower position and another is in the middle of the oven. Preheat the oven to 400°F (200°C). Line a baking sheet with parchment paper.

3. Combine the tomatoes, raisins, nuts, dates, and sugars in a large bowl. Mix well. Add the vinegar, flour, cinnamon, ginger, cloves, salt, and lemon zest. Mix again. Let stand for 10 minutes.

4. Roll the other dough portion into an 11-inch circle. Turn the filling into the pie shell and smooth it out. Dot the filling with the butter. Lightly moisten the rim of the pie shell. Drape the top pastry over the filling, pressing along the edge to seal. Trim the overhang with scissors, leaving an even ½ to ¾ inch all around, then sculpt the edge into an upstanding ridge. Flute or crimp the edge, as desired. Poke several steam vents in the top of the pie with a large fork or paring knife. Put a couple of the vents near the edge so you can check the juices. Brush the pie sparingly with the egg wash glaze and sprinkle with granulated sugar.

5. Put the pie on the prepared baking sheet and bake on the lower rack for 30 minutes. Reduce the heat to 375°F (190°C) and move the pie up to the middle rack, rotating it 180 degrees. Bake for 30 to 35 minutes longer, until the juices bubble thickly at the steam vents.

6. Transfer the pie to a rack and cool for at least 1 hour. Serve warm or at room temperature. Cover and refrigerate leftovers after 24 hours.

Recipe for Success

Green tomatoes can seem so rock hard that you may wonder if they'll ever soften as they bake. They will. Just slice them as thinly as possible, and they'll be fine.

Some green tomatoes will have a few red spots on them, indicating the first signs of ripening. That's okay.

When in doubt, insert a sharp paring knife (or a skewer; see box on page 190) through the top crust in several places and down into the tomatoes to check for tenderness. When the pie is done, the tomatoes will offer little or no resistance.

Green Tomato and Cranberry Pie
with Cornmeal Streusel

Green tomatoes and maple syrup go hand in hand in the North Country, where pies like this aren't uncommon, although this one, with its cornmeal crumb topping, is perhaps more uncommon than most. The dried cranberries are a pleasant surprise, as is the five-spice powder.

Makes 8–10 servings

Buttermilk Pie Dough (page 67) or another single-crust dough

FILLING

4½ cups quartered, cored, seeded, and very thinly sliced green tomatoes

½ cup sweetened or unsweetened dried cranberries

⅓ cup packed light brown sugar

⅓ cup maple syrup

1½ tablespoons lemon juice

1 tablespoon apple cider vinegar

1 teaspoon five-spice powder

Scant ½ teaspoon salt

3 tablespoons all-purpose flour

Cornmeal Streusel (page 450)

Whipped Cream (page 447), for garnish

1. Prepare and refrigerate the pie dough. Roll the dough into a 12-inch circle and line a 9- to 9½-inch standard pie pan with it, shaping the edge into an upstanding ridge. Flute or crimp the edge, then refrigerate the shell until needed.

2. Adjust the oven racks so one is in the lower position and another is in the middle of the oven. Preheat the oven to 400°F (200°C). Line a baking sheet with parchment paper.

3. Combine the tomatoes, cranberries, sugar, maple syrup, lemon juice, and vinegar in a large bowl. Mix well. Stir in the five-spice powder, salt, and flour. Turn the filling into the pie shell, smoothing the top to even out the filling.

4. Put the pie on the prepared baking sheet and cover the filling with a generous layer of the streusel; you may not need all of it. Tamp the streusel down gently.

5. Bake the pie, on the sheet, on the lower oven rack for 30 minutes. Reduce the heat to 375°F (190°C) and move the pie up to the middle rack, rotating it 180 degrees. Bake for 30 to 35 minutes longer, until the juices bubble thickly around the edge of the pie and perhaps through the topping. If the pie starts to get too dark, cover it with aluminum foil.

6. Transfer the pie to a rack and cool. Serve just slightly warm or at room temperature, garnished with whipped cream. Cover and refrigerate leftovers after 24 hours.

Recipe for Success

If you don't have any five-spice powder and you'd like to make the pie with ingredients on hand, substitute the spices used in Green Tomato Mincemeat Pie (page 233).

Another delicious way you can prepare this is to use the double-crust version of Cornmeal Pie Dough (page 68) and make a double-crust pie.

Slow-Cooker Fall Fruit Pie

Years ago I ran across an unlikely recipe for a slow-cooker apple pie. I was incredulous, but it turned out surprisingly well — not like a pie in the traditional sense, with a separate crust and filling, but more like an apple pudding. So I ran with the idea and spun a fall fruit pie made with apples, pears, and cranberries. I think you'll like it. Prepare it late the night before for breakfast, or make it in the morning for dinner.

Makes 8–10 servings

- 4 **cups peeled, cored, and sliced apples**
- 3 **cups peeled, cored, and sliced ripe pears**
- 1 **cup fresh or frozen cranberries**
- 1 **teaspoon ground cinnamon**
- ¼ **teaspoon ground cardamom**
- ¼ **teaspoon ground nutmeg**
- ⅛ **teaspoon salt**
- 1½ **cups baking mix (like Bisquick)**
- ¾ **cup milk**
- ¾ **cup granulated sugar**
- 2 **large eggs**
- 3 **tablespoons unsalted butter, softened**
- ½ **teaspoon vanilla extract**
- ⅓ **cup packed light brown sugar**
- 3 **tablespoons cold unsalted butter, cut into ¼-inch pieces**
- **Whipped Cream (page 447), for garnish**

1. Lightly butter a 5- to 6-quart slow cooker. Add the apples, pears, and cranberries. Sprinkle the cinnamon, cardamom, nutmeg, and salt over the fruit. Toss well to combine.

2. Combine ½ cup of the baking mix, the milk, granulated sugar, eggs, softened butter, and vanilla in a large bowl. Mix well, then pour over the fruit.

3. Combine the remaining 1 cup baking mix and the brown sugar in a medium bowl. Add the cold butter and rub the mixture between your fingers until crumbly. Sprinkle evenly over the fruit.

4. Cover and cook on the low setting for 7 hours. When done, the fruit will be quite soft.

5. Turn off the pot and cool for about 30 minutes before serving, garnished with whipped cream. If you can't wait that long, cool briefly in individual bowls.

Recipe for Success

With such prolonged cooking, don't expect the apples and pears to hold their shape all that well, no matter what variety you use. They'll be quite soft, maybe even mushy, when the pie is finished cooking.

Thanksgiving Dried Fruit Pie

My friend and occasional editor Georgia Orcutt is a serious pie maker. This dried fruit pie is a perennial on her holiday table. The pie is nicknamed "Sally Darr" — a cook, apparently, whose name appeared on the original recipe that inspired Georgia's version. It has a thick filling of mixed dried fruit that's cooked on the stovetop before the pie is baked. You'll have no problem getting ample servings out of this hearty pie.

Makes 12 or more servings

Buttermilk Pie Dough, double-crust version (page 67) or another double-crust dough

FILLING

- 2 **cups pitted prunes, coarsely chopped**
- 2 **cups dried apricots, coarsely chopped**
- 1 **cup dried Bing cherries**
- ½ **cup coarsely chopped dried apple rings**
- 1½ **cups apple cider**
- 1 **cup chopped walnuts**
- ⅓ **cup sugar, plus a little for sprinkling**
- 1 **tablespoon lemon juice**
- 2–3 **tablespoons cold unsalted butter, cut into small pieces**
- **Milk or half-and-half, for glaze**
- **Whipped Cream (page 447), for garnish**

1. Prepare and refrigerate the pie dough. Roll the larger dough portion into a 12½- to 13-inch circle and line a 9- to 9½-inch deep-dish pie pan with it, letting the excess dough drape over the edge. Refrigerate the shell until needed.

2. Combine all the fruit in a large nonreactive saucepan; add the cider. Cover the pan, place over medium heat, and cook, stirring often, until the liquid is absorbed into the fruit, 10 to 15 minutes. Remove from the heat and scrape the mixture into a shallow bowl to cool.

3. Preheat the oven to 375°F (190°C). Stir the walnuts, sugar, and lemon juice into the fruit.

4. Roll the other dough portion into an 11-inch circle. Turn the filling into the pie shell and smooth over the fruit to even it out. Dot the filling with the butter. Lightly moisten the rim of the pie shell. Drape the top pastry over the filling, pressing along the edge to seal. Trim the overhang with scissors, leaving an even ½ to ¾ inch all around, then sculpt the edge into an upstanding ridge. Flute or crimp the edge, as desired. Poke several steam vents in the top of the pie with a large fork or paring knife. Put a couple of the vents near the edge so you can check the juices. Lightly brush the pie with milk and sprinkle with sugar.

5. Put the pie on the center oven rack and bake for about 45 minutes, until the top is golden brown, rotating the pie 180 degrees midway through the baking.

6. Transfer the pie to a rack and cool to room temperature before serving. Cover and refrigerate leftovers after 24 hours.

Recipe for Success

Georgia says: "This recipe is quite flexible. I've substituted some dried blueberries with success, and I have tossed in the remnants of a bag of currants. Just remember to keep the total dried fruit at about 5½ cups."

If the pie filling seems devoid of liquid after it has cooled, stir in an additional ¼ cup cider when you add the sugar.

Since there are no eggs to be concerned with or thickener that needs to "take," the best indication of doneness is total elapsed time.

Holiday Pie-Baking Strategies

A little forethought can go a long way during this crazy busy time of year. Here are a few ways you can keep your pie making on track.

- Nearly all pie doughs freeze well and can be made at least a month ahead. Thaw them overnight in the fridge before using.

- Decide on your pie menu the week ahead, then stock up on the staples. Buy plenty, knowing that you'll need extra flour, sugar, vanilla, and butter in the weeks to come.

- To save time, compartmentalize your movements. Don't make one batch of dough, then the filling, then the dough for another pie. Make a quantity of dough all in one session.

- Make some of your pies the day ahead. Chess pies, custard ones, pumpkin, and others hold up beautifully. If possible, bake fruit pies early in the day on Thanksgiving, or as close to serving as possible.

Splenda Fall Fruit *and* Cherry Pie

Often, when I give a pie-baking demonstration, someone will ask me about sugar-free pies that diabetics can eat. In pie fillings and other baking, you can substitute Splenda measure for measure for sugar, and the results are impressive. I've made a number of fruit pies with it, and all have been a hit. Here's one I particularly like, made with fresh pears and apples and frozen cherries.

Makes 8–10 servings

Old-Fashioned Shortening Pie Dough, double-crust version (page 62) or another double-crust dough made without sugar

FILLING

- 4 **cups peeled, cored, and sliced apples**
- 3 **cups peeled, cored, and sliced ripe pears**
- 1 **cup frozen cherries, partially thawed**
- ½ **cup Splenda sugar substitute**
- 1 **tablespoon lemon juice**
- 1½ **tablespoons cornstarch**
- ¼ **teaspoon ground cinnamon**
- ¼ **teaspoon ground nutmeg**

1. Prepare and refrigerate the pie dough. Roll the larger dough portion into a 12½- to 13-inch circle and line a 9- to 9½-inch deep-dish pie pan with it, letting the excess dough drape over the edge. Refrigerate the shell until needed.

2. Adjust the oven racks so one is in the lower position and another is in the middle of the oven. Preheat the oven to 400°F (200°C). Line a baking sheet with parchment paper.

3. Combine the fruit, Splenda, and lemon juice in a large bowl. Mix well. Let stand for 10 minutes. Mix in the cornstarch, cinnamon, and nutmeg.

4. Roll the other dough portion into an 11-inch circle. Turn the filling into the pie shell and smooth it over to even the fruit. Lightly moisten the rim of the pie shell. Drape the top pastry over the filling, pressing along the edge to seal. Trim the overhang with scissors, leaving an even ½ to ¾ inch all around, then sculpt the edge into an upstanding ridge. Flute or crimp the edge, as desired. Poke several steam vents in the top of the pie with a large fork or paring knife. Put a couple of the vents near the edge so you can check the juices.

5. Put the pie on the prepared baking sheet and bake on the lower rack for 30 minutes. Reduce the heat to 375°F (190°C) and move the pie up to the middle rack, rotating it 180 degrees. Bake for 30 to 40 minutes longer, until the juices bubble thickly at the steam vents.

6. Transfer the pie to a rack and cool for at least 1½ to 2 hours before serving. Cover and refrigerate leftovers after 24 hours.

Recipe for Success

In large measure, the quality of the fruit you use will determine the flavor score for this pie. If you make it with the best fall apples and pears, it will be as good as any fruit pie you could possibly bake, sugar or not.

Dried Pear and Date Pie
with Glazed Nut Topping

When you simmer dried fruit in juice and purée it in a food processor, you end up with a thick fruit sauce that can be used to make a different sort of pie filling, much thicker and with a more concentrated flavor than a fresh fruit pie. That's what you do here with pears, spreading the sauce in the shell, then topping it with buttery-sweet mixed nuts. It makes for a wonderfully dense pie that's best served in thin slices.

Makes 10–12 servings

Oat and Cornmeal Pie Dough (page 69) or another single-crust dough

FILLING

1½ cups coarsely chopped dried pears

½ cup halved and pitted dates

⅔ cup pear juice, plus ¼–1 cup for puréeing

¼ cup granulated sugar

1 tablespoon lemon juice

4 tablespoons unsalted butter, cut into in several pieces

¼ cup packed light brown sugar

3 tablespoons light corn syrup

1¼ cups mixed nuts (any combination, but no peanuts), toasted (page 453) and coarsely chopped

Whipped Cream (page 447), for garnish

1. Prepare and refrigerate the pie dough. Roll the dough into a 12-inch circle and line a 9- to 9½-inch standard pie pan with it, shaping the edge into an upstanding ridge. Flute or crimp the edge, chill the shell, and partially prebake it according to the instructions on page 000.

2. Combine the pears, dates, the ⅔ cup pear juice, and granulated sugar in a medium nonreactive saucepan. Bring to a boil, then reduce the heat, cover, and gently simmer until most of the liquid is absorbed, about 15 minutes. Remove from the heat and let cool.

3. Preheat the oven to 375°F (190°C). Transfer the cooked fruit to a food processor. Add the lemon juice and ¼ to ⅓ cup of the additional pear juice. Process the fruit to a smooth purée, adding more pear juice as needed to make a purée with a consistency of thick applesauce. This may take ½ cup or more of juice. Spread the purée evenly in the pie shell.

4. Combine the butter, brown sugar, and corn syrup in a medium saucepan. Bring to a boil, stirring, and let boil for 1 minute. Add the nuts and stir well, coating them with the liquid. Remove from the heat and spoon the mixture evenly over the filling, smoothing it with a spoon.

5. Put the pie on the lower oven rack and bake for 35 to 40 minutes, until the nut topping is a deep golden brown and is bubbling vigorously, rotating the pie 180 degrees midway through the baking.

6. Transfer the pie to a rack and cool to room temperature. Cut thin slices and serve with a dollop of whipped cream. Cover and refrigerate leftovers after 24 hours.

Recipe for Success

The pear flavor really rules here, even with the dates. If you'd like to tone it down slightly, use equal amounts of the two fruits.

  Use any combination of mixed nuts, except peanuts. Their flavor tends to crowd out the other nuts.

Funeral Pie

The name of this pie turns many people off, but I can assure you that the pie itself turns people on. Funeral pie, with a stovetop-cooked, cornstarch-thickened filling, is traditionally served at the wakes of Old Order Mennonites and Amish. They say the tradition of serving this at wakes evolved because raisins have no season and could always be found in the pantry. There's no reason to wait for a funeral before you try this.

Makes 8–10 servings

Old-Fashioned Shortening Pie Dough, double-crust version (page 62) or another double-crust dough

FILLING

- 2 cups dark raisins
- 2 cups water
- ½ cup granulated sugar, plus a little for sprinkling
- ½ cup packed light brown sugar
- 3 tablespoons cornstarch
- ½ teaspoon ground cinnamon
- ¼ teaspoon salt
- 1½ tablespoons lemon juice
- 1 teaspoon finely grated lemon zest
- 2 tablespoons unsalted butter, cut into ½-inch pieces
- Milk or half-and-half, for glaze

1. Prepare and refrigerate the pie dough. Roll the larger dough portion into a 12-inch circle and line a 9- to 9½-inch standard pie pan with it, letting the excess dough drape over the edge. Refrigerate the shell until needed.

2. Combine the raisins and 1 cup of the water in a large saucepan over low heat. Meanwhile, combine the sugars, cornstarch, cinnamon, and salt in a medium bowl. Whisk in the remaining 1 cup water, then pour the mixture into the saucepan. Increase the heat to medium-high and bring the mixture to a boil, stirring virtually nonstop. When it starts to boil, lower the heat slightly and let it continue to boil for 1½ minutes, stirring nonstop to keep the mixture from spattering. Remove from the heat and stir in the lemon juice, lemon zest, and butter, until the butter melts. Transfer to a large bowl and cool for at least 30 minutes.

3. Preheat the oven to 400°F (200°C). Roll the other dough portion into an 11-inch circle. Turn the filling into the pie shell and smooth it out to even the top. Lightly moisten the rim of the pie shell. Drape the top pastry over the filling, pressing along the edge to seal. Trim the overhang with scissors, leaving an even ½ to ¾ inch all around, then sculpt the edge into an upstanding ridge. Flute or crimp the edge, as desired. Poke several steam vents in the top of the pie with a large fork or paring knife. Put a couple of the vents near the edge so you can check the juices, though this isn't an overly juicy pie. Lightly brush the pie with milk and sprinkle with granulated sugar.

4. Place the pie on the center oven rack and bake for 40 to 45 minutes, until the crust is golden brown, rotating the pie 180 degrees midway through the baking. The color of the pastry and total elapsed time are the best indicators of doneness.

5. Transfer the pie to a rack and cool thoroughly. Serve warm or at room temperature.

Recipe for Success

Since there are no dairy products in this pie, it will keep at room temperature for a couple of days. This room-temperature longevity, according to some accounts, partly explains the pie's popularity during times of grieving when people's attention is elsewhere.

Dried Cranberry *and* Walnut Funeral Pie

This funeral pie has a contemporary twist — dried cranberries. It follows the same basic formula, but with festive flavor embellishments, like cranberries, orange juice and zest, ground cloves, and walnuts. Like the original funeral pie (see page 241), this will remind you of a mock mincemeat pie. Unique and delectable.

Makes 8–10 servings

Flaky Cream Cheese Pie Dough, double-crust version (page 72) or another double-crust dough

FILLING

- 2 **cups sweetened dried cranberries**
- 1 **cup orange juice or cranberry juice cocktail**
- 1 **teaspoon grated orange zest**
- ⅔ **cup sugar, plus a little for sprinkling**
- 3 **tablespoons cornstarch**
- ¼ **teaspoon ground cloves**
- ¼ **teaspoon salt**
- 1 **cup water**
- 1 **tablespoon unsalted butter, cut into ½-inch pieces**
- 1 **tablespoon lemon juice**
- ¾ **cup chopped walnuts**
  Milk or half-and-half, for glaze

1. Prepare and refrigerate the pie dough. Roll the larger dough portion into a 12-inch circle and line a 9- to 9½-inch standard pie pan with it, letting the excess dough drape over the edge. Refrigerate the shell until needed.

2. Combine the cranberries, orange juice, and orange zest in a medium nonreactive saucepan; place over low heat. As the cranberries start to heat, mix the sugar, cornstarch, cloves, and salt together in a small bowl. Stir in the water. Add the mixture to the saucepan, increasing the heat to medium. Bring to a boil, stirring, then reduce the heat slightly and continue to boil for 1½ minutes, stirring nonstop to prevent it from spattering. Remove from the heat and stir in the butter until melted. Stir in the lemon juice and walnuts. Transfer to a large bowl and cool.

3. Preheat the oven to 400°F (200°C). Roll the other dough portion into an 11-inch circle. Turn the filling into the pie shell and smooth it with a spoon. Lightly moisten the rim of the pie shell. Drape the top pastry over the filling, pressing along the edge to seal. Trim the overhang with scissors, leaving an even ½ to ¾ inch all around, then sculpt the edge into an upstanding ridge. Flute or crimp the edge, as desired. Poke several steam vents in the top of the pie with a large fork or paring knife. Put a couple of the vents near the edge so you can check the juices, though this isn't an overly juicy pie. Lightly brush the pie with milk and sprinkle with sugar.

4. Bake the pie on the center oven rack for 40 to 45 minutes, until the crust is golden brown, rotating the pie 180 degrees midway through the baking. The color of the pastry and total elapsed time are the best indicators of doneness.

5. Transfer the pie to a rack and cool thoroughly. Serve warm or at room temperature.

Recipe for Success

Feel free to substitute a bit of other dried fruit for the cranberries. If I have a couple of prunes or dried figs languishing in the pantry, I'll dice them and add to the cranberries. This pie is a good place to salvage even really dry, hard fruit.

Chewy Medjool Date–Nut Pie

I love dates, and I'm always looking for new ways to eat them. Years ago, I saw a date pie recipe in *Maida Heatter's Book of Great American Desserts*, and I instantly knew she was onto something. Using her recipe as my model, I invented my own version — gooey and chewy like hers, and a real treat. I'll repeat her advice that to make a proper date pie, you have to start with the softest dates you can find, not the hard dried ones that come in a box. This pie should be served cold, with whipped cream.

Makes 8–10 servings

Old-Fashioned Shortening Pie Dough (page 62)

FILLING

- 4 **large eggs**
- ½ **cup packed light brown sugar**
- 4 **tablespoons unsalted butter, melted**
- 1 **cup light corn syrup**
- ½ **teaspoon vanilla extract**
- ⅛ **teaspoon salt**
- 1½ **cups pitted and coarsely chopped soft Medjool dates**
- 1 **cup coarsely chopped walnuts or pecans**
- **Whipped Cream (page 447), for garnish**

1. Prepare and refrigerate the pie dough. Roll the dough into a 12½- to 13-inch circle and line a 9- to 9½-inch deep-dish pie pan with it, shaping the edge into an upstanding ridge. Flute or crimp the edge, chill the shell, and partially prebake it according to the instructions on page 36.

2. Preheat the oven to 350°F (180°C). Combine the eggs and sugar in a large bowl. Using an electric mixer, beat on medium-high speed for 2 minutes. Add the butter and beat again briefly. Add the corn syrup, vanilla, and salt. Beat for 30 seconds.

3. Put the pie shell on a baking sheet, near the oven, and scatter the dates and nuts evenly in the shell. Slowly pour the filling into the shell. Gently rake a fork through the filling to distribute the dates and nuts evenly.

4. Bake the pie, on the sheet, on the center oven rack for about 45 minutes, until the perimeter has puffed up as much as 1 inch and the center seems set but perhaps a little jiggly, rotating the pie 180 degrees midway through the baking.

5. Transfer the pie to a rack and cool thoroughly. Refrigerate for at least 3 hours before serving, garnishing the slices with whipped cream. Refrigerate leftovers.

Recipe for Success

If you shake a little flour over the dates, they'll be less likely to stick to the knife and clump up when you cut them. Some cooks prefer to cut them with scissors, which works well.

Very Fig *and* Walnut Pie

If you don't care for figs, this pie won't be of much interest to you, but if you love them like I do, you'll find it heavenly. The filling is made primarily from dried Turkish figs that have been poached in pear juice, then puréed. The walnuts add a bit of crunch to the thick, soft filling.

Makes 8–10 servings

Perfect Pie Dough by Hand (page 56) or another single-crust dough

FILLING

- 1½ cups stemmed and halved dried Turkish figs
- About 2 cups pear juice
- ½ cup packed light brown sugar
- 3 large eggs
- ¾ cup light corn syrup
- 2 tablespoons lemon juice
- Finely grated zest of 1 lemon
- 1½ teaspoons vanilla extract
- 1 cup coarsely chopped walnuts
- Whipped Cream (page 447), for garnish

1. Prepare and refrigerate the pie dough. Roll the dough into a 12-inch circle and line a 9- to 9½-inch standard pie pan with it, shaping the edge into an upstanding ridge. Flute or crimp the edge, chill the shell, and partially prebake it according to the instructions on page 36.

2. Combine the figs and pear juice in a medium nonreactive saucepan; bring to a boil. Reduce the heat, cover, and gently simmer until the figs are very soft, about 30 minutes. Remove from the heat. Using a slotted spoon, transfer the figs to a small bowl. Pour the cooking liquid into a glass measuring cup. Set aside.

3. Preheat the oven to 350°F (180°C). Combine the poached figs, sugar, and ½ cup of the poaching liquid in a food processor. Process to a smooth purée.

   Whisk the eggs in a large bowl, until frothy. Add the corn syrup, lemon juice, lemon zest, vanilla, and fig purée. Whisk again until evenly blended. Stir in the walnuts.

4. Put the pie shell on a baking sheet, near the oven, and carefully pour the filling into the shell. Bake the pie, on the sheet, on the center oven rack for about 45 minutes, until the filling is set and has puffed slightly, rotating the pie 180 degrees midway through the baking.

5. Transfer the pie to a rack and cool thoroughly. Refrigerate for at least 1½ hours before serving, garnishing the slices with whipped cream. Refrigerate leftovers.

Recipe for Success

Because this filling is dense and thick, and not as jiggly as some, it's trickier to know when the pie is done. Don't be surprised if all indications point to the pie being done after 30 to 35 minutes. Nonetheless, bake it a full 45 minutes to be sure the eggs are fully cooked in the dense filling.

Date-Walnut Free-Form Pie

This may be unlike any pie you've ever eaten or baked. Instead of baking it in a pan, you fold the sides up and over the filling and bake it free form — thus the name. The filling is an unabashedly rich spread of Medjool dates simmered in heavy cream, and it tastes unimaginably good.

Makes 8–10 servings

Almond Pie Dough (page 81)

FILLING

- 1 cup heavy cream
- ¼ cup sugar, plus a little for sprinkling
- ½ teaspoon vanilla extract
- 1½ cups pitted and coarsely chopped soft Medjool dates
- 1½ cups chopped walnuts
- ¼ teaspoon ground cinnamon
- 1 egg beaten with 1 tablespoon milk, for glaze

  Vanilla ice cream, for serving (optional)

1. Prepare and refrigerate the pie dough.

2. Combine ¾ cup of the cream and the sugar in a small saucepan over medium heat. Bring the mixture to a simmer, then reduce the heat and simmer gently for 2 minutes, stirring once or twice. Remove from the heat and stir in the vanilla.

3. Put the dates in a large bowl and pour the hot cream over them. Let stand for 10 minutes, then add the walnuts and cinnamon; mix well. Let stand for 20 minutes.

4. Preheat the oven to 375°F (190°C). The best way to assemble this is to roll the dough onto a large sheet of parchment paper, assemble the pie, then lift the pie onto a rimmed baking sheet with the paper. Alternatively, roll the dough onto a piece of floured waxed paper, invert it onto the baking sheet, peel off the paper, then assemble the pie on the baking sheet. Either way, roll the dough into a 13-inch circle.

5. Add the remaining ¼ cup cream to the dates and mix well. Scrape the filling into the center of the pastry and spread it into a 9-inch circle. Go easy because the filling is rather coarse and you don't want to tear the dough. Fold the edge of the pastry over the filling, enclosing it. The pastry will sort of self-pleat as you go. Brush the pastry border lightly with the egg wash glaze and sprinkle with sugar.

6. Put the pie on one of the lower oven racks and bake for about 40 minutes, until the pastry is golden brown.

7. Transfer the baking sheet to a rack and cool. If you used parchment, and you feel confident doing so, you can slide the paper and pie right onto the rack to cool. Serve lukewarm or at room temperature, with vanilla ice cream, if desired. Refrigerate leftovers.

9
The Notable Nut:
PECAN PIE AND BEYOND

I know several people who are more or less indifferent to pie in general. They can't be bothered to make one, and they'll almost never order a slice when eating out. But offer one of these dear souls a slice of pecan pie and everything changes, indifference giving way to a sort of singular pie reverence. The very sight of a tawny pecan pie has been known to make grown men emote and otherwise composed women gasp with delight.

In less dramatic fashion, pecan pie seems to have that effect on almost everyone. No matter how you feel about other kinds of pies, most of us have an undeniable soft spot for pecan. I don't know if it's the buttery crunch, the toasted-rich flavor, or the gooey candylike filling — probably all of the above — but pecan pie holds a place of eminence in the pie world that's almost unparalleled.

This chapter celebrates not just pecan but other nut pies as well — those made with walnuts, pine nuts, hazelnuts, and peanuts, too. Many are made in the traditional pecan fashion, nuts surrounded by that gooey filling people adore. But others are less so, leaning toward a brownie or fudgelike filling. Some feature a single nut; others, like the Fruits of the Forest Pie on page 273, combine several. In every case, however, the nuts are there to make a statement, not simply tossed in as an afterthought.

Even if you've already found the world's best pecan pie recipe, I hope that you'll give this chapter its due. You might pick up a new trick or two, such as using browned butter in your pecan pie (Louisiana Browned Butter–Pecan Pie, page 250) to add a second layer of toasted flavor. Have fun!

❧

Tips for Baking Noteworthy Nut Pies

- Shop around for nuts. You'll generally find the best price buying them in bulk. Shop where there is rapid inventory turnover to be sure you're getting them fresh.

- Store nuts in a cool, dark place, tightly sealed in plastic or glass containers. This is especially important in summer. Nuts can turn rancid quickly if left at room temperature in the warmer months. Buy only enough nuts to last for a month, or freeze them for up to 2 years.

- Taste the nuts from your pantry before using them to make sure they have a fresh flavor.

- In some cases, I like to toast nuts before using them in a pie to give them a toasty flavor. Other times I don't bother if I'm feeling lazy or there aren't enough of them in the recipe to make it worthwhile. You'll find toasting instructions on page 453.

- Pecan halves look most attractive on top of a pie, but they present a problem when you cut into a pie. As you slice, the filling gets squished under the larger nuts. That's why I'll often chop nuts coarsely by hand before adding them to the filling. Or leave the nuts in large pieces, place the pie in the freezer until it is partially frozen, and then slice it.

- Most nut pies contain eggs and, therefore, should not be overbaked or baked too fast or the filling will be adversely affected. If your nut pies puff up very quickly and develop lots of cracks, the oven is probably too hot. Check the temperature with a reliable oven thermometer and adjust the setting as needed, or call in a professional to have the oven recalibrated.

- With few exceptions, don't slice nut pies until they are thoroughly cooled or the filling will not have the proper candylike texture.

Butterscotch-Pecan Pie

I think this is the quintessential pecan pie. There's no state secret to it, just a large handful of butterscotch chips. But when you taste it, you'll think butterscotch chips were invented to fulfill this destiny. This recipe goes heavy on the pecans, incorporating a full two cups. You can use slightly less, if you like. Pretoast the pecans or not; up to you. It's pretty much mandatory to serve this pie with vanilla ice cream.

Makes 8–10 servings

Perfect Pie Dough by Hand (page 56) or another single-crust dough

FILLING

- 1 **cup light corn syrup**
- ½ **cup packed dark brown sugar**
- 4 **tablespoons unsalted butter, cut into pieces**
- ¾ **cup butterscotch chips**
- ⅛ **teaspoon salt**
- 3 **large eggs plus 1 large egg yolk**
- 1½ **teaspoons vanilla extract**
- 2 **cups pecan halves, toasted (page 453) or not, coarsely chopped**
- **Vanilla ice cream, for serving**

1. Prepare and refrigerate the pie dough. Roll the dough into a 12½- to 13-inch circle and line a 9- to 9½-inch deep-dish pie pan with it, shaping the edge into an upstanding ridge. Flute or crimp the edge, chill the shell, and partially prebake it according to the instructions on page 36.

2. Preheat the oven to 350°F (180°C). Gently warm the corn syrup, sugar, and butter in a medium saucepan until the butter melts. Turn off the heat and add the butterscotch chips; scatter them around rather than dumping them in one spot. Let stand for 5 minutes, shaking the pan once or twice to move hot liquid over the chips. After 5 minutes, add the salt and whisk to smooth. Pour the mixture into a large bowl and cool for 5 minutes.

3. Whisk the eggs and egg yolk together in a medium bowl just until frothy. Whisk in the vanilla. Gradually whisk a little less than half of the hot liquid into the eggs until smooth. Add the rest of the hot liquid in a stream and whisk again. Stir in the pecans. Put the pie shell on a baking sheet, near the oven, and carefully pour the filling into shell. Use a fork to gently rake the filling and distribute the nuts evenly.

4. Bake the pie, on the sheet, on the center oven rack for 40 to 45 minutes, until the perimeter of the filling has puffed up a little and cracked slightly, rotating the pie 180 degrees midway through the baking. When done, the center of the pie may wobble, but it shouldn't seem soupy. Just give the pie a little nudge to check.

5. Transfer the pie to a rack and cool. Serve at room temperature, or chill first for several hours before serving; either way, garnish with ice cream. Refrigerate leftovers.

Recipe for Success

Don't worry if the top of this pie bakes up a little darker than the tops of other pecan pies. The dark brown sugar and butterscotch chips are responsible.

Louisiana Browned Butter–Pecan Pie

If you've ever eaten a piece of genuine Louisiana pecan pie and wondered what that elusive nutty taste is, it might not be the pecans; it could be browned butter. Cooks typically learn to not brown the butter or they'll compromise its pure flavor. But there are times when browning butter gives it a toasted quality that's just right for our purposes — like here, where it layers on some genuine Southern charm.

Makes 8–10 servings

Single-Crust Food Processor Pie Dough (page 58)

FILLING

- ½ cup (1 stick) unsalted butter
- 3 large eggs
- 1 cup packed brown sugar
- ½ cup dark corn syrup
- 2 tablespoons honey
- 2 teaspoons vanilla extract
- ⅛ teaspoon ground cinnamon
- 1½ cups pecan halves, toasted (page 453) and coarsely chopped by hand
- Vanilla ice cream, for serving (optional)

1. Prepare and refrigerate the pie dough. Roll the dough into a 12½- to 13-inch circle and line a 9- to 9½-inch deep-dish pie pan with it, shaping the edge into an upstanding ridge. Flute or crimp the edge, chill the shell, and partially prebake it according to the instructions on page 6.

2. Preheat the oven to 400°F (200°C). Using a shiny skillet so you can easily see what's happening in the pan, melt the butter over medium to medium-high heat. Stir with a wooden spoon, keeping a close eye on the butter as you wait for it to brown. Once that starts to happen, it will happen quickly. The trick is to catch the butter while it is dark golden brown and before the little solids get too dark and burn. As soon as the butter reaches the golden brown point, in 2 to 4 minutes, pour it into a bowl and cool slightly.

3. Combine the eggs, sugar, corn syrup, honey, vanilla, and cinnamon in a large bowl. Whisk well to blend. Add the browned butter and whisk again until evenly combined. Stir in the pecans. Put the pie shell on a baking sheet, near the oven, and carefully pour the filling into the shell. Gently rake a fork through the filling to distribute the nuts evenly.

4. Bake the pie, on the sheet, on the center oven rack for 10 minutes. Reduce the heat to 350°F (180°C) and bake for about 30 minutes longer, until the filling is set, rotating the pie 180 degrees midway through the baking. When done, the pie will have puffed slightly and developed fine cracks around the perimeter. There should be no soupiness at the center of the filling.

5. Transfer the pie to a rack and cool thoroughly. Serve at room temperature or chill slightly before serving, with a scoop of vanilla ice cream, if desired. Refrigerate leftovers.

Recipe for Success

A shiny skillet is the best background for monitoring the butter as it darkens. It's much more difficult to gauge the progress if you're using a black cast-iron pan or a nonstick pan.

Vanilla ice cream or whipped cream are the best accompaniments here because they won't hide the browned butter flavor.

Race Day Chocolate-Pecan Pie

This recipe is from Alice Colombo, former assistant food editor with the *Louisville Courier-Journal* in Kentucky. It's her version of the pie traditionally served to mark the running of the Kentucky Derby. You'll love the crusty, cookielike topping and chocolaty pecan filling underneath. Alice's original recipe doesn't specify a prebaked crust, but I think it's worth doing.

Makes 8–10 servings

Single-Crust Food Processor Pie Dough (page 58)

FILLING

- 2 **large eggs**
- 1 **cup sugar**
- ½ **cup cornstarch**
- ½ **cup (1 stick) unsalted butter, melted and slightly cooled**
- 2 **tablespoons bourbon**
- 1 **cup pecan halves, toasted (page 453) or not, coarsely chopped by hand**
- 1 **cup semisweet chocolate chips**
- ¼ **teaspoon salt**
- ½ **teaspoon vanilla extract**

  Whipped Cream (page 447) made with 1 or 2 tablespoons bourbon, for garnish

1. Prepare and refrigerate the pie dough. Roll the dough into a 12-inch circle and line a 9- to 9½-inch standard pie pan with it, shaping the edge into an upstanding ridge. Flute or crimp the edge, chill the shell, and partially prebake it according to the instructions on page 36.

2. Preheat the oven to 350°F (180°C). Whisk the eggs in a large mixing bowl. Mix the sugar and cornstarch together in a small bowl, then gradually whisk the mixture into the eggs. Whisk in the butter and bourbon. Stir in the pecans, chocolate chips, salt, and vanilla.

3. Put the pie shell on a baking sheet, near the oven, and carefully pour the filling into the shell. Don't leave any chocolate chips or nuts behind in the bowl.

4. Bake the pie, on the sheet, on the center rack for 45 to 50 minutes, until the top is crusty and golden brown, rotating the pie 180 degrees midway through the baking.

5. Transfer the pie to a rack and cool. Dollop the slices with the bourbon-laced whipped cream, using a heavy hand. Cover and refrigerate leftovers.

Recipe for Success

Alice says everyone likes to prepare foods ahead for Kentucky Derby Day; this pie is a very good keeper. Here's how she does it. After baking, cool the pie completely. Slip it into a gallon ziplock freezer bag and zip almost closed. Insert a drinking straw into the opening and suck out the air. Slip the straw out of the bag and immediately zip up the opening. Freeze. Remove the pie from the freezer several hours before serving. Rewarm it in the oven. Make the bourbon whipped cream the day you serve the pie.

Snowbird Mountain Lodge's Mocha-Pecan Pie

I can always tell when I've stumbled upon a great pie if I can't stop eating it — before the pie is even baked! Such was the case with this delicious mocha pecan pie, courtesy of Robert Rankin, chef-owner of the Snowbird Mountain Lodge in the southern Appalachian Mountains of western North Carolina. Chef Rankin says it sells out whenever it's on the menu.

Makes 8–10 servings

Single-Crust Food Processor Pie Dough (page 58) or another single-crust dough

FILLING

- 3 tablespoons unsweetened cocoa powder
- 2 teaspoons instant espresso or instant coffee granules
- 3 tablespoons unsalted butter, melted
- 1 tablespoon heavy cream
- 1 cup sugar
- 1 cup light corn syrup
- 3 large eggs, at room temperature
- 2 teaspoons vanilla extract
- ¼ teaspoon salt
- 1½ cups coarsely chopped pecans
- Vanilla ice cream, for serving (optional)

1. Prepare and refrigerate the pie dough. Roll the dough into a 12-inch circle and line a 9- to 9½-inch standard pie pan with it, shaping the edge into an upstanding ridge. Flute or crimp the edge, chill the shell, and partially prebake it according to the instructions on page 36.

2. Preheat the oven to 350°F (180°C). Combine the cocoa, coffee, butter, and cream in a large bowl; whisk to blend. Add the sugar, corn syrup, eggs, vanilla, and salt. Whisk again to smooth, then stir in the pecans. Put the pie shell on a baking sheet, near the oven, then carefully pour the filling into the shell. Gently rake a fork through the filling to distribute the nuts evenly.

3. Bake the pie, on the sheet, on the center rack for 30 minutes. Rotate the pie 180 degrees and bake for 20 to 30 minutes longer, or until the filling has puffed around the edge and the middle of the pie is set. To check, give the pie a quick little nudge. The pie should not move in waves below the crusty surface.

4. Transfer the pie to a rack and cool thoroughly. Serve at room temperature or chilled, topped with ice cream if desired. (I think it has a better texture if it's refrigerated for at least 1 hour before serving.) Cover and refrigerate leftovers.

Recipe for Success

Like most pecan pies, this one forms a crunchy crust on top of the filling. When you test the pie to determine whether it is done, watch what happens below the crusty surface. If it moves, wavelike, bake the pie for 7 to 10 minutes longer.

Robert says that a little orange flavor in the pastry is a wonderful complement to the mocha filling. He adds some grated orange zest to the dough's dry ingredients and substitutes 1 tablespoon orange juice for an equal amount of corn syrup in the filling.

Maple-Pecan Pie

This elegant pie, an arranged marriage of Northern sweetness and Southern charm, makes pie lovers weak in the knees. I like to add a little bit of almond extract to the filling. I think it melts into the pecan flavor without seeming out of place, but you can omit it if you prefer.

Makes 8–10 servings

Old-Fashioned Shortening Pie Dough (page 62) or another single-crust dough

FILLING

- ½ **cup sugar**
- 4 **tablespoons unsalted butter, melted and slightly cooled**
- 3 **large eggs plus 1 large egg yolk**
- ¾ **cup maple syrup**
- ½ **cup light corn syrup**
- 1½ **teaspoons vanilla extract**
- ½ **teaspoon almond extract (optional)**
- 2 **teaspoons lemon juice**
- ¼ **teaspoon salt**
- 1½ **cups pecan halves, toasted (page 453) or not, coarsely chopped**

  Vanilla or butter pecan ice cream, for serving

1. Prepare and refrigerate the pie dough. Roll the dough into a 12½- to 13-inch circle and line a 9- to 9½-inch deep-dish pie pan with it, shaping the edge into an upstanding ridge. Flute or crimp the edge, chill the shell, and partially pre-bake it according to the instructions on page 36.

2. Preheat the oven to 350°F (180°C). Combine the sugar, butter, eggs, and egg yolk in a large bowl. Using an electric mixer (handheld is fine) or a whisk, beat the mixture until evenly blended. Add the maple syrup, corn syrup, vanilla, almond extract (if using), lemon juice, and salt. Beat for several seconds, until evenly blended. Stir in the pecans. Put the pie shell on a baking sheet, near the oven, and carefully pour the filling into the shell. Gently rake a fork through the filling to distribute the nuts evenly.

3. Bake the pie, on the sheet, on the center rack for 50 to 55 minutes, until the filling is set, rotating the pie 180 degrees midway through the baking. When the pie is done, the perimeter will have puffed slightly and the center will not move in waves. Give the pie a quick little nudge to check it.

4. Transfer the pie to a rack and cool thoroughly. Serve at room temperature or slightly chilled, garnished with vanilla or butter pecan ice cream. It has a better consistency for slicing when cold, but let the cold slices sit at room temperature for 15 minutes to enhance the flavor before serving. Cover and refrigerate leftovers.

Recipe for Success

Rich, sweet nut pies like this freeze very well and stay in great shape for at least a couple of months, so think about baking one of these and stashing it in the freezer for a special occasion. Just wrap the pie in plastic and overwrap snugly with aluminum foil. Thaw the pie at room temperature, then unwrap and heat in a 300°F (150°C) oven for about 20 minutes to give it a freshly baked taste. Or use the technique described on page 252 for Race Day Chocolate-Pecan Pie.

Chocolate Brownie–Pecan Pie

Pecan pie is always a special treat, especially when it's this good. As with most versions, the nuts float to the top here, settling over a layer of something akin to a chocolate pudding fudge brownie. As for serving, this pie is good warm but better, I think, at room temperature or chilled, when the texture of the chocolate firms up. Don't forget the whipped cream or vanilla ice cream.

Makes 8–10 servings

Single-Crust Food Processor Pie Dough (page 58)

FILLING

⅔ cup light corn syrup

⅔ cup packed light brown sugar

4 tablespoons unsalted butter, cut into pieces

4 ounces semisweet chocolate, coarsely chopped

⅛ teaspoon salt

3 large eggs plus 1 large egg yolk

1½ teaspoons vanilla extract

1½ cups pecan halves, toasted (page 453) or not, coarsely chopped

Whipped Cream (page 447) or vanilla ice cream, for serving

1. Prepare and refrigerate the pie dough. Roll the dough into a 12½- to 13-inch circle and line a 9- to 9½-inch deep-dish pie pan with it, shaping the edge into an upstanding ridge. Flute or crimp the edge, chill the shell, and partially prebake it according to the instructions on page 36.

2. Preheat the oven to 350°F (180°C). Gently heat the corn syrup, sugar, and butter together in a medium saucepan until the butter melts. Turn off the heat and add the chocolate and salt. Let stand for about 5 minutes, until the chocolate melts, occasionally tilting the pan so the liquid runs over the chocolate. Whisk the mixture to smooth, then it pour into a medium bowl and cool for 15 minutes.

3. Whisk the eggs and egg yolk together in a medium bowl until frothy. Blend in the vanilla. Add about half of the chocolate

mixture and whisk until smooth. Blend in the remaining chocolate mixture. Add the pecans and stir well. Put the pie shell on a baking sheet, near the oven, and carefully pour the filling into the shell. Gently rake a fork through the filling to distribute the nuts evenly.

4. Bake the pie, on the sheet, on the center rack for about 40 minutes, until the filling has puffed and cracked slightly, especially around the edge, rotating the pie midway through the baking. When done, the pie might look a little wobbly or loose at the center, but don't worry — the residual heat will continue to cook the pie.

5. Transfer the pie to a rack and cool. Serve slightly warm or at room temperature, garnished with whipped cream or ice cream. Or cool completely and refrigerate for several hours before serving.

Recipe for Success

Don't be temped to use an unbaked pie shell to save a little time. The filling is fairly wet and may yield a crust with a raw taste.

But don't be afraid to underbake the pie slightly, either. The worst that can happen is that it will turn out a little moist. If that's the case, you can simply refrigerate the pie to firm it up a bit before serving.

Jack Daniel's Chocolate Chip–Pecan Pie

If you like a little kick in your pecan pie, try this one made with Jack Daniel's whiskey, just enough of it to flavor the pie but not so much as to overwhelm it with alcohol. This spirited pie is right at home on the holiday table.

Makes 8–10 servings

Single-Crust Food Processor Pie Dough (page 58)

FILLING

- 4 large eggs, at room temperature
- 1 cup sugar
- ¾ cup dark corn syrup
- 2 tablespoons Jack Daniel's whiskey
- 2 tablespoons unsalted butter, melted
- 1 teaspoon vanilla extract
- 1 cup pecan halves, toasted (page 453)
- ½ cup semisweet chocolate chips

1. Prepare and refrigerate the pie dough. Roll the dough into a 12½- to 13-inch circle and line a 9- to 9½-inch deep-dish pie pan with it, shaping the edge into an upstanding ridge. Flute or crimp the edge, chill the shell, and partially prebake it according to the instructions on page 36.

2. Preheat the oven to 350°F (180°C). Combine the eggs, sugar, and corn syrup in a large bowl. Whisk well to combine. Add the whiskey, butter, and vanilla; whisk again.

3. Put the pie shell on a baking sheet, near the oven, then scatter the pecans and chocolate chips evenly in the shell. Whisk the filling once more, then carefully pour it over the nuts and chips. Rake the filling with a fork to distribute the nuts somewhat evenly. (They will rise during baking.)

4. Bake the pie, on the sheet, on the center oven rack for 40 to 45 minutes, until the filling is set, rotating the pie 180 degrees midway through the baking. When done, the top of the filling will be wobbly, toasted brown on top, and the perimeter will be slightly puffed.

5. Transfer the pie to a rack and cool thoroughly. Serve at room temperature or slightly chilled. Cover and refrigerate leftovers.

Recipe for Success

Not all recipes in this genre call for the pie shell to be partially prebaked, but I find that prebaking virtually guarantees a crisp crust.

This pie freezes well. Thaw at room temperature for 4 to 5 hours before serving. To get a good clean slice, partially freeze the pie before cutting. Use a sturdy knife, as the chocolate chips are very hard when frozen. Serve at room temperature.

Sawdust Pie

This recipe has one of the most un-pie pie fillings you'll ever come across. There's nothing moist or juicy about it, and the name itself could very well scare you off, but somehow it all comes together. If you can imagine something like a coarse graham cracker–coconut cake, that would begin to describe it. You have to try this one to appreciate it. It begs for ice cream and a drizzle of caramel sauce.

Makes 8–10 servings

Old-Fashioned Shortening Pie Dough (page 62) or another single-crust dough

FILLING

7 **large egg whites**

1 **cup granulated sugar**

½ **cup packed light brown sugar**

1½ **teaspoons vanilla extract**

1½ **cups graham cracker crumbs**

1½ **cups sweetened flaked coconut**

1½ **cups finely chopped pecans**

⅛ **teaspoon salt**

3 **tablespoons unsalted butter, melted**

Vanilla or butter pecan ice cream, for serving

Caramel Sauce (page 444), for garnish (optional)

1. Prepare and refrigerate the pie dough. Roll the dough into a 12½- to 13-inch circle and line a 9- to 9½-inch deep-dish pie pan with it, shaping the edge into an upstanding ridge. Flute or crimp the edge, then refrigerate the shell until needed.

2. Whisk the egg whites, sugars, and vanilla in a bowl until evenly mixed. Add the graham cracker crumbs, coconut, pecans, and salt. Stir briefly, then add the butter and stir just until the filling is evenly mixed. Don't overmix.

3. Turn the filling into the pie shell and spread it evenly with the back of a spoon. Bake on the center oven rack for 40 to 45 minutes, until the top is crusty and has risen, rotating the pie midway through the baking. It's fine if the pie develops cracks here and there.

4. Transfer the pie to a rack and cool for at least 2 hours before serving. Serve warm or at room temperature, garnishing slices lavishly with vanilla or butter pecan ice cream and a drizzle of caramel sauce, if desired. Cover and refrigerate leftovers.

Recipe for Success

Chop the nuts by hand, not in the food processor, for the best texture. (The food processor can make them *too* fine if you're not careful.)

Don't overmix the filling. The more you work it, the stiffer and less spreadable the filling becomes.

You'll have a lot of egg yolks left over with this pie. Consider making crème brûlée or custard with them.

A Native Nut

The pecan is the only tree nut that is truly native to the United States. Thomas Jefferson was so taken with the flavor of pecan that he imported trees from Louisiana for his orchards at Monticello.

Cream *of* Coconut–Pecan Pie

Here's a pie that was inspired by one I found, of all places, on the Coco Lopez website. I thought adding some of their cream of coconut to a pecan pie was a novel idea, so I gave it a try. Glad I did. The cream of coconut gives the pie a beautifully dense and creamy texture and a rich coconut flavor. The pecans float to the top; a sort of coconut custard settles on the bottom. This pie is fabulous served cold.

Makes 8–10 servings

Single-Crust Food Processor Pie Dough (page 58) or another single-crust dough

FILLING

3 **large eggs**

½ **cup packed light brown sugar**

1 **cup canned cream of coconut (stirred well before measuring)**

2 **tablespoons unsalted butter, melted**

¼ **cup heavy cream**

1½ **teaspoons vanilla extract**

1 **teaspoon distilled white vinegar or fresh lemon juice**

1 **cup pecan halves, toasted (page 453) or not, coarsely chopped**

Whipped Cream (page 447) for garnish (optional)

1. Prepare and refrigerate the pie dough. Roll the dough into a 12-inch circle and line a 9- to 9½-inch standard pie pan with it, shaping the edge into an upstanding ridge. Flute or crimp the edge, chill the shell, and partially prebake it according to the instructions on page 36.

2. Preheat the oven to 350°F (180°C). Whisk the eggs and sugar together in a large bowl until smooth. Whisk in the cream of coconut, butter, heavy cream, vanilla, and vinegar. Stir in the pecans. Put the pie shell on a baking sheet, near the oven, and carefully pour the filling into the shell. Gently rake a fork through the filling to distribute the nuts evenly.

3. Put the pie, on the sheet, on the center oven rack and bake for 45 to 50 minutes, until the filling has puffed around the edge and looks set, rotating the pie 180 degrees midway through the baking. Give the pie a little nudge to check it: it should wobble, not move in waves below the crusty surface.

4. Transfer the pie to a rack and cool thoroughly, then refrigerate for at least 2 hours before serving. Garnish slices with whipped cream, if desired. Cover and refrigerate leftovers.

What's in a Name?

Archaeologists have found evidence to suggest that Native Americans in what is now Texas used pecans more than 8,000 years ago. The word *pecan* comes from the North American Algonquian word for nut, *pakan*, which became the French word *pacane*, meaning, more or less, "not so hard as to require a stone to crack." As for whether you pronounce it puh-KAHN, puh-CAN, PEE-can, PEE-kahn or something else, I'll let you debate that all you like, while I help myself to another slice of pecan pie.

Molasses-Walnut Pie

Molasses pies like this were probably common among cooks in colonial America, when molasses was much less expensive than refined sugar. This one features walnuts, which our forebears would have gathered and painstakingly shelled. The filling reminds me of Indian pudding. The molasses flavor isn't overpowering because it is well balanced by the other sugars.

Makes 8–10 servings

Single-Crust Food Processor Pie Dough (page 58)

FILLING

- ⅓ cup unsulphured molasses
- ¼ cup light corn syrup
- 4 tablespoons unsalted butter, in several pieces
- ½ cup granulated sugar
- ½ cup packed light brown sugar
- 3 large eggs plus 1 large egg yolk
- 1 teaspoon vanilla extract
- 1 teaspoon fine yellow cornmeal
- 1½ cups walnut halves, toasted (page 453) or not, coarsely chopped

1. Prepare and refrigerate the pie dough. Roll the dough into a 12½- to 13-inch circle and line a 9- to 9½-inch deep-dish pie pan with it, shaping the edge into an upstanding ridge. Flute or crimp the edge, chill the shell, and partially prebake it according to the instructions on page 36.

2. Preheat the oven to 350°F (180°C). Combine the molasses, corn syrup, and butter in a small saucepan and warm gently, stirring occasionally, until the butter melts. Remove from the heat and cool briefly.

3. Combine the sugars, eggs, and egg yolk in a large bowl. Whisk in about one-third of the molasses mixture. Add the vanilla, cornmeal, and the remaining molasses mixture. Whisk again, then stir in the walnuts. Put the pie shell on a baking sheet, near the oven, and carefully pour the filling into the shell. Gently rake a fork through the filling to distribute the nuts evenly.

4. Bake the pie, on the sheet, on the center oven rack for about 45 minutes, until the filling is set, rotating the pie 180 degrees midway through the baking, When the pie is done, the edges will have puffed slightly and the filling will jiggle when you give the pie a nudge. The center should not seem soupy.

5. Transfer the pie to a rack and cool. Serve warm, at room temperature, or slightly chilled. Cover and refrigerate leftovers.

Jeff's Chocolate-Walnut Pie

This brownielike pie recipe is from my friend Jeff Paige, formerly the chef at Canterbury Shaker Village in New Hampshire, from his book *The Shaker Kitchen*. Because it contains cocoa, it isn't as rich as other pies in this book that call for semisweet or bittersweet chocolate. The upside is that you can make a chocolate pie when the only chocolate you have on hands is cocoa.

Makes 8–10 servings

Single-Crust Food Processor Pie Dough (page 58)

FILLING

- ⅔ **cup dark corn syrup**
- 4 **tablespoons unsalted butter**
- ½ **cup sugar**
- ⅓ **cup unsweetened cocoa powder**
- ¼ **teaspoon salt**
- 3 **large eggs, at room temperature**
- 1 **teaspoon vanilla extract**
- 1½ **cups coarsely chopped walnuts**

1. Prepare and refrigerate the pie dough. Roll the dough into a 12½- to 13-inch circle and line a 9- to 9½-inch deep-dish pie pan with it, shaping the edge into an upstanding ridge. Flute or crimp the edge, chill the shell, and partially prebake it according to the instructions on page 36.

2. Preheat the oven to 350°F (180°C). Warm the corn syrup and butter in a small saucepan over medium heat until the butter melts; whisk to smooth. Set aside to cool.

3. Sift the sugar, cocoa, and salt into a large bowl. Add the eggs, one at a time, whisking well after each addition. Whisk in the vanilla, then the warm corn syrup mixture. Stir in the nuts. Put the pie shell on a baking sheet, near the oven, and carefully pour the filling into the shell. Gently rake a fork through the filling to distribute the nuts evenly.

4. Bake the pie, on the sheet, on the center oven rack for about 40 minutes, until the filling is set, rotating the pie 180 degrees midway through the baking. When done, the filling may have puffed slightly around the perimeter.

5. Transfer the pie to a rack and cool thoroughly. Both the texture and the flavor of the pie will improve as it cools. This is best served slightly chilled, but not too cold. Cover and refrigerate leftovers.

Chocolate Crème de Cacao–Walnut Pie

Here's a chock-full-of-walnuts pie with real personality. With its complex and tantalizing flavor, it's a pie that should be on every chocolate lover's bucket list.

Makes 8–10 servings

Single-Crust Food Processor Pie Dough (page 58) or another single-crust dough

FILLING

- 1 **cup light corn syrup**
- 1 **tablespoon unsulphured molasses**
- 4 **tablespoons unsalted butter**
- ¼ **cup semisweet chocolate chips**
- 3 **tablespoons crème de cacao**
- 2 **teaspoons vanilla extract**
- ½ **cup sugar**
- 2 **tablespoons all-purpose flour**
- ¼ **teaspoon ground cinnamon**
- ⅛ **teaspoon salt**
- 3 **large eggs, at room temperature**
- 2 **cups walnut halves, toasted (page 453) and coarsely chopped**

 Vanilla ice cream, for serving

1. Prepare and refrigerate the pie dough. Roll the dough into a 12½- to 13-inch circle and line a 9- to 9½-inch deep-dish pie pan with it, shaping the edge into an upstanding ridge. Flute or crimp the edge, chill the shell, and partially prebake it according to the instructions on page 36.

2. Preheat the oven to 350°F (180°C). Gently heat the corn syrup, molasses, and butter together in a small saucepan until the butter melts. Remove from the heat and add the chocolate chips. Let stand for 5 minutes, then whisk to smooth the chocolate. Whisk in the crème de cacao and vanilla. Set aside.

3. Combine the sugar, flour, cinnamon, and salt in a large bowl. Add the eggs, one at a time, whisking well after each addition. Scrape the chocolate mixture into the egg mixture, whisking to blend. Stir in the walnuts. Put the pie on a baking sheet, near the oven, and carefully pour the filling into the shell. Carefully rake the filling with a fork to distribute the nuts evenly.

4. Bake the pie, on the sheet, on the center oven rack for about 40 minutes, until the center is set and the edge of the pie puffs and cracks slightly, rotating the pie 180 degrees midway through the baking, When done, the center should not be soupy. Give the pie a little nudge to check.

5. Transfer the pie to a rack and cool thoroughly. Serve at room temperature or slightly chilled, garnished with ice cream. Cover and refrigerate leftovers.

Recipe for Success

If you don't have crème de cacao, you can substitute a coffee liqueur, like Kahlúa. You'll wind up with a mocha taste instead of chocolate, but is that such a bad thing?

Chocolate Chip–Macadamia Cookie Pie

When my wife, Bev, and I got married in Hawaii, we ran into a number of pies like this with macadamia nuts, chunks of chocolate, and coconut; they were all wonderful. Back home, I put my own spin on this Hawaiian threesome and created this pie, turning it into a sort of cookie pie. It's really good! Throw a luau and serve it for dessert, or make it to celebrate an impending departure for the islands.

Makes 8–10 servings

Old-Fashioned Shortening Pie Dough (page 62)

FILLING

- ½ cup (1 stick) unsalted butter, very soft
- ¾ cup granulated sugar
- ½ cup packed light brown sugar
- 2 large eggs, at room temperature
- 1¼ teaspoons vanilla extract
- ½ cup all-purpose flour
- ¼ teaspoon salt
- 2 tablespoons milk
- 1 cup semisweet chocolate chips
- ¾ cup coarsely chopped macadamia nuts
- ¼ cup sweetened flaked coconut

1. Prepare and refrigerate the pie dough. Roll the dough into a 12-inch circle and line a 9- to 9½-inch standard pie pan with it, shaping the edge into an upstanding ridge. Flute or crimp the edge, chill the shell, and partially pre-bake it according to the instructions on page 36.

2. Preheat the oven to 350°F (180°C). Cream the butter in a large bowl with an electric mixer (handheld is fine) until smooth, gradually adding the sugars. Add the eggs, one at a time, beating well after each addition. Beat in the vanilla. With the mixer on low, beat in the flour, about half at a time. Beat in the salt and milk, then switch to a wooden spoon and stir in the chocolate chips, nuts, and coconut until evenly mixed.

3. Spoon the filling into the pie shell, smoothing it with a spoon so it is level and evenly distributed. Bake the pie on the center oven rack for 45 to 50 minutes, until the filling is set, rotating the pie 180 degrees midway through the baking. When the pie is done, it will be a rich golden brown and the filling will not jiggle. Don't underbake, to be sure the cookie layer is fully baked.

4. Transfer the pie to a rack and cool thoroughly. Serve at room temperature. If you refrigerate the pie and serve it cold, I recommend heating the slices in a microwave for 15 or 20 seconds to soften the chocolate chips. Otherwise they'll be quite hard. Or just leave the slices at room temperature for 30 minutes before serving. Refrigerate leftovers.

Recipe for Success

I like salted macadamia nuts for this pie, if you can find them, because a little saltiness makes for a good contrast in a sweet pie. If you find only unsalted nuts, by all means use them. Toss them with a big pinch of salt, if you like.

Oregon Caramel-Coffee-Hazelnut Pie

Coffee and hazelnuts, in the best gooey pecan pie tradition? I don't know of many pie lovers who'd have a problem with any of that. This pie was inspired by some of the fabulous pie recipes I've tried from various hazelnut-centric websites, and I've hit upon a winner. I have a feeling you'll think so, too. Savor this with coffee ice cream.

Makes 8–10 servings

Perfect Pie Dough by Hand (page 56)

FILLING

½ cup packed dark brown sugar

1 tablespoon instant espresso or instant coffee granules

½ cup (1 stick) unsalted butter, melted

3 large eggs, at room temperature

1 cup light corn syrup

1 teaspoon vanilla extract

¼ teaspoon salt

1½ cups hazelnuts, toasted (page 453) and chopped by hand

Coffee ice cream, for serving (optional)

1. Prepare and refrigerate the pie dough. Roll the dough into a 12-inch circle and line a 9- to 9½-inch standard pie pan with it, shaping the edge into an upstanding ridge. Flute or crimp the edge, chill the shell, and partially pre-bake it according to the instructions on page 36.

2. Preheat the oven to 350°F (180°C). Combine the sugar, espresso, and butter in a large bowl; whisk well to combine. Add the eggs, one at a time, whisking well after each addition, then whisk in the corn syrup, vanilla, and salt. Stir in the hazelnuts. Put the pie shell on a baking sheet, near the oven, and carefully pour in the filling. Gently rake a fork through the filling to distribute the nuts evenly.

3. Bake the pie, on the sheet, on the center oven rack for 45 to 50 minutes, until the center is set, rotating the pie 180 degrees midway through the baking. When the pie is done, the surface should not move in waves. Give the pie a quick nudge to check.

4. Transfer the pie to a rack and cool thoroughly. Serve at room temperature, or refrigerate and serve chilled. Either way, garnish with coffee ice cream, if desired. Cover and refrigerate leftovers.

Recipe for Success

Hazelnuts can be pretty firm, so chop them well or the pie may present a textural challenge for some.

While we're on the subject, whenever you're chopping nuts for this or any other nut pie, do it by hand unless otherwise instructed. If you use a food processor, it will reduce some of the nuts to a fine, floury consistency. That's fine if that's the texture you're aiming for, but it usually isn't.

Trail Mix Peanut Butter Pie

This is something like pecan pie, only made with peanuts, peanut butter, raisins, and chocolate chips — all the things people like in a trail mix. Take a slice along on your next hike, bike ride, or cross-country ski. Sweet and rich, this pie packs an energy wallop and tastes extraordinary. And it's only slightly more difficult to prepare than a batch of trail mix.

Makes 8–10 servings

Whole-Wheat Pie Dough (page 66) or another single-crust dough

FILLING

- 3 large eggs plus 1 large egg yolk
- ½ cup granulated sugar
- 2 tablespoons packed light brown sugar
- ⅓ cup smooth peanut butter
- 1 cup light corn syrup
- 4 tablespoons unsalted butter, melted
- 1 teaspoon vanilla extract
- ½ cup salted dry-roasted peanuts
- ½ cup dark raisins
- ½ cup semisweet chocolate chips

1. Prepare and refrigerate the pie dough. Roll the dough into a 12½- to 13-inch circle and line a 9- to 9½-inch deep-dish pie pan with it, shaping the edge into an upstanding ridge. Flute or crimp the edge, chill the shell, and partially prebake it according to the instructions on page 36.

2. Preheat the oven to 350°F (180°C). Combine the eggs, egg yolk, and sugars in a large bowl and beat for 15 seconds with an electric mixer. Add the peanut butter, corn syrup, and butter, and beat again until smooth. Blend in the vanilla. Stir in the peanuts and raisins. Scatter the chocolate chips evenly over the bottom of the cooled pie shell. Put the pie shell on a baking sheet, near the oven, and slowly pour in the filling. Gently rake the filling with a fork to distribute the nuts, raisins, and chocolate chips evenly.

3. Bake the pie, on the sheet, on the center rack for about 40 minutes, until the perimeter puffs slightly and the filling is set, rotating the pie 180 degrees midway through the baking.

4. Transfer the pie to a rack and cool thoroughly. Serve at room temperature, or slightly chilled. Cover and refrigerate leftovers.

Recipe for Success

Since this pie freezes well, you can slice it into skinny wedges, wrap them in aluminum foil or freezer bags, and stash them in the freezer. Just throw a couple of slices in your pack and they'll be perfectly thawed by the time you need a snack.

Snack on This

- Peanuts account for more than two thirds of all the snack nuts consumed.

- Americans eat more than 700 million pounds of peanuts each year.

- Peanuts are a valuable source of folate, an important B vitamin.

Roasted Virginia Peanut Pie

Careful — you might like this even more than pecan pie and get hopelessly hooked. It's unabashedly sweet, and the flavor of roasted peanuts comes through loud and clear. (Don't use unroasted peanuts or the flavor won't be nearly as good.) I suggest adding a drizzle of warm Chocolate Ganache to the mandatory vanilla ice cream garnish.

Makes 8–10 servings

Single-Crust Food Processor Pie Dough (page 58)

FILLING

- 3 **large eggs, at room temperature**
- ⅓ **cup packed light brown sugar**
- ¼ **cup granulated sugar**
- 1¼ **cups dark corn syrup**
- 6 **tablespoons unsalted butter, melted**
- ¼ **teaspoon salt**
- 1 **teaspoon vanilla extract**
- 1½ **cups salted dry-roasted peanuts, coarsely chopped**

  Vanilla ice cream, for serving

  Chocolate Ganache (page 445), warmed (optional)

1. Prepare and refrigerate the pie dough. Roll the dough into a 12½- to 13-inch circle and line a 9- to 9½-inch deep-dish pie pan with it, shaping the edge into an upstanding ridge. Flute or crimp the edge, chill the shell, and partially prebake it according to the instructions on page 36.

2. Preheat the oven to 350°F (180°C). Whisk the eggs and sugars together in a large bowl just until frothy. Whisk in the corn syrup, butter, salt, and vanilla until well mixed. Stir in the peanuts. Put the pie shell on a baking sheet, near the oven, and slowly pour the filling into the shell. Gently rake a fork through the filling to distribute the nuts evenly.

3. Bake the pie, on the sheet, on the center rack for about 50 minutes, until the filling is set and doesn't move in waves, rotating the pie 180 degrees midway through the baking. Give the pie a quick nudge to check it.

4. Transfer the pie to a rack and cool thoroughly. Serve at room temperature, or refrigerate for an hour or two before serving with vanilla ice cream and drizzling with warm chocolate ganache, if desired. Cover and refrigerate leftovers.

Peanut Butter Cheesecake Pie *with* Brown Sugar–Sour Cream Topping

This is like a cheesecake disguised as a pie. The filling has a creamy, peanut buttery texture, with the occasional soft crunch of peanut butter chips. It's topped with a sour cream and brown sugar layer that's poured over the top once the pie has cooled a bit. This is a good one for the kids, or for dessert after a Sunday comfort-food supper.

Makes 8–10 servings

Graham Cracker Crust or Nut Crumb Crust (page 82) made with peanuts

FILLING

12 ounces full-fat cream cheese, softened

1 cup smooth peanut butter

1¼ cups granulated sugar

3 large eggs plus 1 large egg yolk, at room temperature

½ cup full-fat sour cream

1½ teaspoons vanilla extract

1 cup peanut butter chips

TOPPING

1 cup full-fat sour cream

¼ cup packed light brown sugar

⅛ teaspoon vanilla extract

1. Prepare the crust and set it aside to cool. It can be made a day or two ahead and refrigerated, if you like.

2. Adjust the oven racks so one is in the lower position and another is in the middle of the oven. Put about 1 inch of water in a shallow casserole dish and place it on the lower rack; this pie likes a saunalike oven. Preheat the oven to 325°F (170°C).

3. To make the filling, combine the cream cheese and peanut butter in a large bowl. Using an electric mixer, preferably a stand mixer, cream the ingredients on medium speed until evenly combined. Gradually add the granulated sugar, beating until evenly blended and scraping down the sides of the bowl as needed. Beat in the eggs and egg yolk, one at a time, until evenly combined. Beat in the sour cream and vanilla. Fold in the peanut butter chips. Put the pie shell on a baking sheet, near the oven, and pour the filling into the pan, smoothing it with a spoon or rubber spatula.

4. Bake the pie, on the sheet, on the center rack for 45 to 55 minutes, until the filling is set, rotating the pie 180 degrees midway through the baking. When the pie is done, the filling may be slightly puffed, though not too much, and the center will be wobbly but set. Also, the very center may have a shiny finish, whereas the perimeter will appear dull or flat. Transfer the pie to a rack and cool for about 30 minutes.

5. To make the topping, combine the sour cream and brown sugar in a small saucepan over low heat, stirring well until evenly mixed. Remove from the heat and stir in the vanilla. Immediately pour it over the center of the pie, then tilt the pan this way and that so the topping runs up to the edge. Return the pie to the rack and cool thoroughly. Cover with loosely tented aluminum foil and refrigerate for at least 6 hours or overnight before serving.

Recipe for Success

Take care not to overbeat the filling. You don't want to beat too much air into it, causing it to puff dramatically during baking and then fall and crack. A stand mixer with a flat beater is best.

Pine Nut Pie

Mild and buttery tasting, pine nuts give this sweet pie a soft crunch, a delicious flavor, and a golden mosaic surface pattern. A touch of cinnamon complements the nuts without overpowering them, and the brown sugar caramel-like filling will make you swoon. A real treat served with butter pecan ice cream.

Makes 8–10 servings

Single-Crust Food Processor Pie Dough (page 58) or another single-crust dough

FILLING

- ½ **cup packed light brown sugar**
- 2 **tablespoons all-purpose flour**
- ¼ **teaspoon ground cinnamon**
- ⅛ **teaspoon salt**
- 5 **tablespoons unsalted butter, melted**
- 3 **large eggs**
- ¾ **cup light corn syrup**
- ½ **teaspoon vanilla extract**
- 1 **cup pine nuts**

  Butter pecan, coffee, or vanilla ice cream, for serving (optional)

1. Prepare and refrigerate the pie dough. Roll the dough into a 12-inch circle and line a 9- to 9½-inch standard pie pan with it, shaping the edge into an upstanding ridge. Flute or crimp the edge, chill the shell, and partially pre-bake it according to the instructions on page 36.

2. Preheat the oven to 350°F (180°C). Combine the sugar, flour, cinnamon, and salt in a large bowl. Rub with your fingers to combine and break up any clumps. Whisk in the butter. Add the eggs, one at a time, whisking well after each addition. Whisk in the corn syrup and vanilla. Stir in the pine nuts. Put the pie shell on a baking sheet, near the oven, and carefully pour the filling into the shell. Gently rake a fork through the filling to distribute the nuts evenly.

3. Bake the pie, on the sheet, on the center rack for 40 to 45 minutes, until the filling is set and the top of the pie is a rich golden brown, rotating the pie 180 degrees midway through the baking. When done, the top will be a deep golden brown and the filling will be set; give the pie a little nudge to check it.

4. Transfer the pie to a rack and cool thoroughly. Serve at room temperature or refrigerate before serving. Either way, don't forget the ice cream, if desired. Cover and refrigerate leftovers.

Recipe for Success

Don't bother to toast the pine nuts before adding them to the pie; they will rise to the surface during baking and toast up nicely.

Toasted Almond Pie

One of the most appealing things about this delicious almond pie (that borders on almond cake) is the fact that the entire filling is made in a food processor; you won't leave a pile of bowls, beaters, and dirty utensils in your wake. The coffee cake–like filling will have you slicing this pie for breakfast to enjoy with your morning coffee.

Makes 8–10 servings

Almond Pie Dough (page 81) or Single-Crust Food Processor Pie Dough (page 58)

FILLING

1½ cups whole almonds, toasted (page 000) and coarsely chopped by hand

⅔ cup granulated sugar

¼ cup all-purpose flour

¼ cup sweetened flaked coconut

1½ teaspoons baking powder

¼ teaspoon salt

½ cup (1 stick) unsalted butter, at room temperature, cut into in several pieces

2 large eggs, at room temperature

½ cup heavy cream

½ teaspoon vanilla extract

Confectioners' sugar, for garnish (optional)

1. Prepare and refrigerate the pie dough. Roll the dough into a 9-inch circle and line a 9- to 9½-inch standard pie pan with it, shaping the edge into an upstanding ridge. Flute or crimp the edge, then refrigerate the shell until needed.

2. Preheat the oven to 400°F (200°C). Combine the almonds and granulated sugar in a food processor. Pulse the machine five or six times to partially chop the nuts. Add the flour, coconut, baking powder, and salt; pulse until the mixture is well combined and the nuts are more finely chopped, but not pulverized. Add the butter and pulse until well incorporated. Add the eggs, cream, and vanilla, and process until well blended, 6 to 8 seconds. Scrape the filling into the pie shell, smoothing the top with a spoon.

3. Place the pie on the center oven rack and bake for 20 minutes. Reduce the heat to 350°F (180°C) and rotate the pie 180 degrees. Bake for 20 to 25 minutes longer, until the filling rises a bit and is set.

4. Transfer the pie to a rack and cool. Serve just barely warm or at room temperature. Put confectioners' sugar in a small fine-mesh sieve and shake it over the top of the pie, if you like, before serving. Cover and refrigerate leftovers.

Recipe for Success

To help this pie retain as much moisture as possible, I cover it with plastic wrap while it is still a tad warm. Whether you do this or not, you'll notice that the pie is a little moister on the second day than it is on the first.

The reason I suggest hand chopping the almonds before processing them is because whole almonds sometimes fly around in the processor before the machine cuts them up. Hand chopping helps the processor do its job better.

Fruits of the Forest Pie *(Nut Version)*

As I mentioned in the headnote to the fruit version of this recipe (page 161), fruits of the forest pies are often made with fruit, but nuts are probably the more authentic way. Here's how I do the nut version, with mixed nuts and nut liqueurs. Buy a bag of roasted mixed nuts; that's much easier than buying the separate nuts. Rather than chop them, I leave most of them whole to give this granddaddy of nut pies a big, bold personality.

Makes 8–10 servings

Whole-Wheat Pie Dough (page 66) or another single-crust dough

FILLING

- 4 **large eggs, at room temperature**
- 1 **cup light corn syrup**
- ⅔ **cup packed light brown sugar**
- 6 **tablespoons unsalted butter, melted**
- 1 **tablespoon hazelnut liqueur**
- 1 **tablespoon almond liqueur**
- 1 **teaspoon vanilla extract**
- ¼ **teaspoon almond extract**
- ¼ **teaspoon salt**
- 2½ **cups roasted mixed nuts**

  Whipped Cream (page 447), for garnish

1. Prepare and refrigerate the pie dough. Roll the dough into a 12½- to 13-inch circle and line a 9- to 9½-inch deep-dish pie pan with it, shaping the edge into an upstanding ridge. Flute or crimp the edge, chill the shell, and partially prebake it according to the instructions on page 36.

2. Preheat the oven to 350°F (180°C). Gently whisk together the eggs in a large bowl. Whisk in the corn syrup, sugar, butter, liqueurs, vanilla, almond extract, and salt. Set aside.

3. Remove any nuts that are too large for comfort — such as Brazil nuts — and chop them coarsely. Spread all the nuts in the pie shell. Put the pie shell on a baking sheet, near the oven, and carefully pour the filling over the nuts. Push the nuts down into the filling with the back of a large spoon to make sure they're well coated; they'll quickly pop back up. Rake them around with a fork to get them evenly distributed.

4. Bake the pie, on the sheet, on the center oven rack for 40 to 45 minutes, rotating the pie 180 degrees midway through the baking. The pie is done when the filling is just set and no long soupy in the middle. Give it a little nudge to check.

5. Transfer the pie to a rack and cool thoroughly. Serve at room temperature, with a dollop of whipped cream. Cover and refrigerate leftovers.

Recipe for Success

Look for a nut mixture without peanuts, as they tend to overwhelm other nuts. My ideal combination would include Brazil nuts, hazelnuts, cashews, pecans, and maybe almonds. I like having a little of the rain forest in my fruits of the forest pie.

Unlike some of my nut pies, I don't chop the nuts here, for the most part, because I love the way the pie looks with whole nuts and large pieces. The big nuts might squeeze out some of the filling when you cut the pie, but you can make cleaner cuts by slicing it when it is very cold.

10
Rich, Sweet, and Simple:
CHESS, BUTTERMILK, AND OTHER CUSTARD PIES

Chess, buttermilk, and custard pies are close enough relatives that I've joined them here in a single chapter. Although each category has its distinguishing characteristics, they share a noteworthy common ingredient: eggs. When a pie is made with eggs, the rules change. Unlike the chapters on fruit pies where you heard me harp relentlessly about not underbaking them — lest the thickener not thicken — I'll now implore you to go slow and easy, taking care not to overbake your pies.

Cautionary notes aside, the thing I love most about these pies is their accessibility. For the most part, these pies have long been the stock-in-trade of the everyday cook. Their history dates back to a day when the main concern of busy home-makers and farm wives was getting a good meal on the table without contrivance or flourish. So they did what came naturally: they whipped up some pie shells, beat some eggs and milk or cream together with some sugar, and slid the pans into the oven. If it was August and they had more berries on hand than they knew what to do with, they'd toss in some of those, too.

What makes these pies most interesting and delicious, however, is not their similarities but their differences. As great composers know, the theme can remain constant without diminishing the variations. Maple syrup adds a change of color and the subtle flavor of New England to a custard pie. The combination of coffee and hazelnuts gives an exotic Mediterranean flair. A spoonful of cornmeal provides body and texture to a chess pie, making it distinct from one made without. Such is the beauty of these pies, and my hope is that you'll have a chance to try them all.

Tips for Baking Egg-Based Pies

- Bottom line is, you can do little damage to an egg-based pie if it's baked too slowly, but plenty if it's over-baked. Rather than acting as a thickener, the eggs can "break," or lose their ability to hold moisture. If you've ever cooked cup custard too long, you have some idea what awaits: a weepy pie and weepy cook.

- If your custard pies seem to puff up excessively, the edge of your crust gets overbrowned, or your crust looks done before your fruit filling is fully baked, it's a sure sign the oven is too hot. Check the temperature with a reliable oven thermometer and adjust the setting as needed, or call in a professional to have the oven recalibrated.

Classic Chess Pie

One of the interesting things about the category of chess pies is the various methods for mixing them. In many of the recipes, the butter — and no shy amount of it — is melted and stirred or whisked into the filling. Here, however, it is creamed with the other ingredients, resulting in what looks like a creamy cake batter that curdles when lemon juice is added. The baked pie has a dark brown crust, which is not uncommon with a genuine chess pie. This version is excellent.

Makes 8–10 servings

Old-Fashioned Shortening Pie Dough (page 62) or another single-crust dough

FILLING

- ½ cup (1 stick) unsalted butter, softened
- 1½ cups sugar
- 3 tablespoons all-purpose flour
- ⅛ teaspoon salt
- 4 large eggs, at room temperature
- ⅓ cup lemon juice
- Grated zest of 1 lemon

1. Prepare and refrigerate the pie dough. Roll the dough into a 13-inch circle and line a 9- to 9½-inch deep-dish pie pan with it, shaping the edge into an upstanding ridge. Flute or crimp the edge, chill the shell, and partially prebake it according to the instructions on page 36.

2. Preheat the oven to 350°F (180°C). Cream the butter in a large bowl with an electric mixer, gradually adding the sugar about ¼ cup at a time. Beat in the flour and salt; the mixture will be quite grainy. Beat in the eggs one at a time, beating well on medium speed after each addition. Blend in the lemon juice and zest on low speed. Place the pie shell on a baking sheet, near the oven, and carefully pour the filling into the shell, smoothing the top with a spoon.

3. Bake the pie, on the sheet, on the center oven rack for about 45 minutes, turning the pie 180 degrees midway through the baking. The pie is done when the filling is just set and no long soupy in the middle. Give it a little nudge to check.

4. Transfer the pie to a rack and cool to room temperature. Refrigerate for at least 2 hours before serving. Refrigerate leftovers, covered with tented aluminum foil.

Recipe for Success

Don't worry about the curdled look of the filling when you're mixing. The filling will bake up smooth and creamy.

The top of the pie will have a thin, spongelike layer, so it can be difficult to judge doneness. Look carefully at the center of the pie when you nudge it. The sponge is also why I suggest covering the pie with tented aluminum foil, so you don't damage the nice sponginess.

Brown Sugar and Toasted Pecan Chess Pie

I love brown sugary baked goods, and this is one of my favorites. The tablespoon of molasses gives the filling a dark, handsome profile and a deep, satisfying flavor. The toasted pecans are a fancy touch for a chess pie.

Makes 8–10 servings

Perfect Pie Dough by Hand (page 56) or another single-crust dough

FILLING

- 1½ cups light brown sugar
- 3 tablespoons all-purpose flour
- ¼ teaspoon ground cinnamon
- ¼ teaspoon salt
- ½ cup (1 stick) unsalted butter
- ½ cup milk or half-and-half
- 1 tablespoon unsulphured molasses
- 1 teaspoon vanilla extract
- 3 large eggs plus 1 large egg yolk
- 1 cup pecan halves, toasted (page 453) and finely chopped by hand

1. Prepare and refrigerate the pie dough. Roll the dough into a 12½- to 13-inch circle and line a 9- to 9½-inch deep-dish pie pan with it, shaping the edge into an upstanding ridge. Flute or crimp the edge, chill the shell, and partially prebake it according to the instructions on page 36.

2. Preheat the oven to 350°F (180°C). Combine the sugar, flour, cinnamon, and salt in a large bowl. Rub well by hand to smooth out the mixture. Combine the butter and milk in a small saucepan and gently heat until the butter melts. Pour over the sugar mixture. Add the molasses and vanilla, and whisk until smooth. Cool to lukewarm.

3. Whisk the eggs and egg yolk in a large bowl. Gradually whisk in the sugar mixture. Stir in the pecans. Place the pie shell on a large baking sheet, near the oven, and carefully pour the filling into the shell.

4. Bake the pie, on the sheet, on the middle oven rack for 40 to 45 minutes, until the filling is set and slightly puffy. When done, the filling will wobble, but not move in waves under the nut topping. Give the pie a little nudge to check.

5. Transfer the pie to a rack and cool thoroughly. Refrigerate for at least 2 hours before serving; I prefer it well chilled. Cover and refrigerate leftovers.

Recipe for Success

Don't use more than 1 tablespoon of molasses. Molasses has a strong flavor and can quickly overwhelm everything else.

Homestead Chess Pie

This classic of the chess pie genre originated at the famed Homestead Restaurant in Lexington, Kentucky, and first appeared in the *Louisville Courier-Journal* in 1954. It's perfectly delicious and embodies everything I love about chess pies — mainly, how just a few ingredients can make such a delicious pie.

Makes 8–10 servings

Old-Fashioned Shortening Pie Dough (page 62) or another single-crust dough

FILLING

- 3 **large eggs**
- 1½ **cups sugar**
- 7 **tablespoons salted or unsalted butter, very soft**
- 1 **tablespoon fine yellow cornmeal**
- 1 **tablespoon white vinegar or apple cider vinegar**
- 1 **teaspoon vanilla extract**

1. Prepare and refrigerate the pie dough. Roll the dough into a 12-inch circle and line a 9- to 9½-inch standard pie pan with it, shaping the edge into an upstanding ridge. Flute or crimp the edge, then refrigerate the shell until needed.

2. Preheat the oven to 350°F (180°C). Combine the eggs, sugar, butter, cornmeal, vinegar, and vanilla in a large bowl. Whisk well to mix thoroughly. Place the pie shell on a baking sheet, near the oven, and carefully pour the filling into the shell.

3. Bake the pie, on the sheet, on the center oven rack for 35 to 40 minutes, rotating the pie 180 degrees midway through the baking. When done, a knife inserted in the center of the pie will come out clean, and the top of the pie will be a rich golden brown.

4. Transfer the pie to a rack and cool for at least 30 minutes. You can serve the pie lukewarm, but I think it, like virtually all chess pies, tastes best chilled.

Recipe for Success

The original recipe calls for an unbaked pie shell, the way it is written here, but I prefer a partially prebaked shell so the bottom crust stays crisper.

The original recipe does not specify the kind of vinegar to be used. I tend to use apple cider vinegar, but I've also used distilled white vinegar and it works just fine.

Canadian Butter Tarts

At the risk of oversimplifying things, a butter tart is something like a miniature version of our pecan pie, minus the pecans — just the lovely gooey filling and a buttery crust. It's perhaps the closest thing Canadians have to a national sweet, though even they can't seem to agree whether their beloved tarts should contain raisins or chopped nuts; feel free to use either, none, or both. But do make these cute little tarts — they're out-of-this-world delicious.

Makes about 12 servings

Single-Crust Food Processor Pie Dough (page 58)

FILLING

- ⅔ cup packed light brown sugar
- ⅓ cup maple syrup
- 4 tablespoons unsalted butter, very soft
- 1 large egg
- 1½ teaspoons white vinegar or apple cider vinegar
- 1 teaspoon vanilla extract
- ¼ teaspoon salt
- Small handful of raisins, dried currants, chopped pecans, or chopped walnuts (optional)

1. Prepare and refrigerate the pie dough.

2. Roll the dough as you would for most pies, about ⅛-inch thick or a tad thinner. Don't worry about keeping it nice and round like you normally would.

3. Using a 4-inch-diameter cookie or biscuit cutter, cut the dough into as many circles as possible. Line each cup of a standard 12-cup muffin pan with one of the circles, gently nudging it down into the bottom creases of the pan. Try not to stretch the dough as you work; it can help to use something blunt, like a narrow jar, to nudge the dough. The top edge of the dough circle should come to about the middle of the cup. Gather the scraps and reroll the dough if you need additional circles. Chill the pan in the freezer for 20 to 30 minutes.

4. Adjust one oven rack so it is in the lower position, and preheat the oven to 425°F (220°C). Combine the sugar, maple syrup, and butter in a mixing bowl. Whisk briefly. Add the egg, vinegar, vanilla, and salt, and whisk again.

5. Set the muffin pan on your work surface. If you're using the fruit or nuts, put a few pieces in as many of the shells as you wish, but don't crowd them. Use a ladle or ¼-cup measuring cup with a handle to divide the filling evenly between the shells.

6. Bake for 15 to 18 minutes, until the filling bubbles and darkens somewhat.

7. Transfer the pan to a rack and cool for 5 minutes, then carefully run a butter knife around the edge to loosen each tart. Let the tarts cool in the pan, then remove. Store, refrigerated, in a single layer in a covered tin or container, but let them come to room temperature before serving.

Recipe for Success

The trick with these tarts is knowing precisely how long they should be baked, but that depends on personal preference. A lot of people like them slightly runny (shorter baking time), while others prefer the filling to be more like pecan pie (longer baking). You may need to make the recipe a few times — what a shame — and note the visual clues that will help you bake them to your liking.

Typically these will not stick to the pan so long as the filling has not bubbled over the edge of the shell. Those, in particular, are the ones you have to loosen with a butter knife.

If you can manage it, these tarts benefit from a brief rewarming before serving if they've been refrigerated. Arrange them on a baking sheet and place in a 300°F (150°C) oven for 5 or 6 minutes. That will crisp the shells and soften the filling.

Maple-Buttermilk Chess Pie

Most chess pies are pretty sweet, which is why you find buttermilk in so many of them; its tartness provides just the right counterbalance to the sweetness. Here's a buttermilk chess pie that's all about pure maple flavor without distractions. Serve with unsweetened whipped cream, or lightly sweetened and with a dab of almond extract.

Makes 8–10 servings

Whole-Wheat Pie Dough (page 66) or another single-crust dough

FILLING

- 1 **cup packed light brown sugar**
- 2 **tablespoons fine yellow cornmeal**
  - **Scant ½ teaspoon salt**
- 3 **large eggs plus 1 egg yolk**
- ⅔ **cup buttermilk**
- ½ **cup maple syrup**
- ½ **cup (1 stick) unsalted butter, melted**
- 1½ **teaspoons vanilla extract**
  - **Whipped Cream (page 447), unsweetened or lightly sweetened, for garnish**

1. Prepare and refrigerate the pie dough. Roll the dough into a 12-inch circle and line a 9- to 9½-inch standard pie pan with it, shaping the edge into an upstanding ridge. Flute or crimp the edge, chill the shell, and partially prebake it according to the instructions on page 36.

2. Preheat the oven to 350°F (180°C). Combine the sugar, cornmeal, and salt in a large bowl. Rub with your fingers to work out any lumps in the sugar. Add the eggs and egg yolk, buttermilk, maple syrup, butter, and vanilla. Using a hand-held electric mixer, beat the mixture on medium speed until well blended, about 1 minute. Put the pie shell on a baking sheet, near the oven, and carefully pour the filling into the shell.

3. Bake the pie, on the sheet, on the middle oven rack for 20 minutes. Lower the heat to 325°F (170°C) and rotate the pie 180 degrees. Bake for 25 to 35 minutes longer, until the pie is a rich golden brown and the filling is set. Give the pie a little nudge. The filling should wobble, but there should be no soupiness at the center.

4. Transfer the pie to a rack and cool thoroughly. Serve at room temperature, or refrigerate the pie first, garnished with whipped cream either way. Refrigerate leftovers.

Recipe for Success

Be sure to use fine cornmeal here. Coarse-ground cornmeal will not give the pie the same sort of smooth, uniform texture.

Angus Barn Chocolate Chess Pie

The Angus Barn has been an institution in Raleigh, North Carolina, for more than 50 years. It's best known for its steaks, and perhaps second best for this incredible version of chess pie that owner Van Eure tells me was perfected by her parents, the original owners. Van thinks it tastes best at room temperature with whipped cream or ice cream. You'll love everything about this, especially the brittle top that forms.

Makes 8–10 servings

Old-Fashioned Shortening Pie Dough (page 62)

FILLING

- ½ **cup (1 stick) unsalted butter**
- 2 **ounces semisweet chocolate, coarsely chopped**
- 1 **cup sugar**
- 2 **large eggs**
- 1 **teaspoon vanilla extract**
- ⅛ **teaspoon salt**

1. Prepare and refrigerate the pie dough. Roll the dough into a 12-inch circle and line a 9- to 9½-inch standard pie pan with it, shaping the edge into an upstanding ridge. Flute or crimp the edge, chill the shell, and partially prebake it according to the instructions on page 36.

2. Preheat the oven to 350°F (180°C). Melt the butter over low heat in a medium saucepan, preferably nonstick. Turn off the heat and add the chocolate. Let the mixture sit until the chocolate has melted, about 5 minutes, occasionally tilting the pan so the hot butter runs over the chocolate. Cool briefly, whisking to smooth.

3. Whisk together the sugar, eggs, vanilla, and salt in a medium bowl. Add the chocolate mixture and whisk until evenly blended. Slowly pour the filling into the cooled pie shell.

4. Place the pie on the center oven rack and bake for 35 to 40 minutes, until set, rotating the pie 180 degrees midway through the baking. When the pie is done, the top will be crusted over and the filling may puff slightly, but don't expect it to rise much.

5. Transfer the pie to a rack and cool completely. Serve at room temperature, or refrigerate for an hour or two before serving. Refrigerate leftovers.

Recipe for Success

As a matter of record, the original Angus Barn recipe doesn't specify prebaking the crust. That's my own preference.

Where Did Chess Pie Get Its Name?

There are two possible stories that sound somewhat credible. The first has to do with a piece of furniture known as a pie safe or pie chest. Traditionally a cupboard with perforated tin panels, the name might come from the fact that Southerners stored their pies in such a chest for safekeeping.

In the more charming version, it's said that a creative Southern housewife threw a few ingredients together, baked them in a pie shell, and served it to her husband. The husband loved it and made quite a fuss, to which she replied — you supply the accent — "Why honey, it's ches' pie."

Fancy Chocolate Chess Pie

This slightly fancier version of chocolate chess pie is made with bittersweet chocolate and cornmeal, which is used as a thickener in many chess pie recipes. Here you wind up with the same thin, crispy top layer as the previous pie, but with a rich, oozing, chocolate pudding–like layer underneath. Cold, it has a texture like gooey caramel; warm, it's slightly runny. Either way, it's superb.

Makes 8–10 servings

Single-Crust Food Processor Pie Dough (page 58) or another single-crust dough

FILLING

- ½ cup (1 stick) unsalted butter, cut into in several pieces
- 4 ounces bittersweet chocolate, coarsely chopped
- 1¼ cups sugar
- 2 tablespoons fine yellow cornmeal
- ¼ teaspoon salt
- 3 large eggs plus large 1 yolk, at room temperature
- ¼ cup whole milk or half-and-half
- 1 teaspoon vanilla extract

1. Prepare and refrigerate the pie dough. Roll the dough into a 12-inch circle and line a 9- to 9½-inch standard pie pan with it, shaping the edge into an upstanding ridge. Flute or crimp the edge, chill the shell, and partially prebake it according to the instructions on page 36.

2. Preheat the oven to 325°F (170°C). Put the butter in the top insert of a double boiler set over, not in, barely simmering water. (Alternatively, use a heatproof bowl, suspended by the sides of a saucepan, over barely simmering water.) Scatter the chocolate over the butter. Let the mixture sit until melted, about 5 minutes, stirring once or twice. Remove the insert, whisk the mixture to smooth it, then let the chocolate cool briefly.

3. Combine the sugar, cornmeal, and salt in a large bowl, tossing with your hands to mix. Add the eggs, egg yolk, milk, and vanilla, and whisk until evenly mixed. Pour the chocolate mixture into the bowl and whisk briefly to smooth. Put the pie shell on a baking sheet, near the oven, and carefully pour the filling into the shell.

4. Bake the pie, on the sheet, on the center oven rack for 45 to 55 minutes, rotating the pie 180 degrees midway through the baking. When done, the pie will have developed a uniformly thin upper crust, and it will puff slightly.

5. Transfer the pie to a rack and cool for at least 1 hour. Serve slightly warm, at room temperature, or chilled. Cover and refrigerate leftovers.

Recipe for Success

With the chocolate pies in this collection, the chocolate and butter are sometimes melted in a saucepan over direct heat, and other times in a double-boiler setup. Given chocolate's temperamental behavior, the double-boiler method is safer and generally preferred because you're less likely to scorch the chocolate.

However, sometimes it's just easier to start melting the butter in a small saucepan over low heat, drop in the chocolate, and turn off the heat. The residual heat in the pan and cooktop is usually sufficient to melt the chocolate. If necessary, you can always turn the heat back on, very low, for 30 seconds to boost the process. Swirling the pan allows the butter to run over the chocolate, which also helps the melting.

Finally, never use the direct stovetop method to melt chocolate without the butter — always use a double boiler.

Lemon Chess Pie

A common thread among traditional chess pie recipes is a little cornmeal to help thicken the filling, like you see here. It's a uniquely Southern touch that adds just a bit of coarseness to an otherwise silky-smooth lemon filling in this classic pie.

Makes 8–10 servings

Old-Fashioned Shortening Pie Dough (page 62)

FILLING

1½ cups sugar

2 tablespoons fine yellow cornmeal

¼ teaspoon salt

2 large eggs plus 1 egg yolk, at room temperature

½ cup milk or half-and-half

4 tablespoons unsalted butter, melted

3 tablespoons lemon juice

Finely grated zest of 1 lemon

½ teaspoon lemon extract or vanilla extract

1. Prepare and refrigerate the pie dough. Roll the dough into a 13-inch circle and line a 9- to 9½-inch deep-dish pie pan with it, shaping the edge into an upstanding ridge. Flute or crimp the edge, chill the shell, and partially prebake it according to the instructions on page 36.

2. Preheat the oven to 350°F (180°C). Combine the sugar, cornmeal, and salt in a large bowl. Mix with your hands to combine. Add the eggs and egg yolk, whisking well to blend. Whisk in the milk, butter, lemon juice, lemon zest, and lemon extract. Put the pie shell on a baking sheet, near the oven, and carefully pour the filling into the shell.

3. Bake the pie, on the sheet, on the center oven rack for 45 to 50 minutes, rotating the pie 180 degrees midway through the baking. When the pie is done, the top will be a rich golden brown and the filling will be set.

4. Transfer the pie to a rack to cool. Serve at room temperature or refrigerate for several hours first. Cover and refrigerate leftovers.

Recipe for Success

If you like a very lemony pie filling, you can increase the lemon juice by another tablespoon or two. You could also include more zest or even use more lemon extract.

Honey-Lemon Chess Pie
with Crystallized Ginger

I love honey and often use it in baking. It adds moisture to quick breads and muffins, and its delicate flavor works perfectly in this lemony chess pie. The crystallized ginger is a little bonus, if you'd like to sprinkle it over the pie while it's still baking. (The trick is to time the addition of the ginger so it barely sinks into the filling.) I typically serve this in summer, garnished with fresh berries and unsweetened whipped cream.

Makes 8–10 servings

Buttermilk Pie Dough (page 67) or another single-crust dough

FILLING

3 **large eggs, at room temperature**

¾ **cup buttermilk**

½ **cup clover honey or other delicate-tasting honey**

½ **cup sugar**

3 **tablespoons fine yellow cornmeal**

2 **tablespoons lemon juice**

1 **teaspoon lemon extract or 2 tablespoons finely grated lemon zest**

⅛ **teaspoon salt**

6 **tablespoons unsalted butter, melted**

3 **tablespoons chopped crystallized ginger (optional)**

1. Prepare and refrigerate the pie dough. Roll the dough into a 12-inch circle and line a 9- to 9½-inch standard pie pan with it, shaping the edge into an upstanding ridge. Flute or crimp the edge, chill the shell, and partially prebake it according to the instructions on page 36.

2. Preheat the oven to 350°F (180°C). Whisk the eggs briefly in a large bowl. Add the buttermilk, honey, sugar, cornmeal, lemon juice, lemon extract, and salt. Whisk well, then add the butter and whisk again until everything is evenly combined.

3. Put the pie shell on a baking sheet, near the oven, and carefully pour the filling into the shell. Bake the pie, on the sheet, on the middle rack for 20 or 25 minutes. If you're using the ginger, slowly slide out the rack and scatter the ginger over the filling. (Doing this midway through the baking will keep it from sinking to the bottom.) If you're not using the ginger, simply continue to bake the pie.

4. Bake the pie for 15 to 20 minutes longer, until the filling is set. When done, the filling should wobble when you nudge the pan, with no soupiness in the center.

5. Transfer the pie to a rack to cool. Serve at room temperature or refrigerate for several hours first. Cover and refrigerate leftovers.

Recipe for Success

If you're wondering why I don't use all honey here, rather than honey with sugar, the answer is that all honey can make the pie cloyingly sweet. The combination of the two provides the delicate flavor of honey without overstating it.

Be sure to use fine cornmeal here. Coarse-ground cornmeal will not give the pie the same sort of smooth, uniform texture.

Amish Milk Pie

This Amish specialty is the simplest sort of pie you're likely to encounter, but it's unusual in several respects. It's not thickened with eggs, like a custard pie, so the result is charmingly runny and meant to be eaten with a spoon. And the filling is mixed in the pie shell itself. Some milk pies call for molasses, others for brown or regular sugar. Many specify evaporated milk, while others use half-and-half or sour milk. This one is a hybrid of the best ones I've tried.

Old-Fashioned Shortening Pie Dough (page 62) or another single-crust dough

FILLING

- ¼ cup granulated sugar
- ¾ cup packed light brown sugar
- ¼ cup all-purpose flour
- ⅛ teaspoon salt
- 1½ cups evaporated milk or half-and-half
- 2 tablespoons cold unsalted butter, cut into small pieces
- ½ teaspoon vanilla extract
- ¼ teaspoon ground cinnamon

1. Prepare and refrigerate the pie dough. Roll the dough into a 12-inch circle and line a 9- to 9½-inch standard pie pan with it. Trim the pastry overhang so it is flush with the outer edge of the pan. Crimp the edge with a fork or simply leave it as is. (The filling of this pie is very thin, so you don't want to build up the edge of the pie or the filling will look awkward.) Refrigerate the shell until needed.

2. Preheat the oven to 375°F (190°C). Put the sugars, flour, and salt in a pile in the pie shell. Rub the mixture together with your fingers to combine, then spread it evenly in the shell. Drizzle the evaporated milk over the sugar mixture, but don't mix everything together. Dot the filling with the butter, then drizzle on the vanilla. Sprinkle the filling with the cinnamon.

3. Place the pie on the center oven rack and bake for 50 to 60 minutes, until the filling has turned golden brown and bubbly, rotating the pie 180 degrees midway through the baking. The filling may seem a little soupy even when the pie has finished baking, but the entire filling should wobble, not move in waves.

4. Transfer the pie to a rack and cool for at least 30 minutes before serving at any temperature. If you're not serving right away, cool the pie thoroughly and refrigerate until ready to serve.

Recipe for Success

It's not traditional to prebake the shell for this pie, which is why I don't.

Indiana Buttermilk Pie

Dug up from my handwritten files, the original source of this recipe is a mystery to me now, but I love this farm-country pie as much as ever. It's the perfect balance of creamy and tangy-sweet, with a touch of caramel from the brown sugar.

Makes 8–10 servings

Perfect Pie Dough by Hand (page 56) or another single-crust dough

FILLING

- ½ cup packed light brown sugar
- ½ cup granulated sugar
- 3 tablespoons all-purpose flour
- ⅛ teaspoon salt
- 3 large eggs plus 1 large egg yolk
- 1 teaspoon vanilla extract
- 1½ cups buttermilk
- 3 tablespoons unsalted butter, melted

1. Prepare and refrigerate the pie dough. Roll the dough into a 13-inch circle and line a 9- to 9½-inch deep-dish pie pan with it, shaping the edge into an upstanding ridge. Flute or crimp the edge, chill the shell, and partially pre-bake it according to the instructions on page 36.

2. Preheat the oven to 350°F (180°C). Combine the sugars, flour, and salt in a food processor; pulse to combine. Add the eggs, egg yolk, and vanilla, and pulse again. Add the buttermilk and butter, and process for 5 or 6 seconds, until well blended. Put the pie shell on a baking sheet, near the oven, and carefully pour the filling into the shell.

3. Bake the pie, on the sheet, on the center oven rack for 40 to 45 minutes, until the top is golden brown and the filling is set, rotating the pie 180 degrees midway through the baking. The filling should show no sign of soupiness in the center when it's done. Give the pie a little nudge to check.

4. Transfer the pie to a rack and cool thoroughly. Serve at room temperature, or refrigerate for several hours first. Cover and refrigerate leftovers.

Recipe for Success

If the food processor feels a bit prissy for a recipe that originated decades ago in Indiana farm country, just use an old-fashioned whisk to blend the filling.

Blueberry-Buttermilk Pie

This is even better than it sounds: cool buttermilk custard shot through with plump ripe summer berries, all on top of a buttery crust. Pretty as can be, too. If ever there was a can't-miss pie for blueberry season, this is it.

Makes 8–10 servings

Perfect Pie Dough by Hand (page 56)

FILLING

- ½ cup (1 stick) unsalted butter, melted
- 1¼ cups sugar
- ¼ teaspoon salt
- 5 large egg yolks and 3 large egg whites, in separate bowls
- 1½ tablespoons fine yellow cornmeal
- 1½ tablespoons all-purpose flour
- 2 tablespoons lemon juice
- ¼ teaspoon ground nutmeg
- 1½ cups buttermilk
- ½ cup heavy cream
- 1 teaspoon vanilla extract or ½ teaspoon each lemon and vanilla extracts
- 1½ cups fresh blueberries

1. Prepare and refrigerate the pie dough. Roll the dough into a 12½- to 13-inch circle and line a 9- to 9½-inch deep-dish pie pan with it, shaping the edge into an upstanding ridge. Flute or crimp the edge, chill the shell, and partially prebake it according to the instructions on page 36.

2. Preheat the oven to 375°F (190°C). Combine the butter, sugar, salt, and the egg yolks in a large bowl. Using an electric mixer (handheld is fine), beat the mixture on medium speed until well blended, about 1 minute. Add the cornmeal, flour, lemon juice, and nutmeg, and beat again. Add the buttermilk, cream, and vanilla, and beat on medium-low speed until evenly combined.

3. Clean the beaters. Beat the egg whites in a separate bowl until they're billowy and almost able to hold soft peaks. Add the whites to the batter and whisk well. You don't have to worry about deflating the whites; we're not making a soufflé. Just make sure the filling is well mixed.

4. Put the pie shell on a baking sheet, near the oven, and spread the blueberries in the shell. Carefully add the filling, pouring slowly so the berries don't all end up on one side of the pie. (Rake them around with a fork to even them out, if you need to.)

5. Bake the pie, on the sheet, on the middle oven rack for 20 minutes. Reduce the heat to 350°F (180°C) and bake for 30 to 40 minutes longer, until the filling is set and no longer soupy. To check, give the pie a little nudge. The filling should wobble, not move in waves.

6. Transfer the pie to a rack and cool thoroughly. Refrigerate for at least 2 hours before serving. Refrigerate leftovers.

Recipe for Success

After you rinse the berries, be sure to blot them dry on paper towels before adding them to the pie. You don't want extra water in the filling.

Be sure to use fine cornmeal here. Coarse-ground cornmeal will not give the pie the same sort of smooth, uniform texture.

Hominy Grill Buttermilk Pie

One of the best buttermilk pies you'll ever taste, this has a spongelike top layer, like lemon pudding cake, with lemon pudding underneath. The recipe comes courtesy of Robert Stehling, chef-owner of the popular Hominy Grill restaurant in Charleston, South Carolina. The layers are the result of creaming the butter with the sugar, a somewhat unusual step for a pie, then incorporating beaten egg whites. I'm crazy about this pie and know you will be, too.

Makes 8–10 servings

Single-Crust Food Processor Pie Dough (page 58) or Cornmeal Pie Dough (page 68)

FILLING

- 6 **tablespoons unsalted butter, softened**
- 1 **cup sugar**
- 2 **large eggs, separated**
- 3 **tablespoons all-purpose flour**
- 1 **tablespoon lemon juice**
- ½ **teaspoon ground nutmeg**
- ¼ **teaspoon salt**
- 1 **cup buttermilk**

1. Prepare and refrigerate the pie dough. Roll the dough into a 12-inch circle and line a 9- to 9½-inch standard pie pan with it, shaping the edge into an upstanding ridge. Flute or crimp the edge, chill the shell, and partially pre-bake it according to the instructions on page 36.

2. Preheat the oven to 350°F (180°C). Using an electric mixer (handheld is fine), cream the butter in a large bowl, gradually adding the sugar until it is completely incorporated. The mixture looks clumpy; that's fine. Add the egg yolks and blend again. Add the flour, lemon juice, nutmeg, and salt, and beat until thoroughly combined. With the mixer on low speed, gradually blend in the buttermilk. Don't worry if the filling looks curdled.

3. Using a large clean dry bowl and clean beaters, beat the egg whites until they almost hold soft peaks. Pour a ladleful of the buttermilk mixture into the whiles, folding gently to combine. Gently fold the egg white mixture into the remaining buttermilk mixture until just combined. Put the pie shell on a baking sheet, near the oven, and slowly pour the filling into the shell.

4. Bake the pie, on the sheet, on the middle rack for 35 to 45 minutes, until the top is golden brown and the sides have puffed slightly, rotating the pie 180 degrees midway through the baking. When the pie is done, the entire filling should wobble and the center of the pie should show no sign of soupiness.

5. Transfer the pie to a rack and cool thoroughly. You may serve the pie at room temperature, but I prefer chilling it first. Cover the pie with tented aluminum foil before refrigerating.

Coconut-Buttermilk Pie

This recipe is adapted from Joyce White's book *Brown Sugar* and is one of the best buttermilk pies I've ever tried. The author says it's a composite of three recipes, each sent to her by good friends around the time she was experimenting with recipes for buttermilk pie. Creamy and coconutty, it has a little bit of flour to help firm up the filling and a small measure of canned cream of coconut to accentuate the tropical vibe.

Makes 8–10 servings

Old-Fashioned Shortening Pie Dough (page 62)

FILLING

- 3 large eggs, at room temperature
- ⅔ cup sugar
- 3 tablespoons all-purpose flour
- ¼ cup canned cream of coconut, well stirred
- 2 cups buttermilk
- 1 teaspoon vanilla extract
- ⅛ teaspoon salt
- 1 cup sweetened flaked coconut
- ¼–½ teaspoon ground nutmeg

1. Prepare and refrigerate the pie dough. Roll the dough into a 13-inch circle and line a 9- to 9½-inch deep-dish pie pan with it, shaping the edge into an upstanding ridge. Flute or crimp the edge, chill the shell, and partially pre-bake it according to the instructions on page 36.

2. Preheat the oven to 350°F (180°C). Whisk the eggs, sugar, and flour together in a large bowl. Whisk in the cream of coconut, buttermilk, vanilla, and salt. Stir in the coconut and nutmeg to taste until evenly combined. Put the pie shell on a baking sheet, near the oven, and slowly pour the filling into the shell.

3. Bake the pie, on the sheet, on the center oven rack for 40 to 45 minutes, just until set, rotating the pie 180 degrees midway through the baking. When done, the filling will wobble, not move in waves. Give the pie a little nudge to check. Also, the edge of the pie may puff slightly. Expect to see minimal, if any, browning on top of the filling.

4. Transfer the pie to a rack and cool thoroughly. Some like this pie served at room temperature, or even lukewarm, but I much prefer it chilled first. Cover and refrigerate leftovers.

About Buttermilk

Buttermilk today is not the same by-product of churned butter that our ancestors knew. Generally speaking, today you can find two kinds: cultured and acidified. Cultured buttermilk is made much like yogurt is: milk is inoculated with a bacterial culture and fermented. Acidified buttermilk is soured with tartaric or citric acid. I prefer the cultured variety, which I think has a smoother flavor in buttermilk pies and other baked goods.

By the way, there is no butter in buttermilk. In fact, it has only about 100 calories per cup, since most of it is made with low-fat or nonfat milk. So go right ahead and have that second piece of pie!

Maple Sugar Pie

Sugar pie is a French Canadian sort-of relative to shoofly pie. They have in common a thick layer of crumbs, which helps thicken the filling. Some of them float to the top of the pie to form a lovely layer there. Under the crumbs, you get a layer of soft maple goo. Don't even consider using pancake syrup for this in place of real maple syrup; the pie just wouldn't be the same. This is pretty sweet, so you will want to serve it with fresh unsweetened whipped cream.

Makes 8–10 servings

Single-Crust Food Processor Pie Dough (page 58) or another single-crust dough

FILLING

- 1 **cup all-purpose flour**
- ¾ **cup packed light brown sugar**
- ¼ **teaspoon salt**
- ¼ **teaspoon ground cinnamon**
- 6 **tablespoons cold unsalted butter, cut into ¼-inch pieces**
- 1 **cup maple syrup**
- ½ **teaspoon baking soda**
- 1 **large egg plus 1 egg yolk**
- ½ **teaspoon vanilla extract**

  Whipped Cream (page 447), preferably unsweetened

1. Prepare and refrigerate the pie dough. Roll the dough into a 13-inch circle and line a 9- to 9½-inch deep-dish pie pan with it, shaping the edge into an upstanding ridge. Flute or crimp the edge, chill the shell, and partially prebake it according to the instructions on page 36.

2. Preheat the oven to 350°F (180°C). Combine the flour, sugar, salt, and cinnamon in a large bowl. Add the butter and cut it into the dry mixture with a pastry blender until it is broken into very small pieces. Using your fingers, rub the mixture until you have crumbs that clump together when pressed in your palm.

3. Gently heat the maple syrup in a small saucepan until it is slightly warmer than body temperature. Transfer to a large bowl and whisk in the baking soda. Whisk the egg and egg yolk in a small bowl until frothy, then whisk this into the warmed maple syrup. Stir in the vanilla.

4. Place the pie shell on a baking sheet, near the oven. Spread about half of the crumbs in the shell. Slowly pour the filling over the crumbs. Scatter the remaining crumbs evenly over the filling.

5. Bake the pie, on the sheet, on the center rack for about 30 minutes, rotating the pie 180 degrees midway through the baking. When done, the pie will puff up considerably and turn a dark golden brown.

6. Transfer the pie to a rack and cool thoroughly. It can be eaten lukewarm, but I think it's best served at room temperature or slightly chilled. Refrigerate leftovers.

Recipe for Success

Don't be tempted to bake the pie much more than 30 minutes, even if the filling is a little loose. The crumbs will spread throughout the pie, absorb a good deal of moisture, and help thicken the filling.

Maple-Walnut Vinegar Pie

The idea for this recipe — which will remind you of pecan pie — originated with my friend Richard Sax, the late food writer, who was given a similar recipe by a friend's Canadian cousin. He introduced me to the recipe almost 30 years ago, and I've been making it ever since. Don't be turned off by the mention of vinegar. Vinegar, or for that matter, lemon juice, is often used to take the edge off sweet pie fillings. The vinegar is barely noticeable, but I think it makes this pie special.

Makes 8–10 servings

Single-Crust Food Processor Pie Dough (page 58) or another single-crust dough

FILLING

- 3 **large eggs plus 1 large yolk**
- ¾ **cup sugar**
- ¼ **cup orange juice**
- 2 **tablespoons apple cider vinegar**
- ¾ **cup maple syrup**
- 4 **tablespoons unsalted butter, cut into in several pieces**
- ¼ **teaspoon salt**
- 1¼ **cups walnut or pecan halves, toasted (page 453) or not, coarsely chopped**

1. Prepare and refrigerate the pie dough. Roll the dough into a 13-inch circle and line a 9- to 9½-inch deep-dish pie pan with it, shaping the edge into an upstanding ridge. Flute or crimp the edge, chill the shell, and partially prebake it according to the instructions on page 36.

2. Preheat the oven to 350°F (180°C). Combine the eggs, egg yolk, sugar, orange juice, and vinegar in a medium bowl and whisk to blend. Gently warm the maple syrup with the butter in a small saucepan until the butter melts. Slowly whisk the warm liquid into the egg mixture along with the salt. Stir in the walnuts. Put the pie shell on a baking sheet, near the oven, and carefully pour the filling into the shell. Gently rake a fork through the filling to distribute the nuts evenly.

3. Bake the pie, on the sheet, on the center rack for 40 to 45 minutes, until the surface is golden brown and slightly puffy, rotating the pie 180 degrees midway through the baking. When the pie is done, the filling will be set. Give it a little nudge to check.

4. Transfer the pie to a rack and cool the pie thoroughly. Serve at room temperature or slightly chilled. Cover and refrigerate leftovers.

Recipe for Success

Whenever you have a pie with a soupy filling, like this one, do the final assembly right near the oven. That's why I will often tell you to be near the oven when you pour the filling into the shell. You want to avoid walking across the kitchen with filling sloshing this way and that onto the baking sheet, or worse.

Red Currant Jelly Pie

Jelly pie and Tipsy Transparent Pie (see opposite page) have much in common with chess pies — primarily the fact that they're made with everyday ingredients you'd probably have even if the cupboard was almost bare. Depending on the jelly available in the pantry, the flavor of this pie might vary. Red currant is a fairly common option and makes for an attractive pie with a sweet, jellylike custard filling. Serve it with unsweetened whipped cream.

Makes 8–10 servings

Buttermilk Pie Dough
(page 67)

FILLING

- ¾ cup red currant jelly
- ½ cup (1 stick) unsalted butter, softened
- 1 cup sugar
- 2 teaspoons fine yellow cornmeal
- 1 tablespoon lemon juice
- 2 large eggs plus 1 large egg yolk, at room temperature
  Whipped Cream (page 447), preferably unsweetened

1. Prepare and refrigerate the pie dough. Roll the dough into a 12-inch circle and line a 9- to 9½-inch standard pie pan with it, shaping the edge into an upstanding ridge. Flute or crimp the edge, chill the shell, and partially prebake it according to the instructions on page 36.

2. Preheat the oven to 350°F (180°C). Heat the jelly in a small saucepan over low heat (or microwave it in a small bowl), whisking until smooth. Set aside to cool. Using an electric mixer (handheld is fine), beat the butter in a medium bowl, gradually adding the sugar. Blend in the cornmeal and lemon juice. When the jelly has cooled, beat it into the butter mixture until evenly blended.

Blend in the eggs and egg yolk, one at a time, beating until smooth after each addition. Put the pie shell on a baking sheet, near the oven, and slowly pour the filling into the pie shell, smoothing it out with a spoon.

3. Bake the pie, on the sheet, on the center oven rack for 40 minutes, rotating the pie 180 degrees midway through the baking. Reduce the temperature to 325°F (170°C) and bake for 10 minutes longer, until the filling is set and puffy and the surface has browned nicely.

4. Transfer the pie to a rack and cool thoroughly. Cover with tented aluminum foil and refrigerate for at least 2 hours before serving, garnished with whipped cream.

Recipe for Success

Don't worry if the pie puffs up more than you're used to; it does that. Just continue to bake until the center is set. Give it a little nudge to check.

If you detect a slight burning aroma near the end of baking, don't panic — the top of the pie is caramelizing, which won't detract from the flavor.

Tipsy Transparent Pie

Transparent pie is to Kentucky what chess pie is to the Carolinas and a handful of other Southern states — a simple pie made from everyday ingredients you'd have on hand. Unlike most chess pies, however, vinegar or lemon juice is seldom called for, and transparent pie often contains cream. I'm guessing the name comes from the nearly transparent filling which, sliced thinly enough, you can almost see through. (Rich and sweet as it is, you will want to cut thin slices.) If you don't want yours tipsy, leave out the whiskey.

Makes 10–12 servings

Old-Fashioned Shortening Pie Dough (page 62) or another single-crust dough

FILLING

- 6 tablespoons unsalted butter, very soft
- 1½ cups sugar
- ⅛ teaspoon salt
- 3 large eggs, at room temperature
- ¾ cup heavy cream
- 1 teaspoon vanilla extract
- 2–3 tablespoons whiskey (optional)
- 2 tablespoons all-purpose flour
- Unsweetened whipped cream, for serving

1. Prepare and refrigerate the pie dough. Roll the dough into a 13-inch circle and line a 9- to 9½-inch deep-dish pie pan with it, shaping the edge into an upstanding ridge. Flute or crimp the edge, chill the shell, and partially pre-bake it according to the instructions on page 36.

2. Preheat the oven to 350°F (180°C). Combine the butter, sugar, and salt in a large bowl. Using an electric mixer (handheld is fine), beat on medium speed until well combined, 2 to 3 minutes. Add the eggs, one at a time, beating well after each addition. Add the cream, vanilla, and whiskey (if using), and beat again. Shake the flour over the liquid and beat briefly on medium speed, scraping down the sides, until evenly blended.

3. Put the pie shell, on a baking sheet, near the oven, and carefully pour the filling into the shell. Bake the pie, on the sheet, on the center oven rack for about 45 minutes, until the filling has puffed up and the top is a rich golden brown. Note that the top will crust over and the pie may look prematurely done, but if you nudge the pie you will see that the filling still moves in waves beneath the surface. When the pie is done, you should be able to nudge the pan and see the entire filling wobble, not move in waves.

4. Transfer the pie to a rack and cool. Serve lukewarm, at room temperature, or chilled, with whipped cream. Refrigerate leftovers.

Osgood Pie

Both Southern and Midwestern cooks lay claim to this pie, which in the words of one writer is "a chess-like pie with a glistening, tangy custard with walnut pieces and fat, juicy raisins." That was enough to hook me, and enough of a distraction that I never did find out where this recipe originated. Most accounts maintain that the name is a shortened version of oh-so-good, and that makes total sense to me.

Makes 8–10 servings

Buttermilk Pie Dough (page 67) or another single-crust dough

FILLING

- 1 **cup dark raisins**
- **About 1 cup very hot water**
- 4 **large eggs, separated**
- 1½ **cups sugar**
- 4 **tablespoons unsalted butter, melted and slightly cooled**
- 3 **tablespoons apple cider vinegar**
- ¾ **cup chopped pecans or walnuts**
- ½ **teaspoon vanilla extract**
- ½ **teaspoon ground cinnamon**
- ½ **teaspoon ground nutmeg**
- ¼ **teaspoon ground cloves**

1. Prepare and refrigerate the pie dough. Roll the dough into a 13-inch circle and line a 9- to 9½-inch deep-dish pie pan with it, shaping the edge into an upstanding ridge. Flute or crimp the edge, chill the shell, and partially pre-bake it according to the instructions on page 36.

2. Preheat the oven to 400°F (200°C). Put the raisins in a small bowl and add enough of the water to cover. Let stand for 10 minutes.

3. Combine the egg yolks, sugar, butter, and vinegar in a large bowl. Using a handheld electric mixer, beat on medium-high speed for 2 minutes. Drain the raisins and stir them into the egg mixture along with the pecans, vanilla, cinnamon, nutmeg, and cloves.

4. Using clean, dry beaters, beat the egg whites in a medium bowl until you have soft peaks. Add the whites to the filling, folding them in gently but thoroughly. Put the pie shell on a baking sheet, near the oven, then slowly pour the filling into the shell. Gently rake a fork through the filling to distribute the raisins and nuts evenly.

5. Bake the pie, on the sheet, on the middle oven rack for 15 minutes. Reduce the heat to 350°F (180°C) and bake for about 35 minutes longer, until the filling is set, rotating the pie 180 degrees midway through the baking.

6. Transfer the pie to a rack and cool thoroughly. Serve at room temperature, or refrigerate for an hour or two before serving. Refrigerate leftovers.

Recipe for Success

While we're on the subject of beating eggs, remember that eggs are easier to separate when they're cold, but the whites beat up better when they're at room temperature. Keep that in mind when you make any recipe that calls for beaten egg whites: separating them should be one of your first orders of business.

Cherry Custard Pie

I often add a handful of berries — or in this case, cherries — to my custard pies. There's something very appealing about a custard fruit pie, even if the fruit does tend to bleed into the custard. But that's merely cosmetic and no reason not to try this delicious pie. Canned sweet cherries work nicely here. Or you can use pitted and halved fresh cherries.

Makes 8–10 servings

Single-Crust Food Processor Pie Dough (page 58) or another single-crust dough

FILLING

- 2 large eggs plus 1 large egg yolk
- ⅔ cup sugar
- 1 cup half-and-half
- ½ cup heavy cream
- ½ teaspoon vanilla extract
- 1½ tablespoons kirsch, Grand Marnier, or triple sec (optional)
- Pinch of salt
- 1 (15-ounce) can pitted sweet cherries, drained, or 1½ cups pitted and halved fresh sweet cherries

1. Prepare and refrigerate the pie dough. Roll the dough into a 12-inch circle and line a 9- to 9½-inch standard pie pan with it, shaping the edge into an upstanding ridge. Flute or crimp the edge, chill the shell, and partially pre-bake it according to the instructions on page 36.

2. Preheat the oven to 350°F (180°C). Combine the eggs, egg yolk, and sugar in a large bowl. Using an electric mixer, mix briefly on medium speed. Add the half-and-half, cream, vanilla, liqueur (if using), and salt; mix briefly.

3. Put the pie shell on a baking sheet, near the oven, and carefully pour the filling into the shell. Drop the cherries into the filling, one by one, spacing them throughout.

4. Bake the pie on the middle oven rack for 15 minutes. Reduce the heat to 325°F (170°C) and bake for 30 or 35 minutes longer, rotating the pie 180 degrees midway through the total baking time. When the pie is done, the custard will be just barely set and show no signs of soupiness.

5. Transfer the pie to a rack and cool thoroughly. Refrigerate for at least several hours before serving. Refrigerate leftovers.

Rich Lemon Custard Pie

There's no secret or anything fancy about this pie — it's simply a rich lemon custard filling in a flaky crust. Aside from the crust, it requires very little preparation time, which is one of the reasons it makes the perfect summer pie. The other, naturally, is that anything lemon makes a great summer dessert. Serve alone or with a berry garnish.

Makes 8–10 servings

Perfect Pie Dough by Hand (page 56) or another single-crust dough

FILLING

- ½ **cup half-and-half**
- ½ **cup sugar**
- 5 **large egg yolks**
- 1 **cup heavy cream**
- ¾ **teaspoon lemon extract**
- ½ **teaspoon vanilla extract**
- 1 **tablespoon finely grated lemon zest**
- **Fresh berries and/ or Whipped Cream (page 447) for garnish (optional)**

1. Prepare and refrigerate the pie dough. Roll the dough into a 13-inch circle and line a 9- to 9½-inch deep-dish pie pan with it, shaping the edge into an upstanding ridge. Flute or crimp the edge, chill the shell, and partially prebake it according to the instructions on page 36.

2. Preheat the oven to 325°F (170°C). Whisk the half-and-half, sugar, and egg yolks together in large bowl. Add the cream, lemon extract, vanilla, and lemon zest. Whisk again, just until evenly blended. Put the pie shell on a baking sheet, near the oven, and slowly pour the custard into the shell.

3. Bake the pie, on the sheet, on the center rack for 30 minutes. Lower the heat to 300°F (150°C) and rotate the pie 180 degrees. Bake for 20 to 25 minutes longer, until the filling is just barely set in the center. Give the pie a little nudge and make sure it isn't soupy in the center.

4. Transfer the pie to a rack and cool to room temperature. Refrigerate for at least 2 or 3 hours before serving. Garnish with berries and whipped cream, if desired. Refrigerate leftovers.

Recipe for Success

Some cooks like to strain their custard when it goes into the shell, to remove anything that shouldn't be there, like shell and unincorporated whites. It's probably a good idea, but I rarely bother.

Maple Custard Pie

This is more like maple crème brûlée in a crust than it is an everyday cup custard, which is to say, it's rich! But no one I've served this to has ever complained. Because it is so rich, I like to serve it after a light meal. Better still, serve it in late winter or early spring to celebrate the arrival of maple syrup season.

Makes 8–10 servings

Whole-Wheat Pie Dough (page 66) or another single-crust dough

FILLING

- 1½   cups heavy cream
- ½   cup half-and-half or milk
- ½   cup maple syrup
- ⅓   cup sugar
- ¾   teaspoon vanilla extract
- ⅛   teaspoon salt
- 5   large egg yolks

1. Prepare and refrigerate the pie dough. Roll the dough into a 13-inch circle and line a 9- to 9½-inch deep-dish pie pan with it, shaping the edge into an upstanding ridge. Flute or crimp the edge, chill the shell, and partially pre-bake it according to the instructions on page 36.

2. Preheat the oven to 325°F (170°C). Combine the cream, half-and-half, maple syrup, and sugar in a medium saucepan. Heat the mixture, stirring over medium heat, until the sugar has dissolved, but do not boil. Stir in the vanilla and salt. Remove from the heat and cool for 10 minutes.

3. Using a wooden spoon, stir the egg yolks in a medium bowl. Gradually stir in the warm cream mixture, a ladleful at a time. Place a fine-mesh strainer over a large bowl and pour in the filling, to strain. Put the pie shell on a baking sheet, near the oven, and carefully pour the strained filling into the shell.

4. Bake the pie, on the sheet, on the center oven rack for 55 to 65 minutes. When the pie is done, the edge of the filling will likely have puffed slightly. To check for doneness, give the pie a gentle nudge: the filling should wobble as a whole, with no sign of soupiness in the middle. If the center is not quite done, turn off the oven, open the door halfway, and let the pie sit undisturbed in the oven for 15 to 20 minutes.

5. Transfer the pie to a rack and cool thoroughly. Refrigerate for at least 4 hours before serving. Refrigerate leftovers, covered with tented aluminum foil.

Recipe for Success

As with many other egg-based pies, the rule for our Maple Custard Pie is baking it "low and slow." Virtually no harm can come to the pie baking it too slowly, but bad things can happen to custard pies baked too fast; think tough or curdled filling.

Ginger Custard Pie

Candied or crystallized ginger is a simple and somewhat novel way to flavor a custard pie. The ginger makes this pie especially good with fruit garnishes. I like to dollop the pie with a small mound of unsweetened whipped cream, then spoon a tablespoon of pear or fig preserves on top of that.

Makes 8–10 servings

Cornmeal Pie Dough (page 68) or another single-crust dough

FILLING

- **1 cup heavy cream**
- **1 cup half-and-half**
- **⅔ cup sugar**
- **¼ cup plus 2 tablespoons minced crystallized ginger**
- **1 large egg plus 4 large egg yolks**
- **1 teaspoon vanilla extract**
- **Unsweetened Whipped Cream (page 447), for garnish (optional)**
- **Fig or pear preserves, for garnish (optional)**

1. Prepare and refrigerate the pie dough. Roll the dough into a 13-inch circle and line a 9- to 9½-inch deep-dish pie pan with it, shaping the edge into an upstanding ridge. Flute or crimp the edge, chill the shell, and partially prebake it according to the instructions on page 36.

2. Preheat the oven to 350°F (180°C). Combine the heavy cream, half-and-half, and sugar in a medium saucepan over low heat. Cook, stirring, until the sugar dissolves, 3 to 4 minutes. Remove from the heat and stir in the ¼ cup ginger. Cool for 5 to 10 minutes.

3. Gently whisk the egg and egg yolks in a large bowl until blended. Stir in the cream mixture, a ladleful at a time, adding all of the ginger that's in the saucepan. Stir in the vanilla. Put the pie shell on a baking sheet, near the oven, and carefully pour the filling into the shell. Be sure to scrape out all of the ginger.

4. Bake the pie, on the sheet, on the center rack for 40 to 45 minutes, rotating the pie 180 degrees midway through the baking. Sprinkle the 2 tablespoons ginger over the pie about 10 minutes before it comes out of the oven. When done, the filling is set and no longer soupy in the center.

5. Transfer the pie to a rack and cool thoroughly. Refrigerate for at least 3 or 4 hours before serving, topping with the garnishes you want to use, if desired. Cover and refrigerate leftovers.

Recipe for Success

For a less rich version, substitute whole milk for the half-and-half.

In case you're wondering, the terms "candied ginger" and "crystallized ginger" seem to be used interchangeably in recipes.

Rose-Water Custard Pie

Rose water — liquid distilled from rose petals — makes a delicate flavoring that's the perfect complement to summer fruit. So as you can imagine, this rose-water custard pie tastes lovely with a garnish of fresh sliced peaches or halved strawberries. The trick is to use it sparingly: as with perfume, a mere suggestion is more enticing than a bold statement.

Makes 8–10 servings

Single-Crust Food Processor Pie Dough (page 58) or another single-crust dough

FILLING

- 2 **large eggs plus 2 large egg yolks**
- ¾ **cup half-and-half**
- ¾ **cup heavy cream**
- ½ **cup sugar**
- 2½ **teaspoons food-grade rose water**
- ½ **teaspoon vanilla extract**
- ½ **teaspoon lemon extract**
- **Pinch of salt**
- **Sliced peaches, halved strawberries, or other berries, for garnish**

1. Prepare and refrigerate the pie dough. Roll the dough into a 12-inch circle and line a 9- to 9½-inch standard pie pan with it, shaping the edge into an upstanding ridge. Flute or crimp the edge, chill the shell, and partially pre-bake it according to the instructions on page 36.

2. Preheat the oven to 350°F (180°C). Gently whisk the eggs and egg yolks in a large bowl, then whisk in the half-and-half, cream, and sugar. Stir in the rose water, vanilla, lemon extract, and salt. Put the pie shell on a baking sheet, near the oven, and carefully pour the filling into the shell.

3. Bake the pie, on the sheet, on the center rack for 45 to 50 minutes, turning the pie 180 degrees midway through the baking. When the pie is done, the entire filling should wobble and the center of the pie should show no sign of soupiness. Give the pan a little nudge to check.

4. Transfer the pie to a rack and cool thoroughly. Refrigerate for at least 2 or 3 hours before serving, garnished with your choice of fruit. Cover and refrigerate leftovers.

The Shakers and Rose Water

The Protestant sect known as the Shakers, who settled in colonial America, knew well the charms of cooking with rose water. They especially loved it in their baked goods, using it as freely as people use vanilla extract today in pies, cakes, and breads. Many Shaker recipes pair rose water with apples. They used it in their ice cream, whipped cream, and even in French toast batter.

Toasted Almond–Coconut Custard Pie

This pie will remind you of a Toasted Almond Bar, the kind I used to get as a kid for 15 cents when the Good Humor truck went jingling through the neighborhood. The toasted almond coating ends up on top of this pie; underneath is a thick layer of cool almond custard. Yum!

Makes 8–10 servings

Buttermilk Pie Dough (page 67) or another single-crust dough

FILLING

- 1 **cup whole almonds, toasted (page 453) and cooled**
- 1¼ **cups sugar**
- 3 **large eggs plus 2 large egg yolks**
- ¾ **cup heavy cream**
- ¾ **cup half-and-half**
- 1 **teaspoon vanilla extract**
- ¾ **teaspoon almond extract**
- ⅛ **teaspoon salt**
- 1 **cup sweetened flaked coconut, toasted**

1. Prepare and refrigerate the pie dough. Roll the dough into a 13-inch circle and line a 9- to 9½-inch deep-dish pie pan with it, shaping the edge into an upstanding ridge. Flute or crimp the edge, chill the shell, and partially prebake it according to the instructions on page 36.

2. Preheat the oven to 350°F (180°C). Put the almonds and ¼ cup of the sugar in a food processor. Pulse the machine until the almonds are finely ground. Don't overdo it; you don't want to make almond flour.

3. Combine the eggs and egg yolks in a large bowl and beat with an electric mixer (handheld is fine), gradually adding the remaining 1 cup sugar. Add the cream, half-and-half, vanilla, almond extract, and salt; beat briefly on medium speed. Stir in the almond mixture and coconut. Put the pie shell on a baking sheet, near the oven, and carefully pour or ladle the filling into the shell. Gently rake a fork through the filling to distribute the nuts and coconut evenly.

4. Bake the pie, on the sheet, on the middle oven rack for about 50 minutes, until the top of the pie is golden brown and the filling set, turning the pie 180 degrees midway through the baking. When the pie is done, the filling will wobble, not move in waves. Give the pie a little nudge to check.

5. Transfer the pie to a rack and cool. Serve lukewarm, at room temperature, or chilled. Cover and refrigerate leftovers.

Recipe for Success

As with vanilla extract, it pays to spend a little more on pure almond extract. Imitation extracts never measure up to real ones, and the difference can be evident in a delicate custard filling. A tablespoon of amaretto makes a good substitute here.

Butterscotch-Nut Custard Pie

This luscious custard pie separates into three layers: a thick layer of light golden custard on the bottom; a thin, dark gold butterscotch layer where the melted butterscotch chips settle; and a crunchy nut layer on the surface. Real nursery food, this is.

Makes 8–10 servings

Old-Fashioned Shortening Pie Dough (page 62) or another single-crust dough

FILLING

- ¾ cup butterscotch chips
- ¾ cup heavy cream
- ¾ cup half-and-half or milk
- ⅛ teaspoon salt
- 3 large eggs plus 1 large egg yolk
- ½ cup granulated sugar
- ½ cup packed light brown sugar
- 1 teaspoon vanilla extract
- 1 cup pecan or walnut halves, toasted (page 453) and chopped
- Whipped Cream (page 447), for garnish

1. Prepare and refrigerate the pie dough. Roll the dough into a 13-inch circle and line a 9- to 9½-inch deep-dish pie pan with it, shaping the edge into an upstanding ridge. Flute or crimp the edge, chill the shell, and partially pre-bake it according to the instructions on page 36.

2. Preheat the oven to 350°F (180°C). Put the butterscotch chips in a large bowl. Heat the cream and half-and-half together in a medium saucepan until they come to a near boil, 3 to 4 minutes. Immediately pour over the butterscotch chips. Add the salt. Let stand for 5 minutes, then whisk to smooth the melted chips. Set aside to cool briefly.

3. Combine the eggs, egg yolk, and sugars in another large bowl and beat with an electric mixer (hand-held is fine) on medium speed just until blended. Whisk the melted chips again to smooth, then gradually stir the cream mixture into the egg mixture. Stir in the vanilla and nuts. Put the pie shell on a baking sheet, near the oven, and carefully ladle or pour the filling into the shell. Gently rake a fork through the filling to distribute the nuts evenly.

4. Bake the pie, on the sheet, on the middle oven rack for 50 to 55 minutes, until the custard is set and the top is well browned, rotating the pie 180 degrees midway through the baking. The filling should wobble, not move in waves. Give the pie a little nudge to check.

5. Transfer the pie to a rack and cool. Serve lukewarm or at any temperature you like, with whipped cream; I like this chilled. Refrigerate leftovers.

Some Unsettling Thoughts

When you make a custard pie — and this goes for a lot of things you cook and bake — ingredients like sugar, melted butterscotch chips, and chopped nuts and fruit often settle to the bottom of the bowl. So it's a good idea to stir or whisk ingredients before you combine them, or when you're getting ready to pour the filling into the pie shell, just to be sure everything is evenly mixed and nothing gets left behind.

Coffee-Hazelnut Custard Pie

Here's a custard pie for lovers of coffee and hazelnut, two flavors that were destined to be together. Like the previous Toasted Almond–Coconut Custard Pie (page 000), this one forms a crunchy layer on top. It's a delectable adult pie for anyone looking for novelty in their custard.

Makes 8–10 servings

Single-Crust Food Processor Pie Dough (page 58) or another single-crust dough

FILLING

1 cup hazelnuts, toasted and skinned (page 000)

1 cup sugar

1½ cups half-and-half

1½ tablespoons instant espresso or instant coffee granules

¾ cup heavy cream

3 large eggs plus 1 large egg yolk

1½ tablespoons hazelnut or coffee liqueur

1 teaspoon vanilla extract

⅛ teaspoon salt

Whipped Cream (page 447), for garnish (optional)

1. Prepare and refrigerate the pie dough. Roll the dough into a 12½- to 13-inch circle and line a 9½-inch deep-dish pie pan with it, shaping the edge into an upstanding ridge. Flute or crimp the edge, chill the shell, and partially pre-bake it according to the instructions on page 36.

2. Put the hazelnuts in a food processor with ¼ cup of the sugar. Pulse the machine until the nuts are finely ground, but don't overdo it: you don't want to make a flour.

3. Preheat the oven to 350°F (180°C). Heat the half-and-half, coffee, and the remaining ¾ cup sugar together in a medium saucepan, whisking until the coffee has dissolved. Remove from the heat and stir in the heavy cream. Whisk the eggs and egg yolk in a large bowl until combined. Add the cream mixture, liqueur, vanilla, and salt, and whisk briefly. Stir in the hazelnut mixture. Put the pie shell on a baking sheet, near the oven, and slowly pour or ladle the custard into the shell. Gently rake a fork through the filling to distribute the nuts evenly.

4. Bake the pie, on the sheet, on the middle oven rack for about 50 minutes, until the custard is set, turning the pie 180 degrees midway through the baking. When the pie is done, the entire filling should wobble and the center of the pie should show no sign of soupiness. Give the pie a little nudge to check.

5. Transfer the pie to a rack and cool. Serve lukewarm, at room temperature, or chilled, garnished with whipped cream, if desired. Cover and refrigerate leftovers.

It Must Be the Pie Diet

When you look at the tremendous quantities of desserts they cook and eat, it's amazing that any Midwesterners are able to fit through a normal size doorway. Strangely enough, the majority of people in the Midwest are quite thin. . . . Many Midwestern community and church cookbooks, instead of starting out conventionally with chapters on appetizers and soups and proceeding through the rest of the meal to dessert and beverages, plunge right in and start off with the sweets. First things first.

— *Glenn Andrews,* Food from the Heartland: The Cooking of America's Midwest

Sweet Summer Corn Pie

Here's a sweet idea for using up some of that wonderfully fresh corn on the cob folks can't get enough of every summer: turn it into dessert. Folks have told me that this reminds them a little of a cold corn soufflé, but I don't think that description does justice to this creamy summer pie. Out of season, you could use thawed frozen corn, but I only make this when fresh corn is at its peak.

Makes 8–10 servings

Cornmeal Pie Dough (page 68) or another single-crust dough

FILLING

- 1½ **cups fresh-cut corn kernels**
- ⅔ **cup half-and-half**
- ¾ **cup sugar**
- 1 **cup heavy cream**
- 1 **teaspoon vanilla extract**
- ⅛ **teaspoon salt**
- **Big pinch of ground nutmeg**
- 4 **large egg yolks**
- 2 **egg whites**

1. Prepare and refrigerate the pie dough. Roll the dough into a 12½- to 13-inch circle and line a 9- to 9½-inch deep-dish pie pan with it, shaping the edge into an upstanding ridge. Flute or crimp the edge, chill the shell, and partially prebake it according to the instructions on page 36.

2. Preheat the oven to 350°F (180°C). Combine ¾ cup of the corn, the half-and-half, and sugar in a blender. Process until the corn is well chopped but not fully puréed. Whisk the cream, vanilla, salt, nutmeg, and egg yolks together in a large bowl just until evenly blended. Stir in the corn mixture and the remaining ¾ cup corn.

3. Beat the egg whites in a medium bowl with an electric mixer (handheld is fine) until they hold soft peaks. Add them to the corn mixture and fold everything together until the filling is uniformly mixed. Put the pie shell on a baking sheet, near the oven, then slowly pour or ladle the filling into the shell. Gently rake a fork through the filling to distribute the corn kernels evenly.

4. Bake the pie, on the sheet, on the middle oven rack for about 50 minutes, just until the custard is set, turning the pie 180 degrees midway through the baking. When the pie is done, the entire filling should wobble and the center of the pie should show no sign of soupiness. Give the pie a little nudge to check. The top of the pie will be a rich golden brown.

5. Transfer the pie to a rack. Cool thoroughly, then refrigerate for at least a couple of hours before serving. Cover and refrigerate leftovers.

Recipe for Success

You may be wondering why you don't cook the corn before adding it to the pie. Fresh corn kernels should be tender enough that they'll soften up as they bake in the filling. But if you have doubts, you can always boil the kernels in a small saucepan, in 1 inch of water, for just 2 to 3 minutes. If using frozen kernels, boil for several minutes.

Creamy Coconut Custard Pie

Note to coconut custard pie lovers: you won't find a recipe any better than this one. It's the picture of perfect custard pie creaminess, with just the right amount of coconut.

Makes 8–10 servings

Old-Fashioned Shortening Pie Dough (page 62)

FILLING

- 3 large eggs plus 2 large egg yolks
- 1 cup sugar
- 1 cup heavy cream
- ⅔ cup milk
- 1¼ teaspoons vanilla extract
- 1 teaspoon coconut extract (optional, but highly recommended)
- ⅛ teaspoon salt
- 1½ cups sweetened flaked coconut
- Whipped Cream (page 447), for garnish (optional)

1. Prepare and refrigerate the pie dough. Roll the dough into a 12½- to 13-inch circle and line a 9- to 9½-inch deep-dish pie pan with it, shaping the edge into an upstanding ridge. Flute or crimp the edge, chill the shell, and partially prebake it according to the instructions on page 36.

2. Preheat the oven to 350°F (180°C). Combine the eggs and egg yolks in a large bowl and beat on medium speed with an electric mixer (handheld is fine), gradually adding the sugar. Add the heavy cream, milk, vanilla, coconut extract (if using), and salt; beat briefly, just until evenly combined. Stir in the coconut. Put the pie shell on a baking sheet, near the oven, then slowly pour or ladle the filling into the shell.

3. Bake the pie, on the sheet, on the middle oven rack for about 50 minutes, until the custard is set, turning the pie 180 degrees midway through the baking. When the pie is done the entire filling should wobble and the center of the pie should show no sign of soupiness. Give the pie a little nudge to check. The top of the pie will probably not brown much.

4. Transfer the pie to a rack and cool. If you like warm custard, cool for about 1 hour before serving. I like mine cold, so I'll cool thoroughly and then refrigerate the pie for at least several hours before serving. Garnish each serving with whipped cream, if desired. Cover and refrigerate leftovers.

And You Thought Making One Pie Was a Chore

The brick ovens of colonial times were rated in terms of pies; there were 10-pie and even 20-pie ovens. Pies were eaten at every meal including breakfast, a pleasant custom that still persists. In the old days, especially on farms and especially in winter, pies were turned out by mass production. Enough for a week were routinely baked and put aside in a cold closet or unheated back room. Some housewives baked 100 pies at a time, froze them out in the snow (which did them no harm) and then thawed and warmed them for each meal in front of the fire blazing on the hearth. Pies went into the woods with logging crews and put out to sea on sailing ships as last, loving offerings of relatives ashore.

— Jonathan Norton Leonard, American Cooking: New England

Tyler Pie

Sometimes called Tyler pudding pie, this pie is thought to be named for John Tyler, our tenth president. According to James Beard in his *American Cookery*, pies of this sort were often known as sugar pie in the South and maple sugar pie in the North, depending on the type of sugar it was made with. In any event, it's basically a very sweet custard pie with a caramel flavor — uncomplicated and quite delicious.

Makes 8–10 servings

Old-Fashioned Shortening Pie Dough (page 62) or another single-crust dough

FILLING

- ½ cup (1 stick) unsalted butter
- 1½ cups packed light brown sugar
- 1 cup half-and-half or ½ cup milk plus ½ cup heavy cream
-   Scant ¼ teaspoon salt
- 1½ teaspoons vanilla extract
- 1 tablespoon granulated sugar
- 1 tablespoon all-purpose flour
- ¼ teaspoon ground nutmeg or cinnamon
- 3 large eggs

1. Prepare and refrigerate the pie dough. Roll the dough into a 12½- to 13-circle and line a 9- to 9½-inch deep-dish pie pan with it, shaping the edge into an upstanding ridge. Flute or crimp the edge, chill the shell, and partially pre-bake it according to the instructions on page 36.

2. Preheat the oven to 350°F (180°C). Begin melting the butter in a medium saucepan over a medium heat. Add the brown sugar, half-and-half, and salt. Heat, stirring often, until the butter has fully melted. Remove from the heat and stir in the vanilla. Let cool for 10 minutes.

3. Mix the granulated sugar, flour, and nutmeg in a small bowl; whisk into the half-and-half mixture.

4. Whisk the eggs in a large bowl until foamy, then slowly stir in the half-and-half mixture. Put the pie shell on a baking sheet, near the oven, then slowly pour or ladle the filling into the shell.

5. Bake the pie, on the sheet, on the middle oven rack for 40 to 45 minutes, just until the custard is set, turning the pie 180 degrees midway through the baking. When the pie is done the entire filling should wobble and the center of the pie should show no sign of soupiness. Give the pie a little nudge to check.

6. Transfer the pie to a rack and cool right on the sheet. Serve at room temperature or chill for several hours before serving. Cover the pie with tented aluminum foil and refrigerate leftovers.

Shaker Boiled Cider Pie

This pie holds special meaning for me because early in my career I had the good fortune to interview two of the last Shakers — Eldress Bertha and Eldress Gertrude — not long before they passed away at their home at the Shaker Village in Canterbury, New Hampshire. As these gentle women explained to me, the Shakers commonly used boiled cider and maple syrup to sweeten their baked goods and other dishes. It adds a real punch to fresh apple pies. Here it's combined with maple syrup in what is essentially a custard pie with a thin layer of quasi meringue that rises to the top. Garnish with unsweetened whipped cream, because this is pretty sweet.

Makes 10 servings

Old-Fashioned Shortening Pie Dough (page 62)

FILLING

- ¾ **cup boiled cider**
- ¾ **cup maple syrup**
- 3 **tablespoons unsalted butter, in several pieces**
- ⅛ **teaspoon salt**
- 4 **large eggs, separated**
- **Whipped Cream (page 447), preferably unsweetened**

1. Prepare and refrigerate the pie dough. Roll the dough into a 12-inch circle and line a 9- to 9½-inch standard pie pan with it, shaping the edge into an upstanding ridge. Flute or crimp the edge, chill the shell, and partially prebake it according to the instructions on page 36.

2. Preheat the oven to 350°F (180°C). Gently warm the boiled cider, maple syrup, and butter in a medium saucepan until the butter melts. Pour the mixture into a large bowl and stir in the salt. Cool to lukewarm.

3. Put the egg yolks in a large bowl and gradually whisk in a ladleful of the warm liquid. Repeat several times until all the liquid is added.

4. Using a clean bowl and clean dry beaters, beat the egg whites with an electric mixer (handheld is fine) until they form soft, droopy peaks. Add a third of the whites to the liquid and fold in gently. Add the remaining whites and fold again, then whisk gently to combine. The mixture doesn't have to look uniform, and it's okay if the whites lose some of their volume; they will. Put the pie shell on a baking sheet, near the oven, and carefully pour the filling into the shell.

5. Bake the pie, on the sheet, on the middle oven rack for 40 to 45 minutes, until the filling has set, turning the pie 180 degrees midway through the baking. When the pie is done, the filling should wobble, not move in waves. Give the pie a little nudge to check. The top will be dark brown.

6. Transfer the pie and baking sheet to a rack and cool thoroughly. Serve slightly warm, if you like, garnished with whipped cream, but I prefer to chill this first. Cover the pie with tented aluminum foil and refrigerate leftovers, but be sure the foil doesn't come in contact with the delicate top or it will pull off.

Variation

Adding a layer of sautéed apples gives this pie extra character and flavor. Prepare and partially prebake the shell as instructed, but use a 9- to 9½-inch deep-dish pie pan instead of a standard one.

Melt 1 tablespoon butter in a large skillet. Stir in 2 large peeled, cored, and sliced Golden Delicious or other firm baking apples. Cook over medium heat until the slices are almost tender, about 5 minutes, stirring often. Cool.

Just before adding the custard to the pie in step 4, spread the apples in the shell. Slowly pour the custard over the apples and bake as instructed.

What Is Boiled Cider?

It's fresh apple cider boiled down to roughly one-seventh of its original volume, until it becomes a dark syrup. (Maple syrup, by comparison, is boiled down to about one-fortieth of its original volume.) It makes a great pancake syrup and can be used in place of honey in many recipes, or to glaze ham and pork tenderloin. There aren't many commercial producers, but my favorite one, Woods Cider Mill, has been at it for decades and makes the best.

How to Make Boiled Cider

Start with good, fresh, preservative-free cider, preferably from a local producer. Pour 7 cups into a large saucepan. Bring the cider to a boil and keep it there until it looks like it has reduced to about 1½ cups. At that point, check by pouring the cider into a heatproof measuring cup. Make a mental note of how much liquid you have, then pour it back into the pan and continue to boil until the liquid is reduced to just over 1 cup. Err on the side of caution: if you boil it too much, you'll end up with apple jelly. That's no tragedy, it's just not what you're aiming for. Pour the syrup into a clean jar, seal, and refrigerate. It will keep for months.

Those Inventive Shakers

Shaker men found time to develop a mechanical apple parer, a pea sheller, a water-powered butter churn, an automatic cheese press, a superior wood-burning stove, matches, and a revolving oven for baking dozens of pies at a time. The women charged with the community cooking did inventive things with all kinds of ingredients. Shakers perfected a way to produce dried corn — and thereby helped provide Americans generally with year-round supplies that would not spoil easily. . . .They created their own excellent architecture, designed furniture that is much coveted in the twentieth century, devised methods to increase productivity of soil and livestock, and became superior mechanics, responsible for inventions that helped improve the lives of many outsiders.

— *Evan Jones,* American Food: The Gastronomic Story

Creamy Maple-Yogurt Pie

Pure maple syrup gives this satiny yogurt-custard pie a pretty butterscotch hue and an unmistakable maple flavor. You can use full- or low-fat yogurt, but I think you get a better result with the former. There are so many good yogurts on the market today that I don't have a particular favorite, but if you do, then by all means use it.

Makes 8–10 servings

Single-Crust Food Processor Pie Dough (page 58) or another single-crust dough

FILLING

- 3 **large eggs plus 1 large egg yolk**
- ⅓ **cup sugar**
- 2½ **tablespoons all-purpose flour**
- ½ **cup maple syrup**
- 3 **tablespoons unsalted butter**
- 1 **teaspoon vanilla extract**
- ⅛ **teaspoon salt**
- 2 **cups plain yogurt**

1. Prepare and refrigerate the pie dough. Roll the dough into a 12½- to 13-inch circle and line a 9- to 9½-inch deep-dish pie pan with it, shaping the edge into an upstanding ridge. Flute or crimp the edge, chill the shell, and partially prebake it according to the instructions on page 36.

2. Preheat the oven to 350°F (180°C). Whisk the eggs and egg yolk in a large bowl until frothy. Mix the sugar and flour together in a small bowl. Add to the eggs and whisk until smooth. Gently warm the maple syrup and butter together in a small saucepan until the butter melts. Cool to lukewarm, then gradually whisk into the eggs along with the vanilla and salt. Add the yogurt and blend until smooth. Put the pie shell on a baking sheet, near the oven, and carefully pour the filling into the shell.

3. Bake the pie, on the sheet, on the middle oven rack for 45 to 50 minutes, until the filling is set, turning the pie 180 degrees midway through the baking. When the pie is done, the filling should wobble, not move in waves. Give the pie a little nudge to check. Like most custard pies, it will puff very slightly around the edges, but you don't want to see it puff way up, an indication that the pie is overbaked.

4. Transfer the pie to a rack and cool thoroughly, then refrigerate the pie for at least 2 or 3 hours before serving. Cover and refrigerate leftovers.

Recipe for Success

If you think of it, take the yogurt and eggs out of the fridge a couple of hours before you assemble the filling for this pie. It's not a huge deal, but if the ingredients are at room temperature when you put the pie in the oven, it will bake just a little faster. Don't, however, try to accomplish the same thing by raising the oven temperature.

Cottage Cheese *and* Nutmeg Pie

This recipe is adapted from one by the incredibly gifted vegetarian cookbook author Deborah Madison, whose work I've long admired. The recipe originally caught my eye because I reflexively thought that her use of a full teaspoon of nutmeg would overwhelm the delicate flavor of this pie, but it does nothing of the sort; it's just right. Thanks to Deborah for inspiring my own version of her creamy nutmeg pie.

Makes 8–10 servings

Single-Crust Food Processor Pie Dough (page 58) or another single-crust dough

FILLING

3   large eggs plus 1 large egg yolk

⅔   cup sugar

½   cup half-and-half or heavy cream

2   cups small-curd cottage cheese

1   teaspoon ground nutmeg

⅛   teaspoon salt

1   teaspoon finely grated lemon zest

½   teaspoon vanilla extract

1. Prepare and refrigerate the pie dough. Roll the dough into a 12½- to 13-inch circle and line a 9- to 9½-inch deep-dish pie pan with it, shaping the edge into an upstanding ridge. Flute or crimp the edge, chill the shell, and partially prebake it according to the instructions on page 36.

2. Preheat the oven to 350°F (180°C). Whisk the eggs, egg yolk, and sugar together in a large bowl until well blended. Add the half-and-half, cottage cheese, nutmeg, salt, lemon zest, and vanilla, and stir until evenly mixed. Put the pie shell on a baking sheet, near the oven, and carefully pour the filling into the shell.

3. Bake the pie, on the sheet, on the middle oven rack for 40 to 45 minutes, until the filling is just set, turning the pie 180 degrees midway through the baking. Like most custard pies, it will probably puff very slightly around the edges, but it shouldn't puff way up, an indication that the pie is overbaked. Because of the modest amount of sugar in the pie, the surface isn't likely to brown very much.

4. Transfer the pie to a rack and cool thoroughly. Refrigerate for at least 2 or 3 hours before serving. Cover and refrigerate leftovers.

Recipe for Success

Deborah and I both once worked with the same editor, Fran McCullough, who constantly chided me to use only freshly grated nutmeg. To her mind, anything else was heresy. I can't say I've always followed her admonition, but I've used fresh nutmeg enough to know that I can't argue her point.

Sweet Cottage Cheese Pie
with Plumped Raisins

If the phrase cottage cheese pie doesn't exactly rock your taste buds, I get it: for many of us, cottage cheese is strictly diet food. But if I told you that this pie tastes something like a light lemon cheesecake, perhaps you'd come around. You should, because this one is delicious.

Makes 8–10 servings

Buttermilk Pie Dough (page 67) or another single-crust dough

FILLING

¾ cup dark or golden raisins

1 cup orange juice

1 pound small- or large-curd cottage cheese

⅔ cup sugar

2 large eggs plus 1 large egg yolk

½ cup half-and-half

1 tablespoon lemon juice

2 teaspoons finely grated lemon zest

¾ teaspoon vanilla extract

1 tablespoon all-purpose flour

¼ teaspoon ground nutmeg

Big pinch of salt

1. Prepare and refrigerate the pie dough. Roll the dough into a 12½- to 13-inch circle and line a 9- to 9½-inch deep-pie pan with it, shaping the edge into an upstanding ridge. Flute or crimp the edge, chill the shell, and partially prebake it according to the instructions on page 36. Let cool.

2. Put the raisins in a small bowl and add just enough of the orange juice to cover. Let stand for 1 hour.

3. Preheat the oven to 350°F (180°C). Combine the cottage cheese, sugar, eggs, egg yolk, half-and-half, lemon juice, lemon zest, and vanilla in a food processor. Process for 15 seconds. Sprinkle the flour, nutmeg, and salt over the mixture and process until quite smooth, another 15 seconds.

4. Drain the raisins and scatter them evenly in the pie shell. Put the pie shell on a baking sheet, near the oven, and carefully pour the filling into the shell.

5. Bake the pie, on the sheet, on the center oven rack for 45 to 50 minutes, until the filling is set, rotating the pie 180 degrees midway through the baking. When the pie is done, the perimeter will have puffed slightly, though it's best if the filling doesn't puff too much or it may develop cracks. The center of the pie will be wobbly and seem barely done.

6. Transfer the pie and sheet to a rack and cool to room temperature. Refrigerate for at least 4 hours or overnight before serving. Cover and refrigerate leftovers.

Recipe for Success

Add a second layer of citrus flavor to the pie by incorporating the orange juice you used to plump the raisins. Simply drain the raisins and reserve the juice, pouring it into a 1-cup glass measuring cup. Add enough half-and-half to equal ½ cup liquid, then add to the processor instead of using all cream.

Slipped Custard Pie

This pie is an anachronism, a recipe from an earlier time and one I hope never disappears from the American pie-making tradition. The idea is simple enough: you bake a crust and a custard filling separately, slide the latter into the former — hopefully without incident — and end up with a lovely rich custard inside a delightfully crispy shell. Don't be intimidated. Indeed, gather your friends and family and have them film the final "slipping" scene on their phones. Might be good for some laughs.

Makes 8–10 servings

Old-Fashioned Shortening Pie Dough (page 62) or another single-crust dough

FILLING

- ¾ **cup sugar**
- 2½ **cups half-and-half, warmed**
- 4 **large eggs**
- 1½ **teaspoons vanilla extract**
- ⅛ **teaspoon salt**

1. Prepare the pie dough and refrigerate. While the dough chills, select two matching 9½-inch deep-dish pie pans. I prefer glass, since it won't tinge or color the custard in any way. Lightly butter the one you will cook the custard in.

2. Roll the dough into a 12½- to 13-inch circle and line the unbuttered pie pan with it, shaping the edge into an upstanding ridge. Flute or crimp the edge, chill the shell, and fully prebake it according to the instructions on page 36.

3. Pour about ½ inch water into a large, shallow, ovenproof casserole dish — one large enough to accommodate the pie pan — and place it in the oven on one of the lower racks. Move any higher racks out of the way so you have headroom. Preheat the oven to 350°F (180°C).

4. While the casserole dish and water heat up, put the sugar in a large bowl and whisk in the half-and-half. Cool for several minutes, then whisk in the eggs, vanilla, and salt. Working near the oven, so you don't have far to walk, slowly pour the filling through a fine-mesh sieve into the buttered pie pan to remove any egg lumps. If there's enough room for you to maneuver, reach into the oven and carefully place the pie pan in the casserole. Otherwise, slide the oven rack out a little so you have enough room to put the custard pan in the water. Then carefully — so you don't splash — slide the rack back in. Bake the custard for 25 to 30 minutes, until it is just set. When done, the custard will wobble but won't be soupy.

5. Transfer the custard to a rack and cool to room temperature. Transfer to the fridge for 1 to 2 hours to firm the custard slightly. Carefully slide a butter knife or flexible spatula around the edge of the custard to loosen it. With the pie shell on the counter, tilt one edge of the custard away from you, into the awaiting pie shell. Tilt gently at first; once the custard starts slipping, it will keep moving. As the custard slides into the shell, move the custard pan as necessary so the custard slips right into place. Serve immediately, and refrigerate leftovers.

Sugar Cream Pie #1

By all rights Indiana's most famous pie, this version varies somewhat from the one on the opposite page. That's a leaner version, made with milk, and the filling is cooked on the stovetop and added to a prebaked pastry crust. Made with cream, this pie is richer, and the uncooked filling gets baked in the shell. (Neither contains eggs.) You can't go wrong with either because both are creamy masterpieces.

Makes 10 servings

Old-Fashioned Shortening Pie Dough (page 62)

FILLING

- ½ cup granulated sugar
- ½ cup dark brown sugar
- 2 tablespoons all-purpose flour
- ⅛ teaspoon salt
- 2 cups heavy cream
- ¾ teaspoon vanilla extract
- Confectioners' sugar, for garnish

1. Prepare and refrigerate the pie dough. Roll the dough into a 12-circle and line a 9- to 9½-inch standard pie pan with it, shaping the edge into an upstanding ridge. Flute or crimp the edge, chill the shell, and partially prebake it according to the instructions on page 36.

2. Preheat the oven to 400°F (200°C). Combine the granulated sugar, brown sugar, flour, and salt in a large bowl. Rub the mixture with your fingers to break up all the lumps. Slowly stir the cream, then the vanilla, into the sugar mixture until smooth. Do not whisk. Put the pie shell on a baking sheet, near the oven, and carefully pour the filling into the shell.

3. Bake the pie, on the sheet, on the middle oven rack for about 40 minutes, until the filling is set, rotating it 180 degrees midway through the baking. When the pie is done, the filling will wobble and there will be no sign of soupiness in the center.

4. Transfer the pie to a rack and cool completely. Refrigerate for at least a couple of hours. Dust the pie with confectioners' sugar just before slicing. Cover and refrigerate leftovers.

Recipe for Success

This recipe, for the most part, comes from my friend Paula Haney, the founder of the famed Hoosier Mama Pie Company in Chicago. The only slight changes I've made are a touch of salt in the filling and a smidge more vanilla than she uses, but 99 percent of the credit goes to her, with gratitude.

When this pie reaches its last few minutes, it does something you rarely see with other liquid pies: the filling bubbles away, almost like you're seeing boiling caramel in a saucepan. Don't be alarmed.

Sugar Cream Pie #2

Sugar cream pie is the unofficial Hoosier State pie, but — as these things often go — there's no official version of it, but rather many variations on a the same theme. Unlike the other version of sugar cream pie on the opposite page, the filling for this one is cooked on top of the stove and poured into a prebaked pie shell. In that respect, it's more like a traditional cream pie, though without the eggs, so the filling is nearly pure white, rather firm, and delicious.

Makes 8–10 servings

Old-Fashioned Shortening Pie Dough (page 62)

FILLING

- 1 **cup sugar**
- ¼ **cup plus 1 tablespoon cornstarch**
- 2¼ **cups whole milk**
- ½ **cup (1 stick) unsalted butter, cut into pieces**
- **Big pinch of salt**
- 1 **teaspoon vanilla extract**
- **Whipped Cream (page 447) (optional)**

1. Prepare and refrigerate the pie dough. Roll the dough into a 12-inch circle and line a 9- to 9½-inch standard pie pan with it, shaping the edge into an upstanding ridge. Flute or crimp the edge, chill the shell, and fully prebake it according to the instructions on page 36. Cool thoroughly.

2. Combine the sugar, cornstarch, milk, butter, and salt in a medium saucepan. Place over medium heat and cook, whisking virtually nonstop, until the mixture starts to boil, 6 to 8 minutes. Reduce the heat slightly and cook for about 2 minutes longer, whisking rapidly to prevent the filling from spattering.

3. Remove from the heat and whisk in the vanilla. Pour the filling into the pie shell, smoothing the top. Transfer the pie to a rack and cool thoroughly, then refrigerate for at least a couple of hours, or overnight. Serve on its own, or with a dollop of whipped cream, if desired.

Peanut Butter Custard Pie

I think custard pies are way underappreciated on the whole, and peanut butter custard pie falls somewhere below that. This creamy version will help get the pie the love it deserves.

Makes 10 servings

Graham Cracker Crust (page 82) or another crumb crust

FILLING

- 1 **cup milk**
- 1 **cup heavy cream**
- ¾ **cup smooth peanut butter**
- ⅔ **cup sugar**
- 6 **large egg yolks**
- 1 **teaspoon vanilla extract**
- **Big pinch of salt**
- **Jelly, for garnish (optional)**

1. Prepare the crust and press it into the bottom and up the sides of a 9½-inch standard pie pan. Refrigerate, prebake, and cool as directed. Refrigerate until needed.

2. Preheat the oven to 350°F (180°C). Combine the milk, cream, and peanut butter in a large saucepan. Gradually bring to a simmer — but don't let it boil — occasionally stirring and then whisking gently to smooth out the peanut butter. Remove from the heat.

3. Whisk the sugar and egg yolks in a large bowl until smooth and pale-colored, 2 or 3 minutes. Slowly add the heated milk mixture to the egg yolk mixture in a thin stream, whisking as you pour. Whisk in the vanilla and salt. Put the pie shell on a baking sheet, near the oven. Stir the custard one more time, then carefully pour or ladle it into the shell. The custard should come close to the top of the crust, but don't let it run over.

4. Bake the pie, on the sheet, on the center oven rack for 20 minutes, then reduce the temperature to 325°F (170°C) and bake for 20 to 30 minutes longer, just until the custard is set in the center and no longer soupy.

5. Transfer the pie to a rack and cool completely. Refrigerate the pie at least 1 or 2 hours before serving, though I prefer it good and cold. If you are garnishing with the jelly, heat a few tablespoons in a small microwavable bowl, to smooth it out, then drizzle it over individual slices to serve. Looks pretty that way and tastes wonderful. Cover and refrigerate leftovers.

Recipe for Success

Custard pies like to be coddled. The key thing with this pie is to bake it nice and slow, watch it closely near the end of the baking time, and take it out of the oven as soon as it is done.

Using half granulated sugar and half light brown sugar adds a nice caramel note.

Shoofly Pie

I've learned from experience that most folks prefer this traditional Amish pie when it's made with both molasses and brown sugar, instead of the usual all molasses. Either way, if you're a fan of molasses, you'll enjoy this full-flavored pie with a thick layer of crumbs on top.

Makes 8–10 servings

Simple Press-In Pie Dough (page 73) or another single-crust dough

FILLING

- 1 cup all-purpose flour
- 1 cup packed light brown sugar
- ¼ teaspoon salt
- ¼ teaspoon ground cinnamon
- 6 tablespoons cold unsalted butter, cut into ¼-inch pieces
- ½ cup unsulphured or blackstrap molasses
- ¾ cup boiling water
- ½ teaspoon baking soda
- ½ teaspoon vanilla extract
- 1 large egg, lightly beaten
- Whipped Cream (page 447), for garnish

1. Prepare and refrigerate the pie dough, pressing it into a 9- to 9½-inch deep-dish pie pan according to the recipe on page 73. Refrigerate the shell until needed.

2. Adjust one of the oven racks so it's in the lower position, and preheat the oven to 425°F (200°C).

3. Combine the flour, ½ cup of the sugar, the salt, and cinnamon in a large bowl. Add the butter and rub or cut it into the dry ingredients with your fingers or a pastry blender, mixing until the mixture resembles a fine meal that forms small clumps when you press it in your palm.

4. Combine the molasses and the remaining ½ cup sugar in a medium bowl. Add the boiling water and stir to dissolve the sugar. Whisk in the baking soda, vanilla, and egg. Slowly pour the liquid into the pie shell. Scatter the crumb mixture evenly over the filling; do not press it down.

5. Bake the pie for 15 minutes. Reduce the heat to 350°F (180°C) and rotate the pie 180 degrees. Bake for 25 to 30 minutes longer, until the filling is set. When done, the entire filling should wobble and the center of the pie should show no sign of soupiness. Give the pie a little nudge to check.

6. Transfer the pie to a rack and cool thoroughly before serving at room temperature, garnishing slices with whipped cream. Refrigerate leftovers after 24 hours.

Recipe for Success

Unsulphured molasses is sweeter and less assertive than blackstrap molasses. If you've never had blackstrap before, I suggest using unsulphured molasses.

To make what's known as a "dry-bottom" shoofly pie, spread half of the crumb mixture in the shell, add the filling, then spread the remaining crumbs on top.

The Origin of Shoofly Pie

Each version of [shoofly pie] has passionate advocates among the [Pennsylvania] Dutch. There's a rather dry one that is dunked in coffee, a wet bottom one that is much moister and spicier, and a cake-like kind in which the filling and crumbs are mixed together. No one seems to know, incidentally, how the pie got is name. Logical thinkers tend to the theory that the sweet stickiness attracted flies, but there are various other theories, including one rather unlikely claim that the name came from the French chou-fleur, since the crumbs on the surface look like cauliflower.

—*José Wilson,* American Cooking: The Eastern Heartland

11
Small Packages:
MINI PIES, TURNOVERS, AND OTHER HAND PIES

The popularity of small pies has soared in the past decade. Gone are the days when the only small pies you'd come across were the mass-produced, glazed turnover-type at the checkout counter of your local quick mart.

❧

Today you can find pie shops that specialize in pint-size pies. Pretty, handcrafted mini pies are showing up at wedding receptions in place of multitiered cakes and at fancy parties, showers, and neighborhood potlucks.

Home bakers have caught the mini-pie bug in a big way, and why not? A personal pie is a surefire way to make friends and family feel extraspecial. The pies can be customized to suit virtually any occasion or season, and the pie shells can be made ahead and frozen for later assembly and baking.

In this section, I create a tempting lineup of downsized pies, beginning with those baked in individual pie pans, then moving on to little cream pies. You'll see a variety of turnover-style pies, including one with sticks — the "pop pies" kids love. A number of these recipes are suitable for making with children; they adore this type of kitchen project. I'll tip you off when you come across those.

I think you'll enjoy these little personal pies, and I've no doubt that once you've gotten a few of these recipes under your belt, you'll be dreaming up your own creations and signature touches. At least, I hope so.

Mini Pies Baked in Pie Pans

Every pie maker should own a varied collection of small pie pans, at least that's what I tell my wife every time I come home with a few new ones. I have stacks of disposable aluminum pie pans in several sizes. (Love the fact that I can just give these away and not worry about retrieving the empties.) I have a few dozen 1-cup capacity stoneware pans made by Le Creuset and Emile Henry, a couple of well known brands. There are the inexpensive metal pie pans that you find in HomeGoods and places like that. Not to mention slightly larger pot pie pans for savory pies. And I will often use my standard 12-cup muffin pan to make mini pies or tartlets.

The following recipes include pan size guidelines and suggestions. If you don't have the exact size pans I recommend, you can make substitutions and improvise, adjusting filling quantities and baking times; that's fine. But if mini pies become a regular feature in your kitchen, you'll eventually want to buy the recommended size for a given recipe.

Mini Pie Math

Virtually all of the panned pies in this chapter require a crumb crust or one of the pie dough recipes.

Mini-pie pans come in all different sizes, but most of the ones you'll find are either 1-cup or ½-cup capacity. Most of the single-crust pie dough recipes will make four or five pastry shells, and the double-crust recipes will make eight to ten.

Bear in mind that if you're making a mini fruit pie and you need both a bottom and top pastry, a single-crust dough recipe will make just two double-crust mini pies and perhaps one additional shell, whereas a double-crust dough recipe will make four or five double-crust mini pies.

If you make cream pies in ½-cup capacity pans, you should be able to make about six pie shells; four or five if you're using 1-cup capacity pans. I give a range here because some of this hinges on how thick or thin you like to make your crusts.

Dividing the Dough for Mini Pies

Dividing a crumb crust for your mini pies is simple: you just line up the pie pans, divide the crumbs evenly between them, and press the crumbs into place. Refrigerate the shells for 10 or 15 minutes, then bake.

It's a little more involved when there's pie dough to divide up. Let me discuss a couple of methods, in order of preference. We'll assume, for now, that you're working with a single-crust dough recipe and making shells for four or five mini pies in 1-cup-capacity pans.

METHOD 1. Right after you make the dough and flatten it into a disk, place it in the center of a gallon freezer bag, or between two sheets of plastic wrap. Take a rolling pin and gently roll the dough into an even 8-inch circle. Seal the bag, or wrap up the dough in the plastic, and refrigerate for 1 hour.

Remove the cold dough from the fridge and place it on your work counter. Using a 3-inch-diameter biscuit cutter, cut the dough into four rounds. Gather the scraps, shape them into a ball, and flatten into a disk; cut another circle out of these scraps. (If you want only four pie shells, gather the scraps and gently press an equal amount onto the top of each of the four rounds.)

Working with one piece at a time, roll each round into a 7½- to 8-inch circle. The beauty of starting with these perfect rounds is that it's easy to keep the dough nice and round as you roll it.

Line each of the pans with the rolled-out dough and shape the edge as if you were making a full-size pie (page 34.) Refrigerate until needed.

METHOD 2. This method is a little faster and a little less fussy, but you don't end up with such perfect circles when you roll.

Right after you make the dough, divide it into four or five pieces, as required. Shape each one into a ball, then flatten each ball into a disk about ½ inch thick. Wrap these pieces in plastic and refrigerate for 1 hour. Roll each one into a 7½- to 8-inch circle and line the pans.

With either method, I suggest refrigerating the pastry shells for 30 minutes before using or prebaking them.

Prebaking Mini Shells

Typically with crumb crusts, and sometimes with pie pastry crusts, you will need to prebake the mini-pie shells before filling them. Crumb crusts taste more "baked" when you prebake them. And prebaking pastry crust ensures that the bottom crust is crusty, not damp and flabby, when your pie is done.

In both cases, it's much easier to prebake small pan pies on a baking sheet than directly on the oven rack, where they won't be nearly as stable. Choose a baking sheet large enough to accommodate the shells. A dark sheet is preferable to a shiny one.

Crumb crusts are easy: just place them on the sheet, leaving a little space between them, and bake on the middle rack in a preheated 350°F (170°C) oven for 8 minutes. Cool the whole sheet on a rack.

With pastry crusts, you'll need to weigh down the pastry so it doesn't puff up as it bakes. By far the easiest way to do this is with standard 8- to 12-cup flat-bottom coffee filters. Put one in each shell, add about 1 inch of dried beans to weigh the pastry down, and arrange the shells on the sheet.

For partially prebaked shells, bake with the beans in a preheated 375°F (190°C) oven for 25 minutes. Slide out the rack, remove the filters and beans, and bake for 10 to 12 minutes longer, until the bottom starts to crust over.

For fully prebaked shells, bake an additional 15 to 18 minutes after you remove the beans. When done, the crust should be golden and crusty.

For a more detailed indoctrination to the whys and wherefores of prebaking pie shells, read the appropriate section on page 36. It pertains to full-size pies, but the same logic applies here.

Little Fruit Pie Tip

Don't worry about exact measure of fruit that goes into the pie shell. You may not have the same pans that I recommend. As a rule of thumb, pile the filling level with the top edge of the pastry, or mounded slightly above it. Mounding is good because fruit cooks down and the pie is less likely to look sunken after it bakes.

Little Fruit Crumb Pies

You'll find several other mini fruit pies in this chapter, but here is an easy formula to follow if you want guidelines for creating your own flavors. I sometimes call these "refrigerator fruit pies" because I make them out of whatever fruit I have on hand that needs to be used up. These use a crumb topping, as do most of my mini fruit pies, but by all means add a pastry lid if that's the way you like your pies.

Makes 4 or 5 mini pies

Old-Fashioned Shortening Pie Dough (page 62) or another single-crust dough

FILLING

4½ cups fresh fruit, alone or in combination

⅓ cup sugar

1 tablespoon cornstarch

2 teaspoons lemon juice

1 teaspoon freshly grated lemon zest

¼ teaspoon ground nutmeg (optional)

Pinch of salt

Oatmeal Crumb Topping (page 449)

1. Prepare the pie dough as directed, dividing it into four or five equal pieces using one of the methods described on page 325. Refrigerate for up to 1 hour. Working with one piece of dough at a time, roll each piece into a 7½- to 8-inch circle and line the pans with them, shaping the edges into upstanding ridges. Flute or crimp the edges (page 34), then refrigerate the shells until needed.

2. Prepare the fruit as for any pie — peeled, cored, or pitted as appropriate, and cut into small chunks. Put the fruit in a large bowl, add the sugar and cornstarch, and mix well. Stir in the lemon juice, lemon zest, nutmeg (if using), and salt.

3. Adjust the oven racks so one is in the lower position and another is in the middle of the oven. Preheat the oven to 375°F (190°C). Line a large baking sheet with parchment paper.

4. Put the pie shells on the prepared baking sheet. Divide the fruit evenly between the shells. The fruit should be even with the top edge of the pastry or mounded slightly higher. Cover the top of each pie with a generous ⅓ cup of the crumb topping; spread it around and tamp it down gently.

5. Bake the pies, on the sheet, on the lower over rack for 25 minutes. Move the pies up to the middle rack and bake for 25 to 30 minutes longer, until the juices bubble thickly around the edge of the pies.

6. Transfer the pies to a rack and cool for at least 1 hour before serving. I think fruit pies taste best when they're served barely warm. If you plan to serve them within 24 hours, simply leave the pies at room temperature, stored under a screen dome or in a large paper bag. Don't cover them tightly with plastic wrap or aluminum foil. For longer storage than that, cover and refrigerate.

Cherry-Berry Crumb Cup Pies

Fresh fruit always cooks down and loses volume in the process. That can make your pies look sunken. One way around that is to precook the fruit before adding it to the pie shells, a neat trick that accounts for the compact layer of fruit filling in these mini pies. The blueberry lovers in your circle will adore these.

Makes 12 mini pies

Double-Crust Food Processor Pie Dough (page 60) or another double-crust dough

FILLING

Cherry-Blueberry filling from the Cherry-Blueberry Slab Pie (page 131)

Oatmeal Crumb Topping (page 449) or another crumb topping

Vanilla ice cream or Whipped Cream (page 447), for garnish

1. Prepare the pie dough according to the recipe. Wrap the halves separately in plastic wrap and refrigerate until firm enough to roll, about 1 hour. Prepare the fruit filling, if you haven't already, and cool.

2. When you're ready to assemble the pies, place half of the dough on a sheet of floured waxed paper or parchment paper and roll it just a little thinner than you usually would for a pie. Don't worry if it isn't round.

3. Using a 5-inch round cutter or template, cut out as many circles of dough as you can, probably five or six. Gently press each circle into one of the cups of a 12-cup muffin pan. Repeat the process with the other dough half. Put the muffin pan in the refrigerator. (Gather and roll the scraps, line other individual pans, and freeze these shells for another use.)

4. Preheat the oven to 375°F (190°C). Divide the filling evenly among the pie shells. Spread a small handful of crumb topping over each little pie. Put the pan on the middle oven rack and bake for 30 to 35 minutes, until the fruit bubbles and the topping browns slightly.

5. Transfer the pan to a rack and cool for 10 minutes. Run a knife around the edge of the pies, to loosen them. Cool for 15 minutes longer, then remove the pies from the cups. Serve warm or at room temperature, with vanilla ice cream or whipped cream.

Recipe for Success

Don't underbake these. They have a relatively short baking time, and you want to be sure the crust browns.

Mason Jar–Lid Pies

Makes 6 or 7 mini pies

Single-Crust Food Processor
Pie Dough (page 58) or
another single-crust dough

FILLING

2	tablespoons sugar
1	tablespoon all-purpose flour
⅛	teaspoon ground nutmeg
1½–2	cups peeled and finely diced peaches
½	cup peach or apricot preserves
	Oatmeal Crumb Topping (page 449) or another crumb topping

Variations

APPLE. Use peeled and finely diced apple in place of the peaches, apple butter instead of the preserves, and cinnamon instead of nutmeg.

PEAR. Use peeled and finely diced pears, fig or apricot preserves, and cardamom or cinnamon.

BLUEBERRY. Use small wild blueberries, blueberry or peach preserves, and cinnamon.

STRAWBERRY. Use diced ripe strawberries, peach or strawberry preserves, and nutmeg.

I'm always on the lookout for novel ways to build a pie, especially with everyday items I have around the house, so this idea really appealed. The concept could not be simpler: use a large mason jar lid as the "pan" for your small pies. Functionally, a mason jar lid is no different from a traditional bottomless flan ring that bakers use to constrain tarts, or a tart pan with removable bottom, so why not? Because mason jar lids aren't as tall as the sides of a flan ring, I cut the circles of dough a bit large, then use the excess dough to build up the sides. The basic recipe is for a peach version of the pie, followed by several fruit variations. These are great for parties or anytime you need portable little pies. Kids love them because it's fun to invent their own signature pie.

1. Prepare and refrigerate the pie dough. Get out six or seven large (3½-inch) mason jar rings; you just need the rings, not the lids, because the baking sheet acts as the "bottom" of the pie pans. Make sure they're clean and rust-free. Place the rings on a large parchment-lined baking sheet with the bottoms of the lids facing up.

2. Preheat the oven to 375°F (190°C). Roll the dough as for a pie, but don't worry about keeping it round since you'll be cutting it up. Using a 5-inch round cutter or template, cut the dough into six or seven 5-inch circles; you may have to gather up the scraps and reroll them to get that many. Center the circles over the lids and gently nudge them down into the lids so they fit snugly, but don't stretch the dough. Fold the excess dough down and press it against the sides of each lid, so the sides of the dough push up a little higher than the actual sides of the lid. Refrigerate for 10 to 15 minutes.

3. Mix the sugar, flour, and nutmeg in a small bowl. Spread 1 to 1½ teaspoons of the sugar mixture in the bottom of each shell. Add enough diced peaches to almost fill the shell, then spoon 1 tablespoon preserves over each one, smearing it into the fruit with a spoon. Top with a generous layer of the crumb topping. Tamp the crumbs down lightly. By now the lids will be full to overflowing.

4. Bake the pies on the middle oven rack for 35 to 40 minutes, rotating the baking sheet 180 degrees midway through the baking. When the pies are done, the topping will be golden brown and the filling will have pushed up in the lids and look bubbly juicy.

5. Transfer the sheet to a rack and cool for at least 30 minutes. Remove the pies from the lids and serve warm or at room temperature.

Mini Cream Pies

This is not so much a recipe as it is a blueprint for creating a variety of small cream pies, based on the full-size recipes in chapter 13. The essential building blocks — the pastry cream, whipped cream, and add-ins — remain the same; they're simply divided among smaller pans of your choosing. Cream pies being rather rich, I prefer mini 4- to 4½-inch (½-cup capacity) pans to 1-cup pans; the former makes an ample serving for most of us, the latter is almost a two-person pie.

Makes 4–6 mini pies

Graham Cracker Crust (page 82) or another crumb crust

FILLING

Vanilla Pastry Cream (page 377) or another flavor of pastry cream

Whipped Cream or Stabilized Whipped Cream (page 446)

Toppings, sauces, fruit, and any other extras, as desired

1. Prepare the crumb crust mixture and divide it equally among five or six 4- to 4½-inch-diameter (½-cup capacity) buttered pie pans, pressing it against the bottoms and sides of the pans. (If you only have 1-cup capacity pans, use four or five of them.) Refrigerate the shells for 10 to 15 minutes.

2. Preheat the oven to 350°F (180°C). Arrange the shells on a rimmed baking sheet, evenly spaced. Bake on the middle oven rack for 8 minutes. Transfer to a cooling rack.

3. To assemble the pies — preferably within 1 hour of serving them — spoon a generous amount of pastry cream into each shell. Mound some of the whipped cream on each, or pipe it on with a pastry bag. Then arrange the toppings and extras on each pie. Refrigerate until serving.

Recipe for Success

Crumb-crust shells freeze beautifully, so I tend to make several batches at a time. Prebaking them in aluminum pans before they go into the freezer makes it even easier.

To assemble the pies, follow the same guidelines for layering the pastry cream, whipped cream, and toppings as for full-size pies, making any necessary adjustments. For instance, if you're making mini Caramel Banana Cream Pies (page 382), cut the banana into small chunks instead of large sections — that sort of thing.

If you have leftover ingredients and not enough shells, you can always build crustless pies in ramekins. Nobody will complain.

Little Cherry Pies *with* Mascarpone Whipped Cream

I make these for Valentine's Day and during fresh cherry season, and everybody loves them. Aside from the graham cracker shells, there's nothing to bake because the filling is cooked on the stove. It's then divided among the shells and topped with a heavenly version of whipped cream. What's not to love?

Makes 4 or 5 mini pies

Graham Cracker Crust (page 82)

FILLING

- 3 **cups pitted fresh or frozen cherries (about 1 pound)**
- ½ **cup sugar**
- 1 **tablespoon lemon juice**
- ⅓ **cup apple, cherry, or cranberry juice**
- 1½ **tablespoons cornstarch**
- ½ **teaspoon vanilla extract**

    Mascarpone Whipped Cream (page 448)

1. Prepare the crumb crust mixture and divide it evenly among four or five buttered mini-pie pans. (My favorite pans measure 4¼ inches in diameter and have a capacity of about ½ cup, but virtually any small pie pans will do.) Press the crumbs firmly and evenly against the bottom and up the sides of the pans. Refrigerate the shells for 10 to 15 minutes.

2. Preheat the oven to 350°F (180°C). Arrange the shells on a baking sheet, evenly spaced. Bake on the middle oven rack for 8 minutes. Transfer to a rack and cool thoroughly.

3. Gently heat the cherries in a medium saucepan, covered, until they come to a simmer. Add the sugar and lemon juice. Cover and simmer until quite juicy, 2 to 3 minutes. Mix the fruit juice and cornstarch in a small bowl and immediately stir the mixture into the fruit. Bring the fruit to a boil, then lower the heat slightly and cook, stirring nonstop, until thick and glossy, about 1½ minutes. Remove from the heat and stir in the vanilla. Scrape the fruit onto a plate and cool thoroughly.

4. When you're ready to serve the pies, spoon some of the filling into each of the shells. Mound the whipped cream on top of the filling, or pipe it on with a pastry bag. Serve at once.

Recipe for Success

Make sure the cornstarch and fruit juice liquid are well mixed just before you add them to the fruit.

I'll deny it if anyone asks if I really said this, but you could always use those premade mini graham cracker shells from the supermarket.

Peanut Butter *and* Butterfinger Pies

This and the next few recipes are simple to prepare and geared toward children, who — speaking from experience — will gladly act as your accomplices, that is, assistants. Aside from cooking the crumb crust shells, there's no other baking involved, a real bonus if you're working with youngsters. The filling is delish, something like a peanut butter mousse with Butterfinger candy under it and on top. You'd have a hard time finding another little pie that's this kid friendly and scrumptious.

Makes 4–6 mini pies

Graham Cracker Crust (page 82)

FILLING

- 1 **(8-ounce) package full-fat or reduced-fat cream cheese, softened**
- 1 **cup confectioners' sugar, sifted**
- 2 **tablespoons packed light brown sugar**
- ½ **cup smooth peanut butter**
- ½ **teaspoon vanilla extract**
- ¾ **cup cold heavy cream**
- 1 **Butterfinger candy bar, finely chopped**

1. Prepare the crumb crust mixture, dividing it equally among four to six mini-pie pans, pressing the crumbs evenly against the bottom and up the sides of the pan until they're even with the top of the pan. If your pans have a capacity of 1 cup, you'll have enough crumbs for four pies; less than that and you'll have enough for five or six. Refrigerate the shells for 10 to 15 minutes.

2. Preheat the oven to 350°F (180°C). Arrange the shells on a large baking sheet, evenly spaced. Bake on the middle oven rack for 8 minutes. Transfer the shells to a rack and cool.

3. Beat the cream cheese in a large bowl with an electric mixer (handheld is fine) until smooth and creamy. Add the sugars and beat until smooth, scraping down the sides. Add the peanut butter and vanilla, and beat again until smooth. Wash and dry the beaters. Chill a mixing bowl to beat the cream in.

4. Using the clean beaters and chilled bowl, beat the cream until it holds firm peaks. Set aside a big spoonful of it to garnish the pies. Add the larger portion of whipped cream to the peanut butter mixture and fold it in gently but thoroughly.

5. Using about half of the chopped candy, sprinkle some in the bottom of each pie shell. Divide the filling evenly among the shells. Sprinkle more candy over each pie, reserving a little bit for decorating. Refrigerate the pies for at least 2 hours.

6. Right before serving, dollop some of the reserved whipped cream over each pie. Top with any remaining candy and serve.

Kid Safety

A recipe like this is the perfect teachable moment for young cooks. Before starting, take a moment to give them a lesson in the safe operation of an electric mixer, stressing the importance of keeping hands out of harm's way. And don't leave a child's side when the mixer is running.

Little Berry Pies
in Vanilla Custard Sauce

These are sweet little pies. You'll want to make them all summer long as the parade of fresh fruit marches on. Simply bake up a half-dozen mini crumb crusts, pour some vanilla custard sauce (crème anglaise) into each, then add fresh berries and a dollop of whipped cream. Couldn't be simpler or more delicious.

Makes 6 mini pies

Graham Cracker Crust (page 82) or another crumb crust

FILLING

Vanilla Custard Sauce (page 446), well chilled

1 **pint fresh raspberries, blackberries, blueberries, or hulled and sliced strawberries**

Whipped Cream (page 447), for serving

Ground nutmeg, for garnish

1. Prepare the crumb crust mixture and divide it equally among six 4- to 4½-inch-diameter (½-cup capacity) buttered pie pans, pressing it in evenly against the bottoms and sides of the pans. (If your pans are slightly larger, use four or five pans.) Refrigerate the shells for 10 to 15 minutes.

2. Preheat the oven to 350°F (180°C). Arrange the shells on a rimmed baking sheet, evenly spaced. Bake on the middle oven rack for 8 minutes. Transfer to a rack and cool.

3. Fill each cooled shell about halfway with the vanilla custard sauce. Make a nice little mound of berries in each. Dollop with whipped cream, dust with nutmeg, and serve. Refrigerate leftovers.

Recipe for Success

To be clear, the custard sauce is a sauce; it doesn't firm up like cup custard. It will ooze thickly when you spoon it into the pie, as it should, but that's no concern since it will be contained in the pan.

Nobody would blame you for drizzling a little caramel sauce into the shell before you add the custard sauce.

Charleston Tarts

My wife, Bev, who lived in Charleston, South Carolina, for 25 years, tells me that these little two-bite pies are a Lowcountry tradition. Her treasured recipe for them was handwritten on a kitchen-worn index card, the origin long since forgotten, but trust me when I tell you the recipe has held up nicely. You'll notice similarities between these and the Canadian Butter Tarts on page 280, though they're unique and tasty enough to warrant space of their own.

Makes 8–10 tarts

Single-Crust Food Processor Pie Dough (page 58) or Old-Fashioned Shortening Pie Dough (page 62)

FILLING

- 1 **large egg**
- ⅓ **cup light corn syrup**
- ⅓ **cup sugar**
- 3 **tablespoons unsalted butter, melted**
- ½ **teaspoon vanilla extract**
- ⅛ **teaspoon salt**
- ½ **cup dark raisins**
- ½ **cup pecan halves, toasted (page 453) and coarsely chopped**

Variation

Instead of raisins, use chocolate chips or even butterscotch chips.

1. Prepare the pie dough and divide it in half. Wrap the halves separately in plastic wrap and refrigerate until firm enough to roll, about 1 hour.

2. When you're ready to assemble the tarts, roll half of the dough slightly thinner than you would for a regular pie. Don't worry if it isn't round. Using a 4-inch round cutter, cut out four or five circles of dough. Gently press each circle into one of the cups of a 12-cup muffin pan. Repeat the process with the other dough half. Then gather up any scraps, roll, cut out another circle or two, and add those to the pan. Refrigerate the pan.

3. Preheat the oven to 375°F (190°C). Whisk the egg lightly in a medium bowl. Add the corn syrup and sugar; whisk again. Whisk in the butter, vanilla, and salt until evenly blended.

4. Divide the raisins and pecans evenly among the muffin cups. Ladle some of the filling into each pastry shell, dividing it equally. Keep the filling slightly below the upper edge of the pastry.

5. Put the pan on the center oven rack and bake for about 25 minutes, until the tops are golden brown and puffed.

6. Transfer the pan to a rack and cool for 5 minutes. Run a knife around the edge of each tart and cool for 30 to 45 minutes longer. Slide a knife under each one, lift it out, and continue to cool. Serve at room temperature. Store leftovers in a covered container at room temperature for up to 24 hours. Refrigerate for longer storage, but serve at room temperature.

Mini Cheesecake Pies

These make for a great party dessert, whether your guests are big or little. Or throw a pie party: Bake up as many as you need, then serve them up with a variety of toppings for a build-your-own buffet. Everyone loves making a signature pie!

Makes 6 mini pies

Graham Cracker Crust (page 82)

FILLING

- 6 **ounces cream cheese, softened**
- ½ **cup sugar**
- 1 **large egg, at room temperature**
- ¼ **cup sour cream**
- ½ **teaspoon vanilla extract**
- ¼ **teaspoon lemon extract or grated lemon zest**

1. Prepare the crumb crust mixture and divide it equally among six 4- to 4½-inch-diameter (½-cup capacity) pie pans, pressing it in evenly against the bottoms and sides of the pans. Refrigerate the shells for 10 to 15 minutes.

2. Preheat the oven to 350°F (180°C). Arrange the shells on a rimmed baking sheet, evenly spaced. Bake on the middle oven rack for 8 minutes. Transfer to a rack and cool the shells right on the sheet. Set aside.

3. Set the oven to 325°F (170°C). Using a handheld electric mixer, beat the cream cheese in a medium bowl, on medium speed, gradually adding the sugar. Add the egg and beat briefly. Add the sour cream, vanilla, and lemon extract, and continue to beat until smooth and evenly combined.

4. Ladle the batter into the pie shells, dividing it evenly. Fill it close to the top, but leave a little room for toppings.

5. Bake the pies, on the sheet, on the center rack for about 20 minutes, until they puff slightly and have a dull, not glossy, surface. Do not overbake.

6. Transfer the baking sheet and pies to a rack and cool thoroughly. Cover loosely with tented aluminum foil and refrigerate for at least 3 hours before serving.

Variations

CARAMEL NUT. Spoon a little caramel sauce over the filling, then sprinkle with chopped nuts. Drizzle with chocolate syrup for an over-the-top finish.
FRESH BERRY. Top with fresh blueberries, raspberries, or hulled and sliced strawberries. Brush with warmed red currant jelly to make the fruit shine.
GLAZED FRUIT. Spread with a simple fruit topping or glaze (there's no shame in store-bought).
CANDY FANTASY. Pipe whipped cream over the filling. Top with rainbow or chocolate sprinkles, mini M&M's, or other small candies.

Mini Lemon Pies *with* Mascarpone Whipped Cream

These adorable mini pies filled with lemon curd are just right for summer entertaining, in large part because the components are easily made in advance. Once prepared, these can be assembled in about five minutes. Choose perfect little berries to go around the perimeter of each one, perhaps using blueberries for some and raspberries for others.

Makes 6 mini pies

Graham Cracker Crust (page 82) or other crumb crust

FILLING

Lemon Curd (page 450)

Mascarpone Whipped Cream (page 448)

1 cup fresh blueberries or raspberries

Ground nutmeg, for garnish

1. Prepare the crumb crust mixture and divide it equally among six 4- to 4½-inch-diameter (½-cup capacity) pie pans, pressing it in evenly against the bottoms and sides of the pans. Refrigerate the shells for 10 to 15 minutes.

2. Preheat the oven to 350°F (180°C). Arrange the shells on a rimmed baking sheet, evenly spaced. Bake on the middle oven rack for 8 minutes. Transfer the shells to a rack and cool.

3. When you're almost ready to assemble the pies — preferably within 1 hour of serving them — spoon a generous amount of lemon curd into each shell. Mound some of the mascarpone whipped cream on each, or pipe it on with a pastry bag. Arrange a circle of berries around the perimeter of each whipped cream mound. Lightly dust each pie with a sprinkle of nutmeg, then serve.

Recipe for Success

The reason I don't recommend assembling these too far in advance is that you want the pie shells to stay as crisp as possible. The longer they sit in the fridge, assembled, the softer the shells will become. But an hour or so won't be a problem.

Briana Carson on Pie and Community

Many people who visit Crave Pie Studio have never had a real pie that is baked entirely from scratch, so our pies set a new standard for them. People who are seeking real, local, and sustainable food love the connection with the local farmers and growers whose ingredients are baked into our pies.

Pie has the ability to take people with differences, whether generational, regional, or cultural, and bring them together over a common shared pleasure. Customers have blessed me with stories of how our pie has brought back memories and created new traditions for them. Our pies have been served during some of life's most meaningful moments — holiday dinners, weddings, baby showers, and to comfort the ill and bereaved.

The most memorable thing a customer has told me was, "Our mom is visiting from out of state and we just had to show her our pie shop." They referred to us as "our pie shop"! I could not have received a more meaningful compliment. To know that my little business has been embraced by the community and become a part of the lives of my customers still sustains me.

— Briana Carson, owner and artisan pie baker, Crave Pie Studio, Duluth, Georgia

Fruit Preserve Finger Pies

When my kids were young, they used to make these every time I baked a pie. They'd scoop up my dough trimmings, press them into little rounds, top with preserves, then fold the dough over to seal. We'd bake them on a little pan next to my big pie, and they'd disappear as soon as they were cool enough to eat. Eventually, I turned their little sideline into an actual recipe, which I hope you'll try the next time you're looking to entertain kids or grands with a fun project.

Makes about 12 mini pies

Flaky Cream Cheese Pie Dough (page 72)

FILLING

1 **jar raspberry, strawberry, peach or other fruit preserves**

Handful of white chocolate chips or semisweet chocolate chips (optional)

1½ **cups confectioners' sugar, sifted**

1. Prepare and refrigerate the pie dough. Line a large baking sheet with parchment paper.

2. Roll the dough as you would for a pie, but just a bit thinner. It doesn't need to be round. Using a 3½-inch round cutter, cut out as many circles as you can. Leaving the circles in place, gather up the scraps. Press them together and refrigerate to firm the dough before rolling out to make the rest of the rounds.

3. Spoon about 2 teaspoons fruit preserves into the center of each circle. Scatter some chocolate chips, if you're using them, on top of the preserves. Moisten the edge of the pastry with a damp fingertip, then fold the dough over, line up the edges, and press along the edge to seal. Crimp the edge with a fork. Evenly space the pies on the baking sheet and refrigerate for 15 minutes.

4. Preheat the oven to 375°F (190°C). Using or fork or the tip of a paring knife, poke a small steam vent in the top of each pie. Bake on the middle oven rack for 25 to 30 minutes, until golden brown. Transfer the hot pies to a rack.

5. Put the confectioners' sugar in a shallow bowl. As soon as the pies are cool enough to handle, roll each one in the sugar, coating them heavily, then return them to the rack to finish cooling. Serve warm or at room temperature. Refrigerate leftovers in a tightly sealed container.

Half-Moon Peach Pies

Peaches are my favorite fresh fruit, so it should come as no surprise that these hand pies are among my favorites, too. I use a thickened filling to prevent a major juice breech, an extra step that keeps the filling good and juicy and plain delicious. Don't let summer pass without baking a batch.

Makes 4 large hand pies

Flaky Cream Cheese Pie Dough (page 72) or another single-crust dough

FILLING

- 3 cups peeled and pitted ripe peaches, cut into bite-size chunks
- ⅓ cup granulated sugar, plus a little extra for sprinkling
- 2 tablespoons orange juice
- 2 teaspoons lemon juice
- 2 tablespoons cornstarch
- ¼ teaspoon vanilla extract
- ⅛ teaspoon ground nutmeg

  Pinch of salt
- 1½ tablespoons cold unsalted butter
- 1 egg beaten with 1 tablespoon milk, for glaze

  Confectioners' sugar (optional)

1. Prepare the pie dough. Divide it into four equal-size balls. Flatten each one into a ½-inch-thick disk and wrap in plastic wrap. Refrigerate for at least 1 hour.

2. Combine the peaches and granulated sugar in a saucepan over medium heat. Bring to a boil, stirring occasionally. Reduce the heat and let the fruit simmer gently for 3 to 4 minutes.

3. While the filling simmers, stir the orange juice, lemon juice, and cornstarch together in a small bowl. When the fruit has simmered for 3 to 4 minutes, stir the cornstarch liquid into the peaches. Increase the heat slightly and cook the fruit, stirring nonstop, until thickened, about 1½ minutes. Remove from the heat. Stir in the vanilla, nutmeg, and salt. Cool thoroughly. (This can be made the day ahead and refrigerated.)

4. Line a large rimmed baking sheet with parchment paper. Working with one piece of dough at a time, roll it into an 8-inch circle. Spoon one-quarter of the cooled filling over half of the dough, leaving a ¾-inch border around the edge. Dot the top of the filling with a little of the butter. Moisten the edge of the pastry, then fold the uncovered half of dough over the filling. Pinch the edges together, then crimp it with a fork or roll it into a sort of rope edge. Put the pie on the lined baking sheet and refrigerate. Refrigerate all the pies for 15 minutes.

5. Preheat the oven to 400°F (200°C). When the oven is preheated, brush each pie lightly with the egg wash glaze and sprinkle with granulated sugar. Poke the surface of each a couple of times, to make vents. Bake on the middle oven rack for 15 minutes. Reduce the heat to 375°F (190°C), rotate the pies 180 degrees, and bake for about 20 minutes longer, until golden brown.

6. Transfer the pies to a rack and cool for 10 minutes. While they're still warm, dust with confectioners' sugar, if desired.

Recipe for Success

For a pop of flavor and color, scatter a few fresh blueberries or raspberries on top of the peach filling before sealing the pastry.

Sprinkling the confectioners' sugar through a fine-mesh sieve on the hand pies while they're still warm allows the sugar to sort of melt into the pastry. Bakeries often do this, followed by another coat on the cooled pies.

Fried Peach Pies
with Frozen Peaches

Frozen peaches aren't as good as fresh, but sadly, fresh peach season is very brief. Plan B is to use frozen ones. The quality of frozen fruit is typically commendable, so I'm all in favor when that's the best option. Mix peach, apple, or white grape juice in with the fruit, but don't use a red one; you want to keep the peachy color.

Makes 6 or 7 hand pies

Dough for Fried Pies (page 65)

FILLING

- 1 **(20-ounce) bag frozen sliced peaches**
- ½ **cup granulated sugar**
- **Pinch of salt**
- ¼ **cup peach, apple, or white grape juice**
- 2 **teaspoons lemon juice**
- 1 **tablespoon cornstarch**
- 1½–2 **quarts peanut, canola, or vegetable oil, for deep-frying**
- **Confectioners' Sugar Glaze (page 452) (optional)**

1. Prepare the pie dough and divide it into six or seven equal-size balls. Flatten them into ½-inch-thick disks. Place them on a plate or small baking sheet, cover with plastic wrap, and refrigerate for 1 hour.

2. Combine the peaches, granulated sugar, and salt in a medium saucepan; mix well. Cover and cook on medium-low heat for several minutes. When the juices start to build up, increase the heat, cover, and continue to cook at a low boil until the peaches are quite soft, 10 to 12 minutes.

3. Using a potato masher, mash the fruit, but not too much; it's nice to have chunks in the filling. Combine the fruit juice, lemon juice, and cornstarch in a small bowl. Mix well, then stir into the fruit. Cook the fruit at a low boil, stirring non-stop, for 1½ minutes. It will thicken up nicely. Remove from the heat, scrape into a bowl, and cool thoroughly. (You may also refrigerate for up to 24 hours.)

4. Line a baking sheet with plastic wrap. Working with one piece of dough at a time, roll it into an 8-inch circle. Spoon about ⅓ cup filling over half of the dough, leaving a ¾-inch border all around. Lightly moisten the edge of the pastry, then fold the uncovered half of dough over the filling. Line up the edges and press to seal. Crimp the edge with a fork or roll it into a sort of rope edge. Place the pies on the baking sheet and refrigerate for at least 15 minutes.

5. When you're ready to fry the pies, heat 2½ to 3 inches of oil to 375°F (190°C) in a deep fryer or heavy pot. When the oil is hot, gently lower two or three pies into the fat — don't crowd them — and fry until golden and crispy, 3½ to 4 minutes. Using a long-handled wire strainer, transfer the pies to a baking sheet lined with a paper bag or paper towels and drain. Repeat until all of the pies are fried. When they've cooled enough to handle, dust them with confectioners' sugar, if desired, or drizzle with the glaze. Wait for 10 to 15 minutes before serving because the insides stay hot for a while.

Fried Cherry Pies

Unlike the fried pies on the facing page, which use dried fruit, these cherry pies combine fresh and dried fruit. The fresh ones add juiciness and the dried ones pack a lot of flavor, so you get the best of both worlds. I use pitted fresh cherries when they're at their peak in summer, but the rest of the time I use frozen ones.

Makes 8 hand pies

Dough for Fried Pies (page 65)

FILLING

- **3 cups pitted sweet cherries, fresh or frozen**
- **½ cup dried sweet or sour cherries**
- **½ cup granulated sugar**
- **2 tablespoons orange juice**
- **1 tablespoon lemon juice**
- **¼ cup apple or other fruit juice, or water**
- **1½ tablespoons cornstarch**
- **½ teaspoon vanilla extract**
- **1½–2 quarts peanut, canola, or vegetable oil, for deep-frying**
- **Confectioners' sugar, for garnish (optional)**

1. Prepare the pie dough and divide it into eight equal-size balls. Flatten them into ½-inch-thick disks. Place them on a plate or small baking sheet, cover with plastic wrap, and refrigerate for 1 hour.

2. Combine the fresh or frozen cherries, dried cherries, granulated sugar, orange juice, and lemon juice in a medium saucepan. Cover and gradually bring the fruit to a simmer over moderate heat. Simmer until the mixture is quite juicy, 3 to 4 minutes.

3. Mix the apple juice and cornstarch in a small bowl. Add this slurry to the fruit. Bring the mixture to a low boil and cook, stirring nonstop, until thickened and glossy, about 1½ minutes. Stir in the vanilla. Remove from the heat and scrape the fruit onto a plate. Cool thoroughly.

4. Line a baking sheet with plastic wrap. Working with one piece of dough at a time, roll it into a 7-inch circle. Spoon 3 or 4 tablespoons filling over half of the dough, leaving a ¾-inch border all around. Lightly moisten the edge of the pastry, then fold the uncovered half of dough over the filling. Line up the edges and press to seal. Crimp the edge with a fork or roll it into a sort of rope edge. Place the pies on the baking sheet and refrigerate for at least 15 minutes.

5. When the pies go in the fridge, heat about 2½ inches oil to 375°F (190°C) in a deep fryer or heavy pot. When the oil is hot, gently lower several of the pies into the fat — don't crowd them — and fry until golden and crispy, 3½ to 4 minutes. Using a long-handled wire strainer, transfer the pies to a baking sheet lined with a paper bag or paper towels and drain. Repeat until all of the pies are fried. When they've cooled enough to handle, dust them with confectioners' sugar, if desired. Wait for 10 to 15 minutes before serving because the insides stay hot for a little bit.

Recipe for Success

If you roll the dough onto waxed paper, then fill the dough circle, you can fold over the dough just by lifting up on the paper and folding that over. This helps if the dough gets frayed or fragile.

Skip the dried cherries if you like and simply use 3½ cups regular sweet cherries.

Fried Pies *with* Dried-Apple Filling

Using dried, reconstituted apples instead of fresh makes for a dense filling, almost like thick applesauce. It's an interesting and quite delicious variation. You can also prepare these with the fresh apple filling used for the Fall Fruit Turnovers (page 347). Substitute pears for apples or dried cranberries for the raisins. See which version you like best!

Makes 8 hand pies

Dough for Fried Pies (page 65)

FILLING

- 2 cups coarsely chopped dried apple rings
- ½ cup dark raisins
- 1 cup water
- ⅔ cup orange juice
- ½ cup granulated sugar
- 1 tablespoon lemon juice
- ½ teaspoon ground cinnamon
- ¼ teaspoon ground nutmeg
- 1½–2 quarts peanut, canola, or vegetable oil, for deep frying
- Confectioners' sugar, for garnish (optional)

1. Prepare the pie dough and divide it into eight equal-size balls. Flatten them into ½-inch-thick disks. Place them on a plate or small baking sheet, cover with plastic wrap, and refrigerate for 1 hour.

2. Combine the apples, raisins, water, and orange juice in a medium saucepan over moderate heat. Bring to a simmer, cover tightly, and simmer until the apples are quite soft and have absorbed much of the water, about 10 minutes. Add the granulated sugar, lemon juice, cinnamon, and nutmeg. Continue to simmer, stirring often, until all of the liquid has cooked off and the fruit is syrupy, 5 to 8 minutes. Transfer the filling to a plate and cool thoroughly.

3. Working with one piece of dough at a time, and leaving the others in the fridge as you work, roll it into a 7-inch circle. Spoon about 3 to 4 tablespoons filling over half of the dough, leaving a ¾-inch border all around. Lightly moisten the edge of the pastry, then fold the uncovered half of dough over the filling. Line up the edges and press to seal. Crimp the edge with a fork or roll the edge to make a sort of rope. Place the pies on a baking sheet lined with plastic wrap and refrigerate for at least 15 minutes.

4. When you're ready to fry the pies, heat about 2½ to 3 inches of oil to 375°F (190°C) in a deep fryer or heavy pot. When the oil is hot, gently lower two or three pies at a time into the fat — don't crowd them — and fry until golden and crispy, 3½ to 4 minutes. Using a long-handled wire strainer, transfer the pies to a baking sheet lined with a paper bag or paper towels and drain. When all the pies are fried and cooled enough to handle, dust them with confectioners' sugar, if desired. Wait for 10 to 15 minutes before serving because the insides stay hot for a while.

Recipe for Success
Unlike baked pies, deep-fried pies shouldn't have vent holes. It isn't necessary to vent them, and any holes will take on oil and make the pies unappetizing.

Fruit Pie Pops

Pie pops have been all the rage for some time now, and for good reason: they're simple to make, fun to eat, and an ideal baking project for kids. They also make a great gift: slide a small cellophane bag over each one and tie it with a ribbon.

The only specialty item you need are lollipop sticks, which you can buy at any craft store. The size and shape of the pops are up to you, so the yield will vary according to your choices. Bigger pie pops have more filling, but smaller ones hold more securely to the sticks. After you've made these a couple of times, you'll be a pro.

Makes 10–12 pie pops

Single-Crust Food Processor Pie Dough (page 58)

FILLING

1-2 dozen lollipop sticks

1 cup fruit preserves or any of the fruit fillings suggested in Variations

1 egg beaten with 1 tablespoon milk, for glaze

Sugar, for sprinkling

Confectioners' Sugar Glaze (page 452) (optional but highly recommended)

1. Prepare and refrigerate the pie dough, adding 1 tablespoon of sugar to the dry ingredients. This will help the crust develop a golden color. If you use a 3-inch round cutter — about the largest size I'd recommend — you will probably have enough dough for about 10 pops. As you go smaller in size, you increase the number of pops you get. I think a good place to start is with a 2½-inch round cutter, preferably a scalloped or ruffled one because it makes such a pretty edge.

2. To assemble the pops, roll the dough out as you would for a pie-crust, but make it a little thinner than normal and don't worry about keeping it round since you're going to cut it anyway. Line a large baking sheet with parchment paper.

3. Using the cutter, and keeping the cuts as close together as possible, cut out as many rounds as you can. Arrange half of them on the baking sheet, evenly spaced and about an inch from the sides.

4. Take a lollipop stick and place it on top of one of the rounds, overlapping it by about half of the diameter. Gently press the stick into the dough. Spoon 2 to 4 teaspoons of the preserves or other filling into the center of the circle, leaving a generous border of dough all around. Using a fingertip, lightly moisten the dough border with the egg wash glaze. Place a second circle over the filled circle, line up the edges, and press along the border to seal. Using one of your pop sticks or a fork, press around the edge to seal the dough. Refrigerate the pops on the sheet for 20 to 30 minutes.

5. Preheat the oven to 375°F (190°C). Brush each pop sparingly with the egg wash glaze and sprinkle with sugar. Bake on the middle oven rack for about 25 minutes, until golden brown. Transfer the pops to a rack and cool them thoroughly right on the sheet.

6. When the pops have cooled, drizzle some of the confectioners' sugar glaze over each one, if desired, and serve. Store flat side down in a sealed container; refrigerate after 24 hours.

Variations

FOR THE FILLING: Instead of fruit preserves, use the peach filling from the fried peach pies on page 340; the cherry filling from the fried cherry pies on page 342; or the fall fruit filling from page 347. Any of these would work beautifully. Thick apple butter is another good option, as is just about any thick, fruity spread.

FOR THE POP SHAPES: You can use heart cutters for Valentine's Day, apple and pumpkin cutters in the fall, ornament cutters during the holidays. Decorate with cookie icing to make them even more fun and appealing. (Or add food coloring to the confectioners' sugar glaze.)

ONE POPULAR VARIATION is cutting a small design in the top layer to show the filling. The drawback is that some of the filling oozes out. Little cutters are notoriously difficult to work with, so chill the top rounds until the dough is firm. This makes it easier to remove the dough from the small cutter. (I will often nudge it out with a thin bladed paring knife or cake tester.)

Apple *and* Fig Jam Pockets

Here's my take on toaster pastries, which I adored as a child. It's been decades since I've eaten one of the original ones, but when I get the urge, I make a batch of these; store-bought ones can't compare. Use a different single-crust recipe if you want, but the Hand Pie version of the Whole-Wheat Pie Dough makes a wonderfully flaky, tender, and slightly sweet crust.

Makes 6 hand pies

Whole-Wheat Hand Pie Dough (page 66)

FILLING

- 1 large apple, peeled, cored, and very finely diced
- 1 tablespoon sugar, plus a little for sprinkling
- 1½ teaspoons all-purpose flour
- ½ teaspoon finely grated lemon zest
-   Pinch of ground cinnamon, nutmeg, or cardamom
- ⅓ cup fig preserves
- 1 egg beaten with 1 tablespoon milk, for glaze
-   Confectioners' Sugar Glaze (page 452)

1. Prepare the pie dough. Instead of shaping it into a disk, shape it into the best square or rectangle you can. Refrigerate for at least 1 hour.

2. Combine the diced apple, sugar, flour, lemon zest, and cinnamon in a small bowl. Mix well. Stir in the preserves; refrigerate while you roll the dough.

3. Roll the dough into a 12- by 12-inch square. Using a pastry wheel or paring knife, cut the dough into 4- by 3-inch rectangles — two cuts in one direction, three in the other — leaving you with 12 rectangles. Set half of them off to the side, and space out the other six on your counter in front of you.

4. Line a large baking sheet with parchment paper. Working with one piece of dough at a time, smear a large spoonful of the apple filling lengthwise in the center of the rectangle, leaving a pastry border of about ½ to

¾ inch on all sides of the filling. Using your fingertip, moisten the edges with the egg wash glaze. Place a second rectangle over the first, line up the edges, then press along the edges to seal. Place the filled pastries on the prepared baking sheet and refrigerate for 15 to 20 minutes.

5. Preheat the oven to 375°F (190°C). Brush each pastry sparingly with the egg wash glaze and sprinkle with sugar. Bake on the middle oven rack for about 25 minutes, until golden brown.

6. Transfer the sheet to a rack and let the pastries cool on the sheet. When the pockets have cooled, drizzle some of the confectioners' sugar glaze over each one and serve. Store leftovers in a sealed storage container. Refrigerate after 24 hours.

Recipe for Success

After I press along the edges to seal, I trim the very edge of each side with my fluted pastry wheel for a ruffled look.

This recipe is easily doubled. Just make a second batch or double batch of dough, or use some of the pastry scraps you've been saving in the freezer. And double the filling quantities.

Fall Fruit Turnovers

Fall is such a great time of year to make these portable pies using fresh seasonal fruit. They travel easily to tailgate parties and on long bike rides and hikes. They're a welcome treat for leaf rakers and firewood choppers. When I can, I assemble them ahead, put them on a parchment-lined baking sheet, and bake them off about an hour before I plan to serve them. That's a useful strategy when you're having guests.

Makes 4 turnovers

Buttermilk Pie Dough (page 67) or Flaky Cream Cheese Pie Dough (page 72)

FILLING

- 2 tablespoons orange juice
- 1 large Golden Delicious apple, peeled, cored, and diced
- 1 ripe pear, peeled, cored, and diced
- ½ cup sweetened dried cranberries
- 3 tablespoons granulated sugar, plus a little for sprinkling
- 2 teaspoons cornstarch
- ⅛ teaspoon ground cinnamon
- ⅛ teaspoon ground nutmeg
- 1 teaspoon finely grated lemon zest
- 1½ tablespoons cold unsalted butter
- Milk or half-and-half, for glaze
- Confectioners' sugar (optional)

1. Prepare the pie dough, dividing it into four equal-size balls. Flatten each one into a ½-inch-thick disk and wrap in plastic wrap. Refrigerate until needed.

2. Combine the orange juice, apple, pear, cranberries, and 2 tablespoons of the granulated sugar in a medium saucepan. Gradually bring to a boil over medium-high heat, cover, and cook for 3 minutes, stirring occasionally. Meanwhile, mix together the cornstarch, cinnamon, nutmeg, and the remaining 1 tablespoon sugar in a small bowl. Stir the mixture into the fruit and cook, stirring nonstop, for 1½ minutes. Remove from the heat and stir in the lemon zest. Spread the fruit on a plate and cool completely.

3. Working with one piece of dough at a time — and keeping the others refrigerated — roll it into a 7½- to 8-inch circle. Spoon about one-quarter of the filling over half of the dough, leaving a ¾-inch border around the entire edge. Dot the filling with a little of the butter. Lightly moisten the edge of the dough, then fold the dough over to cover the fruit, lining up the edges. Pinch the edges to seal. Either crimp the edge with a fork or roll it to make a sort of rope edge. Place on a large rimmed baking sheet lined with parchment paper. Refrigerate the turnovers for at least 15 minutes.

4. Preheat the oven to 400°F (200°C). Brush each chilled turnover with a little milk, then sprinkle with sugar. Poke the surface of each turnover two or three times with a fork, to make vents. Bake on the center oven rack for 15 minutes. Reduce the heat to 375°F (190°C), rotate the pan 180 degrees, and bake for 15 to 20 minutes longer, until golden brown.

5. Transfer the turnovers to a rack and cool slightly. While the pies are still warm, dust them with confectioners' sugar, if desired.

Recipe for Success

The easiest way to dust these is to put the confectioners' sugar in a fine-mesh sieve and shake it right over the turnovers on the rack. For the best coverage, sprinkle once while they're warm, then again when they've cooled to room temperature.

12
Icebox Pies:
CHIFFONS, A CHOCOLATE SILK, AND OTHER COOL PLEASURES

The icebox has pretty much gone the way of the horse and buggy, but icebox pies are every bit as popular as they've always been. Perhaps that's because icebox pies often require very little hands-on time — a big bonus for time-pressed cooks.

What exactly is an icebox pie? Generally speaking, the term refers to almost any pie that isn't baked. The crust, whether a crumb crust or pastry one, will be prebaked, of course. But the expectation of an icebox pie is that it will not require the same sort of skills and diligence as, say, a baked fruit pie.

Technically speaking, classic cream pies are icebox pies, but they're so closely linked by specific techniques that we've given them their own chapter. But that hardly leaves us without options. On the contrary, you'll find plenty of chiffon pies here. Many home cooks think of airy chiffon pies as a throwback to another era, but once you try one of the ones here, you'll banish that idea forever.

The pages ahead feature cold, creamy pies made with peanut butter, another with malted milk and malted milk balls, and an outrageous dulce de leche pie layered with sliced bananas and a mountain of whipped cream. And we're just getting warmed up.

So settle in, get ready to dog-ear some pages, and pick some pies that sound as irresistible as I can assure you they really are.

Lemon Chiffon Pie

This is the pie most people think of when they hear "chiffon pie." The sweet-tangy lemon filling is light as a cloud and to my mind tastes best in a graham cracker crust, although it's often teamed up with a pastry crust (see Recipe for Success). It's the quintessential summer pie, providing a lovely pale backdrop for a garnish of fresh berries.

Makes 8–10 servings

Graham Cracker Crust (page 82)

FILLING

- ¼ cup cold water
- 1 envelope unflavored gelatin
- ½ cup lemonade
- ½ cup lemon juice
- 1 cup sugar
- 4 large eggs, separated, whites brought to room temperature
- 1–2 teaspoons finely grated lemon zest
- Big pinch of salt
- ¼ teaspoon cream of tartar
- ½ teaspoon vanilla extract
- Whipped Cream (page 447) and fresh berries, for garnish

WARNING: *Consuming raw eggs may increase your risk of foodborne illness, especially if you have a medical condition.*

1. Prepare the crust and press it into the bottom and up the sides of a 9½-inch deep-dish pie pan. Refrigerate, prebake, and cool as directed. Refrigerate the shell until needed.

2. Pour the water into a small bowl and sprinkle the gelatin over it; let stand. In a medium heavy-bottom saucepan, whisk together the lemonade, lemon juice, ½ cup of the sugar, the egg yolks, lemon zest, and salt. Place over medium-low heat and cook gently, stirring nonstop, until the mixture thickens enough to coat the back of a spoon, 7 to 9 minutes. Do not let the mixture boil or it will curdle. Remove from the heat, stir in the softened gelatin, and immediately pour into a large bowl. Cool for 10 minutes, then refrigerate just until the mixture turns lumpy, indicating that the gelatin is starting to thicken it, 50 to 60 minutes.

3. Beat the egg whites in a large bowl with an electric mixer (handheld is fine) until they hold soft peaks. Beat in the cream of tartar. Gradually add the remaining ½ cup sugar, beating on high speed until the whites are thick and glossy. Beat in the vanilla. The whites should be firm but not dry. Gently fold about one-third of the whites into the lemon mixture. Add the remaining whites and continue to fold until the filling is evenly blended.

4. Turn the filling into the cooled pie shell and smooth the top with the back of a large spoon. Cover with loosely tented aluminum foil and refrigerate for at least 3 hours or overnight. Garnish individual slices with a dollop of whipped cream and a scattering of berries.

Recipe for Success

If you do use a pastry crust, it will need to be fully prebaked according to the instructions on page 36.

It's a little tricky judging when the lemon mixture has thickened sufficiently and is ready to be removed from the heat. Pay close attention, noting the subtle changes in consistency. When thickened, the mixture will be like heavy cream.

Be careful not to overbeat the egg whites or they'll turn dry and be difficult to fold into the lemon mixture.

Lime Margarita Pie

Here's a refreshing tropical dessert with a mousselike texture and an adult kick. The filling is a lime custard spiked with tequila and triple sec and combined with fresh whipped cream. The pie takes a trip to the freezer for several hours before serving, so time the recipe accordingly if you plan to serve it in the evening.

Makes 8–10 servings

Graham Cracker Crust or Shortbread Cookie Crust (page 82)

FILLING

- ¼ cup tequila
- 3 tablespoons triple sec
- 1½ teaspoons unflavored gelatin
- 4 large eggs
- 1 cup sugar, plus a little for garnish
- ½ cup lime juice
- 1 tablespoon lemon juice
- Finely grated zest of 1 lime
- 1¼ cups cold heavy cream
- 2 limes, for garnish

1. Prepare the crust and press it into the bottom and up the sides of a 9- to 9½-inch deep-dish pie pan. Refrigerate, prebake, and cool as directed. Refrigerate the shell until needed. At the same time, chill a medium bowl and a set of mixer beaters.

2. Combine the tequila and triple sec in a small bowl. Sprinkle the gelatin into the bowl and let stand for 4 to 5 minutes to soften.

3. Combine the eggs, sugar, lime juice, lemon juice, and lime zest in a small heavy nonreactive saucepan. Place over medium heat and cook, whisking more or less nonstop, until the mixture thickens, 5 to 6 minutes. Remove from the heat and blend in the tequila mixture, whisking to dissolve the gelatin. Scrape into a large bowl, cool to room temperature, and refrigerate until the mixture is cool to the touch, stirring occasionally.

4. Using the chilled medium bowl and beaters, beat the cream with an electric mixer (handheld is fine) until it is firm but not grainy. Fold about one-third of the whipped cream into the custard with a large rubber spatula. Add the remaining whipped cream and fold together until the filling is evenly combined. Turn the filling into the pie shell and smooth the top. Cover with loosely tented aluminum foil and place in the freezer for at least 4 hours or overnight. If the pie gets very firm from an extended stay in the freezer, move it to the refrigerator for 30 minutes or so before slicing.

5. Shortly before serving, prepare the garnish. Slice the center portion of each lime into four or five thin slices. Place the slices on a paper towel and blot well. Dip the slices into a shallow bowl of sugar, coating both sides well. Set the slices aside on a plate for 5 minutes. Repeat twice more, waiting 5 minutes between each coating. Just before serving, cut each slice from the edge to the center, leaving the center attached. Twist the halves in opposite directions and garnish each slice of pie with a twist.

Recipe for Success

Custards like this one are often cooked in the top insert of a double boiler to prevent them from curdling. If you maintain a moderate temperature and keep whisking, however, the custard shouldn't curdle.

If you can find it, use genuine Key lime juice, available bottled in most upscale kitchenware shops. Fresh Key limes are also showing up increasingly in the produce section of many supermarkets.

Watermelon Chiffon Pie

This featherlight chiffon pie has the subtle but unmistakable flavor of watermelon, thanks to the nearly three cups of watermelon juice in the filling. The juice is thickened with gelatin, then blended with whipped cream and beaten egg whites to get that airy chiffon texture people love. This pie makes a luscious summer dessert for any gathering.

Makes 10 servings

Graham Cracker Crust or Shortbread Cookie Crust (page 82)

FILLING

- 6 cups watermelon flesh (seeds are fine)
- ½ cup granulated sugar
- 2 envelopes unflavored gelatin
- 1 tablespoon lime juice or lemon juice
- 2 large egg whites, at room temperature
- 1 cup cold heavy cream
- 1 cup confectioners' sugar, sifted, plus a little for garnish
- Whipped Cream (page 447), for garnish (optional)

WARNING: *Consuming raw eggs may increase your risk of foodborne illness, especially if you have a medical condition.*

1. Prepare the crust and press it into the bottom and up the sides of a 9½-inch deep-dish pie pan. Refrigerate, prebake, and cool as directed. Refrigerate the shell until needed.

2. Combine the watermelon and granulated sugar in a very large bowl. Using a potato masher, mash the flesh until it is quite liquid. Let stand for 30 minutes. Drain the mixture through a fine-mesh strainer, reserving 2¾ cups of the watermelon juice. Discard the pulp and seeds.

3. Put ¼ cup of the juice in a medium bowl and sprinkle the gelatin over it. Let stand for 4 to 5 minutes to dissolve the gelatin. Meanwhile, heat ½ cup of the juice in a small saucepan over medium heat (or in the microwave on high) to a near boil. Whisk the hot juice into the dissolved gelatin. Pour the remaining 2 cups watermelon juice into a large bowl and stir in the gelatin mixture. Stir in the lime juice, then put the bowl in the refrigerator.

4. Using an electric mixer (handheld is fine), beat the egg whites in a medium bowl until stiff peaks form; set aside. Clean and dry the beaters. Chill them, along with a medium bowl, for 5 to 10 minutes. Using the chilled bowl and beaters, beat the heavy cream with the mixer until it holds soft peaks. Add the confectioners' sugar and continue to beat until the cream is firm but not grainy. Refrigerate.

5. When the watermelon juice mixture starts to firm up, add about one-quarter of the whipped cream and beat with the electric mixer until smooth. Add the beaten egg whites and remaining whipped cream, and gently fold them together with a large rubber spatula. If necessary, briefly whisk the mixture to break up any large globs of whites or whipped cream.

6. Turn the filling into the pie shell, shaking the pan gently to settle the filling. Cover with loosely tented aluminum foil and refrigerate for at least 4 hours, or preferably overnight. Garnish individual slices with a dusting of confectioners' sugar and a dollop of whipped cream, if desired.

Strawberry Chiffon Pie

Frozen strawberries, available any time of year, are used here to make a blushing chiffon pie with bits of strawberry scattered throughout. If you prepare this in summer, use the frozen strawberries in the pie (they're less expensive, and texture isn't an issue when you're going to cook them) and garnish the top with perfect, medium-size berries around the edge, piping swirls of whipped cream in between.

Makes 8–10 servings

Graham Cracker Crust or Shortbread Cookie Crust (page 82)

FILLING

- ⅔ **cup cold lemonade**
- 1½ **envelopes unflavored gelatin**
- 1 **(1-pound) bag frozen strawberries, partially thawed**
- ½ **cup plus 3 tablespoons sugar**
- **Finely grated zest of 1 lemon**
- 2 **large egg whites, at room temperature**
- **Pinch of salt**
- 1 **cup cold heavy cream**
- **Fresh strawberries**

WARNING: *Consuming raw eggs may increase your risk of foodborne illness, especially if you have a medical condition.*

1. Prepare the crust and press it into the bottom and up the sides of a 9- to 9½-inch deep-dish pie pan. Refrigerate, prebake, and cool as directed.

2. Pour the lemonade into a small bowl and sprinkle the gelatin over it. Let stand for 4 to 5 minutes to soften the gelatin. Combine the frozen strawberries, the ½ cup sugar, and the lemon zest in a large nonreactive saucepan over medium heat. Gradually bring to a simmer, lightly crushing the berries with a potato masher as they heat but leaving some chunks. Simmer the berries gently for 2 to 3 minutes, then remove from the heat. Immediately add the softened gelatin, stirring for 1 minute. Pour the fruit into a bowl and cool to room temperature. Refrigerate, stirring often, until the fruit is just starting to set. (To hasten the cooling, put the bowl in a second, larger bowl of ice water, stirring often.)

3. Beat the egg whites and salt in a medium bowl with an electric mixer (handheld is fine) on medium-high speed until they hold soft peaks. Gradually add the 3 tablespoons sugar, 1 tablespoon at a time, until the whites are thick and glossy but not dry. Fold the whites into the strawberry mixture until evenly blended.

4. Clean and dry the beaters. Chill them, along with a medium bowl, for 5 to 10 minutes. Using the chilled bowl and beaters, beat the cream with the mixer until firm but not grainy. Reserve about ⅓ of the whipped cream for decorating (store it in the refrigerator). Fold the remaining cream into the strawberry mixture until evenly combined. Turn the filling into the pie shell, smoothing the top with the back of a spoon. Cover with loosely tented aluminum foil and refrigerate for at least 4 hours or overnight. Just before serving, decorate the pie with whole fresh strawberries, piping the reserved whipped cream between them.

Recipe for Success

The more you fold the ingredients together, the more likely you are to deflate the filling. I like to add the whipped cream before the egg whites are fully incorporated to shorten the overall folding time required.

   It really does speed the cooling to use an ice-water bath. I like to use my big stainless steel "everything bowl" for this purpose.

Pick-Your-Own Triple-Strawberry Cream Pie

Makes 8–10 servings

Graham Cracker Crust (page 82)

FILLING

- 1½ **quarts fresh strawberries, hulled**
- ⅓ **cup sugar**
- 1 **teaspoon finely grated lemon zest**
- 1½ **tablespoons cornstarch**
- **Stabilized Whipped Cream (page 446)**

Recipe for Success

Given that you'll be making this pie in the hot days of summer, it's particularly important that you chill the bowl and beaters used for whipping the cream. High temperatures can make whipping cream a relatively sluggish process, and the cold bowl and beaters will speed the process.

Don't slice the remaining berries until right before assembling the pie. Ripe summer berries can be very juicy, and you want the juice to stay in the berries rather than leak into the pie.

When my four children were young, I used to take them to a local pick-your-own farm where I would pick boxes of ripe strawberries and they would manage to do everything but. What they didn't eat straight off the vine, they'd smoosh into their shirts, toss at one another, or simply squeeze between their fingers because anything is more fun than filling containers when you're a youngster. (The farm closed its operation to the public at some point, but I like to think we weren't the sole reason.)

Those berries were unsurpassed for this pie, where only the best ripe berries will do. Here you have three distinct strawberry layers: a cooked, thickened strawberry sauce; a layer of fresh berries; and a topping of freshly whipped cream blended with some of the sauce. There are a few steps, but nothing complicated. Most of the elements can be prepared a day or hours ahead and the pie put together at the last minute. Think of this as a special treat for summer get-togethers.

1. Prepare the crust and press it into the bottom and up the sides of a 9½-inch deep-dish pie pan. Refrigerate, prebake, and cool as directed. Refrigerate the shell until needed.

2. Halve half of the strawberries and put them in a large bowl. Stir in 1 tablespoon of the sugar and the lemon zest; let stand for 10 minutes to juice.

3. Using a large fork or potato masher, crush the juiced berries just enough to make a coarse purée; you want some chunks. Transfer to a medium nonreactive saucepan. Mix the cornstarch and the remaining sugar in a small bowl. Stir into the purée and gradually bring to a boil over medium heat, then cook the mixture, stirring nonstop, until thickened, 1½ minutes. Scrape the sauce into a bowl and cool thoroughly. Cover with plastic wrap and refrigerate until cold, at least 1 hour.

4. Prepare the stabilized whipped cream. Reserve one quarter of it for another use. Fold ½ cup of the strawberry sauce into the larger portion of whipped cream.

5. To assemble the pie, spread the remaining strawberry sauce over the bottom of the pie shell. Halve the remaining strawberries — or quarter them if they're very large — and arrange the berry pieces in a tight layer on top of the sauce. If you run out of room, chop the remaining berries and scatter them over the larger pieces. Spoon the strawberry whipped cream on top and smooth with the spoon. Put the pie in the freezer for 15 to 20 minutes, no longer, then serve.

Strawberry-Peach Icebox Pie

Cooked peaches folded with fresh strawberries are a natural summer duo. Like all icebox pies, this one requires no baking (aside from the crust) and just a few minutes of stovetop work to simmer and thicken the peaches. To lighten the load even more, you could use a graham cracker crust instead of a pastry shell. Plan on at least 3 hours to chill the pie. It's best eaten the day it's made because the longer the fresh strawberries sit, the more moisture they put off, resulting in a looser filling.

Makes 8 servings

Old-Fashioned Shortening Pie Dough (page 62), Graham Cracker Crust (page 82), or another single-crust dough

FILLING

- 4 **cups peeled ripe peaches, cut into bite-size chunks**
- ½ **cup sugar**
- 1 **teaspoon finely grated lemon zest**
- ½ **cup lemonade**
- ¼ **cup cornstarch**
- 1½ **cups hulled and halved fresh strawberries; quartered if they're very big**

  Stabilized Whipped Cream (page 446)

  Ground nutmeg, for garnish

1. Prepare and refrigerate the pie dough. Roll the dough into a 12-inch circle and line a 9- to 9½-inch standard pie pan with it, shaping the edge into an upstanding ridge. Flute or crimp the edge, chill the shell, and fully prebake it according to the instructions on page 36.

2. Combine the peaches, sugar, and lemon zest in a medium nonreactive saucepan, preferably nonstick. Place over medium heat, cover, and bring to a low boil, stirring often. Reduce the heat to medium-low and simmer until very juicy, 3 to 4 minutes.

3. Blend the lemonade and cornstarch in a small bowl and add to the peaches. Bring to a boil, then lower the heat slightly and cook at a low boil, stirring nonstop, until it thickens up nicely, about 1½ minutes. Scrape into a shallow bowl and cool to room temperature.

4. Fold the strawberries into the cooled peach mixture. Scrape the filling into the pie shell, smoothing the top with a spoon. Cover with plastic wrap and refrigerate for at least 3 to 4 hours.

5. Spread as much of the stabilized whipped cream as you like over the filling and dust the top of the pie with nutmeg. Refrigerate the pie if you're not serving it right away.

Recipe for Success

Be sure not to underbake the crust if you're using a pastry dough. In cases where cooled filling sits on a baked pastry, the crust should be as crisp as possible to guard against sogginess.

This method of making a pie — folding fresh fruit into a cooked fruit filling — invites all sorts of variations. Instead of strawberries, you could fold in fresh blackberries, blueberries, or raspberries. If you use raspberries, fold gently, as they're quite fragile.

Lemon-Raspberry Icebox Pie

A center of fresh red raspberries, a shortbread cookie crust, and a creamy filling and topping — this pie has a lot going for it. It takes just five minutes to blend the filling and get it into the crust. You have to wait a while for the filling to chill and firm up, then add a layer of fresh raspberries and top with whipped cream. Make this wonderful summer pie when local raspberries are fresh and perfectly sweet-tart.

Makes 8 servings

Shortbread Cookie Crust (page 82)

FILLING

- 6 **ounces cream cheese, softened**
- 1 **(14-ounce) can sweetened condensed milk**
- ⅓ **cup lemon juice**
- 1 **teaspoon vanilla extract**
- 1 **pint fresh raspberries, plus more for garnish (optional)**
- 1 **cup cold heavy cream**
- 2 **tablespoons confectioners' sugar, sifted**

1. Prepare the crust and press it into the bottom and up the sides of a 9- to 9½-inch standard pie pan. Refrigerate, prebake, and cool as directed. Refrigerate the shell until needed.

2. Beat the cream cheese and condensed milk together in a large bowl with an electric mixer (handheld is fine) on medium-high speed until smooth and fluffy, about 2 minutes. Add the lemon juice and beat for 1 minute. Blend in the vanilla. Scrape the filling into the pie shell and smooth the top with the back of a spoon. Cover with loosely tented aluminum foil and refrigerate for at least 3 or 4 hours, preferably overnight. In the meantime, wash and dry the beaters, and chill them along with a medium bowl.

3. Shortly before serving, scatter the raspberries evenly over the pie. Using the chilled bowl and beaters, beat the cream until it holds soft peaks. Add the sugar and continue to beat until stiff but not grainy. Spoon over the raspberries, smoothing it with a spoon. Slice and serve right away, garnishing each slice, if desired, with additional raspberries.

Recipe for Success

It's best not to rinse the raspberries before using them. Water is bound to end up in the cavities and then on the pie. If you must rinse, drain the berries upside down on paper towels.

Blueberries, blackberries, or sliced strawberries will also work well here.

White Russian Pie

This featherlight chiffon pie is flavored with coffee, coffee liqueur, and bourbon. Mounded into a delicious pecan graham cracker crumb crust, it's the perfect ending — served with strong coffee — to an informal dinner party.

Makes 8–10 servings

Nut Crumb Crust made with pecans, or Graham Cracker Crust (page 82)

FILLING

- ⅔ cup granulated sugar
- 5 large egg yolks
- 2 tablespoons bourbon
- ½ cup cold, strong-brewed coffee
- 1 envelope unflavored gelatin
- 1½ cups cold heavy cream
- 2 tablespoons Kahlúa or other coffee liqueur
- 1 teaspoon vanilla extract
- ⅓ cup confectioner's sugar
- Chocolate-covered coffee beans, for garnish (optional)

1. Prepare the crust and press it into the bottom and up the sides of a 9- to 9½-inch standard pie pan. Refrigerate, prebake, and cool as directed. Refrigerate the shell until needed. At the same time, chill a medium bowl and a set of mixer beaters.

2. Combine the granulated sugar and egg yolks in the top insert of a double boiler set over, not in, barely simmering water. (Alternatively, use a heatproof bowl, suspended by the sides of a saucepan, over barely simmering water.) Heat the mixture, whisking nearly nonstop, until thick enough to coat the back of a spoon, 7 to 8 minutes. Remove from the heat and whisk in the bourbon. Remove the insert and let the custard cool.

3. Once the custard has cooled, pour the coffee into a small bowl and sprinkle the gelatin over it. Let stand for 4 to 5 minutes to soften. Transfer the coffee mixture to a small saucepan and gently heat, whisking until the gelatin has dissolved, 1 to 2 minutes. Remove from the heat and gradually whisk into the custard. Scrape the custard into a large bowl and refrigerate, whisking every few minutes.

4. As soon as you refrigerate the custard, and using the chilled medium bowl and beaters, beat the cream with an electric mixer (handheld is fine) until it holds soft peaks. Add the liqueur and vanilla, and beat briefly. Add the confectioner's sugar and beat briefly again, until firm but not grainy.

5. When the refrigerated custard shows signs of thickening, remove it from the refrigerator and whisk in about ½ cup of the whipped cream until smooth. Add the remaining whipped cream in two parts, gently folding everything together until evenly combined. Mound the filling in the pie shell, smoothing the top. Cover with loosely tented aluminum foil and refrigerate for at least 4 hours or overnight.

6. Garnish the pie with chocolate-covered coffee beans, if desired, before serving.

Recipe for Success

It's important to catch the custard before it gets too firm (step 5). Otherwise, it will be difficult to fold in the whipped cream smoothly.

Chocolate Silk Pie

It seems like there's no end to our taste for rich, chocolaty desserts, and this one is right up there with the richest of them. The filling tastes like chocolate buttercream frosting piled into a pie shell and refrigerated, yielding a luxuriously smooth chocolate pie. If you have a stand mixer, I suggest using it here, given the lengthy beating involved. Virtually any crumb or cookie crust will work, including the Oreo Crumb Crust on page 85.

Makes 8–10 servings

Graham Cracker Crust (page 82)

FILLING

- 3 ounces unsweetened chocolate, coarsely chopped
- ¾ cup (1½ sticks) unsalted butter, softened
- 1¼ cups sugar
- 3 large eggs
- 2 teaspoons vanilla extract
- Whipped Cream (page 447), for garnish

WARNING: *Consuming raw eggs may increase your risk of foodborne illness, especially if you have a medical condition.*

1. Prepare the crust and press it into the bottom and up the sides of a 9- to 9½-inch standard pie pan. Refrigerate, prebake, and cool as directed. Refrigerate the shell until needed.

2. Put the chocolate in the top insert of a double boiler set over, not in, barely simmering water. (Alternatively, use a heatproof bowl, suspended by the sides of a saucepan, over barely simmering water.) Melt the chocolate, smoothing it with a whisk. Remove the insert and let the chocolate cool, stirring occasionally.

3. Using an electric mixer (handheld is fine), beat the butter in a large bowl until creamy. Gradually add the sugar and continue to beat, scraping down the bowl as needed, until the mixture is light textured, about 5 minutes. Scrape the melted chocolate into the butter mixture. Beat for 30 seconds. Add the eggs, one at a time, beating on medium-high speed for 3 to 4 minutes after each addition. The filling should be very light and creamy. Add the vanilla and blend for 10 seconds to incorporate.

4. Turn the filling into the pie shell and smooth the top with a spoon. Cover with loosely tented aluminum foil and refrigerate for at least 3 to 4 hours, or overnight. Serve slices garnished with a dollop of whipped cream.

Recipe for Success

Some fancier versions of silk pie use bittersweet chocolate for this pie. If that suits you, then by all means use it, but reduce the sugar by ⅓ cup.

If, like me, you can't keep your fingers out of whatever you're mixing, you may notice some sugar grittiness in the filling as you taste it. Don't be too concerned; there should be none by the time the last egg has been beaten in, and any traces will dissolve before the pie is served.

If you prefer, spread or pipe the whipped cream over the entire pie rather than dolloping it on slices.

Chocolate Malted Pie

When I was a boy, malted milk balls were my favorite candy. In the seventh grade, after Sister Therese appointed me the candy clerk for St. Mary's Grammar School, I snitched them well above the recommended daily dosage, a trespass Sister Therese made clear would land me in purgatory for eternity.

I'm not the first one to add malted milk balls and malted milk powder to a chocolate pie, and once you try this pie I think you'll understand why it's a tradition worth preserving. This is more than some childhood fantasy pie. It's plain good eating. If you can't find malted milk powder on store shelves, your local supermarket will probably be happy to order it for you.

Makes 8–10 servings

Oreo Crumb Crust (page 85) or Graham Cracker Crust (page 82)

FILLING

- 2 **cups cold heavy cream**
- 8 **ounces semisweet chocolate, coarsely chopped**
- ⅓ **cup malted milk powder**
- 1 **teaspoon vanilla extract**
- 1½ **cups malted milk balls**

1. Prepare the crust and press it into the bottom and up the sides of a 9- to 9½-inch standard pie pan. Refrigerate, prebake, and cool as directed. Refrigerate the shell until needed. At the same time, chill a medium bowl and a set of mixer beaters.

2. Heat 1¼ cups of the cream in a medium saucepan, preferably nonstick, until it shimmers, 2 to 3 minutes. Remove from the heat and add the chocolate. Let the mixture stand for 5 minutes, tilting the pan from time to time so the hot cream runs over the chocolate. Add the malted milk powder and vanilla, and whisk until smooth. Let cool.

3. When the mixture thickens slightly but is still pourable, pour about two-thirds of it into the pie shell. Cool thoroughly, then refrigerate until fairly firm, at least 2 hours. Reserve the remaining mixture at room temperature.

4. Using the chilled bowl and beaters, beat the remaining ¾ cup cream with an electric mixer (handheld is fine) until it holds soft peaks. Add the remaining chocolate mixture and continue to beat until a firm and full-bodied chocolate whipped cream develops. Cover and refrigerate until ready to use.

5. Put about half of the malted milk balls in a plastic bag and coarsely crush them with a rolling pin. Spread them over the filling and gently press to embed them. Spread the chocolate whipped cream over the filling and garnish with the remaining whole malted milk balls. Cover with loosely tented aluminum foil and refrigerate until ready to serve.

Recipe for Success

This pie can be made a day or two ahead because adding the chocolate to the whipped cream keeps the topping quite stable. This isn't usually the case with whipped cream–topped pies.

Once you've added the chocolate to the whipped cream, it will quickly firm up. As soon as it becomes firm and full bodied, stop beating or it will lose its smoothness.

Bittersweet Chocolate–Mascarpone Pie

This is one of the most decadently creamy pies you'll ever eat. It has a filling of whipped cream–lightened chocolate mascarpone cheese, topped with more whipped cream. This is one to pull out for company or a special occasion.

Makes 8–10 servings

Oreo Crumb Crust (page 85), Shortbread Cookie Crust (page 82), or Graham Cracker Crust (page 82)

FILLING

- **4 ounces bittersweet chocolate, coarsely chopped**
- **2 teaspoons instant espresso or instant coffee granules**
- **1 tablespoon boiling water**
- **12 ounces (about 1½ cups) mascarpone cheese**
- **1 teaspoon vanilla extract**
- **1 cup cold heavy cream**
- **½ cup confectioners' sugar, sifted**

1. Prepare the crust and press it into the bottom and up the sides of a 9- to 9½-inch standard pie pan. Refrigerate, prebake, and cool as directed. Refrigerate the shell until needed. At the same time, chill a medium bowl and a set of mixer beaters.

2. Melt the chocolate in the top insert of a double boiler set over, not in, barely simmering water. (Alternatively, use a heatproof bowl, suspended by the sides of a saucepan, over barely simmering water.) Remove the insert and set the chocolate aside, whisking to smooth.

3. Put the coffee in a small bowl and pour the boiling water over it. Stir to dissolve; let stand for 5 minutes.

4. Stir the mascarpone cheese briefly in a medium bowl, to smooth. Add the chocolate, dissolved coffee, and vanilla, stirring gently until evenly blended. Do not overstir or the filling may become grainy. Let stand at room temperature.

5. Using the chilled medium bowl and beaters, beat the cream with an electric mixer (handheld is fine) until it holds soft peaks. Add the sugar and continue to beat until stiff but not grainy. Add about one-third of the whipped cream to the chocolate mixture and fold it in gently, until evenly combined. Spoon the filling into the pie shell, smoothing the top with a spoon. Smooth the remaining whipped cream over the filling. Cover with loosely tented aluminum foil and refrigerate for at least 2 hours before serving.

Bittersweet Chocolate Turtle Pie

This icebox pie, inspired by a favorite recipe from an old Betty Crocker cookbook, is as delicious as it is attractive. There's a graham cracker crust, a layer of melted caramels and pecans — the turtle part — another of sweetened cream cheese and, to top it off, chocolate whipped cream. Sounds involved, but the hardest part is washing a few bowls when you're done.

Makes 8–10 servings

Graham Cracker Crust (page 82)

FILLING

- 1 cup pecan halves, toasted (page 453) and coarsely chopped
- 30 caramels
- 2 tablespoons unsalted butter
- 2 tablespoons water
- 6 ounces cream cheese, softened
- ⅓ cup confectioners' sugar
- ½ teaspoon vanilla extract

TOPPING

- 3 tablespoons water
- 4 ounces bittersweet chocolate, coarsely chopped
- 2 cups cold heavy cream
- ¼ cup confectioners' sugar
- 1 teaspoon vanilla extract

1. Prepare the crust and press it into the bottom and up the sides of a 9- to 9½-inch standard pie pan. Refrigerate, prebake, and cool as directed. Scatter the chopped pecans in the crust. Set aside.

2. To make the filling, combine the caramels, butter, and water in a medium heavy saucepan over low heat. Heat, stirring occasionally, until the caramels have melted. Whisk to smooth, then slowly pour over the nuts, covering the pie shell evenly. Refrigerate.

3. Using an electric mixer (handheld is fine), beat the cream cheese in a medium bowl until smooth and creamy. Add the sugar and vanilla, and beat until smooth. Scrape the mixture over the chilled caramel, smoothing it with a spoon. Refrigerate for at least 30 minutes. At the same time, wash and dry the beaters and chill along with a medium bowl.

4. To make the topping, combine the water and chocolate in a small heavy saucepan over very low heat, stirring frequently until the chocolate is smooth and melted. Remove from the heat and cool to room temperature.

5. Using the chilled medium bowl and beaters, beat the cream until it holds soft peaks. Add the sugar and vanilla and continue to beat until stiff but not grainy. Transfer about one-third of the whipped cream to a small bowl. Cover and refrigerate.

6. Add the cooled chocolate to the larger portion of whipped cream and fold it in until evenly blended. Spread over the filling. Cover with loosely tented aluminum foil and refrigerate for at least 3 or 4 hours, or overnight. Shortly before serving, pipe the remaining whipped cream decoratively over the pie or dollop it over individual slices.

Recipe for Success

To make an even thicker layer of caramel, use up to 40 caramels instead of 30.

If you have extra bittersweet or semisweet chocolate on hand, you can add a simple garnish by grating some chocolate over the top of the pie. Use the small holes of a box grater.

Chocolate Peanut Butter Pie

If you like peanut butter and chocolate in the same bite — who doesn't? — this is your pie. My wife, Bev, calls it dangerously good.

Makes 10 servings

Oreo Crumb Crust (page 85)

FILLING

1¼ cups smooth peanut butter

8 ounces full-fat or reduced-fat cream cheese, softened

1 cup confectioners' sugar

1 tablespoon vanilla extract

1¼ cups cold heavy cream

Chocolate Ganache (page 445)

1. Prepare the crust and press it into the bottom and up the sides of a 9½-inch deep-dish pie pan. Refrigerate, prebake, and cool as directed. Refrigerate the shell until needed.

2. Using an electric mixer (handheld is fine), cream the peanut butter, cream cheese, and ½ cup of the sugar together in a large bowl. Blend in the vanilla. Wash and dry the beaters. Chill them, along with a medium bowl, for 5 to 10 minutes.

3. Using the chilled bowl and beaters, beat the cream with the mixer until it holds soft peaks. Add the remaining ½ cup sugar and continue to beat until stiff but not grainy. Add about one-third of the whipped cream to the peanut butter mixture. Blend with the mixer until smooth and creamy.

Fold in the remaining whipped cream until the filling is smooth and evenly mixed. Spoon the filling into the pie shell and smooth the top with a spoon. Cover with loosely tented aluminum foil and refrigerate for at least 3 hours or overnight.

4. When the filling is good and firm, prepare the chocolate ganache; you'll need to rewarm it if you've made it ahead. When the ganache has cooled somewhat but is still pourable, pour a generous helping of it over the pie, tilting the pie to spread the sauce up to the edge. Set aside to cool. Re-cover with loosely tented aluminum foil and refrigerate until ready to serve, at least 30 minutes.

Recipe for Success

When you cream the cream cheese and peanut butter, the mixture will remain somewhat grainy. Don't be concerned. It will become smooth when the whipped cream is added.

Be sure the ganache isn't too warm when you pour it on the pie, or the top of the filling will melt and cause uneven coverage.

Andrea's Maple-Pecan Chiffon Pie

Andrea is Andrea Chesman, a prolific food writer and editor with whom I had the pleasure of working early in my career. I adapted this recipe from her book *Mom's Best Desserts*, a wonderful collection of recipes. I've tweaked it a little here and there, like using a graham cracker crust instead of a pastry and substituting pecans for walnuts. But the credit for this featherlight chiffon pie, long a favorite of mine, belongs to Andrea.

Makes 8–10 servings

Graham Cracker Crust (page 85)

FILLING

¼ cup cold water

1 envelope unflavored gelatin

3 large eggs, separated, whites at room temperature

¾ cup lukewarm maple syrup

¼ cup whole milk or half-and-half, heated

1 teaspoon vanilla extract

⅛ teaspoon cream of tartar

⅛ teaspoon salt

¾ cup cold heavy cream

½ cup chopped pecans

WARNING: *Consuming raw eggs may increase your risk of foodborne illness, especially if you have a medical condition.*

1. Prepare the crust and press it into the bottom and up the sides of a 9- to 9½-inch standard pie pan. Refrigerate, prebake, and cool as directed. Refrigerate the shell until needed.

2. Pour the water into a small bowl and sprinkle the gelatin over it. Let stand for 4 to 5 minutes to soften. In the top insert of a double boiler (or a heatproof bowl suspended by the sides of a saucepan), beat the egg yolks with a wire whisk until thick and lemon-colored. Gradually stir in the maple syrup, then the hot milk. Begin to heat water in the bottom of the double boiler (or saucepan), gradually bringing it to a simmer. Stir the mixture virtually nonstop, until it thickens enough to coat the back of a spoon, 10 to 12 minutes. Add the softened gelatin and stir until it has dissolved. Stir in the vanilla.

3. Fill a shallow casserole dish no more than halfway with ice and cold water. Pour the mixture into a heatproof bowl, then set the bowl in the casserole dish. Cool the mixture, whisking often, until it barely begins to firm up. Don't leave it in the cold water until it gets too firm, or it won't combine smoothly with the egg whites.

4. Beat the egg whites in a medium bowl with an electric mixer (handheld is fine) until foamy. Add the cream of tartar and salt, and beat until stiff but not dry. They should hold their shape and look moist. Using a rubber spatula, gently fold the egg whites into the cooled maple mixture.

5. Wash and dry the beaters. Chill them, along with a medium bowl, for 5 to 10 minutes. Using the chilled bowl and beaters, beat the cream with the mixer until firm but not grainy. Fold it into the filling until evenly combined, then fold in half of the pecans. Turn the filling into the pie shell and smooth the top with a spoon. Cover with loosely tented aluminum foil and refrigerate for at least 4 hours or overnight. Serve garnished with the remaining pecans.

Recipe for Success

Just a quick reminder that eggs should be separated cold, but the whites should be beaten at room temperature for the best results.

Banoffee–Peanut Butter Pie

Banoffee pie — layers of sliced banana and caramel or toffee in a crust — has become quite a thing in the last few years. It's pretty simple to put together, especially when the pie is made with a crumb crust. The piece I've always missed in banoffee pie, however, the piece I can hear the bananas practically begging for, is peanut butter. (I'll admit that I believe there are few things that can't be improved with peanut butter.) So I decided to add some. If you're a kindred peanut butter spirit, I know you'll love this.

Makes 8–10 servings

Shortbread Cookie Crust or Graham Cracker Crust (page 82)

FILLING

1   (13-ounce) can dulce de leche

¾   cup sweetened or unsweetened smooth peanut butter

¼   cup hot water

3 or 4   medium-size ripe bananas

Stabilized Whipped Cream (page 446)

Store-bought butterscotch or caramel sauce or Caramel Sauce (page 444)

1. Prepare the crust and press it into the bottom and up the sides of a 9½-inch deep-dish pie pan. Refrigerate, prebake, and cool as directed. Refrigerate the shell until needed.

2. Put the dulce de leche and peanut butter in a medium bowl. Add about half of the hot water. Using a handheld electric mixer, beat the mixture on low speed until the water is incorporated, 45 to 60 seconds. Add the remaining water and continue to beat on low to medium-low speed just until the mixture is smooth and creamy, but no longer.

3. Assemble the pie within a hour or two of serving it, if possible. Spread the dulce de leche mixture evenly over bottom of the pie shell. Slice the bananas crosswise, then layer and stack them over the dulce de leche. Push the first layer of bananas down into the bottom layer slightly. Don't worry if the slices are a bit random; the whipped cream is going to cover up the construction.

4. Pile the whipped cream high over the bananas, mounding it slightly toward the center. You may not need all of the cream, so just use as much as you like. Refrigerate the pie if you're not serving the pie right away. Garnish slices with a little caramel sauce, if desired.

Recipe for Success

The reason to assemble this pie as close to serving time as possible is because bananas start to weep after you cut them. The longer they sit, the weepier they get. You just don't want things to get out of hand.

Eggnog Chiffon Pie

If you're looking for something unique and festive to serve at your next holiday party, here it is. Creamy, rich in egg yolks, and dusted with nutmeg, this pie tastes like the real deal for eggnog lovers. Instead of serving the whipped cream garnish separately, you can spread it over the top of the pie.

1. Prepare the crust and press it into the bottom and up the sides of a 9- to 9½-inch deep-dish pie pan. Refrigerate, prebake, and cool as directed. Refrigerate the shell until needed. At the same time, chill a medium bowl and a set of mixer beaters.

2. Pour the rum and water into a small bowl. Sprinkle the gelatin over the liquid and let stand for 4 to 5 minutes to soften.

3. Prepare the vanilla custard sauce. As soon as you remove it from the heat in step 3, add the soft-ened gelatin, whisking to smooth. Transfer the mixture to a large bowl and let cool, whisking occa-sionally. When it reaches room temperature, refrigerate.

4. Meanwhile, using the chilled medium bowl and beaters, beat the cream with an electric mixer (handheld is fine) until it holds soft peaks. Add the sugar and continue to beat until the mixture is firm but not grainy; refrigerate. Wash and dry the beaters.

5. When the custard sauce mix-ture is just starting to gel — not too long, likely, after it has been refrigerated — fold about half of the whipped cream into it. Add the remaining whipped cream and continue to fold until evenly combined.

6. Beat the egg whites in a medium bowl with the mixer on medium-high speed until they hold firm peaks. Add about ½ cup of the cream-custard mixture and blend on low speed. Add the egg white mixture back to the cream-custard mixture and fold everything together until evenly combined. Scrape the filling into the pie shell, smoothing the top with a spoon. Cover with loosely tented aluminum foil and refrig-erate for at least 4 hours or over-night. Just before serving, dust the top of the pie with nutmeg. Slice and serve, with additional whipped cream on the side, if desired.

Recipe for Success
One of the tricks to making this and other chiffon pies is to catch the gelatinized mixture just as it is starting to firm up, with a consistency similar to raw egg whites. That's when it's easiest to fold the mixture with the other ingredients. If it gets too firm, the filling will be a little lumpy. You can sometimes rescue an overly firm mixture by whisking vigorously to smooth.

Mocha Ricotta Mousse Pie

This is one of my favorite refrigerator pies — a chocolate-coffee ricotta cream lightened with whipped cream and flavored with vanilla and almond extracts. Not only is it simple to prepare, but even with the graham cracker crust it's sophisticated enough to serve at a dinner party.

Makes 8–10 servings

Graham Cracker Crust or Shortbread Cookie Crust (page 82)

FILLING

- ½ cup sugar
- 1 tablespoon instant espresso or coffee granules
- 2 ounces bittersweet or semisweet chocolate
- 1 (15- to 16-ounce) container ricotta cheese
- 2 tablespoons milk
- 1 envelope unflavored gelatin
- 3 tablespoons cold water
- ¾ cup cold heavy cream
- ½ teaspoon vanilla extract
- ¼ teaspoon almond extract

  Chocolate Ganache (page 445), warmed, for garnish

1. Prepare the crust and press it into the bottom and up the sides of a 9- to 9½-inch standard pie pan. Refrigerate, prebake, and cool as directed. Refrigerate the shell until needed. At the same time, chill a medium bowl and a set of mixer beaters.

2. Put the sugar, coffee, and chocolate in a food processor. Pulse repeatedly to chop the chocolate, then let the machine run continuously until the mixture is very finely ground, 30 to 45 seconds. Expect to see tiny flecks of chocolate throughout. Add the ricotta and milk. Process again, nonstop, until the mixture is very smooth, 30 to 45 seconds. Leave the mixture in the machine.

3. Put the gelatin in a small bowl and pour the water over it. Let stand for 5 minutes to soften, then either heat the gelatin in the microwave for 10 to 15 seconds or transfer it to a small saucepan and warm over low heat, stirring. In either case, it should be liquefied. Cool for 2 to 3 minutes, then add to the ricotta mixture. Process for several seconds to combine.

4. Using the chilled bowl and beaters, beat the cream with an electric mixer (handheld is fine) until it is firm but not grainy. Beat in the vanilla and almond extract. Add the ricotta mixture and beat on low speed, scraping down the bowl, until uniformly mixed. Spoon the filling into the pie shell and smooth the top with a spoon. Cover with loosely tented aluminum foil and refrigerate for at least 4 hours or overnight. Serve slices garnished with chocolate ganache.

Lemon Meringue Pie

I get lots of emails from Pie Academy members who want to know my secret for making a winning lemon meringue pie. My answer is always the same: don't complicate it or try to fancy it up. Stick with the basics as outlined here and the accolades will flow. I'm partial to a graham cracker crust, but I realize that a pastry crust is probably the more traditional choice.

Makes 8-10 servings

Graham Cracker Crust (page 82) or Old-Fashioned Shortening Pie Dough (page 62)

FILLING

1⅓	**cups sugar**
¼	**cup plus 2 tablespoons cornstarch**
⅛	**teaspoon salt**
2	**cups water**
½	**cup lemon juice, preferably fresh**
1	**tablespoon lemon zest**
4	**large egg yolks**
2	**tablespoons unsalted butter, cut into several small pieces**
	Swiss Meringue (page 448)

1. If you're using the Graham Cracker Crust, prepare the crust in a 9- to 9½-inch deep-dish pie pan and refrigerate until needed. If using the pastry crust, prepare in a 9- to 9½-inch deep-dish pie pan, making a fluted or crimped edge. Refrigerate, fully prebake, and cool as directed. Refrigerate until needed.

2. Whisk the sugar, cornstarch, and salt in a medium saucepan to combine. Add the water, lemon juice, lemon zest, and egg yolks, and whisk again.

3. Place the pan over medium heat and cook, whisking continuously, until the mixture comes to a boil, 5 to 7 minutes. Reduce the heat slightly and continue to cook, whisking continuously, for 1½ minutes. Remove from the heat and whisk in the butter one piece at a time. Immediately pour the filling into the pie shell, jiggling the pie pan slightly to settle the filling. Gently press a piece of plastic wrap directly over the filling to prevent a skin from forming. Cool to room temperature, then refrigerate the pie for at least 2 to 3 hours.

4. Shortly before serving the pie, prepare the meringue. Smooth and mound the meringue over the filling. Light a kitchen torch or shop torch and wave the flame over the meringue to brown it evenly. Keep the torch moving so you don't scorch the meringue. (See Torch Tips, page 384.) Slice and serve the pie right away, or refrigerate until serving.

Lemon Curd Meringue Pie

This is one of the most delicious desserts you'll ever make with lemon curd. I recommend making your own curd from scratch, of course, but if you must, go right ahead and pick up a jar or two at the market. (You'll need about 20 ounces.) The curd is covered with Swiss meringue and then browned before serving. Browning the meringue in front of onlookers makes for great theater, so bring your pie and torch right to the table.

Makes 8 servings

Shortbread Cookie Crust (page 82)

FILLING

Lemon Curd (page 450), cold

Swiss Meringue (page 448)

1. Prepare the crust and press it into the bottom and up the sides of a 9- to 9½-inch standard pie pan. Refrigerate, prebake, and cool as directed. Refrigerate the shell until needed.

2. Spread the lemon curd evenly in the pie shell. Refrigerate until you're ready to top with the meringue. The curd should be cold and firm when you serve this pie.

3. Smooth and mound the meringue over the curd. Light a kitchen torch or shop torch and wave the flame over the meringue to brown it evenly. Keep the torch moving so you don't scorch the meringue. (See Torch Tips, page 384.) Slice and serve the pie right away, or refrigerate until serving.

13

Cream Pies:
THE DINER CLASSICS COME HOME

Walk into any great diner and the short trip to your booth will very likely take you past a refrigerated display of sweets clamoring for your attention. If you're lucky, front and center will be an irresistible selection of great American cream pies — vanilla, chocolate, lemon, and some specialty house flavors — all topped with a mountain of whipped cream or meringue.

Chances are, you'll have a piece for dessert because, let's face it, these fancy pies are the province of professional cooks, not something an ordinary cook can tackle at home.

Well . . . not so fast! It may be true that folks associate these scrumptious home pies with the best diners and American eateries, but the fact is cream pies are not difficult to make, and they deserve a second look by any home cook who ever thought them too complicated or unattainable by mere mortals.

Indeed, if you can hold a whisk and operate an electric mixer, you can make the two foundational elements of a cream pie — pastry cream and whipped cream — without breaking a sweat.

If you're new to cream pies, start with the basic Vanilla Cream Pie (page 380). You'll learn the tricks for making vanilla pastry cream, variations of which you use for the other recipes in this section. You'll flavor it with chocolate in some recipes, peanut butter in others, or lemon, maple syrup, even chai tea. Each of these pies is a unique flavor experience you'll want to try and share with your circle of friends and family.

So grab your whisk and let's get going.

✌

Tips for Making Memorable Cream Pies

- Be sure to use the recommended saucepan for making pastry cream — a 3- to 3½-quart stainless steel pan, preferably one with a heavy bottom to spread the heat around evenly.

- Don't walk away from the pastry cream while it's cooking. Keep stirring or whisking, as instructed. This keeps the pastry cream smooth and prevents it from forming lumps.

- Immediately cover the pastry cream with plastic wrap, pressing it right against the cream's surface. This will prevent a skin from forming so the pastry cream stays creamy. Give it ample time to chill before you assemble the pie, at least 3 to 4 hours.

- It's not necessary to use stabilized whipped cream (page 446), but it will hold its shape better than unstabilized cream, without weeping. If you want a topping that's even more stable and will hold its shape nicely when you pipe it, use Mascarpone Whipped Cream (page 448).

- Cream pies are best served within 24 hours — the sooner after they're made, the better.

Vanilla Pastry Cream

Even if you don't know it by name, pastry cream — or vanilla pastry cream — is the velvety, puddinglike stuff that goes into some of our favorite filled doughnuts and éclairs and in Boston cream pie (which is actually a cake; go figure). It's also the creamy filling in cream pies. Here is the basic version, which you flavor and enhance a little differently for each of the scrumptious variations that follow on pages 378 and 379. It's not difficult to make, but it does need your undivided stovetop attention during the short time you're preparing it — no running off to take a nap or hang out on social media.

Makes enough for one 9½-inch deep-dish pie

- **1 cup milk**
- **1½ cups half-and-half**
- **½ cup sugar**
- **¼ cup cornstarch**
- **5 large egg yolks**
- **¼ teaspoon salt**
- **2 teaspoons vanilla extract**
- **2 tablespoons unsalted butter, cut into in several pieces**

1. Combine the milk, half-and-half, and ¼ cup of the sugar in a 3- to 3½-quart stainless steel saucepan. Gradually bring to a simmer, stirring often to facilitate the melting of the sugar. Remove from the heat.

2. Rapidly whisk the cornstarch, egg yolks, and the remaining ¼ cup sugar in a large bowl until it turns a shade or two paler, about 2 minutes. Gradually add the half-and-half mixture to the egg yolk mixture, whisking as you pour. Whisk in the salt.

3. Pour the mixture back into the saucepan and gradually bring to a boil over medium heat, whisking virtually nonstop. This should take 5 to 7 minutes. The first sign of thickening you'll notice is the whisk beginning to drag through the cream, meeting with light resistance.

4. When the pastry cream starts to boil, lower the heat slightly and whisk steadily for 1½ minutes, nonstop, scraping the sides, corners, and bottom of the pan with the whisk. Briefly switch to a heatproof spatula to scrape the pan's surfaces, then switch back to the whisk.

5. After 1½ minutes, immediately remove the pan from the heat and scrape the pastry cream into a large bowl. Add the vanilla and butter, and whisk until the mixture is smooth and the butter has melted. Press a piece of plastic wrap directly over the pastry cream to prevent it from forming a skin. Cool the pastry cream in the bowl for about 1 hour, then refrigerate for at least 3 to 4 hours before assembling the pie.

Recipe for Success

It's important to use a stainless steel saucepan to make pastry cream. An uncoated aluminum pan can taint the color of the pastry cream an unappetizing shade of pale green, and the coating on a good nonstick pan will take a beating from all the action with the whisk. The ideal pan size is 3 to 3½ quarts.

It helps to think of cooking pastry cream in three distinct stages. In the first stage, it is pure liquid and milky. In stage two, the liquid develops some body; the whisk feels the slightest bit of resistance. In the final stage, the pastry cream thickens quickly and takes on the texture of yogurt. See if you notice when you make this.

Pastry Cream Variations

VANILLA BEAN PASTRY CREAM

Pastry cream made with a real vanilla bean will have authentic look and flavor and add a gourmet touch to cream pies. I don't make this often because vanilla beans are so expensive, but it's good to know how if you're ever inclined.

1. Cut a vanilla bean in half crosswise, then slice the halves lengthwise. Put the halves on a cutting board and spread them open as best you can. Pressing down firmly with a paring knife, scrape out the seeds.

2. Put both the seeds and the pod pieces in the saucepan with the milk, half-and-half, and sugar before you heat it. When the milk has heated, remove the pan from the stovetop and use a slotted spoon to retrieve the pod pieces.

3. Proceed as usual with the recipe. (Dry off the vanilla bean with paper towels, place it in a plastic bag, and refrigerate. Use it sometime soon to flavor coffee drinks, custard, even hot cereal, always removing it before serving. You can also bury it in your sugar bowl to infuse everyday sugaring needs.)

LEMON PASTRY CREAM

Proceed as for Vanilla Pastry Cream, but in addition to the vanilla extract, add ½ to ¾ teaspoon pure lemon extract, plus 2 teaspoons finely grated lemon zest.

BANANA PASTRY CREAM

Prepare the Vanilla Pastry Cream, reducing the vanilla extract to 1½ teaspoons. Whisk in 1 teaspoon banana extract when you add the vanilla.

CHOCOLATE PASTRY CREAM

Prepare the Vanilla Pastry Cream with the following changes. Whisk 1½ tablespoons unsweetened cocoa powder with the egg yolk mixture until smooth. After you transfer the cooked pastry cream to a bowl, add 4 ounces coarsely chopped bittersweet chocolate to the hot pastry cream with the butter and vanilla. Push the chocolate down into the pastry cream with the whisk and wait a couple of minutes until the chocolate starts to melt. Then whisk until smooth.

PEANUT BUTTER PASTRY CREAM

Prepare the Vanilla Pastry Cream. As soon as you transfer the hot pastry cream to the bowl, stir ¾ cup peanut butter chips (morsels) into the pastry cream along with the vanilla extract and butter. Whisk until the pastry cream is evenly blended and the chips have melted completely.

MAPLE PASTRY CREAM

Prepare the Vanilla Pastry Cream with the following changes. Use 1 cup heavy cream plus 1½ cups whole milk instead of the half-and-half/milk combination. Add ⅓ cup pure maple syrup to the milk mixture instead of the ¼ cup sugar. (Whisk the other ¼ cup sugar with the egg yolks and cornstarch, as usual.) Proceed as usual, adding the butter and vanilla when instructed.

COCONUT PASTRY CREAM

Prepare the Vanilla Pastry Cream with the following changes. Reduce the vanilla extract to 1½ teaspoons and add 1 teaspoon coconut extract. Stir 1 cup sweetened flaked coconut into the filling after you add the extracts.

BUTTERSCOTCH PASTRY CREAM

Prepare the Vanilla Pastry Cream with the following changes.

1. Use 1 cup heavy cream plus 1½ cups whole milk instead of the half-and-half/milk combination.

2. Instead of the granulated sugar, use ½ cup packed dark brown sugar, adding half — as with our main recipe — to the milk mixture and whisking the other half with the egg yolks and cornstarch.

3. Add 1 tablespoon molasses to the milk mixture when you heat it.

4. Use 3 tablespoons butter instead of 2 when you whisk in the vanilla.

CHAI LATTE PASTRY CREAM

Prepare the Vanilla Pastry Cream with the following changes. In a small saucepan or in the microwave, heat the 1 cup milk to a simmer. Add 3 black chai teabags. Let steep for 10 minutes, then remove the teabags. Reheat the chai milk with the half-and-half and proceed as usual.

Vanilla Cream Pie

When someone says "cream pie," this is the one most of us think of. I hesitate to call it "plain" vanilla cream pie because, done well, there's nothing plain about it. It's sheer perfection, and you would be forgiven if your cream pie aspirations never went beyond this one recipe. (Just to be clear, I'm not recommending that.) You also have the option of making this with Vanilla Bean Pastry Cream (page 378) if you want to add a special touch. If you prefer a pastry crust to a crumb crust, remember that it must be fully prebaked. Any of the single-crust pie dough recipes would work.

Makes 8–10 servings

Shortbread Cookie Crust (page 82) or another crumb crust

FILLING

Vanilla Pastry Cream (page 372)

Whipped Cream or Stabilized Whipped Cream (page 446)

Ground nutmeg, for garnish

Variation

If you prefer, you don't have to add any pastry cream to the whipped cream. You can simply fill the shell with all of the pastry cream and top with the whipped cream. Both options are fine.

1. Prepare the crust and press it into the bottom and up the sides of a 9- to 9½-inch deep-dish pie pan. Refrigerate, prebake, and cool as directed. Refrigerate the shell until needed.

2. Prepare the pastry cream at least 3 to 4 hours ahead of assembly. Prepare the whipped cream or stabilized whipped cream, preferably within an hour or so of serving the pie.

3. Spread about three-quarters of the pastry cream in the pie shell, smoothing it evenly right up to the sides of the shell.

4. Add about one-third of the whipped cream to the remaining pastry cream and fold it in with a rubber spatula. Add another third and continue to fold gently until the topping is evenly combined. If you think you'll need more topping than that, fold in more whipped cream. Mound or pipe topping over the pie. Refrigerate the pie until serving, dusting the top of the pie with nutmeg right before serving.

Toasted Coconut Cream Pie

If coconut is your thing, this pie is going to be your thing of things. The tropical vibe makes it the right dessert for summer seafood feasts like fish tacos, peel-and-eat shrimp, or grilled tuna. Don't skip the toasted coconut garnish: it adds a nice contrast to the billowy white whipped cream topping.

Makes 8–10 servings

Shortbread Cookie Crumb Crust (page 82) or another crumb crust

FILLING

Coconut Pastry Cream (page 378)

Whipped Cream or Stabilized Whipped Cream (page 446)

½–⅔ **cup sweetened flaked coconut, toasted and cooled**

Recipe for Success

I like to toast up extra coconut while I'm at it. I store the cooled coconut in a sealed jar and use it on yogurt, in granola, and sprinkled on top of banana bread and muffins before baking them.

1. Prepare the crust and press it into the bottom and up the sides of a 9- to 9½-inch deep-dish pie pan. Refrigerate, prebake, and cool as directed. Refrigerate the shell until needed.

2. Prepare the pastry cream at least 3 to 4 hours before assembling the pie. Prepare the whipped cream or stabilized whipped cream, preferably within an hour or so of serving the pie.

3. When you're ready to assemble the pie, spread all of the coconut pastry cream in the pie shell. Make it nice and even, and smooth it right up to the sides of the crust. Mound or pipe the whipped cream over the filling, then sprinkle on the toasted coconut. Refrigerate until serving.

National Pie Day

You knew there had to be one, right? So mark your calendar: it's January 23. Created by the American Pie Council, National Pie Day is dedicated to the celebration of pie, plain and simple. The council says it's the perfect opportunity to pass on the love and enjoyment of pie eating and making to future generations. How? Here are a few of the council's suggestions.

- Bake your favorite pie and share it with a friend.

- Teach pie making. Go to a local school, senior center, or civic club and show the people there how it's done.

- Hold a pie potluck. Invite friends to bring their favorite pies for an irresistible buffet.

- Hold a pie auction. Donate the proceeds to a worthy cause.

- Throw a pie-making contest. Invite everyone in your community to participate. Ask local chefs and cooking teachers to be judges and award fanciful prizes.

National Pie Day is not be confused with Pi Day, March 14 (3/14 — get it?) when math lovers around the world celebrate the mathematical constant π. But why not celebrate both with everyone's favorite dessert?

Caramel Banana Cream Pie

It's pretty hard to top banana cream pie, but if you're going to try, then reach for the caramel. In this favorite, you cover the pie shell with caramel, then drizzle more over the pie itself. Once you try it, you'll think banana cream pie tastes sad without it. If you're not up to preparing your own caramel sauce, you'll find good bottled ones in your supermarket.

Makes 8–10 servings

Vanilla Wafer Crust (page 82) or another crumb crust

FILLING

Caramel Sauce (page 444)

Banana Pastry Cream (page 378)

3 or 4 medium-size, just-ripe bananas

Whipped Cream or Stabilized Whipped Cream (page 446)

1. Prepare the crust and press it into the bottom and up the sides of a 9- to 9½-inch deep-dish pie pan. Refrigerate, prebake, and cool as directed. Refrigerate the shell until needed.

2. Prepare the caramel sauce and banana pastry cream at least 3 to 4 hours before assembling the pie. Don't slice the bananas until you're ready to assemble the pie. Prepare the whipped cream or stabilized whipped cream, if possible, within an hour or so of assembling the pie.

3. When you're ready to assemble the pie, pour a generous layer of caramel sauce — about ½ to ⅔ cup — over the pie shell, tilting the pan and using a spoon to spread it around. If you've made the sauce ahead and refrigerated it, you may have to warm it to make it pourable. Refrigerate the pie shell for 30 minutes so the sauce firms up slightly.

4. Spread half of the pastry cream evenly over the caramel, smoothing it right up to the edge of the crust. Halve the bananas crosswise, then cut each half lengthwise. Arrange the halves, cut side down, in a single tight layer on top of the pastry cream. Fill in any gaps with diced banana.

5. Spread the remaining pastry cream over the bananas, pressing it between them like grout on tile. Mound or pipe the whipped cream over the top. Refrigerate the pie, uncovered, until serving.

6. Just before serving, drizzle on a little more caramel or drizzle it over each individual slice.

Recipe for Success

Because the caramel will begin to saturate the crumb crust within a few hours, it's best to assemble this pie no more than a couple of hours before you plan to serve it.

Butterscotch Banana Cream Pie

Banana cream pie never had it so good. You may never eat another version once you've tried this one.

Makes 8–10 servings

Graham Cracker Crust (page 82) or another crumb crust

FILLING

Butterscotch Pastry Cream (page 379)

3 or 4 **medium-size, just-ripe bananas**

Swiss Meringue (page 448)

Caramel Sauce (page 444) (optional)

1. Prepare the crust and press it into the bottom and up the sides of a 9- to 9½-inch deep-dish pie pan. Refrigerate, prebake, and cool as directed. Refrigerate the shell until needed.

2. Prepare the pastry cream at least 3 to 4 hours ahead of assembling the pie. Don't slice the bananas until you're ready to make the pie.

3. When you're ready to assemble the pie, spread half of the pastry cream evenly in the pie shell, smoothing it right up to the edge. Halve the bananas crosswise, then cut each one in half lengthwise. Arrange the halves in concentric circles, cut side down, in a single tight layer, pressing them gently into the pastry cream. Fill in any gaps with diced banana.

4. Spread the remaining pastry cream over the bananas, pressing it between them like grout on tile. Place a piece of plastic wrap on top, smoothing it right over the filling. Refrigerate.

5. Prepare the meringue just before serving the pie, if possible, or as close to serving time as you can. Mound the meringue over the filling, then refrigerate. Just before serving the pie, brown the meringue. (See Torch Tips, below.)

Torch Tips

When it comes to browning a meringue topping, your best bet is a handheld torch, either a small butane kitchen torch or a propane shop torch. Both will do the job nicely.

The trick is to wave the flame back and forth over the meringue and keep it moving. Stay in one spot too long, and you'll leave scorch marks. Keep the flame away from the sides of the pan, too; if you're using glass or ceramic, the flame might crack it.

You can also use the traditional run-it-under-the-broiler approach. I don't like this technique as much, because you don't have nearly as much control. Put the pie on a baking sheet so it's easier to move the pie around and make adjustments as it broils. Position the pie at least 8 inches from the broiler unit. Watch it like a hawk: the meringue can go from golden to ghastly in the blink of an eye.

Maple Cream Pie

I've been a pure maple syrup fan all of my adult life, so much so that I wrote an entire book about cooking with it: *Maple Syrup Cookbook*. The flavor of real maple is so much more nuanced than imitation "pancake syrup," and you'll taste the difference in this classic New England cream pie. For a real treat, top off the pie with chopped candied pecans.

Makes 8–10 servings

Nut Crumb Crust (page 82) made with pecans, or another crust

FILLING

Maple Pastry Cream (page 378)

Whipped Cream or Stabilized Whipped Cream (page 446)

1 **cup pecan halves, toasted (page 453) and chopped**

Maple syrup, for drizzling

1. Prepare the crust and press it into the bottom and up the sides of a 9- to 9½-inch deep-dish pie pan. Refrigerate, prebake, and cool as directed. Refrigerate the shell until needed.

2. Prepare the pastry cream at least 3 to 4 hours before assembling the pie. Prepare the whipped cream within an hour or so, if possible, of assembly.

3. When you are ready to assemble the pie, spoon all of the pastry cream into the crust. Smooth it evenly, right up against the sides of the pie shell.

4. Mound or pipe the whipped cream over the filling, then scatter the chopped pecans over the whipped cream. Refrigerate the pie until ready to serve. Drizzle a spoonful of maple syrup over each slice as you serve the pie.

Maple Syrup by the Numbers

Maple syrup is 100 percent boiled sap. It's made by evaporating the sap (or sometimes from a solution of maple sugar) and contains not more than 33 to 35 percent water. It takes up to 40 gallons of pure maple sap to make 1 gallon of syrup.

Imitation maple syrup or pancake syrup contains about 2 to 3 percent of the real thing; it contains mostly corn syrup. Read the labels carefully to know what you are getting.

Nutella Cream Pie
with Hazelnut Crumb Crust

Nutella, the beloved chocolate-hazelnut spread with a texture like creamy peanut butter, is popping up in recipes everywhere, including here. It's addictive — if socially frowned upon — eaten right from the container, and equally so in this luscious cream pie.

Makes 8–10 servings

Nut Crumb Crust (page 82) made with hazelnuts, or another crumb crust

FILLING

¾ **cup Nutella**

Vanilla Pastry Cream (page 377), flavored

1½–2 **tablespoons hazelnut liqueur (optional, but highly recommended)**

Whipped Cream or Stabilized Whipped Cream (page 446)

1 **cup hazelnuts, toasted (page 453) and well chopped by hand**

1. Prepare the crust and press it into the bottom and up the sides of a 9- to 9½-inch deep-dish pie pan. Refrigerate, prebake, and cool as directed. Refrigerate the shell until needed.

2. Before you begin preparing the pastry cream, put the Nutella in a medium bowl and set it aside. Have another bowl standing by. Prepare the pastry cream as instructed. Right after you whisk in the butter and vanilla, transfer slightly less than half of it to the Nutella bowl and the other half to the empty bowl. Whisk the Nutella pastry cream just until it is evenly blended. Using a clean whisk, whisk the liqueur (if using) into the other portion of pastry cream.

3. Transfer the Nutella pastry cream to the pie shell and spread it evenly with the back of a spoon. Press a long piece of plastic wrap directly over the filling. Put the pie in the freezer for 15 minutes to help stabilize this first layer. While this chills, press a piece of plastic wrap directly over the remaining portion of pastry cream. Leave it at room temperature.

4. Remove the pie from the freezer and gently spoon the remaining pastry cream over the first layer, spreading it evenly with a spoon. Press a fresh piece of plastic wrap over the pie and refrigerate for at least 4 hours or overnight.

5. Shortly before serving, spread as much of the whipped cream over the pie as you like. Sprinkle the chopped hazelnuts over the entire surface, or just make a little path of them all around the perimeter. You can't go wrong either way. Refrigerate until serving.

Peanut Butter Cup Cream Pie

For sheer fun, it's hard to top this cream pie. Use a pretzel crust, cover it with a thick layer of chocolate ganache, then scatter chopped peanut butter cups on that. Next, smooth on peanut butter pastry cream, and it just keeps getting better from there. Kids of all ages adore this pie.

Makes 8–10 servings

Pretzel Crust (page 83)

FILLING

> **Chocolate Ganache (page 495)**
>
> **Peanut Butter Pastry Cream (page 378)**
>
> **Whipped Cream or Stabilized Whipped Cream (page 446)**

2–3 cups coarsely chopped peanut butter cups

> **Large handful of roasted, salted peanuts**

1. Prepare the crust and press it into the bottom and up the sides of a 9- to 9½-inch deep-dish pie pan. Refrigerate, prebake, and cool as directed. Refrigerate the shell until needed.

2. Prepare the chocolate ganache so it's ready when you need it. Prepare the pastry cream at least 3 to 4 hours ahead of assembly. Make the whipped cream an hour or so before you assemble the pie.

3. When you are ready to assemble the pie, pour a generous ⅛-inch-thick layer of the ganache over the pie shell. If you've made the ganache ahead, warm it in a microwave, in 7-second increments, until it's just loose enough to pour.

4. Scatter a large handful of the chopped peanut butter cups over the chocolate. Refrigerate for 30 minutes so the sauce can firm a bit.

5. Spoon all of the pastry cream into the pie shell. Smooth it evenly, right up to the sides of the crust, but try not to upset the peanut butter cups; you don't want them to end up in one big pile. Pipe or mound the whipped cream over the filling, leaving a little of the pastry cream showing at the edge. Top the whipped cream with the rest of the peanut butter cups and the chopped peanuts. Drizzle more ganache over the pie. Refrigerate the pie until serving.

Chai Latte–Caramel Cream Pie

If you like the spicy, exotic flavor of chai tea, you'll be delighted with this pie. The various flavors here — Oreo crust, chai latte filling, and caramel garnish — harmonize nicely and demonstrate that you can teach even a traditional American classic like cream pie a few new tricks.

Makes 8–10 servings

Oreo Crumb Crust (page 85)

FILLING

Chai Latte Pastry Cream (page 379)

Whipped Cream or Stabilized Whipped Cream (page 446)

Caramel Sauce (page 444)

Ground nutmeg, for garnish

1. Prepare the crust and press it into the bottom and up the sides of a 9- to 9½-inch deep-dish pie pan. Refrigerate, prebake, and cool as directed. Refrigerate the shell until needed.

2. Prepare the pastry cream at least 3 to 4 hours ahead of assembly. Prepare the whipped cream within an hour or so of assembling the pie, if possible. Prepare the caramel sauce ahead of time as well.

3. When you're ready to assemble the pie, spoon all of the pastry cream into the crust. Smooth it right up against the sides and make it nice and even.

4. Mound or pipe the whipped cream over the pie, then refrigerate the pie until serving. When you're ready to serve the pie, soften the caramel by warming it gently in a saucepan or in the microwave, until it flows thickly. Dust the pie with nutmeg, then drizzle the caramel over the entire pie just before serving, or garnish individual slices with it.

The Dean of American Cooking Weighs In on Pies

If winters were cold, pies were made in quantity and put out to freeze. The varieties were limited to the supplies at hand, but dried fruit was always available to the thrifty housekeeper. Sometimes the pies were layered. For instance, fresh or dried and simmered apple slices might be topped with custard or a cottage cheese custard; and mince might be topped with apple, cranberries, pumpkin, or sometimes apple and custard. Such recipes do not appear in cookbooks, but have come down to us in old diaries or literature of the time.

—James Beard, James Beard's American Cookery

Lemon Cream Pie *with* Fresh Fruit

Lemon is the perfect flavoring for a cream pie with fresh fruit, that according to just about everyone who has sampled this pie. Fresh berries work best here, but you could also use fresh peaches or other stone fruit. I think of this as the quintessential summer dessert, light and refreshing.

Makes 8–10 servings

Graham Cracker Crust (page 82) or another crumb crust

FILLING

Lemon Pastry Cream (page 378)

Whipped Cream or Stabilized Whipped Cream (page 446)

1 **cup (or more) fresh blueberries, strawberries, blackberries, or other fruit**

2 **tablespoons red currant jelly or raspberry jelly**

1. Prepare the crust and press it into the bottom and up the sides of a 9- to 9½-inch deep-dish pie pan. Refrigerate, prebake, and cool as directed. Refrigerate the shell until needed.

2. Prepare the pastry cream at least 3 to 4 hours ahead of assembly. Prepare the whipped cream within an hour or so of assembling the pie, if possible.

3. When you're ready to assemble the pie, spoon all of the pastry cream into the crust. Smooth it right up against the sides and make it nice and even.

4. Mound or pipe the whipped cream over the pie, leaving a large circle of uncovered filling in the middle; mound the fruit in this area. To give the fruit a pretty, jewel-like sparkle, put the jelly in a small bowl and heat in the microwave, in 5-second intervals, until it has melted. Brush the jelly over the fruit. Refrigerate the pie until serving.

Recipe for Success

If you're using peaches, peel and dice them. That way, you get a more even distribution of fruit with each slice. Also, don't put them on the pie until you're ready to serve it. They're juicy and will puddle all over the top of the pie.

Another way you might vary this pie is to top it with Swiss Meringue (page 448) instead of whipped cream, and simply use the fruit as a garnish on the plate instead of putting it on the filling.

Chocolate Coffee Cream Pie

Chocolate cream pie is terrific, period, but it's even more terrific when it's topped with coffee-flavored whipped cream. Put all that in an Oreo crust, top it with shaved chocolate or sprinkles, and you've got a comfort dessert par excellence.

Makes 8–10 servings

Oreo Crumb Crust (page 85)

FILLING

Chocolate Pastry Cream (page 378)

Coffee Whipped Cream (page 447), stabilized or not, or plain Whipped Cream (page 447)

Shaved chocolate (see box), chocolate sprinkles, or finely crumbled chocolate wafers or Oreos

Variations

There are plenty of ways to spin a chocolate cream pie and add your personal signature. Add a layer of bananas like you do with the Caramel Banana Cream Pie (page 382). Garnish the pie with a perimeter of fresh (hulled) whole strawberries. Or add a few drops of mint extract or food-grade mint oil to plain whipped cream for a refreshing spark of flavor.

1. Prepare the crust and press it into the bottom and up the sides of a 9- to 9½-inch deep-dish pie pan. Refrigerate, prebake, and cool as directed. Refrigerate the shell until needed.

2. Prepare the pastry cream at least 3 to 4 hours ahead of assembly. Prepare the whipped cream, if possible, within an hour or two of serving the pie.

3. When you're ready to assemble the pie, spoon all of the pastry cream into the pie shell, smoothing it evenly right up against the sides of the shell.

4. Mound or pipe the whipped cream over the filling, then garnish the top with shaved chocolate, chocolate sprinkles, or the chopped cookies. Refrigerate the pie until serving.

Simple Shaved Chocolate

This is much simpler than making real chocolate curls and makes for an easy garnish for the pie. Take a 4-ounce bar of bittersweet chocolate, hold it over the pie, and run a sharp vegetable peeler down a long edge, letting the little chocolate threads fall directly on top of the whipped cream. Move your hands around as you work so the shavings don't all pile up in one spot.

14
From the Freezer:
INVITING ICE CREAM PIES
AND OTHER ICY TREATS

I don't know anyone who doesn't like an ice cream pie. And if assembling one entails few of the traditional skills required for baking a fruit or other "real" pies, the genre's near-universal popularity is more than enough reason to include a short chapter on the subject here — short because these pies are so easy to make that you barely need a recipe. Once you've seen how it's done, you'll quickly be off and running, creating signature ice cream pies for all sorts of occasions.

At its most basic, an ice cream pie is little more than a crust — typically graham cracker or another crumb crust — with softened ice cream smoothed in the shell. The pie is put back in the freezer to allow the ice cream to harden, then served.

In this chapter, you'll find only ice cream pies with a little something extra, such as an Oreo crust. The Oreo is one of America's favorite cookies, and one of my favorite ways to use it is in a supporting role for a luscious coffee mud pie. If you love dulce de leche ice cream as much as I do, imagine using it in a frozen pie made with pieces of peanut butter cups. Yum! And what about meringue? Top an ice cream pie with a mountain of meringue, and you have something sensational. There are a couple in this chapter, and I can guarantee that you'll find them, and all the others in the following pages, simply fabulous.

Tips for Making Irresistible Ice Cream Pies

- With few exceptions, a crumb crust makes the best pie shell for an ice cream pie. The flavor of a pastry shell, especially cold, is too muted for an ice cream pie.

- Crumb crusts should always be prebaked when making ice cream pies, followed by a thorough cooling and chilling before adding the ice cream. Otherwise, residual heat from the pan can melt the ice cream.

- It's very important that the ice cream does not start to melt. If it does, it will have a gritty, crystallized texture, not all creamy, after it refreezes.

- Ice cream needs to be softened before pressing it into the pie shell. The best way to do this is to move it from the freezer to the refrigerator for about 10 minutes. Use the back of an ice cream spade to press it firmly into the pan, but try not to damage the crumb crust.

- Once filled, an ice cream pie needs to be frozen for up to 3 hours. If it gets too firm, transfer the pie to the refrigerator for a few minutes before serving to soften it a bit.

- When you're browning a meringue on top of a baked Alaska pie, use a kitchen torch or shop torch (see Torch Tips, page 384) rather than running the pie under the broiler. An oven is not a good place for ice cream pies.

- Like ice cream itself, ice cream pies taste great with a fruit or chocolate topping.

Rice Krispies Mud Meringue Pies

Here's a fun pie to put together with the kids. Instead of a traditional crumb crust, this one is made with melted chocolate and Rice Krispies pressed into individual pie pans. In goes a scoop of coffee ice cream and some store-bought fudge sauce. After being chilled, the pies are topped with meringue and browned just before everyone digs in. If the meringue seems like too much trouble, leave it out or use unbrowned marshmallow crème.

Makes 6 individual pies

CRUST

- **5 tablespoons unsalted butter**
- **¾ cup semisweet chocolate chips**
- **3 cups Rice Krispies cereal**
- **⅓ cup sweetened flaked coconut**
- **¼ teaspoon ground cinnamon**

FILLING

- **1 quart coffee ice cream, slightly softened**
- **Chocolate fudge sauce (store-bought)**
- **Swiss Meringue (page 448) (optional)**

Variation

Many other flavor schemes work nicely with this crust. Try butter pecan ice cream and butterscotch sauce, or vanilla ice cream and a fruit sauce, with a drizzle of sauce on top for garnish.

1. Lightly butter six individual (1- to 1¼-cup capacity) pie pans.

2. To make the crust, melt the butter in a medium saucepan, preferably nonstick. When the butter is nearly melted, add the chocolate chips with the heat at the lowest possible setting. Let stand for 1 minute, then turn off the heat, swirling the pan so the butter runs over the chips. Let stand undisturbed for 5 minutes, then whisk to smooth. Add the Rice Krispies, coconut, and cinnamon, and stir until evenly mixed.

3. Divide the crust mixture among the pans, putting enough in each pan to make a thick crust. Gently press the mixture into the bottom and up the sides of each pan. If there's any leftover mixture, save it for garnish. Cool to room temperature, then put the pans in the freezer until firm, about 15 minutes.

4. To assemble the pies, put a large scoop of ice cream in each pie shell, flattening it slightly. Cover with chocolate fudge sauce. Put the pans back in the freezer to refirm everything, 30 to 60 minutes.

5. When you're ready to serve, spoon some of the meringue, if using, over each pie, mounding it nice and high. Quickly brown the meringue (see Torch Tips, page 384). Work fast so you don't melt the ice cream! Serve the pies right away.

Frozen White Chocolate Pie
with Raspberry Sauce

It's almost unfair that such a simple pie should taste so good. Made with an Oreo or graham cracker crust, this is little more than melted white chocolate folded into whipped cream — not quite an ice cream pie, but close. It goes into the freezer for a few hours, and that's all there is to it. The accompanying raspberry sauce can be made in less than ten minutes and makes for a pretty contrast with the pure white filling.

Makes 8–10 servings

Oreo Crumb Crust (page 85) or Graham Cracker Crust (page 82)

FILLING

¼ cup plus 2 tablespoons whole milk

1⅓ cups white chocolate chips

Stabilized Whipped Cream (page 446)*

Raspberry Sauce (page 452), for garnish

Handful of fresh raspberries, for garnish

*Plus 1 teaspoon of vanilla

1. Prepare the crust and press it into the bottom and up the sides of a 9½-inch standard pie pan. Refrigerate, prebake, and cool as directed. Refrigerate the shell until needed.

2. Combine the milk and white chocolate chips in the top insert of a double boiler set over, not in, barely simmering water. (Alternatively, use a heatproof bowl, suspended by the sides of a saucepan, over barely simmering water.) When melted, whisk to smooth. Remove the insert and let the mixture cool to room temperature, stirring occasionally.

3. Prepare the whipped cream, adding 1 teaspoon vanilla extract.

4. Fold the room-temperature white chocolate mixture into the whipped cream until evenly combined. Spoon the filling into the piecrust and smooth the top. Cover with loosely tented aluminum foil and freeze for at least 3 hours or overnight.

5. If the pie is very firm, let it soften at room temperature for a little while before serving. Drizzle raspberry sauce over and around each slice, garnish with a few fresh raspberries, and serve.

Black Bottom Peanut Butter Cloud Pie

One bite of this pie will put you on cloud nine! The cloud in the title is a reference to the light, almost mousselike consistency of the peanut butter filling, lightened with whipped cream and beaten egg whites. This is spread in a graham cracker crust lined with melted chocolate and chopped peanuts — that's the black bottom — and frozen until the filling is good and firm, about four hours. Kids love this pie because of the peanut butter, yet it's fancy enough to serve at a dinner party.

Makes 8–10 servings

Graham Cracker Crust (page 82)

BOTTOM LAYER

- ¾ **cup semisweet chocolate chips**
- ½ **cup chopped salted dry-roasted peanuts**

FILLING

- 1 **cup cold heavy cream**
- 6 **ounces full-fat cream cheese, softened**
- 1¼ **cups smooth peanut butter**
- ¾ **cup granulated sugar**
- ½ **cup packed light brown sugar**
- 2 **teaspoons vanilla extract**
- 3 **large egg whites, at room temperature**
- ½ **cup chopped salted dry-roasted peanuts, for garnish**

WARNING: *Consuming raw eggs may increase your risk of foodborne illness, especially if you have a medical condition.*

1. Prepare the crust and press it into a 9- to 9½-inch deep-dish pie pan. Bake the shell, and as soon as it comes out of the oven, scatter the chocolate chips evenly over the crust. Wait 5 minutes for the chips to melt, then spread the chocolate over the bottom. Sprinkle with the chopped peanuts and set aside to cool.

2. To make the filling, chill a medium bowl and a set of mixer beaters (handheld is fine) for 5 to 10 minutes. Beat the cream until stiff but not grainy. Cover and refrigerate.

3. Cream the cream cheese and peanut butter in a large bowl with the mixer on medium-high speed until evenly blended. Gradually beat in the granulated sugar, then the brown sugar, until evenly mixed. The mixture may look lumpy, like cookie dough; that's fine. Blend in the vanilla. Add the whipped cream, slowly blending with the mixer until smooth.

4. Clean and dry the beaters. Using a clean medium bowl, beat the egg whites until they hold stiff peaks. Fold them into the peanut butter mixture with a rubber spatula or gently beat them in on low speed with the mixer, until evenly blended. Scrape the filling into the pie shell and smooth with a spoon. Sprinkle the chopped nuts over the pie. Cover with loosely tented aluminum foil and freeze until firm enough to slice cleanly but not rock solid, 3 to 4 hours.

Frozen Peanut Butter Meringue Pie

This recipe first appeared in *Gourmet* magazine some years ago, and I've been changing it a little here and there ever since. The filling is essentially a milk-based peanut butter sauce cooked on the stovetop, cooled, and folded with whipped cream. The original topping was whipped cream — and you could use that if you prefer — but I like the way it tastes even more with the meringue. Dessert doesn't get much better than this.

Makes 8–10 servings

Shortbread Cookie Crust (page 82)

FILLING

- 1 **cup whole milk**
- ⅔ **cup sugar**
- 1 **cup smooth peanut butter**
- 1 **teaspoon vanilla extract**
- 1 **cup cold heavy cream**
  Swiss Meringue (page 448)
  Chocolate Ganache (page 445), for serving
- 1 **cup chopped salted dry-roasted peanuts, for garnish (optional)**

1. Prepare the crust and press it into the bottom and up the sides of a 9½-inch deep-dish pie pan. Refrigerate, prebake, and cool as directed. Refrigerate the shell until needed.

2. Gently warm the milk and sugar in a medium saucepan over low heat, stirring until the sugar melts, about 5 minutes; do not boil. Remove from the heat and add the peanut butter, whisking until smooth. Whisk in the vanilla. Pour the mixture into a large bowl, set on a rack, and cool to room temperature, whisking occasionally. Refrigerate until it begins to thicken. (A faster way to do this is to put the bowl into a bowl of ice water.)

3. To make the filling, chill a medium bowl and a set of mixer beaters (handheld is fine) for 5 to 10 minutes. Beat the cream until stiff but not grainy. Fold about one-third of the whipped cream into the peanut butter mixture. Add the remaining whipped cream and fold until evenly combined. Scrape the filling into the chilled pie shell and smooth the top with a spoon. Cover with loosely tented aluminum foil and freeze until firm but not rock hard, 3 to 4 hours.

4. When you're almost ready to serve the pie, prepare the meringue. Mound it thickly over the pie, then put the pie in the freezer for 5 minutes. Brown the meringue evenly with a kitchen torch or shop torch (see Torch Tips, page 384). Serve at once, garnishing each slice with a drizzle of chocolate ganache — warmed, if necessary, to loosen it up — and a sprinkling of peanuts, if desired.

Recipe for Success

As with ice cream, the longer this is in the freezer, the firmer the filling will be. The texture is usually just right after 3 or 4 hours. If it goes much beyond that, you'll probably want to put the pie in the refrigerator for up to 1 hour before topping with the meringue.

Coffee Mud Pie with an Oreo Crust

Here's a classic ice cream pie with layers of coffee ice cream sandwiching a layer of Oreo cookies and chocolate ganache, all in an Oreo crust. I'd have a hard time choosing an ice cream pie I like more. As with other ice cream pies, the key to doing this right is paying close attention to the texture of the ice cream. It needs to be softish and workable, but not starting to melt.

Makes 10 servings

Oreo Crumb Crust (page 85) or Graham Cracker Crust (page 82)

FILLING

½ gallon coffee ice cream

2 cups coarsely broken Oreo cookies (12 or 13 cookies)

Chocolate Ganache (page 445), at room temperature or slightly warm

1. Prepare the crust and press it into the bottom and up the sides of a 9½-inch standard pie pan. Refrigerate, prebake, and cool as directed. Refrigerate the shell until needed.

2. If the ice cream is very hard, put it in the refrigerator for about 10 minutes before you plan to assemble the pie, to soften it up. Spoon half of the ice cream into the pie shell with an ice cream spade. With the back of the spade, press the ice cream firmly and evenly into the shell. Place in the freezer for 10 minutes, and return the remaining ice cream to the freezer, too.

3. Remove the pie from the freezer and spread the broken Oreo cookies over the ice cream, gently pressing them in. Spoon or pour a generous layer of the chocolate ganache over the cookies. Place in the freezer again for 10 minutes.

4. Spread the remaining ice cream over the cookies and sauce. Using the back of the ice cream spade, smooth the ice cream into a nicely rounded mound. (It helps to run the utensil under hot water briefly as you do this.) Drizzle as much of the remaining sauce as you like over the surface. Cover with loosely tented aluminum foil and freeze for at least 1 hour or over-night before serving.

Recipe for Success

When you scoop out the first half of the ice cream, take it from around the edges, where it is the softest.

Make sure the chocolate ganache isn't too warm when you pour it over the ice cream, or the ice cream will start to melt.

It may seem like extra work to put the pie in the freezer twice, but it helps prevent the ice cream from squishing up and out the sides as you add each layer.

The Ultimate Banana Split Pie

A half gallon of ice cream, gobs of whipped cream, sliced bananas, pecans, and two kinds of dessert sauce — if this isn't every kid's idea of the ultimate pie, I don't know what is. A group of kids can work together and assemble this one for a small party, but I wouldn't leave them to their own devices for too long.

Makes 8 servings

Graham Cracker Crust (page 82) or another crumb crust

FILLING

1 **cup cold heavy cream**

3 **tablespoons confectioners' sugar**

Store-bought butterscotch or caramel sauce or Caramel Sauce (page 444)

Chocolate sauce or Chocolate Ganache (page 445), warmed

½ **gallon (or more) ice cream (any flavor)**

2 or 3 **large ripe bananas**

Large handful of coarsely chopped pecans, for garnish

M&M's, sprinkles, or other candy, for garnish

1. Prepare the crust and press it into the bottom and up the sides of a 9½-inch deep-dish pie pan. Refrigerate, prebake, and cool as directed. Refrigerate the shell until needed. At the same time, chill a medium bowl and a set of mixer beaters.

2. Using the chilled bowl and beaters, beat the cream with an electric mixer (handheld is fine) until it holds soft peaks. Add the sugar and continue to beat until firm but not grainy. Refrigerate.

3. If the butterscotch and chocolate sauces are cold and firm, loosen them in the microwave so they're pourable. Pour a generous layer of each sauce into the pie shell. Place in the freezer for 10 minutes. Take the ice cream out of the freezer for a few minutes to soften a bit.

4. Using an ice cream scoop, mound scoops of ice cream in the pie shell on top of the sauce. Pile them on top of one another, if you like. Slice the bananas right over the top, letting the slices fall where they may. With a large spoon, dollop the whipped cream here and there over the ice cream. Garnish with the pecans. Drizzle more of the butterscotch sauce and chocolate sauce over everything. Sprinkle the candy on top. Slice and serve at once.

Recipe for Success

If progress is slow, or you need to delay serving for any reason, you can freeze the scoops of ice cream to refirm them after they're added to the pie shell.

In summer, it's nice to add a garnish of fresh berries to this pie along with the bananas. At other times of the year, I might use canned pineapple — drained chunks or crushed — as a garnish.

Chocolate-Cherry S'mores Ice Cream Pie

This pie rates an A-plus with the kids, in both the assembly and sheer deliciousness. Begin with a graham cracker or Oreo crust, add lots of cherry-vanilla ice cream, a layer of chocolate-covered grahams and mini marshmallows, and more ice cream. (You can use chocolate or vanilla ice cream in place of the cherry vanilla. Chocolate brownie ice cream also tastes great.) The icing on the cake — the pie, I mean — is marshmallow crème. This is a great birthday party pie or rainy-day baking project.

Makes 8 servings

Graham Cracker Crust (page 82), Oreo Crumb Crust (page 85), or another crumb crust

FILLING

- ½ **gallon cherry-vanilla ice cream**
- 7 or 8 **chocolate-covered graham crackers**
- **Handful of mini marshmallows, frozen**
- 1 **(7-ounce) jar marshmallow crème (2 cups)**
- **Chocolate Ganache (page 445), warmed, or store-bought chocolate sauce**

1. Prepare the crust and press it into the bottom and up the sides of a 9½-inch deep-dish pie pan. Refrigerate, prebake, and cool as directed. Refrigerate the shell until needed.

2. If the ice cream is very hard, put it in the refrigerator for about 10 minutes before you plan to assemble the pie. You want it barely spreadable but not too soft. Spoon half of the ice cream into the pie shell with an ice cream spade, smoothing it around to make one nice level layer. (Return the remaining ice cream to the freezer to keep it firm.) Break the graham crackers into little shards and press them down and into the ice cream edgewise. Press 15 to 20 frozen mini marshmallows into the ice cream. Place the pie in the freezer for 20 minutes.

3. Mound the remaining ice cream in the pie, smoothing it with an ice cream spade or spoon. Place the pie in the freezer for at least 1 hour.

4. Spoon the marshmallow crème over the ice cream, smoothing it out as evenly as possible. Be sure to cover all the ice cream to protect it from the heat of the torch if you're planning to brown the marshmallow crème. Freeze the pie if you're not immediately moving to the next step.

5. When you're ready to serve the pie, quickly brown the marshmallow crème (see Torch Tips, page 384). Slice and serve right away, garnishing slices with the chocolate ganache.

Recipe for Success

Instead of browning the marshmallow crème, you can simply spread it on the ice cream and decorate with more chocolate grahams. Cut the graham crackers on the diagonal and stick them into the marshmallow crème edgewise, arranging them like the spokes of a wheel, radiating out from the center. That way, when you go to cut the pie, you can cut between the crackers rather than through them.

Butter Pecan Ice Cream Pie
with Bananas Foster

This sounds fancy and complicated, but it's quite simple. It's less intimidating, too, than making traditional bananas Foster, since you don't have to flambé the bananas — you sauté them with butter, brown sugar, and rum. When the bananas are soft and the juice syrupy, they're spooned right over slices of butter pecan ice cream pie, where the hot and cold elements create a flavor sensation.

Makes 8 servings

Nut Crumb Crust (page 82) made with pecans, or another crumb crust

FILLING

½ **gallon butter pecan ice cream**

10 **pecan halves**

4 **large, firm, just-ripe bananas**

4 **tablespoons unsalted butter**

¼ **cup packed light brown sugar**

Big pinch of ground cinnamon

⅓ **cup dark rum**

1. Prepare the crust and press it into the bottom and up the sides of a 9½-inch deep-dish pie pan. Refrigerate, prebake, and cool as directed. Refrigerate the shell until needed.

2. If the ice cream is very hard, place it in the refrigerator about 10 minutes to soften slightly before you assemble the pie. Spoon the ice cream into the pie shell with an ice cream spade, pressing it in with the back of the spade and smoothing the top. Press the pecan halves around the edge of the pie, evenly spaced, as a garnish for each slice. Freeze until fairly firm, at least 1 hour, preferably longer.

3. When you're almost ready to serve the pie, have someone slice and plate up the pie while you prepare the bananas. Cut each banana into 3 equal-size crosswise sections, then cut each section in half lengthwise. Melt the butter in a large nonstick skillet over medium heat. Add the bananas, cut side down, and fry for about 30 seconds. Flip them over and fry for 30 seconds more. Shake the sugar evenly over the bananas, add the cinnamon, then pour on the rum. Bring to a boil, shaking the pan to "stir" the ingredients. Cook at a low boil until the liquid is good and syrupy, about 1 minute, then remove from the heat.

4. Immediately spoon some of the bananas and syrup over and around each slice of pie. Serve at once.

Recipe for Success

The bananas can't be overly ripe or they'll get too soft in the skillet. Buy them several days ahead, while they're still a little green, and use them when they're just ripe but still firm.

Four bananas makes enough garnish for the whole pie. They don't keep well, so if you're not serving the whole pie, use two or three bananas, then make more when you serve the rest.

Grasshopper Ice Cream Pie

All grasshopper pies have two things in common: crème de cacao and crème de menthe. Typically, these flavorings are combined with melted marshmallows and whipped cream, as they are here. This one is a little different, because you start with a base of vanilla ice cream in a graham cracker crust. With this method, you don't get a green top layer; it's more of a mocha white. If you want green, use green crème de menthe and white crème de cacao. A drop or two of green food coloring will brighten it even more.

Makes 8–10 servings

Graham Cracker Crust (page 82)

FILLING

About 1 quart vanilla ice cream

¼ **cup milk**

5 **cups mini marshmallows**

3 **tablespoons white crème de menthe**

3 **tablespoons crème de cacao**

1¼ **cups cold heavy cream**

¼ **cup confectioners' sugar**

Small chocolate-covered after-dinner mints, for garnish

Mint sprigs, for garnish

Variation

Use mint or mint chip ice cream instead of vanilla, for a more traditional color and a bigger hit of mint flavor.

1. Prepare the crust and press it into the bottom and up the sides of a 9½-inch deep-dish pie pan. Refrigerate, prebake, and cool as directed. Refrigerate the shell until needed. At the same time, chill a medium bowl and a set of mixer beaters.

2. If the ice cream is very hard, put it in the refrigerator for about 10 minutes to soften it slightly. Using an ice cream spade, spoon the ice cream into the pie shell. Press it in evenly and smooth with the back of the spade; try not to crack the crust. Place in the freezer.

3. Combine the milk and marshmallows in a large saucepan, preferably nonstick, and melt over low heat, stirring often. Remove from the heat and cool, stirring occasionally. When the mixture has cooled to room temperature, stir in the crème de menthe and crème de cacao.

4. Using the chilled bowl and beaters, beat the cream with an electric mixer (handheld is fine) until it holds soft peaks. Add the sugar and continue to beat until stiff but not grainy. Fold the melted marshmallows mixture into the whipped cream until evenly blended. Scrape this mixture over the ice cream, smoothing the top. Freeze for at least 3 hours. Once the surface of the pie has firmed up, cover loosely with tented aluminum foil. The top layer should be firm but slightly yielding when the pie is served. To serve, garnish each slice with an after-dinner mint and a sprig of mint.

Dulce de Leche *and* Peanut Butter Cup Pie

This was inspired by one of my favorite ice cream flavors, dulce de leche. If you haven't tried this caramel-flavored ice cream with caramel swirls, you should. This recipe sandwiches a layer of peanut butter cups between two layers of the ice cream and finishes with warm chocolate ganache. Haagen-Dazs and plenty of others make dulce de leche ice cream, too, so if you have a brand loyalty, then by all means go for it.

Makes 10 servings

Graham Cracker Crust (page 82)

FILLING

½ gallon dulce de leche ice cream

12 regular-size (not mini) peanut butter cups, chilled

Chocolate Ganache (page 445), slightly warm and pourable, for garnish

1. Prepare the crust and press it into the bottom and up the sides of a 9½-inch deep-dish pie pan. Refrigerate, prebake, and cool as directed. Refrigerate the shell until needed.

2. If the ice cream is very hard, place it in the refrigerator for 10 minutes or so before you plan to assemble the pie, to soften it slightly.

3. Coarsely chop the cold peanut butter cups. Put them on a plate and refrigerate for 10 minutes.

4. Spoon half of the ice cream into the pie shell with an ice cream spade, pressing it in with the back of the spade and smoothing the top. Scatter the peanut butter cups over the ice cream, arranging the pieces in a more or less even layer, pressing down on them to embed in the ice cream. Put the pie and the remaining ice cream back in the freezer for 15 to 20 minutes.

5. Spoon the remaining ice cream into the shell, smoothing it evenly over the peanut butter cups. Put the pie back in the freezer for about 1 hour. Slice and serve the pie with a generous garnish of the chocolate ganache.

Creamsicle Ice Cream Pie

Here's a pie adaptation of those twin flavors so many of us love on a stick — vanilla ice cream and orange sherbet. A graham cracker crust and a topping of orange-flavored whipped cream create a cool and refreshing patio dessert for warm summer days — without having to chase down the Good Humor truck.

Makes 8–10 servings

Graham Cracker Crust (page 82)

FILLING

- 1 **quart vanilla ice cream**
- 1 **quart orange sherbet**
- 1 **cup cold heavy cream**
- 1 **tablespoon frozen orange juice concentrate, thawed**
- 1 **teaspoon vanilla extract**
- ⅓ **cup confectioners' sugar**

   Canned mandarin orange segments, drained, for garnish (optional)

1. Prepare the crust and press it into the bottom and up the sides of a 9½-inch deep-dish pie pan. Refrigerate, prebake, and cool as directed. Refrigerate the shell until needed.

2. If the ice cream and sherbet are quite hard, put them in the refrigerator for about 10 minutes to soften slightly.

3. Using an ice cream spade, randomly spoon scoops of the ice cream and sherbet into the pie shell. Use the back of the spade to pack them into the shell; try not to crack the crust. Smooth the top, mounding it slightly. Freeze until firm, at least 1 hour. At the same time, chill a medium bowl and a set of mixer beaters.

4. Using the chilled bowl and beaters, beat the cream with an electric mixer (handheld is fine) until it holds soft peaks. Blend in the orange juice concentrate and vanilla. Add the sugar and continue to beat until stiff but not grainy. Spread the whipped cream over the pie, smoothing it with a spoon. Freeze for at least 30 minutes before serving, garnishing each piece with one or two orange segments, if desired.

Recipe for Success

You don't need to use a fancy sorbet to make this pie, just good old sherbet. I actually prefer regular sherbet from a plastic tub because it gives the pie that old-fashioned flavor I remember from my youth.

   For a splash of color, put a sprig of fresh mint on top of each serving.

Cranberry Ice Cream Pie

I'm not sure whether or not you can even buy cranberry ice cream, but you can make it easily enough, and this pie is as good a reason as any to do so. It's a festive pie to have on hand around the holidays and a nice sidekick to traditional pumpkin pie.

Makes 8–10 servings

Graham Cracker Crust (page 82)

FILLING

- 2 **cups fresh or frozen cranberries**
- ⅓ **cup sugar**
- ½ **cup water**
  Finely grated zest of 1 orange
- 1 **quart vanilla ice cream**
- 1 **cup cold heavy cream**
- 1½ **tablespoons orange liqueur**
- 1 **teaspoon vanilla extract**
- 3 **tablespoons confectioners' sugar**

1. Prepare the crust and press it into the bottom and up the sides of a 9½-inch deep-dish pie pan. Refrigerate, prebake, and cool as directed. Refrigerate the shell until needed.

2. Combine the cranberries, sugar, water, and orange zest in a medium nonreactive saucepan over medium heat. Bring to a boil, then continue to boil until the mixture is thick and syrupy, about 4 minutes. Remove from the heat and scrape the cranberries onto a plate to cool. Refrigerate until they're cold.

3. When the cranberries are cold, put the ice cream in the refrigerator for about 10 minutes to soften slightly, if necessary. Place a large bowl, a medium bowl, and a set of mixer beaters in the freezer, to chill.

4. Scoop the ice cream into the chilled large bowl and add the cranberries. Using an ice cream spade, mix the fruit into the ice cream. Spoon the ice cream into the pie shell, smoothing the top. Freeze until pretty firm, at least 2 hours.

5. Shortly before serving, make the topping. Using the chilled medium bowl and beaters, beat the cream with an electric mixer (handheld is fine) until it holds soft peaks. Blend in the orange liqueur and vanilla. Add the sugar and beat until stiff but not grainy. Smooth the topping over the pie, then put it back in the freezer for 20 to 30 minutes before serving.

Recipe for Success

Try not to cook off all the moisture when you cook the cranberries. A little bit of syrupy liquid will help flavor the ice cream.

If you've ever been to one of those ice cream shops where custom "mix-ins" are folded in, on a chilled marble slab, then you'll know why I recommend freezing the bowl before mixing the ice cream in it: a cold bowl helps prevent the ice cream from melting. Partially melted and then refrozen ice cream always taste gritty.

Strawberry Baked Alaska Pie

You're going to like this pie — so much drama and such good looks for so little work. All you do is pile strawberry ice cream in a graham cracker crust, add a thick dome of meringue, and brown it with a torch. Even though there's only about 15 minutes of hands-on time, allow yourself 2 to 3 hours from start to finish so the ice cream has time to firm up in the pie shell.

Makes 8 servings

Graham Cracker Crust (page 82)

FILLING

½ **gallon strawberry ice cream**

Swiss Meringue (page 448)

Sliced ripe strawberries, for garnish (optional)

1. Prepare the crust and press it into the bottom and up the sides of a 9½-inch deep-dish pie pan. Refrigerate, prebake, and cool as directed. Refrigerate the shell until needed.

2. If the ice cream is very hard, put it in the refrigerator for about 10 minutes to soften up, just until workable. Using an ice cream spade or a large metal spoon, spoon the ice cream into the pie shell, pressing it in firmly and mounding it toward the center. Cover with plastic wrap and freeze until the ice cream is firm but not rock hard, about 2 hours.

3. When you're almost ready to serve the pie, prepare the meringue and mound it thickly over the pie. Brown the meringue evenly with a kitchen torch or shop torch (see Torch Tips, page 384). Slice and serve immediately, garnishing pieces with sliced strawberries, if desired.

Recipe for Success

By far the best way to serve this pie is when the meringue is warm, soft, and crusty and the ice cream is firm but not rock solid. The contrasting textures and temperatures are a real treat. So if you can make and apply the meringue just before serving, by all means, do so. It won't be a tragedy if you have to freeze the completed pie for later, but try not to.

15
A Pie Potpourri:
BROWNIE PIES, RICE PIES, AND OTHER DELICIOUS ODDBALLS

A collection as large as this needs a cubbyhole of sorts, a place to put those pies that don't fit neatly into the categories already covered; this is that cubby. Here you'll find a pie made with Arborio rice that will remind you of rice pudding, as well as a polenta pie thickened with fine cornmeal and boasting a texture and flavor reminiscent of Indian pudding, the traditional New England dessert you may be familiar with.

Don't think for a moment that because these recipes are grouped here at the back of the book that they amount to a collective afterthought. Nothing could be further from the truth. Each pie is deliciously unique and worthy of your consideration, just hard to slot. Where else could one find a comfortable home for the likes of two delicious sweet rice pies or the quirky Wheatena Breakfast Pie (page 441)?

So think of these as delicious misfits, if you will. But do think of them. You're bound to find a few unexpected pie treasures here.

Bev's Brownie Pie

My wife has a real weakness for rich brownies. Her favorite cookie is a brownie recipe that I adapted to cookie form. This pie has all the qualities of that cookie: soft and decadently rich, with a deep chocolate flavor. The key is to bake the pie for exactly 30 minutes, so it has the correct moist texture when it reaches room temperature, at which point it should be served with a large scoop of vanilla ice cream.

Makes 10 servings

Graham Cracker Crust (page 82)

FILLING

5   **tablespoons unsalted butter**

3   **ounces unsweetened chocolate**

1   **cup sugar**

2   **large eggs plus 2 large egg yolks**

1   **teaspoon vanilla extract**

½   **cup walnut halves, toasted (page 453)**

1   **cup all-purpose flour**

1   **teaspoon baking powder**

¼   **teaspoon salt**

    Confectioners' sugar, for glaze

    Vanilla ice cream, for serving

1. Prepare the crust and press it into the bottom and up the sides of a 9- to 9½-inch standard pie pan; refrigerate the shell until needed. Do not prebake the crust.

2. Preheat the oven to 325°F (165°C). Put the butter in the top insert of a double boiler set over, not in, barely simmering water. (Alternatively, use a heatproof bowl, suspended by the sides of a saucepan, over barely simmering water.) When the butter starts to melt, add the chocolate. When the chocolate has melted, whisk to smooth, then remove the insert and let the chocolate cool.

3. Reserve 2 tablespoons of the sugar and set it aside. Beat the, eggs, egg yolks, and the remaining sugar in a large bowl with an electric mixer (handheld is fine) on medium-high speed until light and airy, about 4 minutes. Mix in the chocolate mixture and the vanilla until evenly combined.

4. Combine the reserved 2 tablespoons sugar and the walnuts in a food processor. Pulse until finely chopped. Stir into the chocolate mixture. Mix together the flour, baking powder, and salt in a medium bowl; stir into the chocolate mixture until evenly combined. Turn the filling into the pie shell. Dust the top lightly with confectioners' sugar.

5. Place the pie on the center oven rack and bake for exactly 30 minutes, no more and no less. Transfer the pie to a rack and cool to room temperature. Serve the pie at room temperature, garnished with vanilla ice cream.

Recipe for Success

I suggest using a stand mixer, because you can use it to beat the eggs and sugar together while you're working on other parts of the recipe. That's one of the best reasons for owning a stand mixer: it can work while you're doing something else.

The pie can be made up to 2 days ahead and refrigerated. To serve, cut into individual slices while cold and put on dessert plates. Microwave each for 10 or 15 seconds to warm the slices.

Tar Heel Pie

This recipe was inspired by one my wife and I found on our travels through North Carolina, the Tar Heel State. I've made a few minor changes, adding coconut, a bit of salt, and chocolate chips, but it's not the sort of recipe that needs much altering. Since it's essentially a brownie in a crust, the key — as with most brownies — is to underbake it slightly so the center is soft. Vanilla ice cream is the only proper accompaniment.

Makes 8–10 servings

Old-Fashioned Shortening Pie Dough (page 62) or another single-crust dough

FILLING

½ **cup (1 stick) unsalted butter**

1½ **cups semisweet chocolate chips**

2 **large eggs, at room temperature**

½ **cup granulated sugar**

½ **cup packed light brown sugar**

1½ **teaspoons vanilla extract**

½ **cup all-purpose flour**

¼ **teaspoon salt**

¾ **cup pecan halves, toasted (page 453) and coarsely chopped**

⅓ **cup sweetened flaked coconut**

1. Prepare and refrigerate the pie dough. Roll the dough into a 12-inch circle and line a 9- to 9½-inch standard pie pan with it, shaping the edge into an upstanding ridge. Flute or crimp the edge, then refrigerate the shell until needed.

2. Preheat the oven to 350°F (180°C). Melt the butter in a medium saucepan over low heat. When the butter is melted, turn off the heat and immediately add 1 cup of the chocolate chips to the pan. Swirl the pan so that the hot butter runs over the chips. Let stand for 5 minutes, then whisk the chocolate to smooth. Scrape the chocolate into a large bowl and cool for 10 minutes.

3. Whisk the eggs, sugars, and vanilla in another large bowl until evenly mixed. Stir in the chocolate mixture. Add the flour and salt, and whisk just until evenly combined. Stir in the pecans, coconut, and the remaining ½ cup chocolate chips. Turn the filling into the pie shell.

4. Bake the pie on the center oven rack for 30 to 35 minutes, until the top has risen somewhat but the center still seems a little moist. Check it with a skewer or toothpick; it's fine if it emerges with a bit of batter attached.

5. Transfer the pie to a rack and cool. Serve barely warm or at room temperature. Cover and refrigerate leftovers after 24 hours.

Recipe for Success

The original recipe did not specify a partially prebaked crust, but 30 to 35 minutes is a short bake time if you want to brown the crust. If you don't want to prebake the crust, roll the dough on the thin side, trim the excess, and save it to make small pies.

If you're in doubt about whether the pie is done, you should err on the side of underbaking it. Another way to check for doneness is to press down gently on the center of the pie. It should be soft but not too squishy.

Kahlúa Fudge Brownie Pie

This pie is dangerous, being irresistible and way too rich. The secret is a double dose of chocolate — bittersweet and cocoa powder. When I want a chocolate pie to impress, this is the one I bake. Highly recommended for Valentine's Day, it's a surefire way to win that special someone's heart.

Makes 8–10 servings

Single-Crust Food Processor Pie Dough (page 58)

FILLING

- ¾ cup (1½ sticks) unsalted butter
- 4 ounces bittersweet chocolate, coarsely chopped
- ⅓ cup coarsely chopped walnuts
- 1 cup sugar
- ⅓ cup unsweetened cocoa powder
- 2 tablespoons all-purpose flour
- ¼ teaspoon salt
- 4 large eggs, at room temperature
- 1½ tablespoons Kahlúa or other coffee liqueur
- 1 teaspoon vanilla extract
- Whipped Cream (page 447) or vanilla ice cream (optional)

1. Prepare and refrigerate the pie dough. Roll the dough into a 12½- to 13-inch circle and line a 9- to 9½-inch deep-dish pie pan with it, shaping the edge into an upstanding ridge. Flute or crimp the edge, chill the shell, and partially prebake it according to the instructions on page 36.

2. Preheat the oven to 350°F (180°C). Start melting the butter in a small saucepan over very low heat. Add the chocolate. When the butter is completely melted, turn off the heat but leave the chocolate in the pan for 5 minutes, tilting the pan once or twice so the hot butter runs over the chocolate. (Alternatively, you can melt the butter and chocolate in the top insert of a double boiler set over, not in, barely simmering water.) Remove the pan from the heat. Wait for several minutes, then whisk the chocolate to smooth. Set aside to cool.

3. Put the walnuts in a food processor with ¼ cup of the sugar, the cocoa, flour, and salt. Pulse repeatedly until the nuts are finely chopped.

4. Using a handheld or stand mixer, beat the eggs and the remaining ¾ cup sugar in a large bowl until light and airy, about 4 minutes. Add the liqueur, vanilla, and ground nut mixture, and beat again until smooth. Add the melted chocolate and beat briefly, until the filling is uniformly mixed. Pour the filling into the pie shell.

5. Bake the pie on the center oven rack for 35 minutes. There's really no way to check the pie for doneness, visually or otherwise. Total baking time is the best indicator. However, do expect the pie to puff up, and don't be surprised if the top develops a crack or two. Expect the filling to seem relatively loose under the crusted top: that's fine.

6. Transfer the pie to a rack and cool to room temperature. The pie can be sliced once it has cooled, but the texture is better for slicing if you refrigerate it for at least 1 hour first. Serve slices garnished with whipped cream or ice cream, if desired. Cover and refrigerate leftovers.

Recipe for Success

If you don't have coffee liqueur but want the coffee flavor, add 1½ tablespoons instant espresso or coffee granules to the nuts when you process them.

If you want nice neat slices, refrigerate the pie overnight and then put it in the freezer for 30 minutes. It will then be fairly solid and easy to slice. However, leave the slices at room temperature for at least 30 minutes before serving.

Snickers Brownie Pie

Makes 8–10 servings

Graham Cracker Crust
(page 82)

Take a thick layer of fudge brownie, add another of sliced Snickers bars, top it off with peanut butter cream, and you have one incredible candy bar pie. It might sound like a child's fantasy, but don't be fooled: adults love this pie as much as kids. It needs several hours to chill — overnight is better — so make it early in the day or the day ahead.

BROWNIE FILLING

- ½ cup (1 stick) unsalted butter
- 4 ounces semisweet chocolate, coarsely chopped
- 1 large egg plus 1 large egg yolk
- ½ cup granulated sugar
- 1 teaspoon vanilla extract
- ⅓ cup all-purpose flour
- ½ teaspoon baking powder
- ⅛ teaspoon salt
- 2 (3.7-ounce) Snickers bars, sliced crosswise about ½ inch thick

PEANUT BUTTER CREAM

- ¾ cup cold heavy cream
- ⅔ cup confectioners' sugar
- 1 teaspoon vanilla extract
- ⅔ cup smooth peanut butter
- 6 ounces full-fat cream cheese, softened

  Chocolate Ganache (page 445), warmed, or another chocolate sauce (optional)

1. Prepare the crust and press it into the bottom and up the sides of a 9½-inch deep-dish pie pan. Do not prebake. Refrigerate the shell until needed.

2. To make the brownie filling, put the butter in the top insert of a double boiler set over, not in, barely simmering water. (Alternatively, use a heatproof bowl, suspended by the sides of a saucepan, over barely simmering water.) As the butter starts to melt, scatter the chocolate in the bowl and leave it for 5 to 8 minutes. When the chocolate has melted, remove the insert and whisk the chocolate to smooth. Let the chocolate cool for 15 minutes.

3. Preheat the oven to 350°F (180°C). Beat the egg, egg yolk, and granulated sugar in a large bowl with an electric mixer (handheld is fine) on medium speed for 2 minutes. Add the melted chocolate and vanilla, and mix until evenly combined. Mix the flour, baking powder, and salt together in a small bowl. Stir into the chocolate mixture until evenly mixed. Turn the filling into the pie shell, smoothing the top with a spoon.

4. Bake the pie on the center oven rack for exactly 18 minutes. Transfer the pie to a rack and cool for 5 minutes. Arrange the sliced Snickers bars in a single layer over the brownie layer. Set aside to cool. Refrigerate, if desired, to accelerate the cooling. At the same time, chill a medium bowl and a set of mixer beaters.

5. When the brownie layer has cooled completely, make the peanut butter cream. Using the chilled bowl and beaters, beat the cream with the mixer until it holds soft peaks. Add the confectioners' sugar and continue to beat until stiff but not grainy. Blend in the vanilla.

6. Combine the peanut butter and cream cheese in a large bowl. Using the mixer, beat until smooth and evenly combined. Add about half of the whipped cream to the peanut butter mixture and blend on low speed. Add the remaining whipped cream and fold it in until evenly combined. Smooth this peanut butter cream evenly over the Snickers slices. Cover the pie with loosely tented aluminum foil and refrigerate for at least 4 hours or overnight. Serve slices drizzled with warmed chocolate ganache or another chocolate sauce, if desired.

Amaretto-Amaretti Chocolate Fudge Pie

Here's a recipe I discovered years ago at a Vermont inn that's no longer in business. The pie has a delicious amaretti crust and a creamy, fudgy amaretto-flavored filling. The texture firms up as the pie cools, but this is as good warm as it is cold.

Makes 8–10 servings

Amaretti Crumb Crust
(page 85)

FILLING

- ½ cup (1 stick) unsalted butter, cut into several pieces
- 3 ounces unsweetened chocolate, coarsely chopped
- 1½ cups sugar
- 4 large eggs, at room temperature
- ¼ teaspoon salt
- 3 tablespoons light corn syrup
- ¼ cup heavy cream
- 2 tablespoons amaretto
- 1 teaspoon vanilla extract
- **Whipped Cream (page 447)**

1. Prepare the crust and press it into the bottom and up the sides of a 9- to 9½-inch deep-dish pie pan. Do not prebake.

2. Place the butter in the top insert of a double boiler set over, not in, barely simmering water. (Alternatively, use a heatproof bowl, suspended by the sides of a saucepan, over barely simmering water.) Add the chocolate as the butter begins to melt. When the chocolate has melted, whisk to smooth, then remove the insert. Let cool.

3. Preheat the oven to 350°F (180°C). Beat the sugar, eggs, and salt in a large bowl with an electric mixer on medium-high speed, until the mixture is thick, pale yellow, and foamy, about 4 minutes; a stand mixer is preferable here. Beat in the corn syrup, heavy cream, liqueur, vanilla, and melted chocolate, until evenly blended.

4. Put the pie shell on a baking sheet, near the oven, and carefully pour the filling into the shell. Bake the pie, on the sheet, on the center oven rack for about 50 minutes, rotating the pie 180 degrees midway through the baking. When done, the filling will be wobbly but not soupy in the center. Give the pie a little nudge to check. The pie will have puffed considerably around the edge and slightly less in the center.

5. Transfer the pie to a rack and cool. Serve barely warm, at room temperature, or chill the pie for several hours before serving, garnishing slices with whipped cream. Cover and refrigerate leftovers.

Recipe for Success

If you can't find amaretti or would simply rather not use this crust, use either the Graham Cracker Crust (page 82) or the Oreo Crumb Crust (page 85) instead.

Beating the eggs and sugar here results in a filling with quite a bit of volume, and it rises more than a little in the pan. So make sure the filling comes no higher than three-quarters up the side of the pan. If you have extra filling, bake it in buttered custard cups.

Use a touch of almond extract in the whipped cream if you have some on hand.

Oatmeal–Butterscotch Chip Cookie Pie

This pie is an oatmeal cookie lover's dream. The oats give the pie a little extra chewiness, and the butterscotch chips add that old-fashioned flavor kids love. A good keeper and easy to slice, this pie is a real hit at bake sales.

Makes 8–10 servings

Simple Press-In Pie Dough (page 73)

FILLING

½ cup (1 stick) unsalted butter, softened

1½ cups packed light brown sugar

3 large eggs, at room temperature

1½ teaspoons vanilla extract

⅓ cup old-fashioned rolled oats

⅓ cup cake flour or all-purpose flour

Scant ½ teaspoon salt

¼ cup milk or half-and-half

1 cup butterscotch chips

¾ cup pecan halves, toasted (page 453) and coarsely chopped

Vanilla ice cream, for serving

1. Prepare the pie dough and press it into a 9- to 9½-inch deep-dish pie pan according to the recipe on page 73. Refrigerate the shell until needed.

2. Preheat the oven to 350°F (180°C). Place the butter in a large bowl. Using a handheld or stand electric mixer, cream the butter on medium speed, gradually adding the sugar. Beat in the eggs, one at a time, beating well after each addition. Beat in the vanilla. Add the oats, flour, and salt, and mix until evenly combined. Blend in the milk. (Don't be concerned if the filling looks a little curdled.) Stir in the butterscotch chips and pecans. Pour the filling into the pie shell, smoothing the top with a spoon.

3. Bake the pie on the center oven rack for 50 to 60 minutes, until the center is set, rotating the pie 180 degrees midway through the baking. When done, the filling should wobble but not move in waves. Give the pie a slight nudge to check. The top of the pie will be dark golden brown, and that's fine; it doesn't mean the pie is overbaked.

4. Transfer the pie to a rack and cool. Serve slightly warm or at room temperature, garnished with vanilla ice cream. Refrigerate leftovers, but rewarm slices for 10 minutes in a very low oven, or in the microwave for several seconds, to soften the chips.

Oatmeal-Butterscotch Pie

Oatmeal pies became popular during the Great Depression, when cooks devised all sorts of clever ways to stretch a dish for pennies. Thrifty or not, all the oatmeal pies I've had taste wonderful. Here's one I really like, and that's probably no accident when you consider the source: Quaker Oats. I've taken liberties with the original recipe by adding butterscotch chips and a few nuts, which make it taste like a giant oatmeal cookie. Most of the oats settle on top of the pie and form a cookielike coating over the moist interior.

Whole-Wheat Pie Dough (page 66) or another single-crust dough

FILLING

- **2 large eggs, at room temperature**
- **¾ cup sugar**
- **¾ cup dark corn syrup**
- **4 tablespoons unsalted butter, melted**
- **¾ cup old-fashioned rolled oats**
- **½ cup sweetened flaked coconut**
- **2 tablespoons all-purpose flour**
- **1 cup butterscotch chips**
- **1 cup walnut or pecan halves, toasted (page 453) or not, coarsely chopped**
- **1 teaspoon vanilla extract**
- **¼ teaspoon salt**
- **Vanilla or butter pecan ice cream, for serving**

1. Prepare and refrigerate the pie dough. Roll the dough into a 12-inch circle and line a 9- to 9½-inch standard pie pan with it, shaping the edge into an upstanding ridge. Flute or crimp the edge, then refrigerate the shell until needed.

2. Preheat the oven to 375°F (190°C). Combine the eggs, sugar, corn syrup, and butter in a large bowl. Using an electric mixer, beat on medium speed for 1 minute. Stir in the oats, coconut, flour, butterscotch chips, nuts, vanilla, and salt. Pour the filling into the pie shell.

3. Bake the pie on the center oven rack for 30 minutes. Reduce the heat to 350°F (180°C) and rotate the pie 180 degrees. Bake for 25 minutes longer, until the top of the pie is dark golden brown and crusty and the center is set. The filling should wobble but not move in waves. Give the pie a slight nudge to check.

4. Transfer the pie to a rack and cool. Serve slightly warm or at room temperature, garnished with ice cream. Refrigerate leftovers, but warm slices in a very low oven for 10 minutes, or in the microwave for 10 to 15 seconds, to soften the chips.

Hillbilly Pie

In Arkansas, you sometimes see hillbilly pie on restaurant menus. It's been described as the poor man's pecan pie because the filling is made with oats instead of more costly pecans. The most basic versions contain little more than sugar, eggs, corn syrup, and oats. A reference to one such recipe claims the pie has been around for at least 40 or 50 years, maybe longer — long enough, judging from some versions, for modern cooks to start adding embellishments such as chocolate chunks, a shortbread crust, and even, yes, pecans to what began as a rather modest pie.

Oatmeal-Raisin Pie

When I married Bev, her dowry included this tasty pie recipe from her personal files. Like any sensible person, Bev is always looking for an excuse to eat pie for breakfast, and because this gooey, chewy pie has oats in it, she says it's perfectly acceptable breakfast fare. You won't disagree.

Makes 8–10 servings

Flaky Cream Cheese Pie Dough (page 72) or another single-crust dough

FILLING

- 3 **large eggs**
- 1 **cup light corn syrup**
- ½ **cup packed light brown sugar**
- 4 **tablespoons unsalted butter, melted**
- ¾ **cup quick-cooking rolled oats**
- ¾ **cup dark raisins**
- 1 **tablespoon all-purpose flour**
- ½ **teaspoon ground cinnamon**
- ¼ **teaspoon salt**
  Vanilla ice cream or Whipped Cream (page 447)

1. Prepare and refrigerate the pie dough. Roll the dough into a 12-inch circle and line a 9- to 9½-inch standard pie pan with it, shaping the edge into an upstanding ridge. Flute or crimp the edge, chill the shell, and partially prebake it according to the instructions on page 36.

2. Preheat the oven to 350°F (180°C). Whisk the eggs, corn syrup, and sugar together in a large bowl. Whisk in the butter. Add the oats, raisins, flour, cinnamon, and salt, and stir well. Put the pie shell on a baking sheet, near the oven, and carefully pour the filling into the shell. Gently rake a fork through the filling to distribute the raisins evenly.

3. Bake the pie on the middle oven rack for 40 to 45 minutes, until the center is set, rotating the pie 180 degrees midway through the baking. When the pie is done, the top will form an oatmeal cookie-like crust and the center will be set, not soupy. Give the pie a slight nudge to check.

4. Transfer the pie to a rack and cool. Serve barely warm or at room temperature, garnished with a big scoop of vanilla ice cream or a dollop of whipped cream.

Recipe for Success

As with any number of pies, it's a close call whether or not to prebake the crust for this pie. If you're pressed for time, you could skip that step and simply pour the filling into the unbaked pie shell and bake as is. The crust won't be as crisp as it could be, but it will still be good. If you don't plan to prebake the shell, roll the dough a little thinner than normal.

Sour Cream–Raisin Pie

The Norske Nook restaurant in Osseo, Wisconsin, is a pie lover's heaven, and with pies like this on the menu, it's easy to understand why. The filling is what I think of as a classic dairy-country sour cream custard, cooked on the stovetop and teeming with plump raisins. It's spread in a pastry crust, cooled, and topped with delicate peaks of Swiss meringue.

Makes 8–10 servings

Old-Fashioned Shortening Pie Dough (page 62)

FILLING

- 2 cups full-fat sour cream
- 1¾ cups sugar
- 4 teaspoons all-purpose flour
- 4 large egg yolks
- 1½ cups dark raisins
- ½ teaspoon vanilla extract (optional)
- Swiss Meringue (page 448)

Recipe for Success

Be patient when you're stirring the sour cream custard, and don't try to rush it by raising the heat. You want the mixture to thicken gradually.

I like to add ½ teaspoon vanilla extract to the custard, although the original recipe does not call for it.

1. Prepare and refrigerate the pie dough. Roll the dough into a 12-inch circle and line a 9- to 9½-inch standard pie pan with it, shaping the edge into an upstanding ridge. Flute or crimp the edge, chill the shell, and fully prebake it according to the instructions on page 36.

2. Combine the sour cream, sugar, flour, egg yolks, and raisins in a large heavy saucepan, preferably nonstick. Cook the mixture over medium heat, stirring nonstop, until it thickens and turns glossy, 8 to 10 minutes. Stir in the vanilla, if using. Slowly pour the filling into the pie shell. Cool thoroughly on a rack, then refrigerate for at least 4 hours or overnight, loosely covered with aluminum foil.

3. Spread the meringue lavishly over the pie. When you're ready to serve the pie, brown the meringue evenly with a kitchen torch or shop torch (see Torch Tips, page 384).

Peach Preserves *and* Applesauce Strudel Pie

If you want something pieish, but you don't want to mess with involved fillings, fluting, and all that, this is the recipe for you. Simply roll the dough into an oblong and cover half of it with preserves and applesauce. Fold the dough over and bake. Dust the warm strudel pie with confectioners' sugar and slice into thin wedges. If you're entertaining overnight guests, make the dough the night before, then assemble and bake this for breakfast.

Makes 8–10 servings

Flaky Cream Cheese Pie Dough (page 72)

FILLING

- 1 **cup peach preserves**
- ½ **cup sweetened applesauce or apple butter**
- ½–¾ **cup finely diced apples, pears, peaches, or apricots**
- **Milk, for glaze**
- **Granulated sugar, for sprinkling**
- **Confectioners' sugar, for garnish**

Recipe for Success

You can, of course, use other sorts of preserves. Blueberry is good, and you can scatter a few fresh blueberries right over the preserves. The same goes for raspberry preserves and fresh raspberries.

1. Prepare the pie dough, but instead of shaping the dough into a circle, shape it into an oval with blunt ends. Refrigerate the dough until chilled.

2. Preheat the oven to 400°F (200°C). The best way to assemble this is to roll the dough onto a large sheet of parchment paper, assemble the pie, then lift the pie onto a rimmed baking sheet with the paper. Alternatively, roll the dough onto a piece of floured waxed paper, invert it onto the baking sheet, peel off the paper, then assemble the pie on the baking sheet. Either way, roll the chilled dough into a 13- to 14-inch long oblong, about 10 inches wide at the widest point. Smooth the preserves evenly over the lower half of the pastry (the half closest to you), leaving a ¾-inch border of uncovered dough. Spoon the applesauce over the preserves. Scatter the fruit evenly on top, then smooth the filling with a spoon.

3. Moisten the entire edge of the dough with a finger or pastry brush. Using a spatula or dough scraper to help you lift the pastry (or the parchment, if it's under the dough), fold the top half of the pastry over the filled half, line up the edges, and press to seal. Crimp the edge with a fork. Using a paring knife or fork, poke three or four steam vents in the top of the pastry. Do this on an angle to keep from poking through the bottom of the pastry. Hold on to the parchment and lift the pie onto a baking sheet. Brush the pastry sparingly with milk and sprinkle with granulated sugar.

4. Bake the pie on the center oven rack for 10 minutes. Reduce the heat to 375°F (190°C) and bake for 25 to 35 minutes longer, until the top is a rich golden brown, rotating the pie 180 degrees midway through the second part of the baking.

5. Transfer the pie to a rack to cool. While the pie is still quite warm, sift a generous dusting of confectioners' sugar over the pie. Serve warm.

Mango and Pineapple Pie *with* Candied Ginger

I like frozen mango chunks for my pies because they're fast and convenient — you don't have to cut or peel anything or wonder if you're buying good fruit. The mango and pineapple, mixed with candied (crystallized) ginger, give this pie a Caribbean twist with a heavy ginger accent.

Makes 8–10 servings

Perfect Pie Dough by Hand, double-crust version (page 56)

FILLING

- 5 cups frozen mango chunks, partially thawed
- 1 cup canned diced pineapple, drained
- ¼ cup chopped crystallized ginger
- ⅔ cup sugar, plus a little for sprinkling
- 2½ tablespoons cornstarch
- 1 tablespoon lemon juice
- ½ teaspoon finely grated lemon zest
- ½ teaspoon vanilla extract
- Milk or half-and-half, for glaze

1. Prepare and refrigerate the pie dough. Roll the larger dough portion into a 12½- to 13-inch circle and line a 9- to 9½-inch deep-dish pie pan with it, letting the excess dough drape over the edge. Refrigerate the shell until needed.

2. Adjust the oven racks so one is in the lower position and another is in the middle of the oven. Preheat the oven to 400°F (200°C). Line a baking sheet with parchment paper.

3. Mix the mango, pineapple, and ginger in a large bowl. Mix the sugar and cornstarch in a small bowl. Stir into the fruit along with the lemon juice, lemon zest, and vanilla.

4. Roll the other dough half into an 11-inch circle. Turn the filling into the pie shell and smooth it out with the back of a spoon. Lightly moisten the rim of the pie shell. Drape the top pastry over the filling, pressing along the edge to seal. Trim the overhang with scissors, leaving an even ½ to ¾ inch all around, then sculpt the edge into an upstanding ridge. Flute or crimp the edge, as desired. Poke several steam vents in the top of the pie with a large fork or paring knife. Put a couple of the vents near the edge so you can check the juices. Brush the pie lightly with milk and sprinkle with sugar.

5. Put the pie on the prepared baking sheet and bake on the lower oven rack for 30 minutes. Reduce the heat to 375°F (190°C) and move the pie up to the middle rack, rotating 180 degrees. Bake the pie for 30 to 40 minutes longer, until the juices bubble thickly at the vents and the top is golden brown.

6. Transfer the pie to a rack and cool for at least 1½ to 2 hours before serving. Cover and refrigerate leftovers after 24 hours.

Recipe for Success

Be sure to partially thaw the fruit before it goes into the pie filling, or the pie will take longer to cook and the crust may get too brown.

   This pie is also excellent with a Coconut-Almond Crumb Topping (page 451) instead of a top crust.

Chocolate Chip Cookie Pie

This and the Oatmeal–Butterscotch Chip Cookie Pie on page 420 are variations on the famous Toll House cookie pie, essentially big buttery cookies in a crust. This country's signature pie may be apple, but I think cookie pies must be near the top of most people's favorites list. There's nothing to peel and no top crust, and they can be mixed up and popped in the oven in about five minutes. And are they ever good — like eating a big, fat, soft cookie, but better, because there's piecrust.

Makes 8–10 servings

Single-Crust Food Processor Pie Dough (page 58)

FILLING

½ cup (1 stick) unsalted butter, softened

1 cup packed light brown sugar

½ cup granulated sugar

3 large eggs, at room temperature

1 teaspoon vanilla extract

½ cup sifted cake flour

¼ teaspoon salt

¼ cup milk or half-and-half

1 cup semisweet chocolate chips

½ cup walnut halves, toasted (page 453) and coarsely chopped

Vanilla ice cream, for serving

1. Prepare and refrigerate the pie dough. Roll the dough into a 12-inch circle and line a 9- to 9½-inch standard pie pan with it, shaping the edge into an upstanding ridge. Flute or crimp the edge, then refrigerate the shell until needed.

2. Preheat the oven to 350°F (180°C). Using an electric mixer, cream the butter on medium speed in a large bowl, gradually adding the sugars. Beat in the eggs, one at a time, beating well after each addition. Beat in the vanilla. Add the flour and salt, and mix on low speed until evenly combined. Blend in the milk. (Don't be concerned if the filling looks a little curdled.) Stir in the chocolate chips and walnuts. Pour the filling into the pie shell, smoothing the top with a spoon.

3. Bake the pie on the center oven rack for 50 to 60 minutes, until the center is set, rotating the pie 180 degrees midway through the baking. When done, the filling should wobble but not move in waves, even at the very center. Give the pie a slight nudge to check. The top of the pie will be dark golden brown, and that's fine; it doesn't mean that the pie is overbaked.

4. Transfer the pie to a rack and cool. Serve slightly warm or at room temperature, garnished with ice cream. Cover and refrigerate leftovers, but rewarm slices for 10 minutes in a very low oven, or in the microwave for several seconds, to soften the chips.

Recipe for Success

If you don't have cake flour on hand, you can make a substitute. Add 2 tablespoons of cornstarch to a ½-cup measure, then fill the rest with all-purpose flour and mix.

This bears repeating: Don't be concerned if the top of the pie gets a little dark. That darkness is just a very thin crust, because of all the sugar, and it does not indicate that the filling is overcooked.

Shaker Marmalade Pie

This pie has enough in common with Shaker Lemon Pie (opposite page) that, had it not sounded disrespectful, I might have called it Faker Shaker Pie. The difference, and the reason for this pie, is that it can be made easily with a jar of lemon marmalade; authentic Shaker pie requires you to macerate thinly sliced lemons for several hours or overnight. But even though it's not the real deal, it's a fine pie in its own right.

Makes 8–10 servings

Shortening and Butter Dough with Egg (page 63)

FILLING

- 1 **(16-ounce) jar lemon marmalade (1½ cups)**
- 3 **tablespoons unsalted butter, melted**
- 4 **large eggs, at room temperature, lightly beaten**
- ⅓ **cup sugar, plus a little for sprinkling**
- 2 **tablespoons all-purpose flour**
- ⅛ **teaspoon ground nutmeg**
- **Pinch of salt**
- 2 **teaspoons finely grated lemon zest**
- ¼ **teaspoon lemon extract**
- **Milk or half-and-half, for glaze**
- **Vanilla ice cream, for serving**

1. Prepare and refrigerate the pie dough. Roll the larger dough portion into a 12-inch circle and line a 9- to 9½-inch standard pie pan with it, letting the excess dough drape over the edge. Refrigerate the shell until needed.

2. Adjust the oven racks so one is in the lower position and another is in the middle of the oven. Preheat the oven to 400°F (200°C).

3. Combine the marmalade and butter in a large bowl, stirring until smooth. Stir in the eggs. Mix the sugar, flour, nutmeg, and salt in a small bowl; stir into the marmalade mixture along with the lemon zest and lemon extract.

4. Roll the other dough half into an 11-inch circle. Turn the filling into the pie shell and smooth it over with the back of a spoon. Lightly moisten the rim of the pie shell. Drape the top pastry over the filling, pressing along the edge to seal. Using a paring knife, trim the edge of the pastry flush with the sides of the pan; crimp the edge with a fork. Poke several steam vents in the top of the pie with a large fork or paring knife. Lightly brush the top of the pie with milk and sprinkle with sugar.

5. Bake the pie on the center oven rack for 15 minutes. Reduce the heat to 350°F (180°C) and rotate the pie 180 degrees. Bake for 25 to 35 minutes longer, until the top is golden brown. When done, the pie will be set in the center, with no sign of soupiness. Insert the tip of a paring knife into the center to check.

6. Transfer the pie to a rack and cool. Serve barely warm or at room temperature, with a scoop of ice cream. Cover and refrigerate leftovers.

Recipe for Success

If you can't find a marmalade made with at least some lemons, use orange marmalade. A little extra lemon extract and lemon zest will boost the lemon flavor if you'd like to add more.

Don't skip the ice cream. It softens the sharp edges of the marmalade.

Shaker Lemon Pie

This delicious pie is almost always credited to the Shakers, whose thriftiness and cleverness in the kitchen is well documented. Modern cooks are intrigued because it includes the white pith of the lemon, which we're typically told to avoid because it is so bitter. That's not the case here, however, because the paper-thin lemon slices are first macerated with a full two cups of sugar, rendering the pith highly palatable. I think you'll be delighted by how tasty this is.

Makes 8–10 servings

Shortening and Butter Dough with Egg (page 63)

FILLING

- 2 large lemons
- 2 cups sugar
- ⅛ teaspoon salt
- 4 large eggs, at room temperature
- 2 tablespoons all-purpose flour
- 1 tablespoon sugar, plus a little for sprinkling
- 2 tablespoons unsalted butter, melted

  Milk or half-and-half, for glaze

  Vanilla ice cream, for serving

1. The day before you bake the pie, finely grate the zest from the lemons into a small bowl. Using your sharpest knife, slice the lemons paper thin, removing the seeds as you encounter them. Put the slices in a large glass or ceramic bowl and add the sugar, salt, and grated zest; mix well with your hands. Cover the bowl with plastic wrap and leave at room temperature overnight, stirring once or twice.

2. Prepare and refrigerate the pie dough. Roll the larger dough portion into a 12-inch circle and line a 9- to 9½-inch standard pie pan with it, letting the excess dough drape over the edge. Refrigerate the shell until needed.

3. Preheat the oven to 375°F (190°C). Thoroughly whisk the eggs in a medium bowl. Mix the flour and 1 tablespoon sugar in a small bowl, then whisk into the eggs. Add the egg mixture and butter to the lemon slices and mix thoroughly; hands are best here.

4. Roll the other dough half into an 11-inch circle. Turn the filling into the pie shell and smooth it out. Lightly moisten the rim of the pie shell. Drape the top pastry over the filling, pressing along the edge to seal. Trim the overhang with scissors, leaving an even ½ to ¾ inch all around, then sculpt the edge into an upstanding ridge. Flute or crimp the edge, as desired. Poke several steam vents in the top of the pie with a large fork or paring knife. Brush the pie lightly with milk and sprinkle with sugar.

5. Bake the pie on the center oven rack for 50 to 55 minutes, until the top is golden brown, rotating the pie 180 degrees midway through the baking. The best way to judge overall doneness of the pie is total elapsed baking time, so go by that.

6. Transfer the pie to a rack and cool. Serve barely warm or at room temperature, garnished with vanilla ice cream. Cover and refrigerate leftovers after 24 hours.

Recipe for Success

When I say paper-thin slices, I mean paper thin. Use your sharpest serrated knife, or sharpen your chef's knife before you begin cutting. If you're lucky enough to own a mandoline — a mechanical slicing device — now's the time to get it out.

Serve pieces of this pie with a fork and knife so that guests can deal with any large pieces of lemon. Incidentally, I'm not religious about using only whole lemon slices. Try coarsely chopping some of the slices to keep the pieces to a manageable size.

Joe's Stone Crab Key Lime Pie

A lot of folks believe that the Key lime pie at Joe's Stone Crab Restaurant in Miami Beach is one of the best in Florida. Joe's certainly gets enough practice, producing tens of thousands of pies each year. Joe's pie is baked in a graham cracker crust and has a firm texture and taste that's slightly more tart than sweet, the way many regulars prefer it. Rather than a meringue topping, this one is garnished with a dollop of whipped cream.

Makes 8–10 servings

Graham Cracker Crust (page 82)

FILLING

3 **large egg yolks, at room temperature**

Grated zest of 2 limes

1 **(14-ounce) can sweet-ened condensed milk**

⅔ **cup fresh lime juice, preferably Key lime**

Whipped Cream (page 447), for serving

1. Prepare the crust and press it into the bottom and up the sides of a 9½-inch standard pie pan. Refrigerate, prebake, and cool as directed. Refrigerate until needed.

2. Preheat the oven to 350°F (180°C). Place the egg yolks and lime zest in a medium bowl. Beat together with an electric mixer (handheld is fine) on high speed until somewhat fluffy and well aerated, about 5 minutes. (Set the timer; that's a lot of beating and you might be tempted to cut it short.) Gradually add the condensed milk and beat until all of the milk has been added and the mixture is thick and fluffy, about 4 minutes. Slowly add the lime juice, mixing it in on low speed just until evenly blended. Pour the filling into the pie shell.

3. Bake the pie on the center oven rack for about 10 minutes, just until the filling appears set.

4. Transfer the pie to a rack and cool thoroughly. Refrigerate until good and cold, at least 2 to 3 hours. Serve each slice with a big dollop of whipped cream. Cover and refrigerate leftovers.

Recipe for Success

One of the best things about this pie is how simple it is, one of the easiest pies in this entire collection. I suggest keeping a bottle of Key lime juice on hand so you can whip it up for family and friends on short notice.

Even to an experienced pie maker, baking this pie is somewhat counterintuitive in that it takes only 10 minutes. That hardly seems like enough time for the filling to set, but it is. Baking it longer may ruin the filling.

Orange Pie *with* a Pistachio Crumb Crust

Similar to Key lime pie, this version is flavored with reduced orange juice and only a little lime juice. It has a wonderful aroma and a sprightly citrus taste that I love — and love to serve — in summer. The pistachio crust is a special touch. Generously proportioned, this is baked in a deep-dish pie pan and serves ten easily.

Makes 10 servings

Nut Crumb Crust (page 82) made with pistachios

FILLING

- 2 **cups orange juice**
- 2 **cups sweetened condensed milk (from two 14-ounce cans)**
- 5 **large egg yolks**
- 2 **tablespoons lime juice**
- ½ **teaspoon vanilla extract**
- 2 **teaspoons finely grated orange zest**

 Whipped Cream (page 447)

 Threads of orange zest, for garnish (optional)

1. Prepare the crust and press it into the bottom and up the sides of a 9½-inch deep-dish pie pan. Refrigerate, prebake, and cool as directed. Refrigerate until needed.

2. Bring the orange juice to a rapid boil in a medium nonreactive saucepan. Boil until the juice is reduced to about ⅔ cup; keep a heatproof measuring cup nearby to check. Pour the juice into a shallow bowl and cool briefly.

3. Preheat the oven to 350°F (180°C). Combine the condensed milk, egg yolks, lime juice, vanilla, and orange zest in a large bowl, whisking well to combine. Whisk in the reduced orange juice until evenly blended. Pour the filling into the pie shell.

4. Bake the pie on the center oven rack for 20 minutes. Even if the filling does not appear solid, remove the pie from the oven when the time is up; the filling will firm as the pie cools.

5. Transfer the pie to a rack and cool thoroughly. Once it has cooled, refrigerate the pie for at least 4 hours, preferably longer, before serving. Pipe the whipped cream decoratively over the pie, or just smooth it over the top. If you're starting with the entire recipe of whipped cream, you may not need all of it. Decorate the pie with the orange zest, if desired.

Recipe for Success

Note that this recipe is a little different from the previous one in that the ingredients are simply whisked together and not beaten. The Key lime pie has a slightly lighter texture, but this one is delicious, too — creamy and dense.

 It's best to prepare the recipe with fresh orange juice, but in a pinch you can use a good not-from-concentrate blend.

 For the garnish, use a lemon zester or sharp vegetable peeler to peel off long threads of orange zest.

Atlantic Beach Pie

Many written mentions of this pie lead back to Bill Smith, a chef in Chapel Hill, North Carolina. Though the pie is not well known beyond the coastal Carolinas, Bill says similar recipes can be found in community cookbooks, and that there's a long-standing North Carolina tradition of serving lemon pies as a refreshing finish to a fish dinner. This pie is sometimes served with a meringue topping, but a dollop of whipped cream and a sprinkle of coarse sea salt do quite nicely.

Makes 8 servings

Saltine Cracker Crust (page 84)

FILLING

1 (14-ounce) can sweetened condensed milk

4 large egg yolks

½ cup fresh lemon or lime juice, or a combination of the two

Whipped Cream (page 447), for serving

Coarse sea salt, for garnish (optional)

1. Prepare the crust and press it into the bottom and up the sides of a 9½-inch standard pie pan. Refrigerate, prebake, and cool as directed. Refrigerate the shell until needed.

2. Preheat the oven to 350°F (180°C). Combine the condensed milk and egg yolks in a large bowl. Whisk well for about 1 minute, then whisk in the lemon juice until smooth. Pour the filling into the shell.

3. Bake the pie on the center oven rack for 18 minutes. There are virtually no visual clues that the filling is done, so it is best to go by total elapsed time.

4. Transfer the pie to a rack and cool thoroughly. Refrigerate for at least 4 hours; overnight is fine. Serve slices of the pie dolloped with whipped cream and lightly sprinkled with sea salt, if desired. Refrigerate leftovers.

Cherry Cheesecake Pie

I grew up in New Jersey, cheesecake capital of the country, so this is personal. A cheesecake pie is nearly the same thing as a cheesecake, just a little thinner. They're easier to make, too, because there are no special pans to mess with. Here's a really good version with a creamy, lemony filling beneath a sweet cherry topping. Start this well ahead, even the day before, so it has plenty of time to chill.

Makes 10 servings

Graham Cracker Crust (page 82)

FILLING

- 12 ounces full-fat cream cheese, softened
- ½ cup sugar
- 2 large eggs, at room temperature
- ½ cup full-fat sour cream
- 1 teaspoon vanilla extract
- ½ teaspoon lemon extract

TOPPING

- 3 cups frozen sweet cherries
- 2 tablespoons lemon juice
- ½ cup sugar
- 2 tablespoons cornstarch
- ¼ cup water
- ½ teaspoon vanilla extract
- Whipped Cream (page 447), for garnish (optional)

1. Prepare the crust and press it into the bottom and up the sides of a 9½-inch deep-dish pie pan. Refrigerate, prebake, and cool as directed. Refrigerate the shell until needed.

2. Preheat the oven to 350°F (180°C). To make the filling, place the cream cheese in a large bowl. With an electric mixer, cream the cheese, gradually beating in the sugar on medium speed. Add the eggs, one at a time, beating on medium speed until evenly blended. Add the sour cream, vanilla, and lemon extract, and beat on medium speed until smooth. Pour the filling into the pie shell and smooth the top.

3. Bake the pie on the center oven rack for 25 to 30 minutes, until the center of the filling is set. Transfer the pie to a rack and cool to room temperature. Cover with tented aluminum foil and refrigerate for at least 4 hours or overnight.

4. To make the topping, begin an hour or two before serving. Combine the cherries, lemon juice, and sugar in a medium nonreactive saucepan. Cover and bring to a low boil over medium heat, stirring often. Reduce the heat to medium-low and simmer, partially covered, for 2 to 3 minutes. While the cherries simmer, blend the cornstarch and water in a small bowl, then stir the mixture into the cherries. Bring to a boil and continue to boil, stirring, for 1½ minutes. Remove from the heat and stir in the vanilla. Cool to room temperature.

5. Spoon the cooled cherries evenly over the pie, then refrigerate for at least 30 minutes. If desired, pipe whipped cream decoratively around the edge of the pie.

Recipe for Success

Keep in mind that cheesecake is a custard and, like other custards, it will become watery and less tender than it should be if overbaked. That said, keep a close eye on the filling after about 20 minutes of baking. When you see the sides starting to rise slightly, the filling is almost done.

Black Bottom Ricotta Cheese Pie

Lighter than ricotta cheese cheesecake but with a similar texture, this pie is a great way to cap off an Italian feast — if you have room left! The plain appearance hides a razzle-dazzle of flavor: chocolate, citrus, and almond play off one another like the notes of a jazzy song, coming at your taste buds from all directions. I normally prefer creamy pies served cold, but this one is yummy served barely warm, too.

Makes 8–10 servings

Graham Cracker Crust (page 82)

BOTTOM LAYER

- 2 tablespoons unsalted butter
- 1 tablespoon light or dark corn syrup
- ¾ cup semisweet chocolate chips

FILLING

- 1½ cups whole-milk or part-skim ricotta cheese
- ⅔ cup sugar
- 3 large eggs, at room temperature
- ¼ cup heavy cream
- 1 teaspoon finely grated lemon zest
- 1 teaspoon finely grated orange zest
- ¾ teaspoon vanilla extract
- ½ teaspoon almond extract
- ⅛ teaspoon salt

1. Prepare the crust and press it into the bottom and up the sides of a 9- to 9½-inch standard pie pan. Refrigerate, but do not prebake.

2. To make the bottom layer, combine the butter, corn syrup, and chocolate chips in the top insert of a double boiler set over, not in, barely simmering water. (Alternatively, use a heatproof bowl, suspended by the sides of a saucepan, over barely simmering water.) Heat until the chocolate melts, 5 to 6 minutes, then whisk to smooth. Remove the insert and scrape the chocolate into the pie shell. Smooth it over the bottom and part way up the sides of the shell. Refrigerate.

3. To make the filling, preheat the oven to 350°F (180°C). Using an electric mixer (handheld is fine), beat the ricotta, sugar, and eggs together in a large bowl until evenly mixed. Add the cream, lemon and orange zests, vanilla, almond extract, and salt, and beat just until evenly blended. Slowly pour the filling into the chocolate-lined pie shell.

4. Bake the pie on the center oven rack for 30 minutes. Rotate the pie 180 degrees and bake for 15 to 20 minutes longer, until the center is set. When done, the edge of the filling will be golden brown and will likely have risen slightly. The center of the pie will show no signs of soupiness.

5. Transfer the pie to a rack and cool well. Serve barely warm, at room temperature, or chilled. Cover and refrigerate leftovers.

Recipe for Success

You can, if you like, skip the chocolate "lining," but I can't recommend the idea with any enthusiasm. For one thing, the chocolate tastes perfect with the filling. For another, it helps keep moisture in the filling away from the pie shell. I think it's worth the little extra time required to make it.

An almond version of the crust would also be excellent here.

Richard's Rice *and* Ricotta Pie

My friend Richard Sax was one of the most beloved and widely respected food writers of recent time. Not only was he a great cook and writer, but he had a generosity of spirit people found irresistible. I love this recipe of his, which I adapted from one of his early books, *Old-Fashioned Desserts*. It's basically a rice pudding in a crust, only better. The recipe has a couple of fussy little steps, but it's worth every bit of extra effort.

Makes 8–10 servings

Single-Crust Food Processor Pie Dough (page 58) or another single-crust dough

FILLING

2 **cups water**

¾ **cup long-grain white rice**

¾ **cup plus 2 tablespoons whole milk**

⅓ **cup plus ¼ cup sugar**

¼ **teaspoon salt**

1 **cup whole-milk ricotta cheese, pressed through a sieve**

1 **large egg plus 2 large egg yolks**

1 **teaspoon vanilla extract**

½ **teaspoon grated lemon zest**

½ **cup cold heavy cream**

Several pinches of ground cinnamon

Whipped Cream (page 447), for garnish

1. Prepare and refrigerate the pie dough. Roll the dough into a 12½- to 13-inch circle and line a 9- to 9½-inch deep-dish pie pan with it, shaping the edge into an upstanding ridge. Flute or crimp the edge, chill the shell, and partially prebake it according to the instructions on page 36. At the same time, chill a small bowl and a set of mixer beaters.

2. Preheat the oven to 350°F (180°C). Bring the water to a boil in a small saucepan. Stir in the rice and boil, uncovered, for 5 minutes. Drain through a fine-mesh sieve, rinsing with cold water. Return the drained rice to the saucepan along with the ¾ cup milk, the ¼ sugar, and the salt. Place over medium heat and bring to a gentle boil, stirring occasionally. Reduce the heat to medium-low and simmer, partially covered, until the liquid is absorbed and the rice is tender, 15 to 20 minutes.

3. Whisk the ⅓ cup sugar, ricotta, egg, egg yolks, vanilla, lemon zest, and the 2 tablespoons milk in a large bowl. Stir in the rice.

4. Using the chilled bowl and beaters, beat the cream with a handheld electric mixer until it holds soft peaks. Fold the cream into the rice mixture until evenly combined. Put the pie shell on a baking sheet, near the oven, and carefully pour the filling into the pie shell; sprinkle with the cinnamon.

5. Bake the pie, on the sheet, on the center rack for 45 to 55 minutes, until the top is a rich golden brown and the filling is firmly set, rotating the pie 180 degrees midway through the baking.

6. Transfer the pie to a rack and cool. Serve barely warm, at room temperature, or chilled, garnishing slices with the whipped cream. Cover and refrigerate leftovers.

Recipe for Success

If you've never pressed ricotta cheese through a sieve before, it's simple: place it in a sieve, then just press and sweep with the back of a large spoon or rubber spatula to force the ricotta through. It doesn't require much force; the ricotta goes through pretty easily, creating a fine-textured cheese.

Keep an eye on this pie during the last 15 to 20 minutes of baking. Remove it from the oven as soon as it seems done. If you're in doubt, stick a paring knife into the center. If it comes out with uncooked custard on the knife, continue to bake.

Ricotta Pie *with* Chocolate and Toasted Almonds

Some people pick up Italian cookbooks and immediately flip to the pasta dishes; I go right to the dessert section. Ricotta cheese turns up in many Italian pies and tarts, often combined with flavorings like vanilla or almonds and chocolate. Typically, these Italian pies and tarts are baked in a crostata-style pastry like the one on page 80. Here, however, I use cream cheese pastry because I think it pairs well with this lovely ricotta filling. Serve barely warm or chilled, but do save room for this.

Makes 8–10 servings

Flaky Cream Cheese Pie Dough (page 72) or another single-crust dough

FILLING

1 **(15- or 16-ounce) container whole-milk or part-skim ricotta cheese**

¾ **cup sugar**

3 **large eggs, at room temperature**

1½ **teaspoons vanilla extract**

½ **teaspoon almond extract**

1 **teaspoon grated lemon zest**

¼ **teaspoon ground cinnamon**

1 **cup whole almonds, toasted (page 453) and coarsely chopped by hand**

1 **cup semisweet chocolate chips (preferably mini chips)**

1. Prepare and refrigerate the pie dough. Roll the dough into a 12½- to 13-inch circle and line a 9- to 9½-inch deep-dish pie pan with it, shaping the edge into an upstanding ridge. Flute or crimp the edge, chill the shell, and partially prebake it according to the instructions on page 36.

2. Preheat the oven to 350°F (180°C). Combine the ricotta and sugar in a large bowl. Using an electric mixer, beat in the eggs, one at a time, beating well after each addition. Add the vanilla, almond extract, lemon zest, and cinnamon, and blend briefly. Stir in the almonds and chocolate chips. Put the pie shell on a baking sheet, near the oven, and slowly pour the filling into the cooled pie shell, smoothing the top with a spoon. Gently rake a fork through the filling to distribute the nuts and chips evenly.

3. Bake the pie, on the sheet, on the center rack for 40 to 50 minutes, until the top is light golden brown and the filling is set, rotating the pie 180 degrees midway through the baking.

4. Transfer the pie to a rack and cool to room temperature. Cover the pie with tented aluminum foil and refrigerate for at least 4 hours, or overnight, before serving.

Recipe for Success

Anytime you have a pie filling with a combination of liquid and solids like nuts or chocolate chips, take a moment to redistribute things after you pour the filling into the pie shell. Simply take a large fork and rake it carefully through the filling, moving the solids around so they're somewhat evenly distributed. Don't be fanatical about it, but it's nice if everyone ends up with some of the good stuff in their slice.

Arborio Rice Pie

Anyone who loves rice pudding will adore this pie, modeled after an Italian pastry known as *crostata di riso*, or rice tart. The key ingredient in this rice pie is the Italian Arborio rice, an extrastarchy variety that's widely available. The starch is gradually released as the grain is cooked prior to baking the pie, giving the filling a satiny, ultrasmooth texture. Don't use regular white rice: the texture won't be the same.

Makes 8–10 servings

Single-Crust Food Processor Pie Dough (page 58) or another single-crust dough

FILLING

- 3 **cups whole milk**
- ⅓ **cup Arborio rice**
- ½ **cup sugar**
- 2 **tablespoons unsalted butter**
- ¼ **teaspoon salt**
- 2 **large eggs plus 1 large egg yolk**
- ½ **teaspoon finely grated lemon zest**
- 1 **teaspoon vanilla extract**

1. Prepare and refrigerate the pie dough. Roll the dough into a 12½- to 13-inch circle and line a 9- to 9½-inch deep-dish pie pan with it, shaping the edge into an upstanding ridge. Flute or crimp the edge, chill the shell, and partially prebake it according to the instructions on page 36.

2. Combine the milk, rice, sugar, butter, and salt in a medium heavy-bottom saucepan over medium heat. Bring to a simmer, then immediately turn the heat down very low. Watch the rice carefully, because when it first comes to a simmer — and for several minutes after that — the milk may rise quickly and boil over. At the first sign of this, quickly remove the pan from the heat until the liquid settles down. Partially cover and gently simmer the rice, stirring occasionally, until it is tender and the liquid in the pan is starchy thick, 40 to 45 minutes. Remove from the heat, uncover, and cool for 30 minutes.

3. Preheat the oven to 350°F (180°C). When the rice has cooled, whisk the eggs and egg yolk together in a large bowl. Add a ladleful of the rice and whisk again. Add the remaining rice, lemon zest, and vanilla, stirring until evenly blended. Carefully transfer the filling to the pie shell.

4. Bake the pie on the center oven rack for 40 to 50 minutes, until the filling is set, rotating the pie 180 degrees midway through the baking. When done, the perimeter may puff slightly, but other than a few areas here and there, the top of the pie will not brown much.

5. Transfer the pie to a rack and cool. Serve at room temperature, or refrigerate for several hours and serve chilled (my personal preference). Cover and refrigerate leftovers.

Recipe for Success

Not to harp on this too much, but in order for the pie to achieve the perfect texture, it's important to use Arborio rice and to cook it thoroughly. The rice may actually become tender after 30 minutes of cooking, but don't be tempted to remove it from the heat at that point. Continue cooking until you can see and feel an unmistakable thickening of the liquid around the rice, like heavy cream. That rich body is one of the things that makes this pie so good.

Smooth *and* Simple Polenta Pie

Most folks are familiar with polenta, a classy version of cornmeal mush. I love the stuff and set out to make a pie based on the same simple ingredients and preparation method. This is it, and I think you'll like it. The filling is soft and creamy, not overly sweet, and has a hint of lemon. It's a little like Indian pudding, but without all the spices and heavy molasses flavor. Serve cool or cold for the best flavor, perhaps with a dab of mascarpone whipped cream.

Makes 8–10 servings

Perfect Pie Dough by Hand (page 56) or another single-crust dough

FILLING

- 2 **cups milk**
- ¼ **cup plus 1 tablespoon fine yellow cornmeal**
- **Scant ½ teaspoon salt**
- 4 **tablespoons unsalted butter, cut into ½-inch pieces**
- ½ **cup sugar, or ⅓ cup sugar plus 2 tablespoons maple syrup**
- 1 **tablespoon lemon juice**
- 1 **teaspoon finely grated lemon zest**
- ½ **teaspoon vanilla extract**
- 3 **large eggs, at room temperature, lightly beaten**
- **Mascarpone Whipped Cream (page 448) or Whipped Cream (page 447), for garnish (optional)**

1. Prepare and refrigerate the pie dough. Roll the dough into a 12-inch circle and line a 9- to 9½-inch standard pie pan with it, shaping the edge into an upstanding ridge. Flute or crimp the edge, chill the shell, and partially pre-bake it according to the instructions on page 36.

2. Preheat the oven to 350°F (180°C). Combine the milk, cornmeal, and salt in a medium saucepan, preferably nonstick. Gradually bring to a simmer over medium heat, stirring often, and cook until thickened, about 5 minutes. It won't turn extrathick, just full bodied. Reduce the heat slightly and cook for 3 to 4 minutes longer, whisking virtually nonstop to keep it from spattering. Remove from the heat and immediately whisk in the butter, one piece at a time, until melted. Whisk in the sugar, lemon juice, lemon zest, and vanilla. Remove from the heat and cool for 5 minutes, then whisk in the eggs one at a time.

3. Put the pie shell on a baking sheet, near the oven, and slowly pour the filling into the shell, smoothing the top with a spoon. Bake the pie, on the sheet, on the center oven rack for 40 to 45 minutes, until the filling is set, rotating the pie 180 degrees midway through the baking. When done, the filling will look firm in the pan and won't wobble. The edge of the pie may puff slightly, but not much.

4. Transfer the pie to a rack and cool thoroughly. Refrigerate for at least 2 hours, or overnight, before serving, garnishing individual slices with mascarpone or plain whipped cream, if desired. Cover and refrigerate leftovers.

Recipe for Success

I happen to love the subtle flavor of this pie, but you can flavor it more boldly by adding 1 teaspoon pumpkin pie spice and substituting light brown sugar for the granulated sugar.

Wheatena Breakfast Pie

Who can resist the idea of eating pie for breakfast, especially when it's full of things people eat for breakfast anyway? This version is made with Wheatena, a boyhood favorite of mine, as well as raisins, walnuts, and brown sugar. Whole-grain lovers will appreciate the coarse filling baked in a whole-wheat piecrust. For a pie that's a little smoother and more refined, try the Smooth and Simple Polenta Pie on the opposite page.

Makes 8–10 servings

Whole-Wheat Pie Dough (page 66) or another single-crust dough

FILLING

2¼ cups milk

⅓ cup Wheatena cereal

½ cup packed light brown sugar

Scant ½ teaspoon salt

3 tablespoons unsalted butter, cut into ½-inch pieces

½ teaspoon vanilla extract

3 large eggs, at room temperature, lightly beaten

¾ cup raisins

½ cup chopped walnuts

¼ teaspoon ground cinnamon

1. Prepare and refrigerate the pie dough. Roll the dough into a 12½- to 13-inch circle and line a 9- to 9½-inch deep-dish pie pan with it, shaping the edge into an upstanding ridge. Flute or crimp the edge, chill the shell, and partially prebake it according to the instructions on page 36.

2. Preheat the oven to 350°F (180°C). Combine the milk, Wheatena, sugar, and salt in a medium saucepan over medium heat. Bring to a gentle boil, then reduce the heat and simmer, stirring occasionally, until somewhat thickened, about 7 minutes. It won't become pasty thick, just slurry thick. Remove from the heat and stir in the butter, one piece at a time, and the vanilla. Remove from the heat and cool for 10 minutes.

3. Whisk the eggs into the Wheatena mixture. Stir in the raisins, walnuts, and cinnamon. Put the pie shell on a baking sheet, near the oven, and slowly pour the filling into the cooled pie shell. Gently rake a fork through the filling to distribute the raisins and nuts evenly.

4. Bake the pie, on the sheet, on the center rack for about 40 minutes, until the filling is set, rotating the pie 180 degrees midway through the baking. The filling will have a fairly firm texture when the pie is done.

5. Transfer the pie to a rack and cool. Serve warm or at room temperature. Or cover and refrigerate before serving. Cover and refrigerate leftovers.

Recipe for Success

This reheats nicely if you want to serve it several days in a row. Heat slices on a small baking sheet for about 10 minutes in a 300°F (180°C) oven.

Other nuts or dried fruits work beautifully in this pie, too. Consider pecans or almonds, as well as dried cherries or dried cranberries.

16
The Pie Maker's Pantry:
SWEET SAUCES, TOPPINGS, AND MERINGUES

I've always loved pantries, especially the one I grew up with in our big Victorian home in New Jersey. My parents kept all kinds of good stuff in there, including the blue change jar we'd raid for the Good Humor truck, the meat grinder I loved to feed leftover chunks of roast beef for hash, and the desserts Mom tried to hide from us.

You'll find lots of good stuff in this pantry, too, which holds recipes like caramel sauce and Swiss meringue that you'll need for finishing many of the pies in this collection. Don't be fooled by the fact that these recipes appear here, at the back of the book: many of the pie recipes wouldn't be complete without them. I have a feeling you'll find yourself referring to this chapter for tried-and-true versions of recipes — a sauce, a crumb topping — you can trust even when you're not making one of these pies.

❧

Caramel Sauce

The thought of making homemade caramel sauce is daunting for many cooks, but there's no reason to be intimidated. It's simple to prepare and, start to finish, takes only 15 to 20 minutes, after which you have a luscious, full-bodied sauce to drizzle on apple and peach pies, use in and on cream pies, and top off pie à la mode. No fancy equipment needed: just a 3-quart stainless steel saucepan and a candy thermometer.

Makes about 1½ cups

- 1 cup sugar
- ¼ teaspoon salt
- ⅓ cup water
- 1 cup heavy cream
- 1 teaspoon vanilla extract

1. Combine the sugar and salt in a 3- to 3½-quart stainless steel saucepan and pour the water over them. Place the pan over medium to medium-high heat, stirring gently with a wooden spoon. As soon as the mixture comes to a boil, stop stirring.

2. Cook the mixture for 5 to 6 minutes, gently swirling the pan to "stir" the caramel so it colors evenly. As soon as the mixture turns a medium amber color, remove the saucepan from the heat and add the cream all at once. Stir well, and don't be concerned if it clumps up at first; it will smooth out.

3. Put the saucepan back over medium-low heat and boil, stirring virtually nonstop, until the caramel reaches 220 to 225°F (104 to 107°C) on a candy thermometer. Remove from the heat and stir in the vanilla. Cool briefly, then transfer to heatproof jars to store. Cool to room temperature before refrigerating. It will keep for at least several weeks. To reheat, microwave the jar in 5- to 10-second intervals, stirring in between, until pourable.

Lauren's Salted Caramel Sauce

This excellent caramel sauce, used on Lauren's Salted Caramel–Apple Streusel Pie (page 186), is a little different from the previous one. It calls for both cream and butter, and it has that salty edge that's so popular these days. Drizzle it on peach pies, too.

Makes about 1¼ cups

- 1 cup sugar
- 7 tablespoons unsalted butter, in cubes
- ½ cup heavy cream
- ¾ teaspoon coarse kosher salt

1. Put the sugar in a 2½- to 3-quart stainless steel saucepan. Heat the sugar over medium to medium-low heat until it starts to liquefy and brown at the edges. When this happens, begin to pull the sugar from around the edge into the center with a wooden spoon or heat-proof spatula. Continue like this until all of the sugar has melted into an amber-colored liquid, but don't overwork it. Watch it carefully, because at this stage it can darken and burn quickly.

2. When the sugar has melted and is amber in color, quickly stir in all of the butter. The contents of the pan will bubble up. As soon as the butter melts, remove the pan from the heat and add the heavy cream.

3. Continue to stir until the sauce is smooth and even. Stir in the salt. Pour the caramel into a heatproof container. Cool thoroughly, then cover and refrigerate. If you're using the caramel cold, you'll need to gently heat it first to bring it to a drizzling consistency.

CHECK YOUR THERMOMETER

Any time you use a candy thermometer, make sure it is suspended in the liquid you're heating and not resting on the bottom of the pan, or you may get an inaccurate reading. This is why most candy thermometers have some sort of clip, so you can attach them to the side of the pan.

Chocolate Ganache

Chocolate ganache can be used to coat a bottom crust, sometimes thinly, other times thickly. It's also perfect for drizzling on top of pies, from cream pies to nut pies and cookie pies to sweet potato pies. (Try it on pound cakes and Bundt cakes, too.) It's the easiest chocolate sauce you'll ever make, so no excuses for not keeping it on hand. (I've been known, in weaker moments, to spoon it right out of the jar.)

Makes about 1½ cups

- ¾ cup heavy cream
- ½ teaspoon vanilla extract
- 1¼ cups semisweet chocolate chips

1. Bring the cream to a simmer in a small saucepan. Remove the pan from the heat and stir in the vanilla. Immediately add the chocolate chips. Tilt the pan this way and that so the hot cream runs over the chips. Let stand for 5 minutes, then stir the mixture briefly to start smoothing it out.

2. Let the mixture rest for another 2 to 3 minutes, then whisk briefly, until smooth. The glaze will be a little runny at first, perfect for drizzling. If you want thicker coverage, let the sauce cool slightly before using it. If you're not using it right away, transfer the sauce to a microwavable jar and let cool completely. Seal and refrigerate. To reheat, transfer the sauce to a saucepan over low heat, stirring occasionally. Or microwave the uncovered jar in 5- to 10-second intervals, stirring in between, until pourable.

Remove from the heat and gradually whisk it into the egg yolks, adding about ⅓ cup at a time. Return the mixture to the saucepan. Using a wooden spoon, stir the custard over medium-low heat, nonstop, until it thickens enough to coat the back of the spoon, about 5 minutes. If you draw a finger across the spoon, it should leave a path in the sauce. Be careful not to boil the sauce or heat it too aggressively.

3. Remove from the heat and pour the sauce into a bowl. Stir in the vanilla. Let the sauce cool to room temperature, cover with plastic wrap, then refrigerate until cold. It will keep in the fridge for up to 3 days. Whisk briefly before serving.

Whipped Cream (Stabilized)

Typically, to serve whipped cream with pie, you'd just beat it to a billowy consistency, with a bit of sugar added for good measure. When you prepare whipped cream to top a cream pie, however, you want it to "sit tight" on the pie without weeping or drooping, so you'll use stabilized whipped cream. I cover both versions here, starting with the stabilized one. It requires a couple of extra steps to prepare the gelatin stabilizer, but it only adds a minute or two to the entire process.

Makes 3 cups

- 1 tablespoon plus 2 teaspoons cold water
- 1½ teaspoons powdered gelatin
- 2 cups cold heavy cream
- ½ cup confectioners' sugar, sifted

1. I like to use my stand mixer for whipped cream, but a hand mixer will work. Whichever you use, refrigerate a large bowl and beaters for 5 to 10 minutes.

Vanilla Custard Sauce

There's nothing wrong with serving pie with the usual suspects, ice cream and whipped cream, but that's a bit predictable. Enter an unexpected third option that many people are unfamiliar with: vanilla custard sauce. If you're one of the uninitiated, it's just what it sounds like — a rich vanilla custard, only pourable. It doesn't take much imagination to realize how good that tastes, but you'll never know until you try. I like it best served cold. It's also good on pound cakes, fresh berries, pancakes, and so on.

Makes about 2½ cups

- 6 large egg yolks
- ½ cup sugar
- 2 cups half-and-half
- 1 teaspoon vanilla extract

1. Whisk the egg yolks and sugar together in a medium bowl.

2. Bring the half-and-half to a near boil in a medium saucepan over moderate heat.

2. Pour the cold water into a small microwaveable bowl and sprinkle the gelatin evenly over it. Let stand for 5 minutes.

3. After 5 minutes, when the gelatin is slushy, heat the mixture in the microwave in 5- to 6-second increments, until the gelatin has liquefied. This typically happens after the first heating, but you may have to give it a few extra seconds. Stir with a small spoon to smooth the mixture. Set aside until lukewarm.

4. Pour the cream into the chilled bowl. Using the chilled beaters, begin beating the cream with an electric mixer. Start slowly at first, so it doesn't spatter, and gradually increase the speed to high. When the cream starts to thicken and the beaters leave trails in the cream, add the sugar, then add the liquid gelatin in a stream. Continue to beat on medium-high speed just until the cream holds peaks that don't droop or sag. Do not overbeat, or the whipped cream will become grainy. Refrigerate until ready to use.

TECHNIQUE TIP

If you find that your whipped cream has a tendency to turn grainy on you, you're probably overbeating it. Try this: use the electric mixer for most of the process, but stop beating before you typically would, while the cream is still a little droopy. Using a large whisk, continue to whip by hand just until it reaches the right thick and voluminous consistency. It's easier to monitor progress this way, so you're less prone to overwork it.

Whipped Cream (Plain)

When you see a reference to Whipped Cream in this book, it means whipped cream that hasn't been stabilized. To prepare, follow the recipe for stabilized cream but simply omit the liquefied gelatin. Add the confectioners' sugar at the same point, and beat until the cream holds peaks that don't sag.

Variations

COFFEE WHIPPED CREAM

Combine 2 tablespoons coffee liqueur with 2 teaspoons instant coffee powder or espresso in a small microwavable bowl. Microwave for 4 or 5 seconds. Stir and allow to cool. Beat into the whipped cream when you're almost done whipping.

FRUITED WHIPPED CREAM

This is a nice way to add a fruity note to cream pies, especially Lemon Cream Pie with Fresh Fruit (page 390). Begin by adding 2 tablespoons of your favorite fruit liqueur when the cream starts to become billowy. To play up the fruity flavor, gently fold in 3 tablespoons thick, cold fruit preserves when you're done beating.

MINT WHIPPED CREAM

Mint adds a refreshing accent to cream pies and many chocolate pies. Just add a couple of drops mint extract or food-grade mint oil to the cream while you whip it. Use fresh mint leaves for garnish.

VANILLA WHIPPED CREAM

At the risk of stating the obvious, ½ to 1 teaspoon vanilla extract is almost always a good addition to whipped cream.

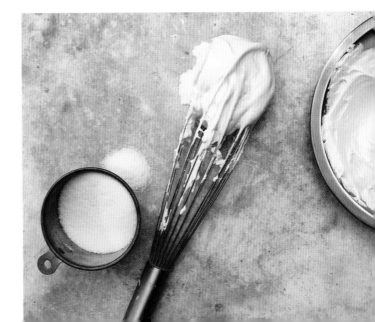

Mascarpone Whipped Cream

Here's another way to make stabilized whipped cream: by beating it with mascarpone cheese. It's a rich indulgence, but when the occasion calls for it (see Little Cherry Pies, page 330), it's a real treat. This whipped cream is easy to pipe from a pastry bag, and it holds its shape very nicely. This recipe makes enough to garnish up to eight mini pies or slices; for thick coverage for a whole pie, double the recipe.

Makes 2–2½ cups

- 4 ounces cold mascarpone cheese
- ⅔ cup cold heavy cream
- ⅓ cup confectioners' sugar
- ¼ teaspoon vanilla extract

1. Chill a medium bowl and a set of mixer beaters for about 10 minutes. If you're doubling the recipe, you might want to use a stand mixer, if you have one.

2. Put the mascarpone in the chilled bowl and beat on medium-low speed for 1 minute to loosen it up; it will not smooth out yet. Start adding the cream in a stream. The mixture will thin out at first, then gradually start to thicken. After all the cream has been added and the mixture begins to mound, stop beating and add the sugar and vanilla. Beat them in slowly at first, then increase the speed and beat the cream just until it holds firm peaks. Do not overmix, or the cream will curdle. If not using the whipped cream right away, cover the bowl and refrigerate until needed.

Swiss Meringue

This is the only type of meringue I use anymore. Denser than the French-style meringue you often find on lemon meringue and cream pies, it has the flavor of a gooey marshmallow. It's outrageously delicious. Also, because the egg whites are heated along with the sugar, you eliminate any concerns about eating raw eggs. Spread it on the pie as soon as it's made. It browns beautifully when you take a torch to it (see Torch Tips, page 00).

Makes enough for 1 large pie

- ⅔ cup egg whites (from 5 or 6 large eggs)
- 1 cup sugar
- ⅛ teaspoon salt
- ¼ teaspoon cream of tartar

1. Pour about 1½ inches water into a medium saucepan, large enough to hold a stand mixer's metal bowl safely suspended in the pan without toppling. If you don't have the appropriate-size saucepan, bunch up about 2 feet of aluminum foil to make a fat collar that supports the pan and keeps it over, not in, the simmering water. Bring the water to a simmer.

2. Combine the egg whites, sugar, salt, and cream of tartar in the mixer's metal bowl. Put the bowl over the simmering water — it should remain at a simmer at all times — and start mixing the egg white and sugar mixture nonstop with a whisk or flexible, heat-resistant spatula. Continue to heat and stir until the mixture reaches 160°F (71°C) on a candy thermometer.

3. Immediately take the mixture off the heat and place the bowl in the stand mixer. Beat slowly for 1 minute, then quickly increase the speed and beat on high speed until the meringue is thick, glossy, and holds firm peaks, about 5 minutes. This meringue is quite stable, but it's still possible to overbeat it and result in less loft, so err on the side of caution.

4. Smooth the meringue over the pie right away. If desired, brown the meringue evenly with a kitchen torch or shop torch.

If you'd like to add a bit of flavoring to the meringue, add ½ teaspoon vanilla extract or almond extract when you start beating the egg whites.

This meringue is best eaten the day it is made, when it's fresh. It will be fine if you keep it overnight, but it will lose some volume and won't have quite the same ultracreamy consistency.

Many crumb toppings behave best if they're cold when they go on the pie. That's why I usually make the topping first, even before I start my pie. Cold toppings don't clump and tend to get more crunchy without "melting" into the pie.

Oatmeal Crumb Topping

This has been my go-to crumb topping since dinosaurs roamed the earth, that's how much I like it. People often tell me that it makes more than enough for most pies, and I tell them that's the entire point: you want extra to use on coffeecakes, muffins, quick breads, fruit crisps, mini fruit pies, and so much more. In fact, I recommend making a double batch. Freeze leftover mixture in a plastic freezer bag; it lasts for months.

Makes enough for 1 large pie, with some left over

- 1 cup all-purpose flour
- ½ cup old-fashioned rolled oats
- ⅔ cup packed light brown sugar
- ¼ teaspoon salt
- ¼ teaspoon ground cinnamon
- ½ cup (1 stick) cold unsalted butter, cut into ¼-inch pieces

1. Combine the flour, oats, sugar, salt, and cinnamon in a food processor. Pulse several times to mix.

2. Scatter the butter pieces over the dry mixture. Pulse until the mixture resembles coarse crumbs. Don't overdo it; you want to see some oat flakes.

3. Empty the crumbs into a large bowl and rub them gently to even out the consistency and make them more "buttery." Refrigerate until using.

Melted Butter Crumb Topping

Unlike the previous topping and the Traditional German Streusel on page 450, this one is made with melted butter instead of cold butter. Using melted butter makes the streusel easy to mix, especially with an electric hand mixer. The crumbs are refrigerated before they go on the pie, and they tend to stay separate and get good and crunchy. A great recipe for virtually any fruit pie.

Makes 2½–3 cups, enough to cover 1 large pie with some left over

- 1¼ cups all-purpose flour
- ½ cup sugar
- ½ cup well-chopped walnuts, pecans, hazelnuts, or almonds
- ½ cup sweetened flaked coconut
- ¼ teaspoon salt
- ½ cup (1 stick) unsalted butter, melted

1. Combine the flour, sugar, nuts, coconut, and salt in a large bowl. Rub together briefly by hand or use an electric mixer.

2. While the butter is still warm, add it to the dry ingredients in a stream as you mix on low speed. When all the butter is added, continue to beat for 1 minute on medium-low speed. The topping will form small, coarse crumbs.

3. Spread the crumbs evenly on a rimmed baking sheet and refrigerate for 1 hour, or longer, until they become firm. Either use them the same day, or transfer the crumbs to a freezer bag and freeze until needed.

Traditional German Streusel

This is a no-frills version of streusel, made in the traditional hand-rubbed way. It has a more sandy texture than the other toppings and bakes up beautifully. If you prefer a stand mixer, use the flat beater. Combine the dry ingredients in the bowl and mix briefly on low. Add the cold butter and mix on low until everything is evenly combined and the mixture has a sandy consistency.

Makes about 2 cups, enough to cover 1 large pie

- 1⅔ cups all-purpose flour
- ½ packed light brown sugar
- ¼ teaspoon salt
- ½ cup (1 stick) cold unsalted butter, cut into ½-inch cubes

1. Combine the flour, sugar, and salt in a large mixing bowl. Toss with your hands to mix. Add the butter and toss it to coat as well.

2. Using your fingers, thoroughly rub the butter and dry ingredients together until all of the butter is incorporated and the topping is evenly mixed. You don't have to rush, but don't dilly-dally because it's best if the butter stays cold. When you're done, the mixture will be fine textured and feel a bit like dry sand.

3. Put the bowl in the fridge, or first transfer the topping to a shallow casserole dish or pie pan, then refrigerate for at least 30 minutes before using. Leftover topping can be stored in plastic freezer bags and frozen for up to a year.

Variation
CORNMEAL STREUSEL

Replace ⅔ cup of the all-purpose flour with fine yellow cornmeal. Use granulated sugar instead of the brown sugar. The cornmeal adds a pleasing crunch. Try it on any of your favorite pies, especially blueberry.

Lemon Curd

If you're not already a fan, once you make real lemon curd and have it in the fridge, you'll think of all sorts of reasons to reach for it. You can smear it on toast and biscuits, use it as a cake filling, and dollop fresh berries with it. You can also use it as a pie filling (see Mini Lemon Pies with Mascarpone Whipped Cream, page 337). Or add it as an extra layer in the Lemon Cream Pie with Fresh Fruit on page 390, smoothing it over the lemon pastry cream before the whipped cream goes on. Lots of possibilities here.

Makes almost 2 cups

- 6 tablespoons unsalted butter, softened
  Scant 1 cup sugar
- 2 large eggs plus 2 large egg yolks
- ½ cup lemon juice
  Finely grated zest of 1 lemon

1. Put the butter in a medium bowl. Gradually add the sugar, beating with a handheld electric mixer on medium speed for about 1 minute. Beat in the eggs and egg yolks, one at a time, beating well after each addition. Add the lemon juice in a stream, beating briefly to combine.

2. Transfer the mixture to a medium heavy-bottom saucepan and add the lemon zest. Heat the mixture, stirring over medium-low heat, until it starts to smooth out and no longer looks curdled. Increase the heat to medium and stir, nonstop, until the mixture thickens enough to heavily coat the back of a spoon. Do not boil.

3. Remove from the heat and immediately scrape the curd into a bowl. Press a piece of plastic wrap directly over the curd to prevent a skin from forming. Cool for about 1 hour at room temperature, then refrigerate until needed. If you're not using it within 24 hours, transfer to one or two smaller jars, seal, and refrigerate.

TEMPERATURE TIP

I seldom use a candy thermometer for this, because it's pretty clear when it has thickened up, but if you'd feel better using one, the curd will register 170°F (77°C) when it is ready to come off the heat.

Coconut-Almond Crumb Topping

This is a delicious topping for virtually any fruit pie, but I think it works best with cherry and peach pies, especially the Peach-Mango Pie on page 137.

Makes enough for 1 large pie or several smaller ones

    1   cup all-purpose flour
    ⅔   cup sugar
    ½   cup whole raw almonds
    ½   cup sweetened flaked coconut
    ¼   teaspoon salt
    6   tablespoons cold unsalted butter,
        cut into ½-inch cubes

1. Combine the flour, sugar, almonds, coconut, and salt in a food processor. Pulse five or six times to chop the nuts coarsely.

2. Scatter the butter over the dry mixture, then pulse until you have coarse, gravelly crumbs. Empty the mixture into a large bowl and rub gently to make uniform crumbs. Refrigerate until ready to use.

Homemade Apple Butter

If you've ever made applesauce, you've come close to making apple butter, which is essentially just applesauce cooked to a thicker consistency. It's used in a few pies in this collection, but you'll find all sort of other great things to do with it, from slathering it on biscuits to serving it with salty hams. For a spiced version, add ½ teaspoon cinnamon plus ¼ teaspoon each ground cloves and nutmeg.

Makes 2½–3 cups

    3–4 pounds apples, peeled, cored,
         and cut into large chucks
    1½   cups fresh apple cider
    2   tablespoons minced crystallized
         ginger (optional)
    ⅓   cup sugar
    1½   tablespoons lemon juice

1. Preheat the oven to 350°F (180°C). Combine the apples, cider, and ginger (if using) in a large nonreactive pot. Bring to a boil. Cover, reduce the heat to medium, and cook at a low boil, stirring occasionally, until the apples turn to mush, 20 to 25 minutes.

2. Remove from the heat and stir in the sugar and lemon juice. Transfer about half of the apple mixture to a food processor and process to a fine purée. Pour into a shallow ovenproof casserole dish. Repeat for the remaining apple mixture, pouring the purée into the same casserole.

3. Bake the casserole for 30 minutes, stirring once or twice. Reduce the temperature to 300°F (150°C) and bake for 45 to 55 minutes longer, stirring occasionally, until the apple butter has darkened, thickened, and reduced by nearly half.

4. Remove from the oven and cool. Transfer to jars, screw on the lids, and refrigerate. It will keep in the fridge for at least a couple of weeks.

Confectioners' Sugar Glaze

Here's a basic glaze with two variations that will jazz up just about any sweet pie. A drizzle of this adds a real wow factor to a plain crust. Simple? You can make it with your eyes closed: just whisk and drizzle. Apply it lavishly to top-crust pies, less so on crumb-topped pies since the topping is already pretty sweet.

Makes about ⅔ cup

PLAIN GLAZE
- 2 cups confectioners' sugar
- 3 tablespoons milk or heavy cream, plus more as needed
- ½ teaspoon vanilla extract

Whisk the sugar, milk, and vanilla in a medium bowl until smooth, adding more milk 1 teaspoon at a time as needed to make a medium-thick consistency. If you use heavy cream, expect to use a little more.

Variations
CITRUS GLAZE

Add ½ teaspoon lemon extract and 1 to 2 teaspoons finely grated lemon zest or orange zest to the plain glaze. This is especially good on berry fruit pies and pound cakes.

MAPLE SYRUP GLAZE
- 3 tablespoons unsalted butter
- ⅓ cup maple syrup
- 1½ cups confectioners' sugar

Combine the butter and maple syrup in a small saucepan. Gently heat until the butter melts, then whisk in the sugar until smooth. Use right away. I drizzle this one on many of my fall fruit pies, especially pear and apple-pear pies. It's wonderful on muffins and quick breads, too, especially pumpkin.

Raspberry Sauce

This pretty fruit sauce is a cinch to prepare. Lean, colorful, and slightly acidic, it's a nice garnish for ice cream pies and other rich, creamy pies, like cheesecake pies. You can make it with fresh berries, but more often than not I use frozen berries because they're so readily available. And frankly, it's hard to tell the difference. Blackberries are also good in place of the raspberries.

To make a sauce with a little more body, whisk in 1 or 2 tablespoons seedless raspberry preserves or red currant jelly that's been warmed and thinned in the microwave.

Makes about 1 cup

- 1 pint fresh raspberries or 1 (12-ounce) bag frozen raspberries
- 3 tablespoons sugar
- 1-2 teaspoons lemon juice

Put the berries and sugar in a food processor and process thoroughly, to a smooth purée. Pour the purée into a fine-mesh sieve placed over a bowl and strain the sauce, pressing it through the sieve with a silicone spatula. It will take several minutes to do a thorough job. Be sure to scrape the sauce off the outside of the sieve, where it tends to build up. Stir the lemon juice into the sauce, to taste.

Transfer the sauce to a jar and seal. Refrigerate, stirring well just before you use the sauce. It will keep for 2 days in the fridge, 3 days tops.

Toasted Nuts

This is not a recipe per se, but the subject is important enough to warrant the space because so many of the pies in this book include nuts.

I think most of us would agree that toasting — technically known as roasting — brings out the best qualities in nuts. Take America's favorite nut, for instance — the peanut. Raw ones, let's face it, taste bland compared to roasted: you get none of that toasted flavor people love. And so it goes for most other nuts, too.

When you consider the taste aspect (not to mention high cost) of nuts these days, it makes sense to get the most flavor from them that you can, and that means roasting.

The first thing you should know is that nuts are full of natural oils, so they roast quickly. You can't wander away from the kitchen when you're on nut-roasting duty. They can go from perfectly toasty to inedibly overdone in just a few minutes.

1. No matter the nut, spread them out on a rimmed baking sheet. Even if you need only 1 cup, you might as well roast 2 or 3 cups while you're at it and freeze the leftovers in a sealed container. They'll keep for months, and you can use them in quick breads, cakes, or other pies.

2. Preheat the oven to 350°F (180°C). Put the nuts on the middle oven rack, leave them there for 8 minutes, then have a peek; they'll probably show their first hint of darkening. It's also when you're likely get your first whiff of toastedness. The color transition you're looking for is just one or two slight shades darker than the original shade. If they don't seem to be done at 8 minutes, check them again at 9 and 10 minutes.

3. As soon as they're done, immediately remove them from the oven, then tilt the nuts out of the pan and onto the counter or a plate. If you leave them on the hot sheet, they will continue to roast and perhaps overroast.

Not all nuts will take exactly the same amount of time. Whole almonds take a little longer than walnut and pecan halves. Make sure you roast the nuts before you chop them. Chopped nuts will scorch very quickly.

Whole hazelnuts are handled a little differently. They usually take 12 to 15 minutes. Shake the pan once or twice as they roast, to "stir" them. When you can see blistered skins on most of the nuts, tilt them onto a clean tea towel. Fold the towel over the nuts and let them cool like this for 10 minutes, then vigorously rub the nuts inside the towel to remove the skins. Don't expect to remove every last bit of skin; some of it always clings to the nuts, and that's fine.

Allow the nuts to cool thoroughly, then transfer them to jars or leftover containers. Seal tightly and refrigerate or freeze. They'll keep for several months.

TROUBLESHOOTING GUIDE

As I suggested earlier, I would like to have a word with the person who coined the expression "as easy as pie." If there's one thing I've learned as dean of The Pie Academy, it's that for many cooks, pie making is anything but easy. Stuff can happen when you make a pie, stuff that's not supposed to, and you're left wondering where things went awry and how to prevent it from happening again. Let's take a look at some of these problem areas, based on the most common complaints I hear.

If you have other troubleshooting questions you'd like me to answer, please feel free to contact me at ken@thepieacademy.com.

DOUGH ISSUES

My dough still seems dry and crumbly even after I add the liquid.

You're probably not adding enough water. When you're just starting out as a pie maker, it's difficult to know whether you've added enough water or not. It's one of those things you need to develop a feel for. There'll be a little trial and error at first. Don't be afraid to add a touch more water — a teaspoon or two at a time. The standard test for knowing whether you've added enough water is to compress a few tablespoons of the dough mixture in your palm. If it holds together without crumbling apart easily, you're good.

It's worth considering, too, that the dough may be dry because you're cramming too much flour into the measuring cup to begin with. Don't push the dry measuring cup down into the flour; you'll overfill the cup. Do this instead: store the flour in a rectangular bin that you can get your hands into. Hold the measuring cup over the bin with one hand. Fluff the flour with your other hand, then lift and deposit flour into the cup. Level off the top with a knife blade or your finger. If you use a scale, all-purpose flour measured this way should come in right at about 4½ ounces.

One other reason the dough may feel dry is that you're not cutting in the fat thoroughly enough. Especially if you're cutting in the fat by hand, you want to make sure all the dry mixture looks like it has been touched by the fat. You should not see lots of dry, floury areas in the mixture. If all the dry mixture is lubricated, there's less chance the dough will seem dry and crumbly.

My dough always seems too wet after I add the liquid.

Unlike the last pie maker, you're probably using a little more liquid than you should. If that's the case, (a) the dough may seem sticky when you go to roll it, and (b) the crust is likely to be more chewy than flaky, because extra water tends to activate gluten,

the stretchy protein strands in dough. So ease up a little on the liquid, cutting back by 2 to 4 teaspoons. Keep in mind that when dough rests in the fridge, dry areas in the dough will take on moisture from the surrounding areas, like a sponge does, and help hydrate the dough evenly.

It's also possible that you're adding too much liquid by accident. When you measure the water, use a 1-cup glass measuring cup, and bend down until you're eye level with the cup so you get an accurate reading. If you're trying to read the liquid level looking down at the cup, your measurement will be off.

My dough cracks when I try to roll it.

This is a common complaint, so take heart; you're not alone. First of all, make sure you're not trying to roll the dough while it is still cold-hard, or the dough will be brittle. You'll end up fighting with it. Next, take care not to dust the dough with extra flour while you're shaping it into a ball, then a disk. Excess flour can get wedged in the dough and cause a fault line where the dough will split when you roll it.

Of course, you may simply not have added enough liquid to the pastry and now it's just plain crumbly. Unfortunately, once you've started to roll the dough it's too late at this point to work in more moisture, but you might be able to minimize the crumbliness by rolling the dough between sheets of plastic wrap.

Finally, it's quite common for dough to crack a little around the edges as you roll it. Don't worry too much about that. If it bothers you or starts to get out of hand, pinch the cracks back together and carry on.

My pie dough always sticks to my counter when I roll it.

Let's start with the obvious: the dough may be too wet, so use a little less liquid next time. Obvious thing #2: you need to dust your counter with a little more flour. Not a blizzard of it, just a nice even and thorough dusting. The moment the dough starts to stick, slide it off to the side and dust again. If the problem persists, try rolling the dough on waxed paper or plastic wrap. You also might be pressing too hard with the rolling pin. Remember that your goal is to flatten out the dough gradually as you roll, and not with the first swipe of the pin. That's asking for trouble.

I can't keep my dough round when I roll. It looks like an amoeba instead of a circle.

One time I was giving a pie-making demonstration and a lady in the audience kept firing comments at me. She was visibly irritated because she never had success keeping her dough round, like the one I was rolling at my demo. I gave her every tip I could think of, and when I ran out of good ideas and started grasping at straws, I told her that she should try to picture something round when she rolled — like the earth, I said. To which she shot back: My dough looks like part of the earth, all right. Florida!

If you've got chronic Florida dough, relax. Start with a nice round disk of dough and make sure it's not too cold-hard. Let it sit at room temperature for 10 minutes if it is. Give the dough a number of short warm-up rolls, rolling away from you, rotating the dough a quarter turn after each one. Keep up these short, gentle rolls and quarter turns. Only roll away from you in the 10:00, 12:00, and 2:00 positions, not off to the sides, and don't roll toward yourself. That's awkward, and awkward makes for funny-looking doughs. Of all the pie-making skills there are to master, this is one of the trickiest, so don't throw in the towel after your first couple of pies. You'll eventually get very good at it. If all else fail, picture the earth when you roll.

My dough falls apart when I transfer it to my pie pan.

This is likely happening for the same reason that dough cracks too much: not enough moisture in the dough. If another few teaspoons of water doesn't do the trick, take stock of how you're attempting to get the dough into the pan. It might need more support on the way there. If you roll directly onto a countertop, try sliding a thin, flour-dusted rimless baking sheet all the way under the dough. Then slide the dough off the sheet and into the pan. Or try rolling directly onto waxed paper. With most doughs,

the paper will grip it. Then you can invert the rolled dough over the pan, center it, and peel off the paper.

Also be aware that all-butter doughs hold together better than doughs with a high proportion of vegetable shortening, which tends to relax the dough. So if the problem persists, prepare a butter dough and see if that makes a difference.

My dough shrinks when I prebake my pie shells.

A couple of things can help. If you're using all butter in the dough, substitute a bit of lard or vegetable shortening for the butter. Either one will help relax the dough and make it less prone to shrinkage. Also, make sure you don't shortchange the time the dough spends in the oven when it prebakes. If the dough is underbaked, it has a tendency to shrink a bit when you remove the bean weights.

This could also be happening because you're stretching the dough when you nudge it into the pie pan. Take care to lift the edge of the dough with one hand as you scoot it into the pie pan with the other.

The edge of my crust always gets too dark and overbaked.

This is a very common problem. Edges overbrown because that's the most exposed portion of the pie, right out there in the oven with virtually nothing to protect it. This is unfortunate when it happens, but it's not the end of the world, because we're only talking about a small percentage of the pie's overall real estate. Still, nobody wants their pie to look char-grilled, so start by eliminating any sugar you may be adding to the dough. Even a small amount of sugar

can cause significant browning, and since the filling is usually sweet enough, you can skip the sugar in the crust. If the problem persists, make a foil ring to protect the edge. You can buy silicone or metal versions, but because they're heavier and sit directly on the crust edge, they often don't work as well as they should and cause browning as well.

I like to flute the edge of my piecrust. The flutes look good when I first make them, but they always lose their shape in the oven when I bake my pie. Could be a number of things. Your dough could be too moist, which activated the gluten and made the dough bouncy. But whatever caused it to happen, there are a couple of things you can try that will help.

First, if you're making a butter crust, use a little bit of shortening or lard. That will help relax the dough. Next, don't make the flutes right after you form the shell. Instead, put the shell in the freezer for 5 to 7 minutes first; when it's gotten just a little firm, then make the flutes. When the dough resists a little, the flutes will hold their shape better. Finally, exaggerate the flutes by pressing firmly when you make them. You want to stretch the dough out of shape; if you look closely, you can actually see where the outer layers of the dough tear a bit. When you exaggerate the flutes like this, they'll hold their shape better.

FILLING ISSUES

My fruit pies turn out runny. They seem underbaked.

If they're runny, and you remembered to add the thickener, they probably are underbaked. The juice in the pie has to come to a boil, and stay there for a few minutes, before the thickener kicks in and does its job. If you take the pie out before that happens, you're in for disappointment. There are a number of indicators that the fruit pie is done, including total elapsed time, but none more important than seeing thick juices bubbling up around the edge, through a hole in the top crust or up through the crumb topping. If you don't see that juice, the pie is probably underbaked by at least 10 to 15 minutes.

My fruit pies spill over onto the oven floor.

Simple: you need to put the pie on a baking sheet, with a sheet of parchment paper under the pie. and bake the pie that way. If you don't have parchment, use aluminum foil. That is, unless you like to spend your time scrubbing the oven. You're probably also filling your fruit pies a tad too generously. Instead of doing that, consider using the extra filling to make mini pies.

My pumpkin pies always develop cracks when they cool.

Yep, pumpkin pie can be cranky that way. It's a little like cheesecake, which has the same tendency. You can minimize this issue by remembering that almost any pie made with eggs is best baked low and slow — meaning 325 to 350°F (170 to 180°C) — for as long as it takes. Check the temperature with an oven thermometer to be sure. Pumpkin pie, again like cheesecake, will sometime crack if it is subject to a quick temperature change. You might want to turn off the oven, open the door about halfway, and cool the pie like that for 15 minutes before removing it from the oven. If all that fails, layer on the whipped cream nice and thick to hide the crack.

Another reason pumpkin pies can crack, if you're using your own baked pumpkin flesh, is the presence of pumpkin chunks in the filling. Use a food processor to make sure the pumpkin is good and smooth before you mix the filling (page 221).

My custard pies are watery and grainy, not silky and smooth.

See above. That graininess is essentially scrambled eggs because you baked the pie too hot or too long or both. Again, low and slow is the order of the day.

My cream pie filling is loose and watery.

If you've cooked your pastry cream correctly — see Vanilla Pastry Cream, page 377 — then I can think of only one thing: you've been taste testing the pastry cream and putting the spoon back into the saucepan or bowl. Turns out that saliva contains an enzyme that breaks down starches, namely the cornstarch you used to thicken the pastry cream. Nothing seems amiss right away, but when you go to assemble the pie or slice it, the pastry cream will be loose and watery. (It's nature's way of scolding you the way your mom did when you snuck a bite of something.) Solution? Do what I do: don't taste while you're cooking the pastry cream. Instead, set aside a little tasting portion after you've whisked in the butter and flavorings. Or keep a pile of tasting spoons nearby, if you can't resist, and only use each of them once.

ACKNOWLEDGMENTS

This strikingly beautiful and hefty book would not have been possible without the faith, support, talents, and generosity of many. I'm incredibly fortunate to have Storey Publishing as my partner in print. Storey "publishes practical books for creative self-reliance" — a mission they've elevated to an art form. I'm proud to count myself among their authors. Publisher Deborah Balmuth has had tremendous enthusiasm for this project from the start; my editor, Lisa Hiley, has made it almost easy to write a book of this size and scope; art director Carolyn Eckert's hand and stylish eye can be seen on every page; and Jennie Jepson Smith played a big role in building the pages. I'm also grateful to Alee Moncy, who coordinates publicity for dozens of authors and hundreds of titles; the seemingly unflappable Jennifer Travis, who does as much as anyone to make you feel a part of the team; and Tina Parent, who faithfully fulfills book orders for me and to outlets everywhere.

A very special thank-you to the wildly gifted photographer and stylist Johnny and Charlotte Autry and their team for contributing their talents to this visual feast. Love working with you guys.

Many thanks to all of the good pie makers and dedicated cooks who have either contributed recipes to this collection or inspired me with their skill at the pie maker's craft.

On the domestic front, my children — Ben, Tess, Ali, and Sam — are a daily source of joy and pride. My siblings — Joe, Barb, Tom, Bill, Joanne, and Mary — make me feel that every day is a gift. And most of all, love and gratitude to my wife, Bev, my partner in The Pie Academy and in life.

Lastly, thanks to all of my loyal readers, fans, followers, and Pie Academy members — my "tribe" as we say today — for tuning in, reaching out, and being such an important part of this community of cooks over the years. I'm very grateful for you and your support.

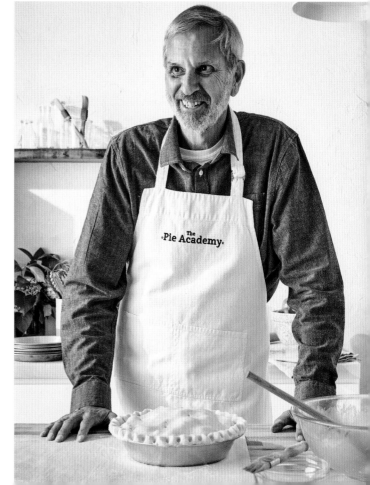

LIST OF PIES BY CHAPTER

INDEX

Page numbers in *italic* indicate how-to photos.

Converting Recipe Measurements to Metric

Unless you have finely calibrated measuring equipment, conversions between US and metric measurements will be somewhat inexact. It's important to convert the measurements for all of the ingredients in a recipe to maintain the same proportions as the original.

TO CONVERT	TO	MULTIPLY
teaspoons	milliliters	teaspoons by 4.93
tablespoons	milliliters	tablespoons by 14.79
cups	milliliters	cups by 236.59
cups	liters	cups by 0.24
pints	milliliters	pints by 473.18
pints	liters	pints by 0.473
gallons	liters	gallons by 3.785
ounces	grams	ounces by 28.35
pounds	kilograms	pounds by 0.454
inches	centimeters	inches by 2.54
feet	meters	feet by 0.3048

US	METRIC
1 teaspoon	5 milliliters
1 tablespoon	15 milliliters
¼ cup	60 milliliters
½ cup	120 milliliters
1 cup	240 milliliters